D1522346

The Joan Palevsky Imprint in Classical Literature

In honor of beloved Virgil—

"O degli altri poeti onore e lume . . ."

—Dante, *Inferno*

The Portrait of the Lover

The Portrait
of the Lover

Maurizio Bettini

Translated from the Italian by
Laura Gibbs

UNIVERSITY OF CALIFORNIA PRESS

Berkeley / Los Angeles / London

THE PUBLISHER GRATEFULLY ACKNOWLEDGES THE
GENEROUS CONTRIBUTION PROVIDED TO THIS BOOK
BY JOAN PALEVSKY.

University of California Press
Berkeley and Los Angeles, California

University of California Press, Ltd.
London, England

Library of Congress Cataloging-in-Publication Data

Bettini, Maurizio.
   [Ritratto dell'amante. English]
   The portrait of the lover / Maurizio Bettini : translated from the
Italian by Laura Gibbs.
     p. cm.
   Includes bibliographical references and index.
   ISBN 0-520-20850-1 (alk. paper)
   1. Love in art. 2. Arts. I. Title.
   NX650.L68B4813 1999
   700'.4543—dc21   99-20905
                                         CIP

Printed in the United States of America
9 8 7 6 5 4 3 2 1

The paper used in this publication meets the minimum requirements
of American National Standard for Information Sciences—Permanence of Paper for Printed Library Materials, ANSI Z39.48-1984.

Contents

Illustrations follow page 137.

Author's Preface

This book is the product of a great passion for stories, but it is also the product of a specific occasion. In 1986 I found myself conducting a seminar at the Villa I Tatti in Florence. The audience consisted mainly of art historians, a situation that prompted me (a classical philologist) to analyze some ancient stories in which painted or sculpted images play a major role. Over the years that followed, I elaborated these observations into a book whose subject is potentially infinite: the anthropological meaning of images. By this I mean not just images that express things, but images that "do" things, engaged as active participants in the ongoing operations of cultural behaviors and models. Such stories about images remain the focus of this book, but I have added many other ancient Greek and Latin texts (and in some cases modern texts as well), both to broaden the field of study and to introduce new topics for consideration.

There was much work involved in the writing of this book, and I would not have been able to bring it to a conclusion without the help of many friends. In particular, I would like to thank Lucia Beltrami, Carlo Brillante, Gianni Guastella, Giulio Guidorizzi, Alessandro Fo, Francesca Mencacci, Renato Oniga, and Salvatore Settis.

Maurizio Bettini
Pisa, May 1992

Translator's Preface

One of the central themes of this book is that of "worsened" reproductions: what Augustine calls resemblance *in deterioribus,* the lamentable situation that arises when a copy fails to resemble its original perfectly and instead resembles it only roughly, partially, insufficiently. As examples of reproductions *in deterioribus,* Augustine lists such phenomena as dreams and optical illusions, family resemblances between parents and children, along with portraits, sculptures, and other works of art. But he could also have included translations under this same heading. Much like the legendary painters and sculptors whose adventures constitute the main subject of this book, translators are likewise condemned to create reproductions that are always *in deterioribus.* Of course, if a goddess were to intervene—as Venus did for Pygmalion, bringing his beloved statue to life—this English *Portrait of the Lover* might become as bright and vibrant as Maurizio Bettini's *Ritratto dell'amante.* But in the absence of divine intervention, I would like to explain something about the original Italian context of this book, and to say a few words about what inevitably gets lost in the translation.

First, Maurizio Bettini represents a school of Italian classical studies that may be rather unfamiliar to American readers, even to American classicists. His focus is on the anthropology of ancient Greece and Rome, and in this effort to elucidate the meaning of ancient cultural models, every bit of textual evidence becomes potentially significant. The canonical authors all have their place here, of course, and the pages of this book are filled with references to Homer, Herodotus, Euripides, Cicero, Vergil, Horace, and so on. But side by side with Homer and

Vergil the reader will find such authors as Palladius, Censorinus, Scribonius Largus, Fulgentius, Hesychius, Pollux, and Minucius Felix, not to mention all the anonymous scholiasts of late antiquity who provide Bettini with some of his most precious insights into the cultural models of ancient Greece and Rome. The results yielded by such an approach are dazzling and extremely persuasive—but the reader may find it disconcerting at times to confront this crowd of oddly named strangers and unfamiliar sources. At such moments, it might be helpful to invoke a metaphor that Bettini often uses to describe this sort of work: what we are looking at is a cultural mosaic made up of thousands of textual tiles, oddly shaped, varicolored, all of which must be continually combined and recombined, so that we are always having to reread each time that we read something new, taking a fresh look at everything over again as we assemble some different part of the puzzle.

Of course, to take such a synthetic approach to these ancient texts (and bits of texts) depends on a particular assumption: in Bettini's words, "this sort of dialogical mosaic implies that there is a given structure in culture, that beliefs are part of a system of meaningful signs." And this is the second point of departure, the other major difference between Bettini's work and that of many American classicists. Bettini is deeply influenced by structuralism and semiotics; consequently, the reader will find frequent references in these pages to such scholars as Claude Lévi-Strauss, Jean-Pierre Vernant, Emile Benveniste, Roman Jakobson, Vladimir Propp, Algirdas Julien Greimas, and Umberto Eco, among others. It is these scholars who provide the methodological assumptions according to which Bettini proceeds, and it is from these authors that he derives some of the key terms of his argument. In particular, Vernant's work on the anthropology of the image in ancient Greece is an essential element in the project that Bettini undertakes in this book. Fortunately for English-language readers, many of Vernant's relevant essays on this topic have recently been translated in a collection entitled *Mortals and Immortals* (edited by Froma Zeitlin). But—I hasten to add—there are no required readings, no prerequisites for *The Portrait of the Lover*. The important thing to keep in mind is simply that Bettini's work here, like that of Vernant, Lévi-Strauss, Benveniste, and the rest, is based on a fundamental belief in the meaningfulness of human culture. The resulting combination of structuralism and semiotics is thus quite different from other varieties of poststructuralism with which English-language readers may be more familiar, as represented by such scholars as Derrida, Foucault, and Lacan. When Bettini uses the terms "signifier" and "signified," he is not preparing to launch into a deconstructionist spiral of philosophical abstraction; instead, he is speaking about *meaning*, and the way that meaning is *communicated* between one person and another. Accordingly, I have often chosen to translate his *significato* as "meaning" or "message" rather than simply as "the signified" (the Italian *significato* is not as technical as the English "signified"), so as not to imply a deconstructionist program, which would be very out of place in the pages of this book. But by and large the reader will find that Bettini writes an almost jargon-free style of scholarship. In fact, the form in which Bettini most often makes his argument is that of a story, and of the meanings that stories can convey: as he himself explains, *The Portrait of the Lover* is a story about two lovers and a portrait, and all the variations that ancient culture played upon this famous theme. The entire book is built around such stories (and of course one story leads to another story, and another . . . as stories tend to do). Along the way, Bettini makes a series of complex arguments about the many different meanings of the image in ancient Greek and Roman societies, and the different cultural models (religious, political, psychological, etc.) in which images could become involved. But the guiding thread of the discourse always takes the form of a story, and it is the succession of stories that gives the book its shape and structure.

Now for the third and final observation in this apology of the translator: Maurizio Bettini is not only an extraordinary scholar, but he is also a writer of immense talent, and a very inspired teller of stories. This, more than anything, is what gets lost in translation. In many cases, I have simply had to resign myself to not being able to translate the elegant wordplay and boundless humor of Bettini's original Italian, with its sly irony and often elaborate allusions. As a rule, when forced to choose between the scholarship and the writing, I have always chosen the scholarship, preferring to make the argument and the method as clear as possible. This was the only choice that I could make, at least according to Augustine's pessimistic (but probably correct) theory of resemblances *in deterioribus*. Because this *Portrait of the Lover* is a translation, it cannot help but prove inferior to the original. But if I have been able to present Bettini's main arguments clearly, I hope that this English version will be of some use to anyone who shares an interest in ancient Greece and Rome, so that we might thus bring to life—again like the lucky Pygmalion—those cultures that have for so long been presented to us only in the frozen inertia of marble statues. The statue that comes to life is just a fantasy, of course, a fairy tale, a story . . . but these are stories that we cannot do without. In the end it is the stories that matter most of all: this is perhaps the principal lesson that Bettini's book has to teach us, and the secret of its success.

I owe many thanks to the other students in Maurizio Bettini's seminars at Berkeley who read various chapters of this book in draft form over the past year, and in particular to the members of our summer reading group: Julie Anderson, Pattie Becker, Bill Jennings, Alesia Mercedes-Alonso, Trevor Murphy, Kim Starr-Reid, and Yasmin Syed. Thanks also to Gianni Guastella for much good advice. Finally, I would like to express my gratitude (endless, as always) to Maurizio Bettini for having written this beautiful book and for having given me the opportunity to translate it.

Laura Gibbs
Berkeley, May 1997

PART I

The Portrait of the Lover

Quando giunse a Simon l'alto concetto
ch'a mio nome gli pose in man lo stile,
s'avesse dato a l'opera gentile
colla figura voce ed intelletto,

di sospir molti mi sgombrava il petto,
che ciò ch'altri à più caro, a me fan vile:
Però che 'n vista ella si mostra humile
promettendomi pace ne l'aspetto.

Ma poi ch'i' vengo a ragionar co llei
benignamente assai par che m'ascolte,
se risponder savesse a' detti miei!

Pigmalïon, quanto lodar ti dei
de l'imagine tua, se mille volte
n'avesti quel ch'i' sol una vorrei.

     —Petrarch, *Canzoniere* 78

When that inspired idea came to Simone, and he took the
stylus in hand on my behalf, if only he had given to his genteel
work a voice and intelligence together with its form! In that
way he would have spared my breast of many sighs that make
what is most dear to others seem worthless to me. But she
does have a very demure expression, and her look is a promise
of peace; when I come to speak with her, she seems to listen
to me, and to be favorably inclined: if only she were able to
respond to my words! Pygmalion, how lucky you are with
that statue: you have enjoyed a thousand times what I would
be glad to enjoy but once.

Introduction

The poet, with a portrait in his hands. It is a familiar scene. The portrait, naturally, is of the woman he loves: rather, of the beloved woman par excellence, of Laura. The poet holds the portrait gently in his hands, moving his lips in a long whisper. He is speaking with her—that is, with it, with the portrait—in the somewhat arcane language of lovers, and poets.

Of course, the poet we are describing here is Petrarch. But this is not a fictional bit of biography. He really did own a portrait of Laura, commissioned from his friend Simone Martini: "my Simone," *Symon noster.* Sadly, the portrait is no longer in our possession; time has swallowed it up, along with Petrarch's lute, and a Madonna by Giotto.[1] There are many people who would have wanted to see that portrait of Laura—indeed, many who would still want to do so, and not only because it was painted by Simone Martini. Perhaps if we could gaze upon her beauty, then we might understand, at last, *why.* But instead we must content ourselves with a far too fragile image of the portrait—the image of an image—that we find in one of Petrarch's poems.[2] And what might have been the fate of that precious effigy? Did it fall into the hands of an ungrateful and indifferent heir, perhaps stolen along with some things packed away in a chest, or ruined by the dampness of a cellar? Poor Laura: we cannot bear to think of her this way. Or perhaps she still exists somewhere, that Laura, hiding under a false name, waiting only for an ingenious art critic or a lucky collector of antiques to bring her back to us again. But are we speaking now of *her,* or of *her portrait?* Indeed, to ask such a question is already the beginning of our story.

I

The Fundamental Story

The subject matter of this book is a story, or rather a set of stories, each of which shares this unusual feature: the characters consist of two lovers and a portrait. We will discover, in fact, that there are very many ways in which these elements can be combined, a large number of stories that can be told about these characters. For example, one of the lovers might disappear and be replaced by a portrait, or one of the lovers might actually *be* a portrait, with no need at all for the referent; not to mention the grim and ominous tale of the enraged portrait, who exacts a surprising revenge after having been scorned by the surviving lover or insulted by a reckless and brazen adulterer. The story created by the moves of this restricted set of pawns—the lover, the beloved, and the image—is what we will call our *fundamental story;* after we begin the game, we will then see just how long the three pieces can be kept in play. But as we consider the various combinations that unfold before our eyes, at a certain moment we must ask whether we are talking now about the *person,* or about the *portrait?* Which is the one that really matters? With this in mind, let us look again to Petrarch, still holding Laura's portrait in his hands.

He is extremely pleased with this portrait. Laura, as Simone has depicted her, wears a sweet and modest expression that seems to offer a promise of peace, *promettendomi pace ne l'aspetto.* And when the poet speaks to her—when he comes to *ragionar co llei*—she actually seems to listen sympathetically. But the portrait is unable to respond to his words, to his *detti:*

Ma poi ch'i' vengo a ragionar co llei
benignamente assai par che m'ascolte,
se risponder savesse a' detti miei!

When I come to speak with her, she seems to listen to me, and to be
favorably inclined: if only she were able to respond to my words!

If only the portrait could speak . . . if only the portrait could love, like
the exquisite statue of a woman that Ovid's Pygmalion carved with his
own two hands—a statue that was finally able to love, thanks to the
intervention of Venus.[1] But Venus has long since ceased to exist and,
outside of literature, lovers no longer have a goddess on whom they
can call.

The image is superior to the model. Even Petrarch is willing to admit as much: the Laura that Simone has painted (faithful to some *alto
concetto*, an "inspired idea," nobly Platonic) is more peaceful, more
gentle, more disposed to love than the real Laura ever could have been.
This is what brings Pygmalion's good fortune to mind. There is a subtle
melancholy in Petrarch's final words—*Pigmalïon, quanto lodar ti dei /
de l'imagine tua*—and this same subtle melancholy no doubt animated
the poet's colloquies, his *ragionamenti*, with the portrait of the lover.
After all, as we know, Laura *is not there* . . . but in some sense she *is there*:
the portrait is simultaneously a sign of her absence and of her presence.
This is the paradox at the heart of our fundamental story. The portrait
is a point of passage, a narrow opening between the light and the dark.
Like a fragile veil of paper, the painted image is delicately poised between these two possibilities, and the slightest pressure in one direction
or the other can summon life, or death. It consoles us, and is also the
source of our greatest anguish.

Petrarch is alone. Solitude, in fact, is the essence of his identity; by
definition, he exists to be alone. The better part of his life begins only
now, when he can collect his thoughts in the company of his books at
the end of an exhausting day, or when he is able to flee the Babylon of
Avignon and escape to Vaucluse. He exists precisely in order to be alone,
there among the woods and springs where, without fail, her *image* will
appear; or in his small study, where he can fill the emptiness that sur-
rounds him by writing about her, or by speaking to her portrait—or by
using words (words that inevitably speak of her) to describe the portrait
he is holding in his hands.[2] All the lovers in our stories will be solitary
lovers, like Petrarch.

So the poet writes, populating his fantasy, furnishing the empty rooms of his longing with words. She is absent, and it could not be otherwise. For if she were present, if she were nearby, the poet would not be writing—for the poet, she *must* be far away. This is what literature, or rather the vocation to literary love, demands. The poet is alone, and an endless flurry of tiny gestures now seems to float up toward the ceiling, like a delicate bubble that swells and expands as it fills with fragile and luminous images. In his hands, the poet always holds the portrait of the lover.

2

A Potter Who Was Not Jealous

Plastice—the art of modeling in clay—was apparently discovered by a man named Butades,[1] a potter from Sicyon who later worked in Corinth.[2] As the story goes, his daughter had fallen in love with a young man who was about to leave on a long journey. On the eve of her lover's departure, she traced his profile on the wall, following the outline of his shadow cast by the light of a lantern. According to Athenagoras,[3] the young woman carried out this task while the young man was asleep (so in a certain sense she stole that silhouette). When her father Butades saw this design on the wall, he made a model of it in clay, which he dried and then hardened in the heat of the oven, along with his other clay pots and bowls. The resulting portrait was reportedly preserved in the Nymphaeum of Corinth until the city was sacked by Lucius Mummius. That is the story of how the art of *plastice* began.[4]

Birth of the Image

We begin with precisely these events because they credit our fundamental story with a vital function. The portrait of the lover is linked to the origin of a particular cultural practice, of an artistic *technē:* the story and the sculpture give rise to one another. The source of this impulse toward artistic creation (or rather, this artistic discovery) is specifically described as the feeling of *regret* for an absent person, that certain unsatisfiable desire which would be called *pothos* in Greek, *deside-rium* in Latin.[5] But at the moment of its birth, this first image shaped by Butades' hands was still fragile and new, unable to stand on its own. The portrait needed something to lean on: the shadow. The original portrait of the lover (and what appears to be the most ancient version of our fundamental story) was produced by a *shadow;* when the lover cast his silhouette on the wall, Butades' daughter traced (or stole) it, and thus discovered a new form of art.[6] According to this etiological account, *plastice* could enter the world of culture only thanks to the intervention of nature. By supplying the shadow, nature served as an unexpected mediator, overseeing the fateful birth of this new technique. The shadow could not remain there, and soon departed with the young man of Corinth as his faithful and ineluctable companion. But in the meantime the lover's astute melancholy (aided by the compassionate cleverness of art) had captured her lover's silhouette unawares. We should take careful note of this: the legendary trick used here by the potter's daughter will be crucial for the further development of our story, and its interpretation.[7]

This account of the origins of *plastice* bestows on our subject matter the quality of a myth. Thanks to Butades and his daughter, something was discovered that had been previously unknown: the technique of modeling in clay, *plastice.* Moreover, if we want to join in the game— so beloved by ancient authors—of deciding who did what first, we could even claim that Butades and his daughter (her *pothos,* and the consolation provided by his art) were the founders not just of modeling in clay, but of all the visual arts. According to Pliny, *plastice* was the first method used to make images that resemble their subjects, *similitudines exprimendi origo.* As such, *plastice* predates the art of making statues,[8] and Pasiteles in fact describes *plastice* not just as the "mother" of making statues, but also of engraving and carving.[9] The first portrait of the lover thus turns out to be the archetype not only of images modeled in clay but of *any sort of three-dimensional image.* In addition, Pliny tells us that the Greeks thought that *painting* was also reportedly discovered in Sicyon (according to some versions), or Corinth (according to others). In any case, "everyone agrees that it was a matter of tracing the outline of a man's shadow."[10] We cannot help but notice that these are precisely the same elements involved in the story of Butades and his daughter: Butades was said to come from Sicyon, and he produced his first portrait in Corinth, while Butades' daughter performed the deed that (as "everyone" agrees) led to the invention of painting: she outlined the contours of a man's shadow on the wall.[11] Were the potter and his daughter thus somehow connected not just to the origins of *plastice* but also to the origins of painting? If so, then it means that *desiderium,* that feeling of regret for the loss of a beloved person (and the motivation for the first portrait of the lover) could proudly claim to have invented the very art of creating images: *any* kind of image.

Whatever the case may be, Butades must also be given credit for having understood and consoled his daughter's lovelorn melancholy—that is, for being a potter who was not jealous. This may come as somewhat of a surprise: in general, fathers are supposed to be rather jealous of their daughters' love affairs. And potters in particular are supposed to be an altogether jealous breed, at least according to a thesis advanced some years ago by Lévi-Strauss: *la poterie, art jaloux.*[12] But perhaps Lévi-Strauss's assertion holds true only for the world of American Indians, not for European potters. What is clear is that the art of creating images began in Greece with an impulse of lovesick *pothos,* of *desiderium:* the story of a young woman who wanted to make a portrait of her absent beloved, assisted by the generosity and affection of a father who wanted to console her. The tables are turned in our next story, which is analogous to this one in every way except that this father will prove to be far less generous in dealing with his daughter and with the portrait that she adores.

Laodamia's Simulacra

The first Greek warrior to disembark on Trojan soil was destined to die, a liminal offering of blood that would mark the beginning of that glorious and accursed war (thus providing us with yet another example of the obscure risks of passage).[13] It was Protesilaus, the husband of Laodamia, to whom that hardly enviable honor was awarded, and his young wife was devastated, completely unable to accept the loss of her husband. According to various versions of the myth, the gods took pity on the young widow and sent Hermes to bring back her husband's shade from the realm of the dead—but the lovers were reunited only briefly. When the divinely allotted time had passed, Laodamia died of grief in the embrace of that beloved shade, and they descended into Hades together.[14] But according to other versions of the myth,[15] Laodamia instead consoled herself with a simulacrum of Protesilaus modeled in wax that she kept in their marriage chamber, venerating it as if it were a sacred image;[16] indeed, she apparently even "had relations" with this simulacrum of her husband.[17] But the slave who delivered the sacrificial fruits each morning decided one day to take a look through a crack in the door, and when he saw Laodamia embracing and kissing the statue, he assumed that she had let an adulterer into her room. The slave went to make a full report to Laodamia's father, Acastus, who in turn felt obliged to burst into his daughter's room—only to discover that it was the effigy, the *effigies,* of Protesilaus in her bed, and nothing more. Acastus then concluded that this fiction was simply tormenting his daughter to no good end, and he resolved to put a stop to it. Unlike Butades, Laodamia's father felt no pity: he ordered his servants to quickly build a pyre with the simulacrum and the sacred vessels thrown on top, and to then set the whole thing ablaze. But Laodamia could not endure this second loss, and cast herself straight into the flames.[18]

With this type of tale (that is, the tale of Butades' daughter, of Laodamia, and of the others yet to come), we enter into the very heart of our fundamental story: this is what we might call the classical variant, the most familiar and expected series of moves that can be made with two lovers and a portrait. The absent lover is replaced by an image: the portrait is a substitute, a consolation. In the centuries that follow, there will be many other solitary lovers who will want to replace an absent person with that person's image. Thomas's Tristan, for example, will possess a portrait of his lovely Isolde. Moreover, in his veneration of that image he will exceed even the devotion of Protesilaus's faithful and disconsolate widow: the sorrowful knight will actually construct around the simulacrum of his beloved a veritable theater of memory, a gallery of images erected in an inaccessible grotto where he will go to alleviate his relentless desire.[19]

Yet this story of the faithful wife and the portrait is already very beautiful. Ovid also sensed its appeal, and cast it in the form of a letter, one of his epistolary *Heroides.* Laodamia was thus enrolled in that unusual assembly of suffering heroines who—in the moment of their greatest distress, or greatest tragedy—decide to take tablet and stylus in hand and set about writing a letter to their lover.[20] Even Ariadne, for example, after Theseus has cruelly abandoned her on the island's shore, apparently can think of nothing better to do than to write him a letter.[21] Likewise, we now find Laodamia writing to her husband, Protesilaus. But the epistolary fiction naturally requires that the recipient still be numbered among the living, and therefore that Laodamia must be consumed by grief over Protesilaus's absence *before* the hero has died. The demands of the literary genre thus modify somewhat the traditional lines of the myth: the faithful wife must now venerate her husband's portrait *prior* to his death.[22] But Laodamia's tormented imagination can already anticipate how that ill-fated voyage to Troy will end (alas); the mere absence of the lover is still more than enough to motivate the existence, again in wax,[23] of Protesilaus's portrait:[24]

Dum tamen arma geres diverso miles in orbe,
    quae referat vultus est mihi cera tuos:
illi blanditias, illi tibi debita verba
    dicimus, amplexus accipit illa meos.
Crede mihi, plus est quam quod videatur imago;
    adde sonum cerae, Protesilaus erit.
Hanc specto teneoque sinu pro coniuge vero
    et, tamquam possit verba referre, queror.

While you, a soldier, are bearing arms in a far-off land, I keep for myself an image in wax that reproduces your face [*vultus*]. I say to it the sweet words I would otherwise say to you; the image receives my embraces. Believe me, that image is more than what it seems [*plus est quam quod videatur imago*]: give the wax a voice, and it would be Protesilaus. I gaze upon that portrait, pressing it to my breast in place of my true husband, and I make my complaints to that portrait, as if it could somehow speak words in response.

This passage provides an excellent description of the portrait of the lover, the image that "is more than what it seems." Ovid's Latin is admittedly very subtle: *plus est quam quod videatur imago*. The image is more than what it seems, and, at the same time, more than its capacity to be seen, more than what it appears (*videatur*). This is not the only time that we will be indebted to Ovid for a consummate definition.[25] But it must also be admitted that his version of Laodamia's story is rather less revealing than some other ancient versions of the tale — even if those other versions have often survived only as fragments, as mere sketches of stories that were once far more rich and spirited.[26]

But when we arrange these variations side by side, a highly meaningful cultural model begins to emerge, a model that explains a great deal about our fundamental story: the *shade* of Protesilaus that returns from the Underworld is somehow equivalent to the *portrait* of Protesilaus that is in his wife's possession. The myth develops along both of these cultural axes; this parallel relationship between the shade and the portrait allows the story to be told in two different ways (precisely as we have seen): this can be the story of a phantom, or the story of a portrait.[27] The portrait of the lover is somehow linked to the lover's ghostly survival in the afterlife, what the Greeks would call his *eidōlon* or *psychē*. The wax effigy of Protesilaus can play the same role as his phantom as it journeys from the Underworld, a melancholy pledge of compassion bestowed by the gods on a faithful and inconsolable wife (if only for a short reprieve). The two alternating plots—Laodamia and the ghost, Laodamia and the portrait—thus define what will prove to be an important cultural synonym for our fundamental story: the absent lover as both phantom and portrait.

The iconographic tradition associated with this story supplies further evidence of a close association between the phantom and the portrait. The most outstanding example is a famous sarcophagus in the Vatican that summarizes the entire myth (see Fig. 1).[28] In this rapid visual explication of the plot, we first see a grief-stricken Laodamia lying on a little bed. Behind the bed there is a portrait of Protesilaus (strongly marked by Bacchic features); meanwhile, seated on the bed next to Laodamia is Protesilaus himself, looking very sorrowful, captured in that brief moment in which the gods have allowed him to rejoin his wife.[29] An identical veiled figure appears to both the left and the right of this central grouping of sorrowful lovers: it is the phantom, depicted on his journeys to and from the Underworld. In this visual representation of the myth, the phantom and the portrait of Protesilaus are made to coexist: the portrait propped on the mantelpiece now witnesses the passage, all too swift, of the very *person* whom the portrait represents. There is also a cameo from the Hellenistic period that illustrates this same close connection—almost a relationship of symmetry or equivalence—between the phantom of Protesilaus and the portrait in Laodamia's possession.[30] This time we see Laodamia actually embracing Protesilaus's shade, while between the two lovers there is a human face, clearly the portrait, which once again serves as the witness and mediator of their impossible love.[31] This iconographic tradition shows us that the person of Protesilaus can apparently be refracted into two simultaneous and symmetrical simulacra: image, and phantom.

This triangle of correspondences between the person, the portrait, and the phantom surely constitutes a profound cultural model. As Vernant has shown, the *kolossos*—the rough-hewn stone statue that was planted upright in the ground as a monument to the dead in archaic Greek culture—was intended precisely as a physical representation of the double of the dead person, a stone equivalent of that person's *psychē*.[32] In archaic Greek religious experience there was thus an association between the stone and the shade, between the simulacrum and the ghostly survival, just as we have seen in the stories of Protesilaus and Laodamia. Moreover, this cultural equation between the portrait and the shade also recalls the melancholy cleverness of Butades' daughter, who traced the portrait of her lover along the lines of his shadow: once again, we find the shadow or shade entwined with the image, providing additional evidence of their proximity. The shadow traced by Butades' daughter was what the Greeks would call *skia*, as opposed to *psychē*, the shade of the dead. The distinction between these two types of shadowy representation further expands the range of cultural synonyms: the lover, the image, the shadow (*skia*), and the shade (*psychē*).[33] Moreover, if we delve somewhat deeper into Laodamia's tale, we can reach one more important conclusion. In the context of this story, the dead man's shade and his image are apparently destined to perform the same, tragic task: they provide the surviving lover with a passageway from the world of the living to the world of the dead. When Laodamia is about to lose her husband's phantom she decides to accompany him on his way to the Underworld; when she is faced with the destruction of her husband's portrait, she again decides to follow that same shadowy path. It is as if the image of the lost lover exerted a perilous, downward attraction to the Underworld. This phenomenon provides another precise parallel to Vernant's analysis of the *kolossos:* like the portrait of the lover in Laodamia's story, the *kolossos* also functioned as a point of passage between the world above and the world below.[34] Therefore, both in the religious experience of archaic Greece and in the mythical imagination of the abandoned lover, the simulacrum marks a gap between life and death; the image is able to open a passageway between the two worlds. In the next chapter, we will observe this same phenomenon in the story of Alcestis and Admetus.

Of course, Ovid should never be underestimated. With a sure sense of the subject in question (and of its structural, or rather its cultural implications), the Roman poet provides another cultural synonym to add to our list: his version of Laodamia's story emphasizes the link between the lover's image and the *dream,* a motif that we will encounter frequently in these pages. As Laodamia explains in her letter to Protesilaus:[35]

> Aucupor in lecto mendaces caelibe somnos;
>   dum careo veris, gaudia falsa iuvant.
> Sed tua cur nobis pallens occurrit imago?
>   Cur venit a verbis multa querela tuis?
> Excutior somno simulacraque noctis adoro.

In my celibate bed I grasp at deceptive dreams; lacking true pleasures, I welcome even false ones. But why does your image appear before me seeming so pale? Why are your words the words of grief? I wake from my sleep and worship the apparitions of the night.

Simulacraque noctis adoro, "I worship the apparitions of the night."
Laodamia venerates these dreams, the *simulacra noctis,* with the same
devotion she displays for the wax simulacrum that is her husband's portrait. Both types of apparition are able to evoke the absent lover, albeit
partially, desperately; Laodamia treats them both as the objects of a cult
of the beloved, thus establishing a tacit correlation, a sort of silent complicity, between the portrait and the dream. Of course, we cannot ig-
nore the role that language plays in this symbolic constellation, and the
way that words themselves make certain demands (or offer certain ad-
vantages): the image seen in a dream or the portrait created by an artist
are both called *eidōlon* in Greek, *simulacrum* or *imago* in Latin.[36] The
lover's dreams, the *simulacra noctis,* will regularly claim a place in the
development of our fundamental story, as in the following (quite famous) example.

A Phantom Reigns in the Palace

The Chorus of Aeschylus's *Agamemnon* describes the
sense of ruin that has seized the court of Sparta and its king since Helen
abandoned Menelaus:[37]

> The soothsayers of the palace greatly lamented, saying, "Alas, alas for
> the palace, the palace and the princes; alas for the bed and the husband-
> loving traces [*stiboi*] she left there. . . . Because of his longing [*pothos*] for
> the woman who has crossed the sea, a phantom seems to reign in the pal-
> ace! The charm of the lovely statues [*eumorphoi kolossoi*] is hateful to the
> husband; in the eyes' emptiness all the charm of Aphrodite has vanished.
> Appearing in dreams, sorrowful apparitions bring empty pleasure—
> because it is surely vanity when a man thinks that he sees joyful things,
> but the vision suddenly slips from his embrace, and wings its way along
> the paths of sleep."

Once again we see that grief for the absent lover teems with images—
in particular, the images seen in dreams. But we are dealing here with
an obscure and difficult text, one that has created many difficulties for
the commentators. What in fact are those "beautiful statues," the *eu-
morphoi kolossoi,* from whose eyes all loveliness has vanished? Are they
images that reproduce Helen's features (and thus another portrait of the
lover, an example of our fundamental story)? Or are we dealing here
simply with decorations, the traditional statues of women called *korai*

that would have adorned the palace of the king? Aeschylus does not appear to have given us enough evidence to reach a definitive conclusion, although the second interpretation does seem somewhat more likely than the first.[38] In any case, despite the difficult and allusive symbolism of Aeschylus's style, something quite noteworthy emerges from the soothsayers' prophecies: Menelaus has been seized by *pothos* (as the text explicitly states), by grief and longing for the wife who abandoned him. And this desire for an absent lover (the same sentiment that led the potter's daughter to trace her lover's shadow on the wall, and that prompted Laodamia to embrace Protesilaus's statue) is once again displayed through *images:* specifically those images constructed by human hands, the *kolossoi* that are now hateful to Menelaus, statues in whose empty eyes the charms of love have vanished.[39] Menelaus's situation is the exact opposite of Laodamia's: the statue of the absent person no longer receives the love of the person left behind; instead, the statues arouse antipathy, and their eyes are empty. This reversal of functions makes perfect sense, given that the *pothos* of Laodamia was grief for a beloved husband from whom she has been sundered by death, while the *pothos* of Menelaus is grief for a faithless and fugitive wife. The consoling image of Protesilaus (whose eyes, presumably, were full) is here transposed into a hateful image lacking integrity and expression: an image whose eyes are empty. But the fact remains that this *pothos* for the absent lover is nevertheless understood in terms of images—in terms of *kolossoi* and (once again) in terms of the images seen in dreams, those phantoms that bring empty pleasures to Menelaus before winging their way along the paths of sleep. In short, Helen's absence is figured in images.

But these are not the only images of Helen mentioned in the passage: we must decide what to make of those *stiboi,* traces of Helen—either "footprints" or "bodily impressions"—that she left behind in the palace. It is not clear if these *stiboi* should be read as the footprints made by Helen's feet when she approached the marriage bed, still in love with Menelaus—or if instead they are the bodily impressions left behind on that same bed.[40] Once again, the sublime obscurity of Aeschylus's style leaves open several ways of reading the text. The first hypothesis ("footprints") seems more likely, at least from a linguistic point of view.[41] But there is no lack of arguments to support the second hypothesis. For example, we know that ancient erotic poetry often focused on the bodily impression that the beloved person left behind in the place of love.[42] But there is something more profound and almost magical at work here: this Aeschylean vision might instead be haunted by the various obscure powers that were attributed to such bodily impressions in ancient culture. One of the so-called *symbola* of Pythagoras required that the body's impression be erased in the morning upon getting up from bed, apparently because the impression of the limbs preserved something of the actual person, something it would be dangerous to expose to others.[43] With strongly erotic overtones, this same prohibition reappears in an unusual rule of etiquette for young men expounded in Aristophanes' *The Clouds:*[44] "At the gymnasium, they should sit with their legs sticking out . . . and when they get up, they should be sure to smooth the sand in order not to leave behind for their admirers any trace [*eidōlon*] of their youth."[45] In Aristophanes' words, the bodily impression is also an *eidōlon,* a "trace," an "image."[46] Indeed, in both ancient beliefs and European folklore (as well as in the "superstitions" of so-called primitive peoples), bodily impressions are considered to be especially significant images.[47] The bodily impression forms a part of the person, magically connected to that person both by contact and by similarity. As such, the bodily impression is very similar to the shadow: like the shadow, the bodily impression reproduces the body's features; and like the shadow, the bodily impression is connected to the body (to the person) by contiguity and belonging.[48] Bodily impressions thus have the extraordinary power to evoke a person, and as such they are subject to specific regulations and beliefs in various cultures, including ancient Greece. In the case of the melancholy, abandoned lover, this bodily impression would be able to perfectly represent both the presence and (paradoxically) the absence of the beloved, serving the same function as the portrait, the shadow, or the image seen in a dream. The *stiboi* of the soothsayers' vision in the *Agamemnon* can thus be understood as a sort of phantom image, sounding a sudden note of ominous estrangement that reverberates throughout the chorus—echoed in the statues whose eyes are empty, and the fleeting shades that are seen in sleep.

Of course, the other (and probably more reasonable) interpretation of Helen's *stiboi*—the footprints made as she approached the marriage bed—also belongs to this same magical realm. If the *stiboi* are understood as footprints, the soothsayers would still be invoking something that recalls the absent woman through signs and contiguity. Indeed, a person's footprints and the impression made by that person's body are subject to the same regulations in many traditional belief systems, because both the trace left by the body and the tracks made by the feet are supposed to retain a part of the person, constituting an evocative sign.[49]

We can find evidence for these traditional beliefs about the specific evocative force of the footprint in another *symbolon* of Pythagoras, which prohibits "cutting a man's footprint with a knife."[50] To wound the footprint was apparently equivalent to a direct assault on the person represented by that footprint.

But beyond these possible "superstitions" of Pythagoras, it must be emphasized that in Greek culture generally, and in the tragedies of Aeschylus in particular, the sign of the *stibos* was assigned a specific semiotic task: this "print" or "impression" was a true and proper identifying feature through which a person could be immediately recognized.[51] Thus, in another play by Aeschylus we find the *stiboi* of Orestes (along with a votive lock of his hair) serving as the signs by which Electra is able to recognize and identify her brother's presence at the tomb of their father, Agamemnon.[52] The *stibos* functions as a strong and very precise sign, able to immediately evoke and identify a person. Certainly those Aeschylean *stiboi* of Orestes might help to explain those other *stiboi*, also Aeschylean, that Helen has left behind in the palace of Menelaus.

The fact is that Helen's *stiboi*, in whatever sense we understand them here (footprints or bodily impressions), belong to a realm of signs and traces endowed with tremendous evocative power. We should not forget that in the mind of Menelaus, inflamed by longing, by *pothos,* the royal palace lives under the rule of a phantom, teeming with deceptive and agonizing apparitions.[53] Nothing exists for itself any more; everything is a trace of something else, endlessly referring elsewhere: empty images (*stiboi, kolossoi,* dreams) that persistently remind the husband of Helen's absence, and of the fact that she has left him for a foreign lover.

3

The Story of Admetus, and the True Portrait of the Lover

"All the rituals have been performed by the king," says the Chorus-Leader in Euripides' *Alcestis*, "and the altars of all the gods are inundated with the blood of sacrifices: nothing is lacking, yet there is still no remedy for our misfortune! But look, here comes a slave woman from the palace of Admetus, her face covered in tears. I will find out from her what has happened . . . [he turns to the slave woman] . . . Does the queen yet breathe, or is she dead? This is what we want to know." The slave replies: "You might say that she is living, and also that she is dead." The Chorus-Leader exclaims, "But how is it possible that the same person can be dead and yet still see the light?" [1]

The Statue of Alcestis

It is possible precisely because the god Thanatos has already arrived; Death itself is waiting (impatiently) at the gate, ready to drag Alcestis away to the Underworld. The story is a famous one. Admetus is supposed to die, but Apollo, in order to save him, obtains a singular privilege for his favorite follower—someone else can die in his place. Yet no one is willing to volunteer for this fatal substitution—not Admetus's father, not even his old mother, who gave birth to him. Only Alcestis, his young wife, agrees to offer her life in exchange for his. The story is an apology for love but it is also a ruthless exploration of what we call "bonds" and the degree to which parents must love their children—in other words, how far one can stretch that biological and cultural law requiring a father to give way before his child, surrendering his place to the next generation, or asking a mother (who alone is able to give life to others) to sacrifice herself in order to sustain the life of her child.[2] In the plot of this tale, the poet and the myth explore together the framework of human relations, that arcane and everyday world of our heartfelt emotions.[3] But this is not the topic that brings us to this text.

Instead, we have already reached the point in the story when Alcestis, after a long and agonized speech to Admetus, is about to begin her sad descent toward the shades. A few moments from now she will collapse, and in front of her fallen body the Chorus-Leader will exclaim: "She is gone; the wife of Admetus is no more!"[4] But now, in Admetus's mind, the gratitude he feels for this gift of life—a gift that can never be repaid—augments his grief for the imminent demise of his remarkable wife. The mounting excess of Admetus's *pathos* finally bursts forth in a lengthy speech.[5]

> While alive, you were my only woman: now that you are dead, no one but you will bear that name; no other Thessalian bride, in your place, will be able to turn to me, calling me her husband. There is no other woman who could excel you in the nobility of her lineage or in her beauty. My sons are enough: I ask of the gods only that I may rejoice in them, because in you I can no longer rejoice. Oh my wife, I will mourn you not just for a year but for as long as I shall live—despising the woman who gave birth to me, hating my father: in name only, not in deeds, did they love me, while you have sacrificed that most precious thing of all in order to save my life. . . .
>
> Shaped by skilled craftsmen's hands, your body will lie in my bed, and falling upon it, I will embrace it, calling out your name. I will think that I have my dear wife in my arms, yet not having her [*doxō gynaika . . . ouk echōn echein*]. A cold delight, I know, but all the same it will lighten the burden of my soul. And coming to me in dreams, you will make me rejoice, because it is sweet at night to see the person you love, for as long as it can last.

As we can see, this text manages to assemble an extraordinary number of the motifs involved in our fundamental story. Indeed, we might even say that they are elaborated here in an analytical, almost discursive, manner. But before examining these motifs in detail, we first need to ask: *who is she* exactly, this Alcestis—a mortal already condemned to death, listening to Admetus's speech after she has collapsed? How might we conceive of her in these moments that the audience knows to be ineluctably her last? There is clearly a wrenching split in Alcestis's identity at this point: she exists, but this is at the same time a nonexistence. The slave has already defined her mistress's condition very precisely: "You might say that she is living, and also that she is dead." The Alcestis who lingers on is a liminal person; life and death are fused together in her. In a certain sense, Alcestis is *doubled:* a dead woman who has the features and voice of a living person, and a living woman whom we expect to turn suddenly rigid, never to move again (an event that will take place just a few moments from now). But this doubled condition, this ambivalence, greatly resembles the nature of an object that will be deeply implicated in our entire discussion: a statue, that realization of a person's presence and, at the same time, also an indisputable sign of the person's absence.[6] The simulacrum of Alcestis that Admetus envisions will serve as a replacement for the deceased Alcestis. But at this moment, on the stage, Alcestis herself is already a mixture of life and death, just like a statue: she already foreshadows the simulacrum that will later replace her. Embracing the statue, the *kolossos* "shaped by skilled hands," Admetus will think that he has his dear wife in his arms, "yet not having her." But if he were to embrace Alcestis now, a moment before her departure, would he actually have her, Alcestis, in his arms, or not? The simulacrum will replace Alcestis, but Alcestis herself already prefigures that simulacrum: it is a game of substitutions that can be played in both directions.[7]

But let us return to our fundamental story and to Admetus's speech, starting with his singular declaration: "I will think that I have my dear wife in my arms, yet not having her." It is certainly not by chance that Euripides again uses almost exactly the same words in his *Helen* to describe the living ghost that Paris brings back to Troy in place of the actual Helen. As she herself explains:[8] "The goddess Hera did not give me to Alexander; she gave him only a living image [*eidōlon*] that resembles me . . . and in vain Paris thinks that he has me, yet not having me [*dokei m' echein . . . ouk echōn*]."[9] Euripides uses essentially the same expression to describe the illusory embrace that grasps at a ghost and the illusory embrace that grasps at a statue: having, yet not having. The very words used in the text of the *Alcestis* thus reveal the close contiguity between the *kolossos* and the *eidōlon*—between the elusive image sculpted by human hands, and the elusive image created by the gods, which they use to deceive mere mortals.

In addition, the beloved's simulacrum and her dream image once again appear together on this stage of absence: "Coming to me in dreams," Admetus says, "you will make me rejoice." As in the case of Ovid's Laodamia and Aeschylus's Menelaus, the bereft lover attempts to reconstruct the beloved's presence by means of two parallel possibilities—the manufactured image and the dream. It is as if he hoped to unite the cold (but corporeal, tangible) presence of the statue with the sweet (but empty, fleeting) visitations of the ghost in dreams. This close contiguity between dream images and artificial simulacra is hardly surprising, given that the same connection surfaces in other aspects of ancient culture, including the sphere of religious experience. As Carlo Brillante has shown, Greek sources provide numerous examples of episodes in which a god appears to the dreamer in a form that resembles his cult image, and other cases in which there are relationships of similarity and interaction between the dream image and the statue of the god.[10] For example, Artemidorus clearly states that there is no difference between dreaming of the divinity as we imagine him to be and dreaming of his cult image. Thus Ptolemy Soter was said to have seen a statue of Serapis in a dream—a vision that was later identified with an actual cult statue of the god venerated at Sinope.[11] Likewise, we can include here a humorous story about a man who had gone to the incubation sanctuary of Asclepius in Athens to seek a response from the god regarding his illness. The god appeared to the man in a dream, and advised him to eat pork. But when he woke up, the patient dared to raise objections to the diet—at which point, the statue of the god intervened directly, prescribing a different regime.[12] In short, as Brillante observes, "by its very nature the dream is already an image (the Greeks emphasized the visual aspect of dreams above all), so the divinity could appear as himself in the dream, or as an effigy that represented him: the final result was in any case always constituted by an image."[13]

At this point, we can draw a first conclusion—or at least make a closer connection between these recurrent, interrelated motifs. The two main versions of Laodamia's story establish an equivalence between the absent person's simulacrum (based on the model of the *kolossos*) and that person's *psychē*, or ghostly shade. Likewise, the story of Butades—the potter who made a portrait of his daughter's lover from the young man's shadow (*skia*) projected on the wall—demonstrates that another type of shade, the corporeal shadow, can also be considered equivalent to the image: the portrait of the lover is somehow born from that shadow, and can then assume (and reinforce) the shadow's representational function.[14] In addition, the symbolic constellation of Aeschylus's vision allows us to add a third player to this game between the image and the shadow: the sign of the *stibos,* either the bodily impression left behind by the beloved, or her footprints as she approached the marriage bed. The series of cultural equivalents thus expands before our very eyes. Deprived of the beloved, the lover nourishes his nostalgic melancholy by evoking the presence of the person who is no longer there: by means of a portrait, a ghost, a stolen shadow on the wall, an impression of the body, a footprint. It is therefore no surprise to find that the *eidōla* of dreams are included among these figures of absence, this panoply of images that populate the solitary lover's world.[15] In the letter written by Ovid's Laodamia, in the soothsayers' vision of Menelaus's palace, or in Admetus's speech to Alcestis (and in still other examples that we will consider), manufactured images are repeatedly associated with dream images in a stable cultural correlation. Any kind of apparition seems drawn to the image, as if by a sort of cultural magnetism.

But before returning (with Admetus) to Euripides' tragic text, we might allow ourselves a brief and more lighthearted interlude. Our ancient sources actually provide us with yet another story that confirms this recurring and deep-seated connection between the phantom apparition (Greek *eidōlon*) and the portrait. According to a famous legend, the unfortunate poet Stesichorus was blinded for having slandered Helen in one of his poems and was thus induced to write the *Palinode* in which he exculpated Menelaus' wife in a most ingenious manner: Helen, it turns out, did not go to Troy after all. That was only her *eidōlon,* a phantom apparition, while the real Helen remained behind in Egypt at the court of Proteus. Menelaus therefore was not betrayed, and Helen, the most beautiful woman in the world, was never a public disgrace. The story was destined to enjoy a certain success (as we saw already in the passage from Euripides' *Helen*), despite the fact that we possess only a fragment of the *Palinode*,[16] along with a few other pieces of indirect (and often contradictory) evidence for the poem.[17] But luckily these philological difficulties are not what interest us here. Instead, we simply want to examine the scholia to Aelius Aristides in which the affairs of this *eidōlon* are narrated in a quite original way.[18]

Like Stesichorus, this scholiast maintains that Helen did not go to Troy but instead remained on the island of Pharos with Proteus. Paris (whom the scholiast calls by his other name, Alexander) did not carry off Helen's actual person, but received the customary phantom: "From Proteus he received her image [*eidōlon*] painted on a tablet [*en pinaki gegrammenon*]. Gazing upon this object, Alexander was able to find a consolation for his love." Paris is thus transformed into a solitary lover of the sort we have seen before—sailing back to Troy with a portrait of the lover in his hands. Stesichorus certainly could not have written anything of the kind, but the invention (whoever it was) is extremely charming, the sort of *Palinode* we might expect from, say, Jules Laforgue—a poem in which Paris arrives at his father's palace only to lock himself away in his room, sighing over Helen's picture, as hosts of warriors covered in blood and dust are being butchered around those accursed walls, not merely for a phantom this time but, still worse, for a piece of painted wood! In the version told by this anonymous scholiast, our fundamental story (the lover, the beloved, and the portrait) produces a bizarre variation on what was already a rather bizarre invention (a Trojan War in which Helen did not go to Troy); the animated phantom that Paris brought to Troy, the *eidōlon* that he believed to be the beautiful Helen, has become another portrait of the lover.[19]

But let us return to Admetus, and with him to the profundity of Euripides' text. We have already examined some of Admetus's gestures, all of them highly symbolic: embracing the simulacrum of his wife as he anticipates the nightly visit of *another* image, the image seen in a dream.[20] But Admetus desires to make one further gesture: he says that he will call out the *name* of Alcestis as he holds her simulacrum in his arms.[21] It is as if the name of Alcestis were somehow able to repair that absence, to restore the life that the simulacrum lacks—because the simulacrum (as we now know) is a presence that can be a sign only of absence. When she is called, Alcestis might return a fragment of herself to her husband; by being called, the simulacrum might somehow become more alive, allowing Admetus to think that he has his dear wife in his arms, "yet not having her." To shout Alcestis's name is clearly something more than an outpouring of grief or a tribute paid to her memory: when it is used in this way, the name actually possesses a tremendous power against death. Likewise, as we will see later in another story, the ghost of Cynthia appears to Propertius in a dream, rebuking him for not having paid his respects at her funeral rites and, in particular, for not having called her back: if Propertius had only called her back (*te revocante*), she might have been able to wrest one more day of life from the gods.[22] In the next chapter, we will see the same words used to describe the poet Lucan who is called by his faithful widow Polla (*vocante Polla*), so that he too can implore one last day of life from the gods.[23]

The name is strictly tied to the image: it is like a vocal tracing of the image, its verbal equivalent. This is why the *damnatio memoriae*—that violent oblivion imposed on a person who is no longer to be loved or honored—specifically involves both the name and the effigy of the *damnatus*.[24] It is precisely the specter of oblivion that terrifies Admetus; this is the enemy he has vowed to defeat. Throughout his monologue, Admetus never even mentions the word "forget" (perhaps because it is too frightening, or too obvious); nor does he mention memory, the faithful opposite of oblivion. In any case, a categorical denial of forgetting fills Admetus's every phrase, taking different shapes at each turn, swelling into the rejection of a new wedding, an insistence that his lineage is already complete ("my sons are enough"), and a vow of perpetual mourning. Admetus vows to *remember,* and thus pledges himself to the name and to the image of the person who has vanished. But there is still something else at work here: the psychology of love tells us that one of the symptoms of feverish passion is that the name and the image of the beloved are invested with tremendous power. As we will see in a later chapter, the solitary lover, tormented by his isolation, feels as if he is surrounded by simulacra of the beloved and, above all, by her *dulce nomen,* her sweet name, which ceaselessly resounds in his ears.[25] Erotic theory thus acknowledges the obscure force that is embodied in the name, a power that makes the name strangely able to replace the beloved. To hear the name, or to pronounce it, is already the outline of a presence; when it is written down, the name becomes a poem of love. Perhaps somewhat abruptly, we can return to the example of Petrarch, and the obsessive care with which he wove the name of Laura like a sort of filigree into the verses that sprang to life at his hands.[26]

The name thus has a complementary relationship to the person's image. It constitutes the other side of an individual's identity, defining the possibility of being precisely that person and not somebody else. If we do not fully appreciate this relationship between the name and the image in the construction of a personal identity, we cannot hope to understand the entire first scene of Plautus's *Amphitruo,* in which poor Sosia desperately tries to defend both his name and his image from being expropriated by Mercury, the god who (at Jupiter's behest) has assumed Sosia's identity.[27] This close connection between the name and the image emerges clearly (even dramatically) whenever the assorted habits of everyday life are disrupted, and the presence—the very identity—of a person becomes an object of dispute, as when Sosia encounters his own double or when Admetus decides to fictitiously reconstruct the identity of a missing person. The same can also be said of magical practices which attempt to bend the forces of nature or human will to their own purposes. This link between the name and the image is one of the most frequently used devices in magic spells, making it possible to harness supernatural forces or exert control over the natural world.[28] The "crisis of presence" that Admetus experiences at the death of his wife provokes him to unleash (consciously or unconsciously) a disturbing series of symbolic substitutes, very much what we might expect to find in any magician's bag of tricks: the simulacrum, the name, the dream.[29]

But there is another important feature that emerges from this Euripidean version of our fundamental story (perhaps the most magnificent version of the story that we possess): Admetus makes a moving declaration of *faithfulness,* swearing absolute fidelity to his dying wife. No other Thessalian woman will call him husband; Alcestis was and will remain the only woman for him so long as he may live.[30] It is in the name of this vow of love, of this pledge, that Admetus decides to have a simulacrum of the absent Alcestis "shaped by skilled hands." The husband's intentions are so urgent that he even plans to place the statue in the marriage bed (as we saw also in one version of Laodamia's story).[31] The marriage chamber is the symbolic kingdom in which the young bride rules, and if that space is occupied by her image, Alcestis can be certain that no other woman will take her place by Admetus's side. The vow of love will triumph even over her absence, with the image serving as a visible and concrete act of faithfulness (a subject to which we will return in a later chapter).[32] In this dramatic speech, Euripides has parted the curtains for us, making it possible to catch a precious glimpse behind the scenes of our fundamental story.

Yet as we bring this discussion to a close, we should not overlook an obvious, but crucial, moment in Euripides' plot. At the end of the tragedy Alcestis succeeds in *returning* from the Underworld, thanks to the assistance of Heracles. No doubt her simulacrum, preserved in the marriage bed, somehow facilitated her return. In the story of Laodamia, the simulacrum of the beloved finally dragged the surviving lover off to the Underworld: confronted with the destruction of that simulacrum, the young bride chose to commit suicide. Here, on the other hand, we find a perfect inversion of the same situation, resulting in an opposite outcome: this time the distant beloved manages to return to the world of the living, as Alcestis rejoins her husband. The simulacrum thus seems to function as a point of passage, a mediator between life and death, a portal that leads in one direction . . . or the other. It is as if the presence of the absent beloved in the form of an image created an open-ended situation, a moment in which the definitive resolution has not yet been reached, or is postponed: the lover is still hoping for an arrival, or waiting to make that (final) exit.

The True Portrait of the Lover

We have spoken here insistently about stories, about tales—and there are many other literary stories that we have yet to consider, of course. But we would not want to leave the impression that such devotion to the portrait of the lover is a purely literary phenomenon, confined to the poets' elegant recreation of ancient topoi or their own highbrow psychological projections. Ovid's Laodamia or Euripides' Admetus are quite famous literary characters—but we should not forget that there are Laodamias and Admetuses to be found among the general population, characters who are totally unknown to us (practically speaking) but who nevertheless might want to leave behind some tangible proof of their special devotion to the image of their beloved.

The literary conventions of poetry clearly exert an influence on these testimonies from the *Carmina latina epigraphica:* but unlike other literary texts, these inscriptions recapitulate a real and actual *life* put into verse (whose meters, admittedly, sometimes falter). Ovid's Laodamia, and all that she professed about Protesilaus's image, was pure fiction; the same must be said of Euripides' Admetus and his speech about Alcestis's image—even if the lies of literature, as we know, often correspond to a higher truth. But what motive could a person like Allius or Cornelia Galla have had to tell lies? These were everyday people from the population at large, who aspired to have their devotion to an image inscribed in stone. We should believe them; that is, after all, what they ask us to do.

This, then, is what Allius says about his deceased wife, Allia Potestas:[33]

Effigiem pro te teneo solacia nostri
quam colimus sancte sertaque multa datur
cumque ad te veniam mecum comitata sequetur.
sed tamen infelix cui tam sollemnia mandem?
si tamen extiterit cui tantum credere possim
hoc unum felix amissa te mihi forsan ero.

Instead of you, I hold an image [*effigies*], my consolation, which I venerate devotedly, and which I crown with many garlands. And when I will come to you, it will follow me, as my companion. But woe is me, to whom can I entrust this sacred task? If only there were someone in whom I could put such trust, this one thing would perhaps be enough to make me happy, despite having lost you.

In making this declaration to his late wife, Allius surpasses even Admetus in his promises. Not only does an image occupy the place of his beloved, he vows to take this image with him into the grave when he too is finally laid to rest; this thought, he insists, is his greatest consolation. Admetus did not envision such a possibility—the statue that he wanted to have "shaped by skilled hands" was not explicitly supposed to last even after death. Yet a very practical worry still disturbs the ingenious joy that Allius has contrived for himself: he is not sure whether there is anyone he can trust to carry out this provision of his will. Perhaps the widower was too well acquainted with mankind (or with the members of his own family) to count on their assistance.

In any case, the quite practical context of Allius's ritual consolation suggests an equally practical question: how should we imagine these portraits of the beloved person in concrete, physical terms? Euripides speaks of a "statue" (*kolossos*) in Admetus's bed, and our mythographical sources also tell us that Laodamia kept a statue in her bed.[34] But surely we cannot suppose that Allius possessed an image of that sort— how would he have been able to take such a statue with him into his tomb?[35] Apparently the portrait is not a complete figure, but only a *face*, made of wax or some other material. This is the most reasonable supposition, and it is supported by a great deal of evidence. Ovid, for example, describes the portrait in Laodamia's possession as a face,[36] and as we will see in the next chapter, Polla possessed and venerated a face of her deceased husband Lucan.[37] Likewise, Cornelia Galla—to whom we will turn in just a moment—consoled herself with an image of the face of her husband Frontonianus.[38]

But in addition to these written descriptions, we can also make use of the two iconographic pieces of evidence that we cited somewhat earlier. Indeed, by looking at these ancient works of art, we are able to speak about the portrait of the lover in the very act of gazing upon it: the image of an image. So let us consider again that Hellenistic cameo in which Laodamia is shown seated in the embrace of Protesilaus's shade. Between the two lovers there is a portrait, and it takes the form of a human face.[39] Similarly, the Vatican sarcophagus also displays a facial portrait, this time in the form of a Bacchic mask,[40] which is propped on the mantelpiece behind the little bed where Laodamia is lying.[41] Thus, in addition to the faces that are described in the poets' powerful (and even somewhat delirious) stories, it appears fairly certain that in real life the portrait of the lover was realized in the form of a face—a face that the other, surviving lover could then devotedly shower with tearful rites of consolation. This presumably is the sort of portrait that Allius wanted to take with him into the tomb—if only he could rely on his executors to carry out this last request.

We can thus consider Allius as a kind of Admetus, passionate but at the same time very pragmatic; Cornelia Galla, meanwhile, seems to be a more reasonable version of Laodamia. Upon the death of her husband, Varius Frontonianus, she commissioned nine quite correct and elegant hexameters as an outpouring of her grief and love.[42] The story of Cornelia Galla is not a famous one; rather, it is one of those countless stories that, having been excluded from books and classical texts, can live only a sort of shadow existence, buried, but not completely lost:

> Hic situs est Varius cognomine Frontonianus
> quem coniunx lepida posuit Cornelia Galla.
> Dulcia restituens veteris solacia vitae
> marmoreos vultus statuit, oculos animumque
> longius ut kara posset saturare figura.
> hoc solamen erit visus. nam pignus amoris
> pectore contigitur memor[i] dulcedine mentis
> nec poterit facili labium oblivione perire,
> sed dum vita manet toto est in corde maritus.

> Here lies Varius Frontonianus, interred by his dear wife, Cornelia Galla. And renewing the sweet consolations of the past, she placed this face [*vultus*] in marble,[43] so that her eyes and soul could yet sate themselves with the sight of his dear features. But this is a comfort for the eyes only, while the pledge of love is kept in the heart through sweet recollections of the mind; his kiss will not fade through easy forgetfulness. As long as she lives, her husband will fill all her heart.

Cornelia Galla, of course, is *not* Laodamia: she is a sensible wife, an average, everyday person. Her husband's image is a consolation for the eyes, she says, but not for the heart: the heart already holds the pledge of love, never forgotten, and has no need of images to revive the bond that united the lovers in life. It is nothing new, this notion that the strongest of all images is the true memory residing in the soul, free from idolatrous effigies or portraits.[44] But it is unusual to hear this thought expressed by a person dedicating a portrait of her beloved—indeed, to hear such a thought expressed in the very act of dedication. Here we glimpse the other side of the image: this poem admits the image's irremediably *extrinsic* character, and the risk of its inability to truly reveal the invisible impulses of emotion. It is almost as if Laodamia were guilty not of having loved Protesilaus *too much* but rather, on the contrary, of not having loved him enough, of being content to display his merely exterior, superficial form, of satisfying herself with his simulacrum. The person who happens to see the image of Varius Frontonianus (a casual or curious onlooker, a *viator* who might take the time to inspect this monument by the side of the road) would not suppose that Cornelia Galla needed *to be there* to remember her husband—and this is precisely what the good Roman *matrona* wanted very much for us to know.

4

A Plaster Dionysus

The *Metamorphoses* of Apuleius are not only a single long story, but also an ongoing occasion for the telling of other stories. In the intricately woven plot, small stories and large ones alternate, creating a flurry of second or third voices to which the internal characters listen, at times distractedly, almost as if they were required to do so by the design of the narrative. But the voices also reach us as well, the actual listeners, who stand outside the text, thus providing a welcome reminder of the existence of literature, and of its pleasures.

At this point, the hero of the *Metamorphoses,* Lucius, has already been transformed into an ass because of his foolish fascination with magic: not a very encouraging state of affairs. To make matters worse, an enraged woman has just burst into his stall, blaming him for the death of her son, and intending to martyr him in a violent act of revenge. But at that very moment, someone arrives from the city, one of Charite's slaves (the same Charite whom the reader of the *Metamorphoses* already knows from her earlier involvement in the episode of Lucius and the bandits).[1] How can we keep from listening to the story that he begins to tell by the fireside, surrounded by all the other slaves? His tale is a baroque and highly refined variation of our fundamental story—but at a certain point the god Dionysus (or rather, Liber) will make an appearance, and this innovation will prove to be of considerable interest in understanding the portrait of the lover.

The Tale of the Playboy's Punishment

Tlepolemus was in love with Charite, and he was loved by her equally in return: the perfect couple.[2] But Charite was also the object of Thrasyllus's attentions. This Thrasyllus was a young man from a distinguished family, although he was given to frequenting taverns and brothels, and even inclined to crime. In order to have Charite all to himself, Thrasyllus was in fact ready to commit murder. Having befriended Tlepolemus under false pretenses, Thrasyllus then invited him to go hunting. But it was all a trap: Thrasyllus led Tlepolemus into the path of a wild boar and then pierced him with a spear, making it look as if the unfortunate young man had been gored by the wild boar's tusk. Charite was disconsolate and took to her bed, ready to die of grief. Yet the relentless Thrasyllus, aided by the young woman's unsuspecting parents, managed to persuade her to remain among the living. Precisely as we would have expected, Charite soon discovered a solace that was also, at the same time, a torturous desire:[3] "She spent whole days and nights in funereal grief [*luctuosum desiderium*] and worshipped with utter devotion a portrait of the dead man represented in the guise of Liber, tormenting herself with this form of consolation." Meanwhile, Thrasyllus, showing no sense of decency or restraint, refused to give up. Mad with desire, he finally asked Charite to marry him. The proposal appalled her, although her soul remained free of any suspicions. Then one night the wretched Tlepolemus, his face still smeared with blood, appeared to her in a dream, and told her the terrible truth. Charite was shaken, but told no one about her vision. Facing the renewed entreaties of Thrasyllus, she pretended to yield, on the condition that they meet in secret. Thrasyllus, willing to do anything to gain possession of her, accepted her invitation. He arrived at the appointed time; he entered the room. Charite was not there yet, but no matter—the old nurse brought out some wine and glasses . . . wine that had been mixed with a sleeping potion. Thrasyllus drank, and drank, until finally he was seized by a deep sleep. Only then did Charite make her entrance. Having removed her hairpin, she addressed her ruthless adversary at length as he was sleeping, and then blinded him in both eyes. Thrasyllus awoke too late; Charite had already grabbed a sword belonging to her husband, and went running like a madwoman throughout the city, telling everyone of her misfortune and her revenge. As the entire city lamented her wretched fate, she finally reached Tlepolemus's tomb, and shouted:[4] "It is long since time that I should have used this sword to seek a downward path that leads to my Tlepolemus!" She then plunged the sword into her breast. Having been informed about this turn of events, and fully aware that a blow of the sword would hardly suffice to atone for all his wicked deeds, Thrasyllus also made his way to the tomb of Tlepolemus. He offered himself up as an expiatory victim to the hatred of those vengeful shades, and descended into the sepulchre. He then had himself sealed inside, consigning himself to a slow death by starvation.[5]

This Charite is a rebellious Laodamia, understandably so, given the pitiless and unjust way in which fate has deprived her of her lover. Her story involves motifs we have seen before: the simulacrum, the dream, and the familiar reunion of the lovers in the realm of the dead. Once again, as in the story of Protesilaus and Laodamia, the image holds open a passageway, leading ever downwards. But Charite's story is also clouded by an atmosphere that is far more cruel and desolate. Her version of our fundamental story involves a theme that will acquire still greater vitality in later versions of the tale: *revenge*.[6] Charite's dream is not a dream of consolation; it is the revelation of a crime, a mysterious summons made by the distant beloved from the remote reaches of the Underworld. The lover responds to his call—but this time it will not be enough for her simply to descend into Hades by herself. The assassin will have to accompany her; the image holds open a passageway for the would-be adulterer as well. These macabre events resound like the tolling of a familiar bell, the chords of some famous melody: in the background we seem to hear the notes of Mozart's *Don Giovanni*, played in some ancient musical key, while the audacious murderer, the brazen adulterer, makes his way to the Underworld through the very tomb of his victim.

Thrasyllus (the "audacious" one, as his very name declares)[7] is actually the worst type of lover, someone who is cynically indifferent to the happiness of his beloved. In order to possess the person whom he desires, he is even willing to sacrifice the life of the person who is loved, in turn, by his beloved—just like Don Giovanni, a character whose adventures we will consider in a later chapter. This scheming *thrasys* has already killed his rival—to make a real Don Giovanni out of him, we need only for him to insult the image of his rival (an image that already makes an appearance in the story, as the object of Charite's devotional cult). If that were the case, if Thrasyllus, this "brazen" man, also insulted the image of Tlepolemus (as Don Giovanni will insult the statue of the Commendatore), then we would of course expect him to descend at last into the tomb of his victim (an excellent way to reach the Inferno)—no longer accompanied by the horror of Apuleius's imperial citizens, but by the howls of a Leporello.[8]

A Plaster Dionysus

Yet we should not conclude that Charite's revenge merely prefigures a story that is yet to come (or, even worse, that her tale is somehow a redundant version of stories we have already examined). Apuleius's account actually features a very specific and characteristic trait distinguishing it from the other stories we have seen so far, a detail we will need to consider at some length. Charite's simulacrum of her dead lover is specifically said to have the appearance *of a god*, the Roman god Liber (Greek Dionysus), and Charite dedicates to it the cult appropriate to that god. Moreover, Charite was not the only woman to realize a Dionysian apotheosis of her beloved.[9] According to Hyginus, Laodamia also conducted her "relations" with the image of her husband *sub similitudine sacrorum*, in the form of a cult ritual,[10] and from other sources we know that this must specifically refer to one of the Bacchic cults.[11] But there is yet another piece of evidence that we can add to this Dionysian inflection of the lover's cult: a poem that Statius wrote for Lucan's widow, Polla. As Statius consoles the widow, he also speaks to (and consoles) her husband:[12]

> Adsis lucidus et vocante Polla
> unum, quaeso, diem deos silentum
> exores. Solet hoc patere limen
> ad nuptas redeuntibus maritis.
> haec non te thiasis procax dolosis
> falsi numinis induit figura,
> ipsum sed colit et frequentat ipsum
> imis altius insitum medullis;
> at solatia vana subministrat
> vultus, qui simili notatus auro
> stratis praenitet incubatque somno
> securae.

Come in your transparency and, called by Polla [*vocante Polla*] may you beseech the gods of the silent places for one more day; that threshold is accustomed to open wide for husbands who are returning to their wives! She does not brazenly endow you with the false semblance of the god in the deceptive dances of Bacchus; it is you whom she vener-

ates, and to you she gives her every moment, you who are firmly set in
the depths of her heart. It is your face [*vultus*] reproduced in a golden
semblance that offers her an empty solace; it shines above her bed,
standing vigil over her safe slumber.

A familiar scene: once again, the portrait in the form of a face, along
with a wife who evokes her husband's transparent and shadowy presence
by calling his name (*vocante Polla*). The fleeting dream image is also
mentioned, suggesting that the golden simulacrum itself can exercise an
evocative power in Polla's sleep, capable of summoning apparitions.[13]
Similarly, the Vatican sarcophagus (see Fig. 1) also shows an image
located behind the bed where Laodamia is reclining.[14] The image is a
mask, placed on the mantelpiece and surrounded with cultic attributes
of Bacchus, generally recognized as the portrait of Protesilaus in the
guise of Bacchus.[15] Indeed, we cannot help but notice how much the
arrangement of the story on the sarcophagus resembles the cult of Polla
described by Statius. The sarcophagus relief depicts Protesilaus aban-
doning Hades accompanied by Hermes (compare Statius: "that threshold is accustomed to open wide / for husbands who are returning to
their wives"). Likewise, after the ghost makes his silent entry into the
house, the sarcophagus again shows a face that similarly keeps watch
over the bed of the woman: but that face is a Bacchic mask, a form of
representation to which Polla does *not* consent.

Above all, Statius wants to reassure the dead man: it is Lucan, he
insists, and only Lucan, whom Polla is venerating. She has not given in
to the brazen temptations of Bacchic delirium, feigning the false semblance of the god in the features of her late husband's face. The custom
apparently must have been widespread for Statius to rebuke it so sternly.
We know that in Statius's time it was a common practice to portray the
deceased in the form of a divinity.[16] It seems quite possible, in fact, that
the frequent selection of a Bacchic portrayal could be related to the general qualities of the cult of Dionysus and its soteriological mysteries.[17]
In fact, I think that it is worth considering at this point an often over-
looked story about the Orphic Dionysus, a story that might be able to
supply a link between the theological contents of the Dionysian cult on
the one hand and the transformation of the dead man into a Bacchic
portrait on the other. Admittedly, we are dealing here with a euhemeristic story passed down to us by a rather late source, and thus difficult
to locate precisely in the already obscure cycle of myths concerning the
passion of the infant Dionysus.[18] But in any case, the story clearly offers
a very noteworthy variant of our fundamental story.

It is Firmicus Maternus who tells us that Liber/Dionysus was actually an illegitimate son of Jupiter, much adored by his father, but much hated by Juno, who was terribly jealous of the boy.[19] Compelled to go on a journey, Jupiter entrusted Dionysus to guardians whom he considered trustworthy, but they were bribed by Juno to drive the boy out of the palace, where he was then massacred by the Titans. In order to better conceal their crime, each of the Titans seized a piece of their dismembered victim, cooking the pieces in various ways and then eating them. But Dionysus's heart fell by lot to one of Jupiter's daughters, Minerva, and she preserved it in a casket, having decided to denounce the Titans to her father. When he returned from his journey and learned of the crime, Jupiter was enraged and condemned the Titans to a horrible death under torture. Finally, "as he was no longer able to endure the torments of his anguished soul, and could find no way to console himself for the loss of his son, he had a statue [*imago*] made of the boy, modeled in plaster [*ex gypso*], and the sculptor then placed the heart of the boy . . . in that part of the statue which was shaped in the form of the breast. Finally, Jupiter ordered that a temple should be built instead of a tomb, and he appointed the boy's tutor as priest of the cult."[20]

This famous Orphic account of Dionysus slain by the Titans features a finale that is of great importance for our fundamental story.[21] In the course of his mystical tribulations, Dionysus undergoes the experience of being transformed into a portrait: specifically, into an animated portrait, a sort of reliquary in which the most precious and intimate part of his dismembered body is preserved.[22] Clearly, the god's ultimate resurrection, his rebirth from dismemberment, is strongly implied in this body of myth and ritual, and (according to Firmicus) Dionysus awaited this resurrection in the form of a *statue,* a statue to whom a specific devotional cult was dedicated.[23] As we have seen before, the image once again reveals itself to be a point of passage, a gap of expectation suspended between life and death.[24] But above all, this segment of Dionysus's story closely recalls the Bacchic cult connected with the portrait of the beloved person, as in the stories of both Laodamia and Charite.[25] Before his own personal resurrection, Dionysus experiences the condition of being a statue: therefore, to bestow this god's form and features on the dead person's simulacrum was perhaps a way to relive this mythical event and, by analogy, to hope for a miraculous rebirth of the person being honored in this Bacchic guise. Protesilaus, Tlepolemus, and the rest were perhaps represented with the features of this particular god in the hope that their permanence in the form of a portrait might be transformed into a mystical return from the dead.

The heart in a statue: later we will return to this singular metaphor based on putting a part of a person in direct contact with that person's iconic reproduction.[26] But first let us pause for a moment to consider an aspect of this story that at first glance might seem to be a marginal detail: the plaster used to construct the simulacrum of the god. There is nothing unusual in the fact that a simulacrum would be made out of plaster; many authors in fact speak of plaster statues erected to the gods.[27] Given the urgency of the situation, it is certainly easy to understand why Firmicus's Jupiter would have recourse to a substance like plaster that is quick and easy to use (which is why, of course, small statues and dolls of little value were often made of plaster).[28] But especially in a story like this one, we might expect more than just a commonsense explanation.

If we consider the issue more closely, we quickly discover that plaster had many cultural values in the ancient world, including a specific quality that is highly relevant to this particular story here: the gypsum used to make plaster was considered an outstanding preservative. Consequently, all sorts of things could be sealed or preserved with gypsum in order to make them immune to corruption: vintners' amphoras were diligently *gypsatae,* and a fine sprinkling of gypsum dust was used to cover clusters of grapes, apples, quinces, and other fruits picked shortly before they were ripe.[29] Therefore, by being enclosed within a plaster statue, the heart of Dionysus was sealed inside a substance that would supposedly preserve its vital characteristics. The process resembles the way in which the Ethiopians treated the corpses of their dead, as reported in Herodotus:[30] "After desiccating them either as the Egyptians do or in some other way, and then completely smearing them with plaster, the Ethiopians paint them in a way that reproduces the appearance of the person as closely as possible." The statue of Dionysus thus seems to function as a sort of seal that perfectly preserves the enclosed contents (Dionysus's living heart), while at the same time externally reproducing the features of the person: it is both an icon and a reliquary at one and the same time.

But there is something more to be said about that plaster statue. The metaphorical value attested in these ancient cultural practices (plaster as a preservative) seems to need an additional explanation, one specifically connected to the mythical context. Gypsum in fact plays a very important role in the cycle of the slain Dionysus, and the use of this specific material in constructing the god's simulacrum must surely be connected with the various references to gypsum throughout this mythical-ritual context. For example, the Titans are said to have smeared themselves with gypsum when they attacked and dismembered Dionysus.[31] This in turn was supposedly the mythical origin of a particular ritual practice: during the Mysteries, acolytes of the cult would also smear themselves with this same substance.[32] Therefore, both in connection with the mythical foundation story and the actual rite of the cult, gypsum plays a very significant role. The murderous Titans, and the acolytes who are pledged to relive the mythical story, are both described as *gypsati*, "covered with plaster." Moreover, there is a particular type of gypsum that is called *titanos* in Greek, thus providing a direct linguistic link between the Titans and the gypsum used in the making of plaster. In order to explain this coincidence, Eustathius tells us that the first gypsum/*titanos* arose from the ashes of the Titans who were struck by Zeus's thunderbolt: because it was created from the ashes of the Titans, this substance acquired the name *titanos*.[33] The Orphic Dionysus cycle thus involves Titans smeared with gypsum who, in addition, were finally struck by a thunderbolt and turned into a type of gypsum called *titanos*.[34] Similarly, "in order to imitate the myth" (as Eustathius tells us), the acolytes of the cult would smear themselves with this same substance. Clearly, gypsum is a central and recurring feature of this mythical-ritual cycle.

In fact, the ashes of the lightning-struck Titans—or rather the volatile smoke produced at the moment of their destruction— is the key to understanding the symbolic significance of gypsum and plaster within this mythical framework. The Orphic story tells us that "the substance dispersed in the vapors that rose up from [the Titans] then became solid and was the origin of men."[35] Another source states that the lightning-struck Titans were the origin not only of the human race but of every living creature on the earth.[36] The material whose precipitation resulted in the origin of the human race is referred to as *aithalē*, a word that generally indicates the volatile substances dispersed in the fire (soot, ashes, etc.).[37] But we are still probably within the same sphere of meaning that includes plaster, gypsum, and its affiliates, because among the different types of smoke and volatile substances generated by combustion, *aithalē* was specifically said to be "the smoke from which *asbestos* is produced,"[38] and *asbestos* was considered by Eustathius to be synonymous with *titanos*.[39] This Orphic account allows us to conclude that the human race was born not from the generic ashes of the Titans but specifically from the consolidation of a volatile substance linked to *titanos,* and thus linked in turn to gypsum and plaster.[40]

Accordingly, we can add this last characteristic to what we already know about the virtues of gypsum and plaster as a factor in the Orphic cycle of Dionysus: in addition to being a preservative, this substance was apparently endowed with a *generative* power. Gypsum was a material capable of awakening life, and thus there could be no better place for the slain god to await his rebirth than in an iconic container made of plaster, *ex gypso*. The choice of gypsum in the construction of this statue not only guaranteed a close connection between this segment of the myth and the entire mythical-ritual complex in which it was to be inserted, but it also symbolically expressed the most fundamental meanings of the cult: *rebirth*, and the capacity to bestow new life. We might also conclude that the acolytes of this cult of rebirth smeared their bodies with gypsum for the same reason, hoping to attract to their own bodies the generative virtues of *titanos* and *aithalē*.

5

The Sign Stained by Reality

Are there lessons to be found here in the stories? Surely there are. But what sort of lessons exactly? That is a much more difficult question, but one worth at least trying to answer. For example, what about this story, the portrait of the lover? Let's imagine some lonely person with a portrait of his lover: nothing out of the ordinary, it happens (has happened, will happen) over and over again in the endless parade of human cultures and lives. A common enough behavior, but not without its depths of meaning: to possess such a portrait reveals the existence of inner emotions and sentiments, feelings that can sometimes become very violent or exclusive. For example, a person might devote himself entirely to the portrait, unable to part with it, going insane if he happens to lose it, ready to do anything to recover it . . . Just by giving an example and trying to explain it, we have already begun to accumulate the small outlines of a story. This, I believe, is precisely how the system works. Given a fact (or better, a bundle of facts, compounded of behaviors, sensations, and so on), a story is created out of the need to speak; the story takes shape when that bundle of facts demands to be made into an object of discourse. Probably each of us recognizes that certain things we do, certain moments of our lives, are profound. But this profundity does not emerge in our everyday behavior; it forms part of our lived experience, but without being transformed into discourse. A story, on the other hand, is concerned precisely with this aspect of the problem, with transforming that profundity into discourse, expressing a meaning that normally cannot be expressed in everyday life. So, take an abandoned lover, put a portrait in his hands, and then a story slowly but surely begins to explore the situation, uncovering the facts, and speaking about them . . . The ensuing narration then attaches other facts to those initial facts (perhaps a shadow projected on the wall, the return of the distant lover, dreams, revenge, and so on), until it reaches the point of teaching us something, explaining why an abandoned lover might depend so much on the other's portrait, how he feels about it, what it is like to let this torment console him. By the word "teach," of course, I do not mean teaching in the vulgar sense of an *epimythium,* the moral attached to the end of an Aesopic fable. I mean instead the sympathetic sort of teaching accomplished by a story, that marvelous object capable of transforming the "metalanguage" of a culture into an actual *plot.*

Every culture incorporates infinite meanings, ancient deposits, layers of significance whose profundity we cannot begin to measure; in fact, we rarely even realize that it exists. And this is true not only for particular events or behaviors that are slightly out of the ordinary, such as the story we are dealing with here. It also applies (indeed, it applies most of all) to the entirety of everyday life, that most human of all possible spaces. It is precisely the stories, the tales, that have been assigned since time immemorial the task of bringing these hidden treasures to light, like miners in the depths of culture who then entertain us with the results of their labors. At one time the stories were called myths, but no longer. Indeed, we have now almost entirely forgotten that in Greek the word *mythos* simply meant a "story." And it is in their telling that stories matter most: more than in their form or content. A myth is thus to tell a story, to draw forth meanings one after another, stringing them like beads on the thread of the plot and to be able to *speak* them.

Let us then try to imagine the plot as a powerful excavator, the characters as workers, while the narrative designs—those well-worn formulas of folklore and overused cliches of mass culture—can be seen as maps or topographical charts, the product of countless forays into the arduous depths of our cultural terrain. The simplest and most immediate way to articulate the meanings of a culture is precisely to tell them *in a story.* This is what makes it possible to grasp the defining limits of our mental world, to apprehend those impalpable boundaries that, consciously and unconsciously, internally and externally, define a limitless and quotidian space swelling with the entirety of human life into a buoyant sphere of meaning. The story is able to explore and analyze, even to create new meanings, in a cyclical accumulation of cultural understanding. Of course, when it becomes possible to transcribe the stories, recording them in writing, their forms are somewhat changed; once it is written down, the story has the power to turn back and pursue itself, to make allusions, to imitate itself. Above all, it can be transmitted over long stretches of time, and this mounting stockpile of stories (a progressively infinite supply that can never be superfluous) allows us to assemble in a single place the thousands of tales that, before the advent of writing, were scattered and diffused over millions of square miles, seemingly unaware of one another's existence. In short, writing does alter the stories in some nontrivial ways, but their function remains the same. Even today, literature tirelessly continues its quest. From this point of view, myths cannot be called dead in any sense whatsoever.

We therefore possess a cultural artifact—the portrait of the lover—along with a series of stories told about it. The question is then what lessons we might learn from these stories, from the tales that we have seen unfolding thus far before our very eyes.

Creatures of *Pothos*

As we have already had occasion to note, the first portrait of the lover (the portrait that inaugurated the creation of images in general) arose from *grief*, from the absence of the beloved person.[1] To be precise, it was generated by an emotion that in Greek would be called *pothos,* and in Latin, *desiderium.*[2] The mythical beginnings of the image, the very manner of its creation, thus assigned to the image a strongly substitutive function. The image is meant to fill the *emptiness* left behind by someone who is no longer there, serving as an actual substitute for that absent person. For example, in a Roman declamation, a mother whose son has died shouts these words at her husband:[3] "Si mihi aliquam imaginem filii mei . . . auferres, inicerem tamen misera tamquam corpori manum, illam similitudinem flens tenerem, illos oculos . . . et adumbratos artificis manu vultus." (If you were to try to take the image [*imago*] of my son away from me, I would woefully throw my arms around it as if it were his actual body; weeping, I would embrace that likeness [*similitudo*], those eyes and the face outlined [*adumbratos*] by the artisan's hand.) This is precisely the same substitution, the same replacement, that we have seen at work in each of these stories, beginning with the foundational myth of the image and all the later variations on this theme: from the ambiguous behavior of Laodamia, who appeared to be having an actual affair with the image, to the desperate fidelity (and desperate eroticism?) of Admetus, to Charite's vendetta, and so on. This profound feature of the image—its link to *desiderium,* its avowedly substitutive function—is strongly emphasized throughout the classical tradition as, for example, in Seneca:[4] "The images of our absent friends are dear to us because they renew the memory, and they alleviate our grief [*desiderium*] with a deceptive, futile solace." Meanwhile, according to Pliny, the force of this same *desiderium* could even reach the point of "giving rise to the effigies of unknown faces, as in the case of Homer."[5]

Grief gives birth to images: this same idea is also expressed in a story from the apocryphal Wisdom of Solomon.[6] Overwhelmed by the death of his son, a father had an image of him made, and then began to honor that image as if it were the effigy of a god. This then was supposed to be the origin of idolatry. Of course, the Biblical story reaches a different conclusion than the other stories we have looked at; it is a foundational story of the image, but one belonging to a different culture. It begins with the same initial impulse: the loss of a beloved person leads to the *substitution* of that person with an image—but the final result is instead that this regard for the image only increases the distance between mankind and the True God.

Over time, this story from the Wisdom of Solomon, interwoven with euhemeristic tenets about the purely human origins of the gods,[7] prompted Christian authors such as Minucius Felix[8] and Lactantius[9] to argue that idolatrous pagan cults began precisely with the experience of *desiderium,* of people grieving for their lost kings. This emotion was supposed to have led the pagans to create images of those kings in order to alleviate their sorrow. Cults were then devoted to those images, which eventually resulted in the false belief that these were images of the gods. In the words of Minucius Felix:[10] "They venerate their kings in a religious way, desiring to see them depicted in images when they are dead, wanting to fix their memory in statues, and then making into sacred objects things that were intended as a consolation." *Desiderium* gives birth to images and to statues, and consolation gives way to cult. Grief, the father of images, also becomes the father of idolatry. It was Isidore of Seville who transmitted this entire body of ideas to medieval European culture through the immense conduit of his *Etymologiae.*[11] Of course, to analyze the totality of Christian thought on the origins of idolatry extends far beyond the horizons of our subject matter here, but it is worth pointing out that this theme closely reproduces the motifs associated with the origin of the image in cultural representations throughout the classical world. The birth of the image from *pothos* or from *desiderium,* and its avowedly substitutive function, constitutes a dominant and recurrent feature in the mythical history of the image. Following different cycles, accommodating itself to different cultural forms, the ancient roots of the image (nourished by *pothos*) continue to bear fruit—fruit of various shapes, but with a markedly similar taste. Let us consider, for example, what happens to the story when it encounters the singularly fertile imagination of Fulgentius Planciades.[12]

Syrophanes of Egypt had a much-beloved son. This son died, and the father then decided to have an image of him made, but "while he sought a remedy for his sadness, he found instead a source of grief [*seminarium doloris*], ignoring the fact that in times of misfortune the only true remedy is forgetfulness. For in this he found only a way to renew his mourning over and over again, not a way to alleviate it. And thus it was called 'idol' [*idolum*], that is, *idos dolu,* which in Latin would be *species doloris,* 'the image of grief.'" Fulgentius had an undeniable literary skill and (perhaps unexpectedly) a certain amount of common sense as well. The best remedy for disaster is to *forget,* the absent person's image is only an agonizing consolation: these are not simply elegant *sententiae,* but statements endowed with a considerable element of truth.[13] Fulgentius did not know Greek, which accounts for his hybrid "idol," a Graeco-Latin "image of grief."[14] But at least in this case his ignorance has reached a happy conclusion. As often happens with false etymologies, the error of the form is compensated for by the substantial validity of the cultural content. The image is indeed a *species doloris;* grief and absence are a fundamental aspect of its cultural mandate. Fulgentius's odd erudition produces an accurate definition precisely because it is mistaken. We will return to this substitutive function of the image in greater detail later, but first we will pause for a moment, and consider another lesson that these stories of the portrait might be trying to teach us.[15]

The Image and the Shadow

We saw how the potter's daughter drew the first portrait of the lover by tracing the outlines of a shadow cast on the wall. Between the referent and the image, between the model and the portrait, there thus exists a sort of *medium,* a connection: the beloved and the portrait are linked by the shadow. With this simple detail, the story reveals something about the cultural value of this kind of portrait. We are not dealing here with a mere effigy of the person, with a reproduction that is determined purely by an axis of likeness. By being fashioned from the lover's shadow, the portrait possesses a part of the model: there is *contact* between the image and the referent, combining similarity with contiguity. It is as if Butades' daughter had appropriated an actual part of her lover by furtively tracing the shadow of the sleeping young man, acquiring some essential part of his being that she would be able to possess even in his absence.

According to ancient cultural beliefs, the shadow was not only attached to the person: it was also considered to be an expression of that person's most vital and significant characteristics. As Proclus explains:[16] "Shadows . . . are the images of bodies and forms, and they have a close affinity [*sympatheia*] with the beings who project them, as we see in the way that sorcerers invoke them for purposes of magic." Proclus's assertion of the *sympatheia* between the shadow and the person deserves our serious attention. According to Pliny, the Persian Magi observed the following prohibition: "The shadow of any person should not become wet with urine."[17] Urine contaminates, and to wet the shadow in this way would mean contaminating the person. We find the same motivation at work in another *symbolon* of Pythagoras that warns "not to urinate on hair clippings or nail clippings."[18] But the shadow is not only an object of warnings: it is also a source of power. Consider, for example, the curious adventure of the hyena, the dog, and their shadows: as both Aelian and Pliny tell us, the hyena was supposedly able to bewitch the dog and take away his voice merely by casting her shadow upon him (an operation that the hyena was supposed to carry out at night, silently, by the light of the moon);[19] meanwhile, in Proclus's version of the story, the hyena exercises this power not by casting her own shadow, but by stepping upon the shadow that is cast by the dog, her unwitting victim.[20] The shadow of the predator is thus a trap set for its victim—or, alternatively, the victim's own shadow leads him ineluctably into the predator's clutches.

The shadow has the power to destroy, but it also has the power to save, depending on the nature of the person to whom the shadow belongs. The Book of Acts explains that the sick and infirm were brought into the public squares, "so that Peter's shadow [*skia*] would overshadow them [*episkiasēi*]."[21] Peter, the saint, was endowed with a beneficent shadow. A wicked or impure person, on the other hand, would be endowed (by the same principle of *sympatheia*) with a maleficent shadow. This is what we discover in Ennius's *Thyestes,* whose title character is tricked by his brother Atreus into devouring the bodies of his sons. Having realized his crime, Thyestes exclaims:[22]

> nolite hospites ad me adire, ilico istic
> ne contagio mea bonis umbrave obsit.
> Tanta vis sceleris in corpore haeret.
>
> Do not draw near to me, guests; remain where you are, so that the contagion of my shadow [*umbra*] will not wound good people, so great is the power of the crime that clings in my flesh.

We can find additional evidence for the cultural value of the shadow in the beliefs associated with the famous sanctuary of Zeus Lykaios in Arcadia.[23] According to Pausanias, "whoever goes into the sacred enclosure will not live for more than one year, and it is said that anything within the enclosure, human or animal, does not cast a shadow [*skia*]."[24] Being alive and possessing a shadow are thus closely connected values; someone who does not cast a shadow is not long for this world. We find a similar statement in the scholia to Callimachus:[25] "Each creature that goes inside [the birthplace of Zeus in Parrhasia] becomes sterile, and its body no longer casts a shadow [*skia*]." Being condemned to an imminent death or suffering from sterility are thus both equivalent to losing one's shadow. The shadow, *skia,* is a metonymy for life, and the person who is close to death, or who is deprived of the capacity to generate new life, is also deprived of his shadow. By comparison, we can recall here a famous passage from the Gospel of Luke in which the Virgin Mary is promised a son, as the angel explains: "The power of the Most High will overshadow you [*episkiasei*]."[26] The casting of the shadow upon the young Virgin is an appropriate metaphor for the miraculous conception, in the same way that to be deprived of a shadow can serve as a symbol of sterility.[27] The shadow produces or demonstrates life. From another *symbolon* attributed to Pythagoras, we know that the dead supposedly did not cast shadows.[28] Accordingly, when Plutarch's Thespesius recounts his experiences in the afterlife, he explains that he was recognized as a living creature, different from the luminescent souls of the blessed, precisely because "the souls of the dead do not cast a shadow [*skia*]," whereas Thespesius could see around himself "a sort of indistinct, shadowy line."[29]

The shadow was thus assigned to represent the person by somehow assimilating and then expressing that person's most essential characteristics.[30] This series of beliefs connected with the shadow can help us to better understand the meaning of the first portrait, the one that Butades and his daughter extracted from the shadow of her young lover. If we understand the functional meaning of the shadow, we can then place the portrait drawn from the shadow in a larger cultural context. Because it is traced along the shadow—that mysterious entity which contains and expresses the essential qualities of the person who projects it—the portrait is fully able to function as a substitute for that person, confirming a conclusion we had previously reached by other means. At the mythical beginnings of the history of the portrait, it was the shadow that authorized the image; as a result, the image drawn from the shadow is something more than an effigy that merely resembles its referent. The mediation of the shadow (a part of the person able to manifest that person's most vital characteristics) places the image in extraordinarily close proximity to its referent, creating a point of contact, a relationship of equivalence, *sympatheia*.

We can also employ this same analytical strategy to understand some other stories that, at first glance, apparently involve very different symbols and contents, such as the story of the plaster Dionysus in which Jupiter preserved the dismembered heart of his beloved son.[31] This heart-in-the-statue is another example of metonymy, of actual contact between the image and a part of the person (once again, a highly significant part of that person: his heart). This contact (with the heart, with the shadow) intensifies the representational function of the image, causing the image to approach its referent as closely as possible: the image can function as a holy reliquary, a host of its own referent. Even more explicit (although admittedly somewhat horrifying) is the attempt to superimpose the two end points of this relational continuum, fully uniting the image and the person. This is what we find in the story of the old fisherman Aegialeus (a character in Xenophon's *Ephesiaca* whom Habrocomes encounters in Syracuse during his endless peregrinations in search of Anthia). In a macabre variation on the story of Admetus, this widower keeps the woman herself in his bed, that is, instead of a portrait of his wife, he keeps a mummy of her corpse, beautifully attired.[32] Through the mediation provided by the hideous technique of embalming, the simulacrum of the beloved here imitates its referent even more closely, audaciously attempting to achieve that (impossible) identification with the person to whom, by definition, the image is dedicated. Admetus is not so bold, of course, but the simulacrum that he keeps in his bed has a similar meaning. These images of the beloved are not mere facsimiles: in some sense they constitute a part of the missing person. In a scale of fantastic gradations—from the shadow, to the heart, to the mummified corpse—these manifold signs do not function by means of metaphor, but by a metonymical substitution.

This privileged relationship between the image and the shadow can also be used to help explain other narrative connections in our fundamental story, other cultural traits associated with the image. First and foremost, the link between the image and the shadow might help us to better understand the image's connection to the Underworld, and the ability apparently possessed by the portrait of the lover to guarantee a passage, to hold open a gap, between the world of the living and that of the dead—or, similarly, for the portrait to be transformed into the phantom or shade, the *psychē* of the deceased.[33] As we know, the image was originally linked to the shadow, a representation of the person in ghostly form, but also a sign of life. This bond between the image and the shadow of the deceased is expressed very effectively and precisely in a poem that Statius addresses to Priscilla, the late wife of Abascanthus. Statius explains that if he knew how to model wax, or to work in ivory or gold, and thus to extract living figures from these inanimate materials, then he would seek to console Abascanthus with the work of his hands. But he explains to Priscilla that the depths of her husband's devotion would require that such figures be painted with the colors of Apelles or be shaped by the hands of Phidias: only such ideal artistry could restore Priscilla to her grieving husband. Even though it is a futile quest, Abascanthus continues to seek this form of consolation:[34]

> sic auferre rogis umbram conatur, et ingens
> certamen cum Morte gerit, curasque fatigat
> artificum inque omni te quaerit amare metallo.

> He is trying to wrest a shade [*umbra*] from the pyre, waging a colossal war with Death. He exhausts the efforts of the craftsmen; he seeks your love in every metal.

It is a strange invention, even a bit baroque: this husband not only craves manufactured images of his wife, but he wants somehow to "wrest a shade from the pyre" in a struggle against Death itself. Abascanthus realizes that the portrait "recalls" the shade; he understands that portraits work not just by similarity, but by actual contact. In short, the portrait of the lover is not purely an icon, but a sign contaminated with its referent. It is a sign imbued with reality, or—to be more precise—a faded version of reality: its shadow.

This symbolic representation implies a conception of death that is seen not as total annihilation, but instead as *debilitated survival:* the substance of life muted in death.[35] Absence is expressed in the form of a partial presence, and negation—a negation that is so difficult to articulate, so hard to admit—emerges as synecdoche. The deceased is not a nonbeing: he is a being *somewhere or other,* a being *who knows where?* As we already saw, the phantom, the *eidōlon,* is an apparition that reproduces in each and every detail the features of the living person, it is an image that perfectly resembles the deceased—but who would have the courage to assert that it is *only* a reproduction of the living person, a figure that merely looks like that person? When Achilles tries to embrace the shade of Patroclus, it is Patroclus, his beloved friend, whom he really wants to embrace, not an image that only resembles Patroclus. But even Achilles himself would have to admit that while the *psychē* and the *eidōlon,* are real, they are somehow different, and much more wretched, than a living person.[36] These representations are only partial; they lack something important—and this lack is the definition of death itself.

The same is true of our portrait of the lover. Traced along the outline of the model's shadow, the image is worth more than its apparent resemblance: *plus est, quam quod videatur, imago,* as Ovid observed. The portrait of the beloved person—in some admittedly obscure, ambiguous, perhaps even magical way—forms an actual part of that person. The image can therefore be placed on the same level as the corporeal shadow and the ghostly *psychē,* along with footprints and other bodily impressions left behind by the absent person, and highly significant parts of the body, such as the heart, or even the entire body itself in the form of a mummified corpse. We should not let ourselves be misled by the fact that the image is like its referent, by the fact that it reproduces the person. Even though the portrait of the beloved person does resemble that person, this does not mean that it is homologous to just any sort of image—such as a landscape, or the simple depiction of a person. The portrait works by analogy, to be sure, but it is not merely an icon. Traced along the outline of the shadow, the resulting likeness in some sense certifies that the portrait belongs to the person; this likeness is a matter of contiguity, not just similarity.[37] As in the case of the *eidōlon,* it is not a question of a more or less accurate reproduction: this portrait *is* the other person's very existence, this representation embodies his very being. Like the shadow, the portrait is debilitated and mute: but it is that person. It means, somehow, that the person *is still here.*

This explains why the image is able to establish a correspondence with the ashes of the deceased, those mortal remains that, together with the ghostly shade, define the two extremes of symbolic existence after death. In a little Latin poem from late antiquity dealing with the myth of Alcestis, we find a rather unusual variation on the story's traditional simulacrum.[38] In the invention of this anonymous poet, the dying Alcestis now asks Admetus to embrace her *ashes*:[39] "Please take my ashes in your lap, and caress them with your hand, unafraid." What was in Euripides a simulacrum "shaped by skilled hands" has been replaced over the course of the centuries by the ashes of the faithful wife, ashes that are caressed in the lap of her husband—a gesture about which the text is very explicit, suggesting a scenario rather similar to the horrifying mummy that the fisherman Aegialeus kept in his bed.[40] And even if we cannot call it a happy invention, this late variation on our theme once again confirms the cultural value of Alcestis's statue. Like these ashes, the statue also demonstrates that some part of Alcestis escaped from the Underworld. The statue was (and still is) an actual part of the person who is now confined to the Underworld; the statue serves as her representative and as her substitute, not merely an image that resembles her. By an identical logic, both ashes and statues can contain the representation of a dead person's *psychē*.

We should thus consider again what we were saying earlier about the strongly substitutional function of the image.[41] Because it is a replacement born from *desiderium,* a visible sign of grief and absence, the image naturally pushes its fragile appearance in the direction of its referent. As the concrete embodiment of a sorrowful and grievous lack (*idos dolu,* as Fulgentius put it so badly, and so well), the image—the substitute—aspires to become an actual proprietor, invested with reality.[42] Or, at the very least, it attracts to itself material traces of the person whom it is supposed to replace. In this sense, Fulgentius was not so misguided after all; he had good reason to call the image a *seminarium doloris,* a source of affliction rather than consolation. The image opens up an emptiness in front of the one who gazes upon it, a void that draws into itself as much as it can of the other, of the one who is no longer there.

A Sign Stained by Reality

We have spoken about a likeness that depends on contiguity rather than similarity. This seems to be the essential message in what the stories about the image have taught us so far. But we can also develop this discourse with greater precision, reinforcing it with some categories traditionally employed in semiotics. Specifically, we can say that in this type of image there is an explicit tendency to superimpose the nature of an index on that of an icon—following Peirce's definition of the icon as a sign that refers to the object by virtue of its similarity to that object or by virtue of its own intrinsic properties corresponding to that object's properties, as opposed to the index, a sign that demonstrates an actual connection to its object, recalling its referent by virtue of a physical rapport.[43] (So, for example, a painting is typically considered to be an icon, while smoke rising in the distance is a notorious example of the indexical sign.)

This set of terms then opens up a very interesting terrain of semiotics—and interesting not only for our purposes here—in which these two fundamental vectors of meaning appear to intersect. At a certain point in his analysis, Peirce considers an example that deserves our very close attention: photography. In this case, Peirce explains that photographs resemble their subjects because they are physically constrained to correspond in every detail to the object in nature. As such, photographs belong to the category of indexical signs (signs involving a physical connection).[44] The photograph, that quintessential icon (a sign that seems to possess an extraordinary number of features in common with its referent, the maximum amount of resemblance), is thus revealed upon closer examination to also be an indexical sign. This modern technique—which manages to achieve the ancient dream of freezing the apparitions that move about in the mirror—is able to produce images simultaneously defined by two different semiotic natures, both icon and index.[45] I think there is a very similar process at work in the intentions of a person who conceives of the portrait (based on specific cultural models) as the tracing of a shadow, as the equivalent of an *eidōlon* or *psychē,* or as a receptacle for the heart of the beloved. The symbolic narrative devices found in these stories clearly emphasize the *indexical* nature of these particular icons, a physical connection with the object of reference. These portraits are images, icons that recall the beloved person by resemblance, but they also function as indexes, marking a point of relation that puts them "in touch" with the person, even in that person's absence.

Of course, the discourse that we are developing here would require a much broader survey in order to be really and truly complete. As we have said, the image superimposes both icon and index *in the intentions* of the person who conceives of the image as the tracing of a shadow. We might also say, more to the point, that image and index are super-imposed in the intentions of the person *who treats* the image in this way, interacting with the image according to a cultural (or narrative) system that involves this sort of behavior. The fact is that the sign—or, at least, this particular type of sign—is subject to more than merely theoretical mandates: it is also part of a cultural praxis, and thus manifests a *performative* value. It is not enough to say that the purpose of the images is to represent something. Instead, one *does* something with images; the fact that they themselves are representations of other objects does not prevent the images from becoming, in turn, the objects (or also the subjects) of personal intentions and other cultural practices. This holds true for the person who simply keeps a photograph of his girlfriend in his wallet (a photograph to which he might he deeply attached); it is equally true of Admetus, and the densely symbolic apparatus that is implied by the simulacrum of Alcestis that he pledges to keep in his bed. The further development of our analysis—or rather the various combinations that our fundamental story has yet to generate—will thus consist of a progressively deeper examination of the *performativity* of the portrait of the lover. These images are not merely a gallery of beautiful paintings, or a portico adorned with statues: these are images that *do* something, or that become involved in various actions. The stories describe for us the many ways in which people treat the images, relying on them—within the labyrinth of cultural models and private emotions—to represent something that is no longer there.

Images of Faithfulness

But let us return to the stories we have already read, and to the lessons that they are trying to teach us. We have now identified several basic and fundamental features of the relationship between the image and the referent—but the cluster of relationships established between the image, the referent, and the person in possession of that image deserves our further attention. We saw in Euripides' *Alcestis* that the presence of the simulacrum was activated in a context of *fidelity*, of a vow. By placing in their marriage bed a statue that reproduces his dead wife's appearance, Admetus declares his own vow of love, a promise that the bond of love will endure, despite the absence of his wife. In other words, the portrait of the lover—as something that can be possessed and treated with devotion—apparently corresponds to a vow of fidelity. All these variations of our fundamental story will involve only faithful lovers swearing eternal love: from the potter's daughter, whose attachment to her lover inaugurated the very art of making images—and so on to Laodamia, Admetus, Charite . . . Indeed, Charite's story involved both her horrified rejection of the adulterer's advances, and also a heroic strategy for remaining faithful to her dead husband. Meanwhile, in Laodamia's story, a clever twist of the plot managed to momentarily transform the simulacrum of her husband into an adulterous intruder, if only in the eyes of the curious servant and Laodamia's pitiless father.[46] But once the mistake had been explained, it served only as further proof of Laodamia's fidelity, and of her tenacious attachment to (the portrait of) her husband—faithful even unto death, as the story showed. To possess a portrait of the lover thus corresponds, in practice, to a promise of fidelity. Solitary lovers content themselves with images; any new bond would be only a betrayal. In one of his epigrams, Meleager judges Heliodora's faithfulness to him in terms of how she treats his image:[47] "Does some relic of my love remain? Is the memory of my kiss still warm upon the cold image of me that she possesses? Are tears the only companions in her bed? Does she dream of me, embracing and kissing that image which beguiles the soul? Or has she found some new love, some new amusement?" In the mind of the distant (or jealous) beloved, the lover ought to warm his portrait with kisses. This is the behavior that would best express her fidelity: she should adore his image. Moreover, as we would expect, she should also await the usual panoply of dream images to visit her in the night, and she should show the same devotion to those images as she does to the portrait of her lover.[48]

This theme—the portrait as fidelity, the image as a vow—expresses what I believe to be one of the most significant anthropological aspects of the image. To reach a fuller understanding of this phenomenon, we can turn to a famous study by Emile Benveniste, in which he advances a very interesting thesis about the swearing of oaths in Greece.[49] As Beneveniste demonstrates, the sworn oath, called *horkos* in Greek, did not consist of an abstract formula in words, but rather of a *concrete* object representing the oath in material form. This sacred object—whether constituted by the waters of the Styx or by the scepter of Achilles—was something that you touched. More precisely, it was something that you grasped, as "grasping" seems to be the most ancient sense of the Greek word, *omnymi,* used to indicate the act of swearing.[50] This *horkos,* the thing that you grasp, constitutes a sacralizing object, something that visibly displays the act of swearing the oath, and that also "contains the power to punish any violation of that sworn oath."[51]

Moreover, we know of cases in which this sacralizing object, the material *horkos,* was specifically constituted by an *image,* a double, a substitute. For example, the text of an oath specifying the reciprocal obligations between Thera and its colonists in Cyrene describes a ritual procedure in which images are shaped in wax and then thrown in the fire, while the following formula is pronounced:[52] "May the person who betrays this oath and commits perjury be liquefied and disappear just like these *kolossoi;* let this befall him, his family, and all his possessions." In this case the pledge is a *kolossos,* a double, a simulacrum. The vow takes the form of an image, and the image is a manifestation and guarantee of that vow.

We can draw a similar conclusion from the text of a sacred law, also from Cyrene, that describes the procedure for receiving a suppliant from a foreign country. If the person who has sent the suppliant is dead, and the master of the house does not know his name, he pronounces this formula:[53] "O person, whether you are a man or a woman!" He then makes two *kolossoi* from wood and earth, one of a man and one of a woman, and welcomes them at his table, letting them partake of the meal. Once these rituals have been carried out, he takes the *kolossoi* and the portions of food into a stand of uncut trees and plants the *kolossoi* in the ground. The ritual apparently seeks to establish—or better, to reestablish—a bond of hospitality, that quintessential relationship based on a *pledge* of reciprocity between two persons. Given that the other person is dead (and that even the name of that person is unknown), the bond is surreptitiously reestablished by means of a *kolossos.* It is as if to say: "Despite the death of my partner, and despite my ignorance of his name, I accept this foreign suppliant and I respect the bond that unites us." Once again, to manufacture an image is equivalent to establishing (or reestablishing) a bond of reciprocal obligation. This notion of the image as obligation and reciprocity appears to have a wide cultural range. As Denise Paulme has shown, for example, little stone statuettes play a fundamental role in the swearing of oaths throughout many regions of Africa.[54] The image is simultaneously a guarantee and an obligation, a tangible proof of the promise that has been made.[55]

We can thus understand Admetus's story (and the story of other faithful lovers and their portraits) in terms of a general anthropological category: the image expresses a vow of fidelity. Moreover, the need to grasp the sacralizing object that manifests this vow can perhaps add further meaning to the way Admetus treats the image of Alcestis, as he "embraces" his wife's simulacrum while calling out her name.[56] This meaning of the image as a vow can also be adduced in all the other cases in which physical contact with the simulacrum seems to intensify the bond that attaches the solitary lover to the memory of his absent beloved. This same cultural model also explains the act of erecting a statue or other effigy in someone's memory, a custom that is not confined to the past but that is still practiced today. To erect such a statue was (and is) a way of declaring: "We are faithful to you; we still respect your ideals and your actions; we have not forgotten the impression that you made on our lives." . . . at least until the statue is knocked down, or has its head removed to make way for some other person's head. Such actions invert the original declaration, as if to say: "Enough, our relationship with you is over; we have pledged our faith to someone else . . ."

This cultural value attached to the image (the vow to keep the faith, and the potential violation of that promise) obviously encompasses a wide range of social practices, from the most sophisticated political stratagems to simple everyday behaviors. In short, there is a potentially infinite number of examples, as one would expect from such a general phenomenon. For instance: Tacitus tells us that Nero (we now find ourselves in the year 62 C.E.) had decided to banish his wife Octavia, sending her away under armed guard, so that he could marry Poppaea instead. But the people of Rome protested openly, until the emperor (seeming almost contrite) was forced to initiate proceedings for Octavia's return. Once this was done, the citizens "joyfully ascended the Capitol to venerate the gods, knocking down the statues of Poppaea, and carrying images of Octavia on their backs. They then adorned her images with wreaths of flowers, setting them up in the Forum and temples."[57] By knocking down the statues of the reviled Poppaea, the people demonstrated their violent reluctance to accept the emperor's new wife, and by replacing her statues with images of his banished wife, covered in flowers, they affirmed their fidelity to Octavia instead.

For another example of the image as a vow, we can turn again to Tacitus, selecting this time a case in which the breaking of a vow was demonstrated by the *absence* of an image. At the funeral of Junia—an extremely aristocratic Roman woman who was the niece of Cato, the sister of Brutus and the wife of Gaius Cassius—the *imagines* of no fewer than twenty of the most noble Roman families could be seen in the ceremonial parade. But the effigies of Brutus and Cassius were missing, evidently as a sign that all ties and connections with Caesar's assassins had

been prudently severed (even if Tacitus, with sublime malice, notes that
the faces of Brutus and Cassius "were more conspicuous than all the rest
precisely because their effigies were absent").[58] In a case like this, the
display of images can prove to be rather dangerous, possibly demon-
strating a faithfulness that should instead be renounced. In similar circumstances, Cassius Longinus incurred Nero's wrath for having "preserved the effigy of Gaius Cassius, the assassin of Caesar" in his ancient
family tree.[59] In the eyes of the emperor (who was, for that matter, already subject to paranoid delusions), to preserve that effigy clearly suggested a suspicious sort of fidelity, contrary and hostile to the ruling
Caesars.[60]

Images thus occupy a prominent place among the sacralizing objects
that, as such, can provide the material embodiment of a vow, constituting an explicit or implied oath of fidelity. If we want to find a sufficiently
general and profound motivation for this fundamental anthropological
value, we might invoke one of our earlier observations about the nature
of the image.[61] Within the complex web of cultural representations, the
portrait is an icon but it can also serve as an index, an actual part of the
person, a physical representation (even "representative") of that person's agency. This is why the image can also act as a pledge, as the embodiment of a vow. The presence of a portrait somehow implies that the
person is not in fact gone for good. Instead, the person is thought to
still be present, or on the verge of returning—if for no other reason
than to claim what is his. For that matter, our fundamental story has
several times told us that the presence of a portrait of the lover can function as a kind of anticipation or hope of a return, a fragile passageway
between there and here. The portrait somehow restores the person; like
all pledges, this particle of the other person suggests that there is more
to come; it is a sign that the story is still not over. And as we will soon
discover, the substitute that the person leaves behind in his place can
even expand into a colossal and sinister statue, an image endowed with
all the power it needs to enforce the vow that it embodies.[62]

Filiation, Marriage, and Kinship

The stories we have examined so far—from the tale of
Butades' daughter, to Admetus, Charite, and the plaster statue containing Dionysus's heart—have each systematically involved the presence of

three elements: the image, its referent, and the possessor of the image, who is markedly attached to that image in a deeply emotional way. We could also say that the same array of characters is involved whenever any sort of image is dedicated, because both scenarios imply a declaration of fidelity. In this more generic situation we could speak of the image, the dedicatee, and the dedicator, whose interactions manifest a highly significant cultural construct: fidelity. In more abstract terms, it is a situation in which an object (that is, the image) is offered to a receiver by a sender.[63] But we should carefully note this singular detail: in this case, the object happens to reproduce the receiver (the image is a reproduction of the dedicatee). This, then, is the context in which we should locate the value of the oath, the display of faithfulness that we have already seen revealed in the image. A declaration of faithfulness is established between the person who sends an object on the one hand, and another person to whom the object is addressed and who, at the same time, is represented in the object. The receiver can thus be more specifically defined as the "receiver/referent" (or the "dedicatee/referent") of that object. Someone possesses an image of someone else, and manifests that possession in a particularly emphatic way, but at the same time this image undeniably belongs to the person who is represented by it. That is, by being represented in the image, that person is also in some sense a possessor of the image: it is "his" image too.

It is an admittedly complex situation, and in order to clarify this unusual network of relationships and exchanges, we can turn to some reflections in a speech that Dio Chrysostom made to the citizens of Rhodes, a speech in which these cultural categories are examined in terms of a very specific and curious problem.[64] At a certain point there were apparently many men who wished to be honored with statues erected by the city of Rhodes. The citizens of Rhodes thus began to systematically take down the old statues that had been previously dedicated to other people so that they could rededicate the old statues to these new individuals. But Dio Chrysostom thought this was completely unacceptable, and in order to oppose this tendency he developed a series of interesting observations about the bonds between the three members of the relationship we are discussing: that is, the links between what we have called the dedicator, the image, and its dedicatee/referent.

To begin with, Dio Chrysostom clearly recognizes the value of the pledge manifested in the image. He argues that to rededicate a statue that had been previously assigned to someone else corresponds precisely to a transgression, a violation of the rules.[65] It is an insulting gesture of *hubris* toward the image's original dedicatee.[66] The person who treats the images in this way is a "flatterer, a despicable and untrustworthy person."[67] Statues thoughtlessly transferred from one person to another in this way resemble actors who are assigned to play multiple parts, and just as when actors make their entrances playing a different character each time, the deception involved here is also so obvious that the audience immediately realizes what is taking place.[68] But because dedicating a statue is an act "that is more just than any other act," to do so "unjustly" is a sign of not understanding the true nature of things.[69] To transfer the image from one person to another is equivalent to destroying the statue: even if the statues are made of durable materials, the citizens of Rhodes render those statues as impermanent as wax dolls that melt in the heat of the sun.[70] The statue, in short, reveals itself here as the concrete manifestation of a bond—and to break that bond means, in effect, to destroy the object itself.

From his own point of view, Dio Chrysostom also shares our concern with the relationship that is established between the dedicator and the dedicatee/referent by means of the image. To receive a statue is actually seen as a sort of contract: "Each man has paid a price [*timē*] for his statue, and no small price at that: some have paid by their brilliant military service in defense of the city, others as ambassadors," and so on.[71] The contract thus involves a multiple relationship between the person who offers the statue, the person represented by the statue, and the person who receives the statue: but these statues are goods whose possession is actually rather difficult to define. It is not entirely clear just who owns the statue, given that one person erects it (is he perhaps the owner?), but someone else is represented by it (and so therefore it is his image too). Thus, "in a general sense the statues are said to belong to the citizens of Rhodes, but in a particular sense each statue belongs to the man in whose name the statue was erected."[72] This is why the citizens of Rhodes have acted wrongfully. The images are not like houses; one cannot say of a statue that "it used to belong to such and such a person, but now it belongs to so-and-so."[73] Language itself rebels at this absurd-sounding possibility: do the citizens of Rhodes really think that they are able "*to erect* a statue for someone when it was in fact *already erected* five hundred years ago for someone else?"[74]

But Dio Chrysostom makes some even more interesting observations as he turns his attention from the citizens of Rhodes who (against every principle of justice) rededicate statues that had previously been dedicated to other people, and directs his criticism instead toward the recipients of these rededicated statues, their new referents. Clearly, these people find themselves in a very anomalous situation. To define this condition, Dio Chrysostom has recourse to an especially powerful cultural model: kinship relations. It is obvious to everyone, he explains, that "women who pass off the children of other women as their own sons" are behaving in an unacceptable manner. But the citizens of Rhodes "are not ashamed to do the same thing with images, declaring that these statues belong to people to whom they do not actually belong."[75] Therefore, the images can be assimilated to the sons of their referents. The relationship between the image and the person is seen in terms of filiation, as a relationship between parent and child. This means that the statue's transferral to another referent is similar to the act of *hypoballein*, that is, substituting one child for another: such statues are not the true sons of their new owners.[76] This metaphor of kinship once again evokes a strictly contiguous relationship between the image and the referent, as we have already observed in the construction of the portrait of the lover.

But somewhat before advancing this argument, Chrysostom makes use of yet another powerful metaphor: in what is perhaps the most interesting passage of this speech, he interprets the situation of the statues not in terms of filiation, but in terms of marriage. "No honorable man," he says, "would be willing to take a wife by committing adultery with her, because he would thus be committing an injustice against her previous husband. Nor, for that matter, would any man want to receive a wife from another man who is her husband (even if that frequently happens without base motivations)."[77] Yet this is precisely what the citizens of Rhodes are doing with the statues. For Dio Chrysostom, the bond between the dedicatee/referent and the image can be understood as a *matrimonial* bond; the person has a wife in the statue dedicated to him. This means that the person who appropriates a statue previously dedicated to someone else is committing a sort of adultery—and it is obvious that one cannot marry a woman taken in the act of adultery or even a woman freely given away by her husband. For the marriage to make sense, the wife must be consigned by a legitimate "giver of wives" (her father, brother, etc.); she cannot be consigned by a man such as her husband who was (and still is) a "taker" of women.[78]

Continuing with Dio Chrysostom's metaphorical analysis of the dedicatee/referent in terms of marriage, we can turn our attention to the dedicator. Evidently, the dedicator is someone who assigns a sort of wife to someone else, dedicating a statue to that person in exchange for the price, the *timē*, that he has paid. The dedicator is thus seen as a "giver of wives," someone like a father-in-law or a brother-in-law who establishes a relationship of affinity with the dedicatee by means of the image: the dedicator and the dedicatee have a kinship through marriage. This explains why the dedicator cannot just take back the image at will. He and the dedicatee/referent have entered into a kinship relation that cannot be unilaterally severed. A son-in-law or a brother-in-law cannot be made to forfeit his kinship identity without his formal consent. The mutual vow between two persons—a vow represented, as we have seen, by the image—thus finds metaphorical expression in that quintessential cultural vow of affinity through marriage. Like a woman who is given and received within the complex mechanism of matrimonial alliance, the image also serves as a transmitter, a means of establishing relations. This is why kinship, whether of sons or of wives, is able to supply a very precise metaphor for how images are regarded in the intricate social networks of human communities.

6

Incredible Loves

Pigmalïon, quanto lodar ti dei
de l'imagine tua, se mille volte
n'avesti quel ch'i' sol una vorrei.

Pygmalion, how lucky you are with that statue: you have enjoyed a thousand times what I would be glad to enjoy but
once.

Petrarch's words, as he gazes at Laura's portrait.[1] But no
matter what Petrarch may have thought, Pygmalion was hardly an artist;
perhaps he did not even know how to draw. In any case, he certainly did
not enjoy the enviable fate that Ovid attributed to him; no divine creation acquired life—in the true sense of that word—at the caress of his
hands.[2] Ovid (and many poets after him) sought to substitute a magical power for what was originally just a weakness, an insanity. Pygmalion, it seems, was the king of Cyprus, desperately in love with a statue
of Aphrodite. Arnobius, armed with dauntless Christian imagination, is
not ashamed to tell this story in all its lurid detail, describing Pygmalion
in his bed, *demens,* given over to a fruitless libido and the sweetness of
illusory embraces.[3] Only in the king's erotic delirium was the sculpted
statue transformed into a perfect woman; his magical power was nothing more than an illness, a mirage.

Image Mania

Yet Pygmalion was not the only person to have fallen in love with a statue. There are some quite famous stories about this subject, worth repeating briefly here.[4] Praxiteles—whose splendid marbles surpassed even his own outstanding works in bronze—had sculpted two Aphrodites, one clothed and one nude (see Fig. 2). The people of Cos preferred the veiled Aphrodite, as if she were somehow better behaved than the other Aphrodite: being clothed, she showed greater decency and restraint. As a result, the people of Cnidos were able to enjoy the nude Aphrodite, and many captains steered their ships to that port just to get a glimpse of Praxiteles' nude goddess. She was kept in an open temple, so that the statue could be seen from all sides (as the goddess herself wished, so it was said). Eventually, of course, a young man from a quite respectable family was seized with an insane love for her incomparable beauty, and hid himself inside the temple precinct, lying beside the simulacrum under the cover of night. He even left behind a small trace of his mad desire on the immaculate white marble—but the historian Posidippus, who tells us the story, was apparently discreet enough to not reveal the young man's name.[5] Praxiteles had also carved a marble Eros (kept at Parium) that was said to rival the Aphrodite of Cnidos in its beauty, and which was similarly defiled: a certain Alcetas of Rhodes (in this case the man's name is known to us) fell in love with that charming little boy, and likewise left behind an analogous sign of profanation on Praxiteles' splendid marble.[6]

But it is Lucian who tells us in greatest detail just what took place there inside the sacred precinct of Aphrodite's temple at Cnidos; such are the privileges of literature, after all.[7] According to Lucian, the young man would go to the temple every morning, at first light, seemingly moved by incomparable devotion. But the truth was that he acted out of desire—his own. For hours he would sit before the goddess, his eyes staring fixedly at her, his lips whispering the incomprehensible words and secret reproaches of a lover. He yearned for solace, pleading with the goddess, but Aphrodite, of course, did not respond. So he decided to put all his hopes in the dice—and in this (we might add) his madness displayed a sort of paradoxical practicality. Although the gods are mute (or, more precisely, they use a language that cannot be deciphered by mortals), it is nevertheless true that the gods can speak (or "be spoken") by a fortuitous throw of the dice. This use of the dice (called *astragalo-*

manteia) was a well known and widely practiced method of divination in ancient Greece.[8]

Thus the infatuated young man made himself a priest, and the mad language of his passion resorted to the science of divination (that quintessential science of interpretation and translation) in an effort to turn his soliloquy into a dialogue. A good throw of the dice—especially that throw called "the cast of Venus"—would be a sign of the goddess's favor, but any other throw would plunge the young man into a state of despair, causing him to curse all of Cnidos.[9] The first throw was unpropitious, of course, as was the next throw, meant to ameliorate the first, and also the next . . . Thus unappeased, the flames of his passion burned even hotter. In this state of excitement he covered the walls of the temple with words of love, and carved tributes to the exquisite Aphrodite in the bark of every tender tree. Praxiteles was honored as if he were another Zeus, and each precious offering found in the treasury was dedicated to the goddess.[10] As for the rest of the story, there is nothing new or surprising: the veil of night finally gave this young man the insane courage he needed to satisfy his passion. But Lucian adds that in the popular version of the story the young man was said to have committed suicide: having emerged from the temple, he either hurled himself from a cliff or (according to still other popular accounts) he leaped into the waves of the sea.

It is worth noting that these popular versions associate the anonymous lover of images with two particular forms of death that ancient Greek and Roman culture usually assigned to criminals defiled by the most serious of all sexual transgressions: incest. Classical texts frequently tell us that people who committed incest were condemned to be punished (or chose to punish themselves) by being cast into the sea or by irrevocably leaping from a cliff.[11] This form of punishment was meant to indicate that such a monster could have no place whatsoever in human society; it was not possible to come into contact with him even in order to exact punishment. Instead, uncivilized nature is called upon to scatter his remains upon the ocean's waves or in the gorge of some ravine. The popular story thus consigns the anonymous lover of Aphrodite (the lover, that is, of her marble image) to a deeply dramatic death that is also strongly marked in cultural terms. This incestuous aspect of the story will claim our attention again shortly.[12]

Incredible loves—but also comical ones, as proclaimed in Aelian's little collection of comical and paradoxical loves: *Geloioi kai paradoxoi erōtes*.[13] Here for example, we find the story of how Xerxes fell in love with a plane tree, and also how Glauce, the famous lyre player, was adored by a dog (or a ram, or a swan, depending on which version of the story you prefer).[14] Aelian also adds the story, more sad than comical, of a young Athenian who was seized by a passion for the statue of Agathe Tyche. He embraced her, he kissed her, and in his surprisingly pragmatic desperation he even tried to buy her from the Athenian city council. The councilors refused, but the young man continued to decorate his cherished simulacrum with sacred fillets and garlands, even if these sacrifices were not exactly what they seemed to be. It was traditional to offer ribbons and garlands to simulacra of the gods, of course, but rejected lovers were likewise accustomed to adorn images of their beloved with garlands of flowers.[15] In this way the young Athenian hid his amorous delusion behind a veil of ritual practices. The image itself has now become the beloved; the objects of these two relationships are conflated, and two different codes of behavior are confounded and superimposed on one another. But there is nothing ambiguous about the story's finale. Having completed his offerings, the young man killed himself in front of the goddess (her statue), just as we might expect of a real lover scorned by his beloved.[16]

Incredible loves, but also—if we believe a story told in Athenaeus's *Deipnosophistae*—thoroughly repulsive as well.[17] Cleisophus of Selymbria was another lover seized by passion for a statue of Parian marble, and he accordingly had himself locked inside the temple at Samos where the statue was kept.[18] But because of the stone-cold frigidity of the statue he was unable to satisfy his desire, and had to place a slice of meat between himself and the statue.[19] For a more polite variation, we can consider the case of a pilgrim to Delphi (a quite discreet person, in his own way) who also longed to embrace a statue, in this case one of the two male statues standing in the temple of Apollo. After his tryst with the image, the man left behind a garland as an offering. This garland later proved to be his salvation: when the pilgrim was charged with the crime of having violated the statue, the god himself ordered that the man be forgiven, on the grounds that "he had paid his bill."

Pygmalion, therefore, was not alone. Indeed, the Pygmalion found in Ovid—the artist captivated by his own work, the father infatuated with his own offspring—has a curious and rather less well known alter ego in the epistolary collection of Aristaenetus.[20] The story involves a painter this time, not a sculptor, and thus constitutes a new variation in our repertoire of tales. He is an artist who curses his own extraordinary talent for having created a woman of irresistible beauty;[21] despite his desperate passion, no goddess of love appears to intervene with a miracle on his behalf. So once again we find the artist lying in bed, vainly attempting to embrace the image and satisfy his desire. This time, however, it is not the frozen rigidity of marble but rather the delicate veneer of a painting that is subjected to the strange adventure of this incredible love. The anonymous painter consoles himself with thoughts appropriate to the genteel and intellectual sophistry of the epigrammatic tradition in which Aristaenetus is writing: for example, he comforts himself with the thought that Narcissus—another famous actor in a drama of incredible love—would have lost his beloved image if he had plunged his hand into the water of the fountain. But the painter's image does not vanish when he reaches out and touches it with his hand: "she" is still there, laughing sweetly. Indeed, she responds to his offers of love by saying nothing, that tantalizing provocation of the true coquette. It is the painter's irrefutable revenge against the perfection of the mirror: silence paradoxically triumphs over speech; the dead image prevails over the life that it lacks. By saying nothing, the image *seduces*. It is as if Aristaenetus's painter were to say: "Better, far better that Venus does not bring her to life—because then the image would be able to speak, and thus destroy her alluring silence."

The inherent absurdity of being in love with a statue was obviously able to produce all manner of baroque conceits, particularly among the rhetoricians, who found in this subject an irresistible topic for declamation. Libanius, in an exercise entitled "What the Painter Should Do If He Has Fallen in Love with the Girl He Has Painted," pushes his rhetorical imagination to the point of making the artist claim that the story of his love now makes him a subject worthy to be painted.[22] Every aspect of love, says the painter, "was a subject for my paintings: now I have become a subject for others! Paint, you artists, paint my unprecedented love! I am ensnared by my own fictions." But this (somewhat forced) game of inlaid images—the painter in love with a painting who in turn aspires to be painted—still cannot escape the obvious conclusion that to embrace the object of his love and satisfy his desire is simply impossible. In spite of every artistic conceit—the silent seduction of the image, the painter painted while in the painting's embrace—the fact remains that the image has no capacity whatsoever to return the passion of which it is the object. In his *Traité de l'essence et guérison de l'amour ou mélancolie érotique*,[23] Jacques Ferrand applies an Aristotelian logic to this situation.[24] "The affection that is felt for inanimate objects is not real love, because there is no possibility of reciprocal feeling; there is no way to desire the good of the object, which is an essential attribute of love." The greatest source of torment in these incredible loves is precisely a lack of reciprocity, the impossibility of exchange—a failure that can eventually lead the unrequited lover to unleash a sad and bitter curse upon the whole affair.

It is the curse, in fact, that makes the sophist Onomarchus's speech on the subject so exemplary. Although he was upbraided for over-indulging in synonyms,[25] and the opening pages of his declamation—entitled "The Man Who Fell in Love with a Statue"—are rather predictable, Onomarchus completely redeems himself as a writer with the lover's final words:[26]

> O living beauty in a body without life, what god gave you form? Persuasion? Grace? Or Love himself, the father of beauty? Truly, you have everything: your face is full of expression and the bloom of youth; there is a light in your eyes, a smile that enchants, a blush on your cheeks, even a sign that you understand my words. It is as if your voice were always on the point of making itself heard—and suddenly you would be able to speak, I am sure . . . but I will not be there, you cruel woman, because you do not know how to love, you who are unfaithful to your faithful lover. You have not granted me so much as a single word. That is why I will hurl at you the curse that more than any other causes beauty to shudder: may you grow old!

It is an incredible paradox, this statue condemned to grow old. Cold, immobile, lifeless, the statue has but one advantage over living creatures: it does not change. Our sophist is somewhat carried away with his own words, but he nevertheless has a keen understanding of the situation, and has condemned the ungrateful statue to the worst possible punishment: to become a statue that ages. Thus the cold and rigid image, already inherently inferior to living creatures, loses its one and only privilege. We might describe Onomarchus's invention as "the paradox of Pygmalion." Indeed, one wonders if Pygmalion, the infatuated sculptor whom we meet in Ovid's version of the story, ever stopped to think that by obtaining life for his lovely masterpiece, he automatically condemned her to the ravages of time.

Brutus and Other Romans

It is tempting to suppose that Roman civilization was immune to these decidedly paradoxical passions, to these incredible loves.

But that would not be entirely correct. There is nothing particularly worrisome (at least apparently) about the fact that Hortensius always carried with him a Sphinx that he had appropriated from Verres, or that the consul Gaius Cestius could not be separated from his favorite *signum* even in battle.[27] But our suspicions are very much aroused (because of both the character and the proclivities of the person involved) when we learn that Nero never parted with an Amazon sculpted by Strongylion, always keeping her nearby because of the loveliness of her legs, which earned her the epithet "Amazon of the Lovely Legs."[28] And about Caligula there can be no doubt whatsoever. Pliny, for example, tells us that the emperor was so "inflamed with desire" (*libidine accensus*) for two paintings at his residence in Ardea, one of Atalanta in the nude, and another of Helen, that he tried to take them away with him; but because they were frescoes he was unable to remove them from the wall.[29] Finally, there is Tiberius. Pliny tells us that outside his baths, Agrippa had placed a statue of Lysippus's famous Apoxyomenos ("Man Scraping Himself"), which Tiberius found extremely attractive. In the early years of his rule, as Pliny explains, Tiberius "was still able to control himself; in the end, however, he could not resist having the statue moved into his bedroom, replacing it with a substitute outside the baths. But the Roman people were so indignant that they protested loudly in the theater, demanding that the Apoxyomenos be restored to its place, so that the emperor, despite his love for the statue, was compelled to put it back."[30] Of course, there is nothing surprising about Tiberius's inclination to these incredible loves. As we will see somewhat later, a lascivious Archigallus painted by Parrhasius also made its way into his bedroom, soon to be followed by an even more lascivious love scene between Meleager and Atalanta, painted by that same artist.[31]

The most unusual story, however, is one that we owe to Brutus, Caesar's assassin. It is a rather stern story (as we would expect from a man of such character) and is all the more striking on that account. The same Strongylion who had sculpted the Amazon of the Lovely Legs much adored by Nero also sculpted a boy "that Brutus of Philippi loved so much that he bestowed on it the fame of his own cognomen."[32] This was no small privilege: the cognomen of Brutus had been handed down by the Junii without interruption since the year 509 B.C.E., and it formed an integral part of their family heritage.[33] In traditional aristocratic practice, this cognomen was bestowed upon the firstborn son.[34] By being awarded this name, Strongylion's sculpted boy became a member of the family: no small feat! In this case the story of incredible passion for an image leads to an unexpected onomastic conclusion.

A Psychoanalyst for Our Fundamental Story

But let us return to our *paradoxoi erōtes,* the stories of people actually driven mad by their erotic passion for a statue or for a painting. In general, these stories are dramatically different from the story of Butades' daughter or Laodamia and Protesilaus, where we find two lovers, one of whom is absent and must be replaced by the portrait. In a story of incredible love, the beloved simply *is* the portrait itself; the image supersedes the referent. Our fundamental story (two lovers, and the portrait of one of them) is thus drastically transformed: the beloved and his (or her) portrait *are conflated,* abruptly eliminating one of the pawns from play and producing what we might call a more economical variation on our fundamental story. There is no longer any need for an actual lover who precedes the image (and whose place the portrait eventually occupies). The image itself is now more than enough to provoke the lover's passion. As for what can be called the Ovidian outcome of the story, in which the statue is transformed into a woman, this finale only exposes the story's deep content while at the same time diluting it. Love for a statue as if it were a woman becomes love for a statue that turns into a woman. Ovid borrows a metaphor, and deftly extracts from it an ending for his story.

Obviously, it is better *not* to fall in love with a statue. "No man in his right mind," as Clement of Alexandria wrote in a chapter devoted to the lovers of statues, "would embrace a goddess, or wish to be interred with a dead woman, or fall in love with a demon or a stone."[35] That would be the act of a madman. If he is a pleasant and friendly sort of madman, like Ovid's Pygmalion, Venus might help him to rejoin normal society, and with the poet's help his story might have a happy ending. But if he is only a lecherous and *demens* king of Cyprus, Arnobius will not hesitate to execrate him in lurid detail (and if he is one of those desperate young men whose names we do not even know, he might be condemned to die by the end of the story). But it is no good sitting idly by—somebody ought to try to do something. So Philostratus tells us the story of another case involving the Aphrodite of Cnidos, in which the intervention of Apollonius of Tyana in person was required to cure the infatuated young man of his reckless folly.[36] Apollonius, after all, was a renowned worker of wonders, famous for his powers of persuasion—even if the words he uses to cure this particular young man are admittedly rather banal. But in a world without the wonder-working Apollonius, whose job is it to rescue these young lovers—is it a task for the psycho-analyst? In fact, I would like to suggest that there is a modern variation of Pygmalion's tale (specifically, of Ovid's Pygmalion, with a metamorphosis for the moral), a story that can be called a clinical case in every sense of the word. What I have in mind is the not very attractive work that a long essay by Freud did much to improve: the "Gradiva" of Wilhelm Jensen.[37]

The hero of this story is one Norbert Hanold, a young German archaeologist who has fallen in love with an ancient bas-relief of a girl depicted in the act of walking. What strikes him most is her step, the way in which she gracefully arches her foot as she walks.[38] He christens her Gradiva ("She Who Is Walking") and convinces himself that this silent figure could not have inhabited a city like Rome; instead, she must have come from some place far more serene and secluded: Pompeii.

Norbert Hanold thus makes his way to Pompeii, which he finds crowded with German newlyweds. Although he is annoyed by their presence, Hanold is nevertheless certain that he has finally found the right setting for his Gradiva. And much to his surprise, he actually sees a young woman coming toward him, similar in every way to the marble figure, but able to speak and move. Because the apparition takes place at noon, Hanold has no difficulty in immediately recognizing the woman as a *daemon meridianus,* one of those ghosts that appear at midday, a disconcerting revenant of his beloved Gradiva.[39] The same ghost appears to Hanold again and again, gradually causing him to suspect that this is not a ghost at all but perhaps something else entirely—until at last it is revealed that the midday demon is none other than Zoe Bertgang, a woman who has been in love with Hanold since their childhood. Solid, Germanic Zoe has in fact taken it upon herself to cure her friend of his delusion: a delusion that, in the archaeologist's peculiar mind, has transformed his memory of Zoe's face and appearance into an enchanting marble effigy. It goes without saying that the beneficial shock of this discovery frees Hanold from his antiquarian visions, and he agrees at last to an encounter with the female sex from which he has always fled, seeking refuge in marbles and bronzes. In the end, Hanold even reconciles himself to sharing Pompeii with the other young German newlyweds who have come there for their honeymoons.

Bas-relief, ghost, and finally a woman in flesh and blood, the "Gradiva" runs lightly through the same stages of metamorphosis as Ovid's simulacrum, as seen through the eyes of her delirious lover. A neurotic young archaeologist, very *fin de siècle,* has replaced that *demens* Pygmalion, the madman who burned with a hopeless libido; and in place of the artist's magic (or the powers of Venus) we can observe the tricks of the unconscious, in whose cramped, limitless confines an enervating game is played out between the archaeologist-lover, the Gradiva-portrait, and its Germanic, very real referent Zoe Bertgang.

In the myth of psychoanalysis, we might say that Pygmalion has a problem with repressed desire, while the statue who comes to life represents his cure: although in that case it is not the portrait but the lover who is transformed. If we were to pursue this line of thought, we could produce an actual clinical analysis, reducing Pygmalion's story to yet another case of delirium (probably hysterical delirium, or perhaps fetishistic erotomania).[40] Jensen's "Gradiva" might not lose much in such a reading, but it would be a shame to reduce its ancient archetype to this sort of interpretation. Therefore, we feel authorized to stop the analysis at this point—just as Freud himself refrained from the endless tendency to psychoanalyze that is inevitably implied by this sort of approach.[41] Instead, we will set out again along the path that we had abandoned in order to pursue the neurotic young archaeologist in his comings and goings at Pompeii: taking up the thread of our topic, we should ask at this point just what happens to the structure of our fundamental story when it is modified to produce tales like this one.

These stories of "incredible love"—Pygmalion, Alcetas, Norbert Hanold, the painter in Aristaenetus, and the rest—all begin with the same disturbing substitution: a portrait that is *worth more* than the beloved, an icon placed *before* its referent. The image comes first both in temporal terms (the portrait itself is transformed into the beloved) and in hierarchical terms (the lover actually prefers this effigy to a real person). Slowly but surely we find ourselves deeper and deeper inside the game, and as we examine the abstract rules that arrange the basic elements of our fundamental story (the lover, the beloved, the portrait), the surprises continue to multiply. It turns out, in fact, that even with a reduced number of pawns, the game can still go on. The beloved can be rendered superfluous and exit the stage (only to return at the behest of Venus, or of the psychoanalyst); meanwhile, *the portrait itself is more than enough.*

This particular version of our fundamental story is based on an assumption that is fully obvious but nevertheless paradoxical. If the lover seeks perfection in the object of his love, then no human woman could ever bear comparison to the manufactured perfection of an image, of an *effigies.* Ovid (that famous expert in love) described Pygmalion's problem in precisely these terms. According to the version in Ovid's *Meta-morphoses,* Pygmalion had been seized by a sort of weariness with the female sex, a disgust for the limitless vices that Nature had assigned to womankind.[42] This was why the artist sought refuge in his exceptional craftsmanship: he wanted to construct for himself a simulacrum of something that he could not find elsewhere, with which he then fell in love. Of course, we would not want to risk making our paradoxical lover look like the victim of some Stendahlian delusion, condemned to madness after having seen a wrinkle in some woman's stockings . . . But clearly the lover of a statue—Pygmalion, Alcetas, Norbert Hanold, the name hardly matters—is someone who acquiesces to a cruel and burdensome paradox: that nothing human is worthy of love, that there is no human being who deserves to be loved. The only choice is to devote one's love to an ideal image constructed by some extremely talented artist. It is the paradox of stone, or bronze, or ivory: creatures that are flawless but cold, as opposed to living creatures that are full of warmth but flawed. A statue cannot share in one's love, this is true. But as we know from the curse of the sophist Onomarchus, the statue does not age; its beauty is eternal.[43]

We might recall, at this point, what we said earlier about a particular quality assumed by the image, by the portrait, within this cultural model: besides having the nature of an icon, the portrait can function as an index.[44] It is a portrait in touch with the person, a sign imbued with reality; such an image, as Ovid noted earlier, "is more than what it seems." And this is precisely the motivation that makes it possible for the number of pawns in play to be abruptly reduced, allowing the beloved, the referent of the portrait, to exit the stage, at no detriment to the unfolding story. The men in love with these statues—the neurotic Norbert Hanold, or the perverse Pygmalion—thus reaffirm in their own way something that we already knew: the statue *is not* an icon. Indeed, in these cases of incredible love, the situation is even more exacerbated, because for these men the image is not merely a part of the person: the image actually *is* a person. The image does not replace anything: it is not a question of *pothos* or *desiderium;* it is a question, so to speak, of reality. Most likely it is here, in this substitution, that we can identify the illness that plagues these paradoxical lovers. People of so-called sound mind would be willing to admit, more or less explicitly, that the portrait is a sign imbued with reality, whereas people of unsound mind (such as our promiscuous madmen) appear to be convinced of the contrary: that reality is instead imbued with signs.

Figures for the Impossible

Paradoxical loves . . . but perhaps we can try to understand in greater depth the nature of the paradox that characterizes this peculiar aberration, a way to categorize and imagine this deviation. To fall in love with an image is surely a form of sexual transgression—but one so unusual (so paradoxical) that it is worth considering just how it was perceived and represented in the cultural imagination. We must therefore turn again to the stories, and to the lessons that they teach.

If there is a starting point from which to grasp the meaning of a story, then it must surely be the story's conclusion; to make sense of an action we begin by considering its outcome. In this case, our experience as readers is corroborated by a rule (both rigorous and commonsensical) that Propp advocated whenever the specific nature of a narrative function could not be clearly identified: to find a possible explanation of these incredible loves, we should first of all examine their consequences.[45] We saw, for example, that the young man in love with the Aphrodite of Cnidos (at least according to the popular versions of the story) finally hurled himself from a cliff, or cast himself upon the waves of the sea, much like a man guilty of incest.[46] In terms of its outcome, the young man's story thus greatly resembles the situation of someone whose love for a forbidden woman—such as for a mother or a sister—violates a basic law of amatory behavior. The lover of statues has apparently committed a transgression so serious that he must be punished as if he had committed incest: this is what the outcome of the story demonstrates.

The fact that the lover of images would be seen as someone who has committed a grave sexual crime, a monstrous crime similar to incest, is further confirmed by other evidence. First of all, there is the fact that Pygmalion—the real one—was a king, and we have seen other tyrannical emperors (Tiberius, Caligula, Nero) involved in similar stories of a mad passion for images.[47] Kings and tyrants were, of course, supposed to be especially entitled to commit any sort of monstrous sexual transgression, including incest: indeed, they even seem to have preferred it.[48] The tyrant's freedom to commit incest is a direct result of the sexual license entailed by his absolute power; to actually commit incest serves as an explicit declaration and assertion of that power. Above and beyond the laws that regulate everyone else's behavior, the tyrant prefers incest in order to affirm once and for all his right to be an exception to the rule. Thus, when Caracalla hesitated to contract an incestuous marriage with his stepmother, he was told: "Don't you know that you are the emperor? You are supposed to make the laws, not obey them."[49] With this in mind, we are not surprised to discover that among the tyrants who were lovers of images, Nero was also rumored to have been his mother's lover,[50] and Caligula was supposedly his sister's lover.[51] Depraved and incestuous, these tyrants were driven by a desperate desire not only for images, but also for their closest female relations.

Nor should we forget about Narcissus, that young man who was similarly in love with an image—his own—and thus acting out a drama of incredible love.[52] As we will see in a perhaps surprising variation on the story, this refined, sensitive young man was even supposed to have come dangerously close to committing incest: before falling in love with his own image, Narcissus was in love with his twin sister.[53] Moreover, his fatal flaw—falling in love with his own reflected image—associates him with the horse of Greek and Roman folklore, a lascivious creature reportedly inclined to incest and also prone to falling in love with its reflected image (or with the image of another horse).[54] The person who loves images is thus placed outside the realm of culture and enters into the disarming realm of nature, where no laws prevail. To love an image is something very close to loving a sexual partner who is absolutely and strictly prohibited. The lover of images can thus be grouped with the lawless tyrant, the young man hurled from a cliff as if guilty of incest, or someone who loves his own sister, deranged by a passion that is typical of beasts. In short, he is a sort of artistic and sophisticated Oedipus whom society drives away in horror, a scapegoat, a *pharmakos*. The sense of estrangement, of distance, that the paradoxical lover communicates through the form of his story constitutes an essentially negative paradigm. Such a story of the lover—such stories of incredible love—thus provide a true and proper myth of prohibition.

The various stories told about the lovers of images constitute a discourse (and we will soon see that we are dealing here with a discourse strictly "among men") that concerns a subject of no little importance in the organization of culture: the rules according to which one is supposed to behave with those beautiful *substitutes* (perhaps even more beautiful than real people could ever hope to be) whose seductive bodies of marble and whose subtly illusionary, colorful figures populate the cultural landscape with ever increasing frequency. This leads to a risky situation in which a man might want to attach himself even more closely, and in a quite irregular way, to an image with which he is already very closely linked. As a result, the referents of those figures (very often figures of the gods, for that matter) might be put in a defenseless position. The images are creatures entrusted to human care, placed under their *fides* or custody.[55] It would be wrong to violate that trust, to break that *fides* by taking advantage of the weakness of an image that is utterly dependent on its creator, and on the people in whose company it finds itself.

But there is one final question that must be addressed: what sort of temptation is contained within these prohibited creatures, within the images? If there are motives for prohibition, for setting the images off-limits, then there must be equally strong motives for desiring them. It would be too easy to appeal to the sexual attraction that in general is aroused by whatever is prohibited. Above and beyond this possible motive, we should ask ourselves if there is not some peculiar characteristic of the image at work here, something that radically differentiates it from a living creature: specifically, its immobility, its availability, its muteness and *passivity*. The image's total inability to participate in a true exchange of love is matched by its symmetrical and equally total passivity.

This characteristic of the image suggests an explanation, perhaps more profound than it first appears, as to why these particular lovers of images always turn out to be men. One cannot help but notice, after all, that the incredible lovers whose absurd adventures we have described thus far have all been men, without exception.[56] Given a culture in which the practice of pleasure was fundamentally based on the stereotype of penetration, and on a polarized contrast of active and passive, the image would thus be able to represent the very prototype of sexual passivity.[57] This means that the paradox of these incredible loves essentially glorifies the one intrinsically respectable and thoroughly valorized role, the role of being active, of dominating.[58] If we combine this cultural ambition to dominate with the beauty and perfection embodied in a work of art, the result would no doubt serve as a strong provocation to desire. In terms of the cultural imagination, it would also serve as a strong provocation to create stories about this love for images—specifically, stories in which an extreme desire for passivity (perfectly represented by the image) encounters and confronts the prohibition against the violent appropriation of these defenseless, readily available objects of desire.[59]

But maybe we can be a bit more generous with Pygmalion, and all the other kings with their incredible loves. Perhaps it was not only out of a disgust with women, or from a fear of living persons that they preferred instead a substitute that was flawlessly perfect and equally docile and passive. Perhaps it was not so much (or not only) a spiteful scorn for life, but rather that in those sculpted or painted images each of those mad lovers may have glimpsed a gesture, an obsessive phantom that they had endlessly sought in real life, hoping to find this object of their desire in a living person somewhere—a fantasy that was always disappointed or denied by the truthfulness of life.[60] But suddenly one day, as they walked inside the temple, they saw the phantom right before their eyes, visible, if not alive; or, in a situation rather more fortunate if not more noble, they managed—being craftsmen themselves—to fix that phantom in an object, in the work of their own hands, making it possible for the stereotypes of art to sustain, rather than suppress, that sought-after gesture.[61] We can compare the reaction of Goethe's young Werther at the moment when having gone up a flight of stairs and having opened the door, he saw for the first time "the most enchanting spectacle in the world"[62]—Charlotte, the young woman with whom he would fall in love, glimpsed as she was slicing a loaf of black bread for the children's afternoon snack. It is astonishment; it is love. This scene, framed by the door of the foyer, would come to rule both Werther's life and his death, fixing his love in an image. Commenting on this episode, Roland Barthes observed:[63] "At first we love a *picture*. . . . Among all the combinations of objects, it is the picture that seems best when seen the first time: the curtain is torn aside, and something that was never seen before is completely uncovered, and is devoured by our eyes at that moment."[64] Norbert Hanold was transfixed by a gesture, by a step: the Gradiva. And what was the gesture in the statue of Agathe Tyche for which the young Athenian lover paid with his life? What sort of phantom did her marble form contain?[65]

"Poets and painters," as Horace remarked in a famous passage, "have always had the right to dare what they want."[66] Yet this is not merely a banal authorization to infringe upon likely probabilities, but something more. It is as if the image were possessed of an intrinsic power to contain the impossible, something that lies outside the province of living creatures, of the objects and situations that populate the world, something that could never be accommodated in the scope of reality. The realm of images not only reproduces the real world, but expands that world, making room not only for what does (or could) exist, but also for everything that has no conceivable chance of ever existing. Antoninus Liberalis tells us that once upon a time, on the plain of Thebes, the hound of Cephalus (from whom no prey could ever escape) found itself facing the Teumessian fox (an animal able to escape from any pursuer).[67] It is a very clever dramatization of a logical paradox: but how can it be resolved? If we let the chase go on forever, we would obviously be doing the hound an injustice; by stopping the chase, we would be wronging the fox. Zeus recognized that the two creatures were caught in a paradox, so he turned them both into stone.[68] In the figurative language of this mythical story, the statue explicitly gives shape to, and makes room for, the impossible. What the real world could never accommodate (even from a logical point of view) finds refuge in the world of images.

7

The Story of the Cruel Painter

But how would things turn out if the lover were not just any sort of lover, but an artist? Someone, that is, who could combine both roles: someone who loves a person, and someone who makes, with his own hands, that person's portrait? At a minimum, we might anticipate that their rapport—the rapport between the lover and the portrait, that is—would be rather different from what we have come to expect, almost a kind of complicity. The lover would be bound by a twofold relationship, but also a somewhat ambiguous one: being in love with the other person, and being the author of that person's portrait. In some sense he would be doubling one into two, commingling love and filiation, dependency and possession. In other words, it is difficult to say which would come first for the lover-artist: the beloved person, or that person's portrait.[1] The fundamental story, as we see, continues.

This doubling—rather, this dilemma—is also found in literature. Do the poets write about their lovers because they love them, or do they love their lovers in order to write about them? Do we owe Petrarch's *Canzoniere* to a great love, or is it just the opposite? When we read that Polygnotus—decorating the Painted Stoa with images of the Trojan women— "depicted Laodice with the face of Elpinice" (his lover), we immediately assume that Polygnotus loved Elpinice so much that he could not help but insinuate her face among the faces he was painting.[2] Agreed. But we might just as well suspect that the painter also felt such a desire for faces that he could not help falling in love. We should devote a few moments to this problem—if for no other reason than to see just how frequently it arises.

In the ancient world (as in later times), many artists depicted their lovers, more or less *deguisées,* in the subjects of their works. The model for Apelles' Aphrodite Anadyomene was reportedly Pancaspe, the courtesan of Alexander the Great with whom he was in love (and whom Alexander, in his generosity, later gave him as a gift).[3] The painter Pausias, on the other hand, was supposed to have fallen in love with Glycera, the famous maker of garlands; in fact, she was apparently the first person to practice this art. Having been seized by an insistent desire to emulate her ability, Pausias refined his technique until he was able to paint any sort of flower. The beloved thus acquires a singular presence in the art of this painter-lover: emulation and erotic metonymy are interwoven in the career of a man who was able to love while at the same time discovering subjects for his art and perfecting his own artistic technique. Eventually Pausias also painted his beloved Glycera, seated and holding a garland in her hands.[4] With this painting (which was considered to be truly outstanding, *e nobilissimis*) Pausias wanted to synthesize, one might say, the story of his technique with the story of his love, tying his double career in a single knot. Such a painting was certain to be a masterpiece.[5]

At least in the *Republic,* Plato emerges as an adversary of all imitation and thus also of the graphic arts, which were meant to imitate things not as they are but only as they seem. As a result, "the mimetic art is far from truth. It can produce anything, because it takes up only a small part of each object, a part that is only a copy [*eidōlon*]. For example, the painter might paint a shoemaker, a carpenter, or some other artisan without knowing anything about their arts. But, if he is a good painter, when he displays his painting of the carpenter at a distance he is able to fool children and naive persons, making them believe it is a real carpenter."[6] At least in the case of Pausias, the Platonic polemic misses its target. This painter of garlands and of garland makers spent years learning to emulate the technique of the artisan who occupied his thoughts; one certainly cannot say that he knew nothing of Glycera's art. In this case there is a rapport of love between the painter who imitates and the artisan who is imitated, and this is what constitutes the science of the imitator. Pausias would probably not have painted carpenters with as much proficiency.

The story of Pausias is quite beautiful, and would be worth elaborating as a story in all its details. And as its counterstory, we might consider the Roman painter Arellius, who likewise entwined his love and his art, but did so in a far less ennobling manner, at least according to

Pliny:[7] "Arellius was a famous painter at Rome somewhat before the time of Augustus, but he corrupted his art with an extraordinary disgrace. He was always attempting to ingratiate himself with the women he happened to desire at the moment, and therefore he depicted the goddesses with the features of his lovers. It was thus possible to keep track of his various prostitutes by observing his artwork." This time Plato's argument is quite legitimate. What indeed can we say of a painter who paints goddesses based on what he knows of prostitutes? How could one ever hope to know and to represent the divine by relying on such a profane science? Plato's reasoning is very sticky indeed, rather like flypaper. While it cannot be applied to Pausias, in this case there seems to be no escaping its hold. But Plato would actually lead us astray if we were to pursue this line of thought much further: we know, after all, that many painters painted the divine based on a science of prostitutes, and with very beautiful results indeed.

The painter's love is thus strong enough to finally become a portrait. It is a pity that we cannot gaze upon those paintings, because they would no doubt make many things clear. When the lover is also a great artist, as Proust says in *La fugitive,* "the answer to the riddle is revealed."[8] It suddenly becomes possible to understand someone like Swann, to comprehend the whole life of a lover whose follies are otherwise bewildering. "Finally you have before your eyes those lips that the common crowd never noticed in that woman, the nose that no one ever observed, that unsuspected bearing. The portrait says: 'What I have loved, what made me suffer, what has never left my sight—everything is here.'"

But we are still left with our initial suspicion: what if Pausias did fall in love with a maker of garlands because he wanted to paint garlands? And so too with Arellius: one can easily imagine that things were actually the opposite of Pliny's moralizing account, and that perhaps he went hunting for prostitutes only in order to be able to paint goddesses. Indeed, for these artist-lovers the two possibilities might both be true simultaneously. At this point, then, there is nothing left to do except to see what we can discover from our fundamental story, specifically from one of its most famous modern variations.

The narrator of Edgar Allan Poe's "Oval Portrait" is a wounded man who has sought refuge in a chateau, accompanied by his valet. Evidently it is wartime, and the chateau is deserted, having been hastily abandoned by its occupants.[9] Everything in those rooms is therefore still in its place, every item of furniture and all the tapestries and trophies, along with the many paintings on the walls—including the mysterious oval portrait of a young woman. The painting is done in vignette style: only the head and the shoulders of the subject can be seen, and they seem somehow to vanish imperceptibly into the obscure, deepening shadows of the background. But the portrait is set apart in a little niche of its own and the narrator does not notice it at first. It is only later that night, as he is lying in bed, feverish and already half asleep, that the narrator suddenly glimpses the painting. The sight of it overwhelms him, and he feels compelled to close his eyes in order to calm and subdue his mind. But he soon opens his eyes again and stares at the portrait for a long time, as if transfixed. Finally, an explanation makes its way into his consciousness, and he begins to understand why the portrait exerts such a power over him, why it is so exceptional: "I had found the spell of the picture in an absolute *life-likeliness* of expression, which, at first startling, finally confounded, subdued, and appalled me." Is this fantastic sensation something real, a reaction produced by the portrait itself? Or is it simply the result of the wounded man's delirious and dreamy stupor? Poe's ambiguous style of fantasy—always in perfect equilibrium between the impossible and the plausible, between logic and the supernatural—naturally leaves the question hanging, suspended in total uncertainty.

The paintings in the chateau are accompanied by a sort of guidebook, explaining the story and contents of each one. Anxious to learn something more about the oval portrait, the narrator takes up the guidebook and reads. The young woman—as the guidebook explains—was extraordinarily beautiful, and, more to the point, radiant with the joy of life. It was thus an ill-fated moment when she married that painter, a gloomy and eccentric man already wedded to his art. The young woman hated the brushes and palette, recognizing in them a dangerous rival. She was terrified when she learned of her husband's plans to paint her portrait—but being good-natured, she demurred, and even agreed to pose for hours and hours in a remote turret of the chateau. The work progressed, but the young woman suffered. Seized by a maniacal passion for his work, the painter did not see that his wife was increasingly despondent, that she grew paler and paler, that her strength was failing. The portrait was almost complete; only a few brush strokes remained— but the cruel painter did not realize that the colors spread on the canvas were actually stolen from the fair cheeks of the woman who stood before him. The last daub of paint was applied, the final tint. The painter, pallid, rejoicing, thrilled with delight, stood gazing at his painting, and loudly exclaimed, "But this is really *life*, life itself." He turned toward his beloved: she was dead.

The opposite of Ovid's Pygmalion: not an image that is changed into a woman, shedding the rigidity of its shape, but a woman who is changed into an image, forsaking life. This portrait *murders* its referent, usurping her place and her identity. In the painter's perverse mind, wedded to his art, the true identity of the beloved does not reside in the living life of that person, but only in the image that his own hands can extract. Our suspicions about the artist-lover thus turn out not to have been groundless after all. Some of them, it is true, paint because they love; but there are others who love only in order to paint.

We should take a step back here from the story's character to its author, noting that Poe actually did not admire "life-likeliness" in art, nor did he believe that the highest aim of the artist should be to reproduce nature in copies that would be indistinguishable from truth: "Were I called on to define, very briefly, the term 'Art,' I should call it 'the reproduction of what the senses perceive in nature through the veil of the soul.' The mere imitation, however accurate, of what is in nature, entitles no man to the sacred name of 'Artist.' Denner was no artist. The grapes of Zeuxis were *in*artistic, unless in a bird's-eye view; and not even the curtain of Parrhasius could conceal his deficiency in point of genius. I have mentioned the 'veil of the soul.' Something of the kind appears indispensable in art. We can, at any time, double the true beauty of an actual landscape by half closing our eyes as we look at it. The naked senses sometimes see too little, but then always they see too much."[10] Zeuxis and Parrhasius wanted to see too much, and they lost their grasp of art. The cruel painter of the "Oval Portrait" also wanted to see too much, and murdered Nature in the process. The veil of the soul is opposed to the curtain of Parrhasius; the ability to close one's eyes is the indispensable prerequisite of genius. It would come as a terrible blow to that cruel painter if he were to discover that his own author considered him not only an assassin but, even worse, an unsuccessful artist.

Let us proceed. It seems, in fact, that the following morning the narrator (Poe's narrator, that is) had to hastily abandon the mysterious chateau. The roar of the enemy artillery had grown dangerously close and, though still consumed by fever, he realized that there was no other hope of escape. Supported by his silent and faithful valet, he dragged himself toward the door into the garden. As he went out, he had time for just one last look at the young woman's portrait: beneath the painting, propped on a stone mantelpiece, a candle was silently burning. Had it been there earlier, that candle, on the night before? He did not recall having seen it. But the roar of the cannons grew ever more alarming, and in great haste the valet pulled the door shut behind them. As soon as the narrator had gone out . . . two eyes, profoundly restless, unexpectedly flickered behind the vase of flowers that stood in the drawing-room window. From outside, there was something like a gentle pressure against the windowpanes that caused the flame of the candle to respond with a sudden flash of light. In the mountains, the heavy artillery continued to roar; the wounded man would find it difficult to make his escape. Another few seconds passed, then slowly the door to the garden was thrown open, and a human figure, wrapped in a long gray cape, appeared on the threshold. Again, the candle nodded, flaring up suddenly. With long and steady steps the man advanced into the room as if making his way along a familiar path, and turned toward the oval portrait. The intermittent flash of the exploding grenades illuminated the tapestries on the walls, the furniture, and the paintings.

"He is gone," the man whispered, almost imperceptibly, "thank God for that." From the wall, the young woman seemed to stare fixedly at him, with eyes that looked incredibly real. She was dressed in a delicate, sky-blue material, as if she had just returned from a country picnic, except that the reddish glare of the candle had deprived her gaze of all its sweetness. The man raised his hands near his forehead, as if to have a better view, and said, "What's wrong? Are you afraid? Perhaps because he read that old story?" He moved a few steps nearer to the portrait, stopping right in front of it. "In an hour or two at most, he will be dead. If the gangrene doesn't kill him, our soldiers will be sure to finish him off; they show no mercy to stray soldiers." His hand reached out, as if to caress the canvas. His hair was blond, rather long, but upon closer inspection sparse and thinning. His face was also that of a man well advanced in years, but its irregular features were somehow flattened out in a way that was undeniably fascinating. "My little darling," he whispered, with a smile, "surely you do not think I am upset by what he read. He could not possibly have understood. But then, even if he did, what difference would it make? I have never regretted what happened. It could not have been otherwise." The gaze of the young woman grew even darker, and it almost seemed as if her lips twisted slightly, grimacing. All of a sudden, the candle's flame was extinguished by the wind. "We had not even thought about it for all these many years! And now that half-dead officer with his ridiculous meddling has gone and made you remember!"

The man lifted his hands up, placing them against the canvas, and again he seemed to make the delicate gesture of a caress. But it was practically dark by now, and one could see nothing more than shadows streaked with color. A light sigh was heard, suddenly stifled by the roar of an explosion. "Your sister," the man continued, "had guessed what was happening . . . what is it? You don't want me to speak of her that way? It seems to me exactly as if she were your sister." He laughed; his teeth were strong and irregular, like the features of his face, and also worn with age. "She was my wife, that is true . . . but there was not room for both of you." By some miracle (or the height of coincidence), the roar of the cannons abruptly ceased, and there was silence: it could have been anywhere in the world, that place. Suddenly he spoke: "I beg you, one more time. There is no longer any danger that she will come in! And that officer is surely dead by now." The man pressed himself even closer to the portrait, letting his long gray cape fall to the ground. He stood there for several seconds, without speaking, his hands still propped against the canvas—then he began again, in a voice no louder than a whisper but still piercing and sharp: "It is I, the one who made you—the one who *murdered*, for you! And you also committed *murder* that day—don't you forget it!" This time there was not the shadow of a doubt: a hoarse gasp, eerie and unnatural, filled the darkness of the room.

But by this point the boom of the grenades had drawn frighteningly close, shaking the chateau, its walls illuminated by the obscure glare of lights clouded by soot and smoke. All the passes were blocked; there was no longer any way out—one could only go back, swept along by the wave of an advance cascading through the valley like a river in flood. A blast of earth and fire smashed the glass in the windows, sweeping away the flowers in the windowsill. One could only go back. At the door, dumbstruck and consumed by fever, the narrator observed the speechless love between the cruel painter and the portrait.

Of course, this continuation of the "Oval Portrait" is my own invention (for which I hope the reader will forgive me). The desire to pursue its premises further was too strong, creating an irresistible temptation to see just what would happen when such a cult (or love) for the image became the immediate cause of a murder—with *her* portrait as an adulterous woman, an unworthy concubine, acting as *his* accomplice in the referent's assassination. It is the story of a diabolical lover who cloaks himself in a clever veil of deceit, an Admetus who plots Alcestis's assassination, aided and abetted by a simulacrum.

8

Lucretius

"No man in his right mind," as Clement of Alexandria wrote, "would fall in love with a demon or a stone."[1] That is, no man of sound mind would clasp an image in his embrace as he would a real human being. But what might that bishop of Alexandria have said about a man who embraced real, live people as if they in fact were images? Surely Clement would consider that man to be equally insane, and by the end of this chapter we too might reach the same conclusion. In the meantime, however, we can embark upon another variant of our fundamental story, the tale of a lover who does not love his beloved, but loves instead the beloved's image—except that, this time, the image does not take the place of the absent beloved: the beloved is there, the beloved exists. But the lover nevertheless persists in believing that what he loves is only an image, nothing more.

This is not some hypothetical game invented for the sake of symmetry, to complete our repertoire of stories. There was, in fact, someone who played precisely this game, and played it in earnest. And he was not an insane painter (of the sort we encountered in previous chapters), not someone whose mind, crazed with figures, could only seize upon highlights and tints where others perceived actual human beings. We will be discussing here the story of Lucretius, a poet, a philosopher, who suffered from a hallucination that was exactly the opposite of Pygmalion's delusion: he believed that to love real human beings was actually to feed on simulacra.

Remedies for Cruel Love

But in order to understand the paradoxical situation of
the Lucretian lover, we must first consider Lucretius's general notion of
love's painful pleasures, its perpetual grief, *dira lubido*.[2] In his funereal
theory of this sentiment, Lucretius aspires to a literal understanding of
that metaphor which was so dear to literary *erōs*—the wounds of love.
In Lucretius, these wounds actually become festering sores possessed
of an invasive authenticity. The lover is "stricken," "wounded," "bloodied." If the beloved (the "enemy," as Lucretius calls him) also happens
to be in the vicinity, he too will leave the battle "drenched in blood."
And that blood, that gush of love, is supposed to be a pleasure, *voluptas!* Indeed, as Lucretius observes, people generally fall in the direction
of their wound, and physiology dictates that "the blood will gush forth
wherever we have been struck by the blow," *unde icimur ictu*.[3] This, according to Lucretius, is "our Venus":[4]

> Haec Venus est nobis; hinc autemst nomen amoris,
> hinc illaec primum Veneris dulcedinis in cor
> stillavit gutta et successit frigida cura.

> This is our Venus; this is where we get the name of love; this is the Venus
> whose beads of sweetness first drip into our heart, followed by a chill-
> ing anxiety.

But Lucretius is not satisfied merely with having discovered the causes
of this distress; he pushes his materialism so far that it becomes horrific,
and even sarcastic. It also becomes ironic, and irony constitutes one
of the dominant tones in the harmonic arrangement of this bizarre theory of love's true aspect, as Lucretius seems to threaten Nature herself,
"take off your mask, or else!" Further on, Lucretius's irony will become
quite insistent, when the poet will produce his antidotes to love in a sort
of brief pamphlet that explains how we can free ourselves from Venus's
chains if we have chanced to fall into her trap.[5] The beloved will be
shamelessly described in all the gross physicality of the human body, that
topic which—according to the etiquette of love and of polite society—
should be excluded from conversation and kept always at a distance. But
in total disregard for the rules of the game, Lucretius will ingeniously
assume the slave's point of view, reporting the words of the maids who
privately make fun of their mistress and the terrible smells that perme-
ate her room. Meanwhile, the infatuated lover, having finally gained ad-

mittance to his darling's boudoir, can only pray for some excuse to make his escape, having realized at last, much to his dismay, that his sweetheart is only a mortal being, a creature made of flesh and blood.[6]

But Lucretius's strategy seems deceptively simple. Could it really be so easy to free oneself of love? Ovid, in his own list of antidotes to love, the *Remedia amoris,* cannot help but recall—without naming names— Lucretius's heretical advice, while politely insisting that such methods should, in fact, be scrupulously avoided:[7]

> Quid, qui clam latuit reddente obscena puella
>   et vidit quae mos ipse videre vetat?
> Di melius, quam nos moneamus talia quemquam;
>   ut prosint, non sunt expedienda tamen.

> And what about the man who lurks in hiding while the girl exposes all her shame, and who sees what etiquette itself forbids us to see? May the gods save us from suggesting such a remedy! Perhaps it would be effective, but even so it should not be tried.

The fact is that Ovid has a delicate sensibility in matters of love—perhaps somewhat frivolous at times, but undeniably discreet in the advice he gives to the lovelorn. Love is not a brutal god, and you can't just beat him over the head with a club: he is only a little boy, after all; he must be cajoled, perhaps even fooled, but always politely, tactfully, gently. There is a fundamental difference between the remedies that Lucretius and Ovid propose to their readers, and it is the same difference that divides their respective theories of love: Lucretius recognizes that love is real, while for Ovid it is merely a fiction.

Ovid, as we know, wrote an entire treatise on the arts of amorous seduction, the *Ars amatoria,* which is basically an instruction manual on how to lie to others in order to make them fall in love with us. Then, with the same light touch, Ovid also wrote a tiny supplement, a pamphlet apparently dedicated to the victims of his previous book: this sequel, entitled "Cures for Love," the *Remedia amoris,* explains how to lie to ourselves so that we can be convinced that we are no longer in love. *Te quoque falle tamen,* "Fool yourself as well!"—this is the motto of Ovid's *Remedia,* and could also serve as an emblematic précis of its contents.[8] For Ovid, love is a fiction: a fiction that kindly assists at the birth of the little god, and that later effects his circumspect and anticlimatic euthanasia. But for Lucretius such a notion would be simply ridiculous, prompting him to explode in some lines of indignant alliteration, filled with lucid, cerebral contempt. How can telling lies not just once but twice be an antidote for anything? Even if we have been seduced with lies, how on earth can lies set us free? Lucretius will have none of that. He knows that love is an awkward fact of life, not a fiction. To "unlove" must be a moment of revelation: we must tear off the mask, and then never speak of it again.

Indeed, it is precisely because love is such a cunning enemy that you cannot afford to show any mercy. The wound only festers if you allow it to feed. Once it takes root, the madness spreads from day to day, with an ever increasing anxiety. Lucretius's words twist and turn, insidious and sublime, like the very affliction that they describe:[9]

> Ulcus enim vivescit et inveterascit alendo,
> inque dies gliscit furor atque aerumna gravescit

> The wound in fact gains strength and, when fed, it takes hold; day by day the madness swells and the anxiety grows heavier and heavier

Love is a wound and a sickness. The metaphorical link between these two semantic fields, between "love" and "sickness," is not just a coincidence. Elsewhere Lucretius relies on the same equation in reverse, when he describes disease in terms of love and its symptoms.[10] But here, almost as if he were alarmed by his involvement in such an affair (Lucretius is supposed to be above all that; this is not his problem), the poet rushes to supply a remedy that will correctly restore the situation to its demonstrably material nature:[11]

> Sed fugitare decet simulacra et pabula amoris
> absterrere sibi atque alio convertere mentem
> et iacere umorem conlectum in corpora quaeque,
> nec retinere, semel conversum unius amore,
> et servare sibi curam certumque dolorem.
> Ulcus enim vivescit et inveterascit alendo
> inque dies gliscit furor atque aerumna gravescit
> si non prima novis conturbes volnera plagis,
> volgivagaque vagus Venere ante recentia cures,
> aut alio possis animi traducere motus.

> It is appropriate to flee from images, to scare away the things that nourish love and to turn the mind to something else; better to discharge the accumulated liquid in any body whatsoever, and not retain it, fixated on a single love for one person, heaping up anxiety and certain grief for yourself. The wound in fact gains strength and, when fed, it takes hold; day by day the madness swells, and the anxiety grows heavier and heavier if you fail to confuse the old wounds with new blows, and do not cure the fresh wounds in time by rambling about with a roving Venus [*volgivaga Venus*], directing the impulses of your heart in some other direction.

It is a crude remedy.[12] The beloved person is to be replaced by a body, any body in which the seed can be disposed of. It is an altogether material way in which to paraphrase the *Venus volgivaga*, a casual and promiscuous love that knows no attachments or rules.[13] Perhaps there is again some sarcasm in this exhortation. It is a remedy supplied by a man who was, after all, well aware of how prostitutes practiced love, and who was able to describe with great precision their gestures and their knowledge of love, sparing nothing. Indeed, Lucretius was someone who claimed he could detect the courtesans' subtle plots behind their erotic *technē*, the crafty and charming artistry practiced by women who were also experts at avoiding unwelcome pregnancies. (Perhaps we can even glimpse here a trace of Lucretius's conversations with those prostitutes, the confidences they shared with him.) Lucretius, in fact, declared that Roman *uxores* shouldn't behave like prostitutes, precisely because in consorting with their husbands these wives were supposed to beget Roman progeny, whereas acting like a prostitute would instead be an obstacle to procreation.[14] And by this point one might begin to suspect that Lucretius is actually speaking of himself, and of what he did (or tried to do) in order to free himself from Venus's snares.

But just what is it about love that causes such pain? Many things, of course, but there is one thing in particular that experience (or plain common sense) immediately suggests: jealousy. Lucretius provides us with a practical description of this sentiment, both its causes and effects:[15]

Aut quod in ambiguo verbum iaculata reliquit
quod cupido adfixum cordi vivescit ut ignis,
aut nimium iactare oculos aliumve tueri
quod putat in vultuque videt vestigia risus.

Perhaps [his beloved] lets fly some ambiguous phrase that is left hanging, fixed in the yearning heart, flaring up like a fire; or perhaps he thinks that she throws too many glances and looks too often at another man, because he thinks he sees the trace of a smile in her face.

Those ambiguous words are actually spoken with no ill intent, but in the delirious interpretation of the jealous lover they sound as if they were full of mockery.[16] Likewise, the casual visual contact between the beloved and another (and the dialogue that is established by such contact) seems to reveal in a smile the entire subject (presumed? real?) of that silent conversation.[17]

Love thus knows no shame, and shows no mercy; it is wicked, and brings pain. Of this Lucretius is absolutely certain. His sarcasm does not even spare the language of lovers, the delicate terms of endearment with which they speak to one another, all those refined and adoring adjectives, sophisticated metaphors, and elegant pet names (augmented by many compliments and courtesies borrowed from Greek, as modern lovers resort to French)—Lucretius will expose and disgrace all of it, sparing nothing. The following are but a few examples from his ruthless catalog.[18] Your beloved might be a girl of "unadorned loveliness"? Then she is only filthy and stinking. "Tongue-tied"? Then she is surely a stammering idiot, incapable of conversation. She "chatters"? overexcited, unbearable. A "mere wisp of love"? So she is emaciated and consumptive . . . It is precisely the reverse of Da Ponte's Don Giovanni, who (as Leporello informs us) was able to make the best of each and every item in the endless catalog of women's imperfections.[19]

At the risk of seeming pedantic, we must point out that Ovid once again proves to be rather more delicate in the way that he also suggests making the worst, whenever possible, of someone's good qualities as an antidote to love. At most, Ovid suggests calling a woman "insolent" if she happens to be sophisticated, and calling her "unsophisticated" if she happens to be demure, along with similarly restrained and courteous examples of verbal dexterity.[20] Lucretius, on the other hand, is incorrigible. He acknowledges only material stuff, beginning and ending with the body: to invent worlds of words is simply not allowed. It is rather odd for a poet to feel such hatred for the fragile creativity of language, suggesting that Lucretius somehow must have found love to be even more hateful (or terrifying). But how could he have taken such ironic wordplay seriously, so seriously in fact that he would declare it to be the truth? Lucretius demands that we resolve to call things by their true names. But it is as if he were to insist on an axiom such as "the arbitrariness of the sign" while at the same time excluding his own argument from this critique. Shouldn't he, a poet, realize that everything can be rewritten (or resaid) in any manner whatsoever? For example, it is possible to take the Trojan War and suggest (as Horace did) that the Greek heroes who died at Troy perished for the sake of a slut or, even more crudely, for a particular part of her anatomy: *nam fuit ante Helenam cunnus taeterrima belli causa*.[21] Lucretius surely must have realized that his own eulogy of Epicurus or his description of the gods' sublime indifference to mankind could also have been rewritten in this way, given a license to ironize. And no doubt he would have found this disturbing: but love, it seems, disturbed him even more.

So let us return to the lover, wounded and ravenous, wallowing in his bloodied voluptuousness. We have now finally reached Lucretius's discussion of *images*, which are also filled with potential danger for the desperate lover. Even if the lover tries to save himself by keeping his distance, he will be overwhelmed by images, by simulacra of the beloved:[22] "for if the one you love is far away, images of the beloved will still be close at hand," *nam si abest quod ames, praesto simulacra tamen sunt/ illius.* Here Lucretius appears to break notably with Epicurus, who instead maintained that "if the beloved is removed from view, with no more visits, no more contact, then the passion of love will vanish."[23] Lucretius disagrees, and he insists that the presence of the beloved object is inescapable. One immediately thinks of Vergil's Dido, another wounded lover, continuously disturbed by the image of someone who is not there:[24]

> At regina gravi iamdudum saucia cura
> vulnus alit venis, et caeco carpitur igni.
> Multa viri virtus animo multusque recursat
> gentis honos. Haerent infixi pectore vultus
> verbaque.

> The queen, by now suffering a deep anxiety, nourishes the wound in her veins, and an obscure fire consumes her. Her mind is preoccupied with the hero's great valor and the great dignity of his lineage; his face and his words are fixed in her heart.

And a few lines later:[25]

> Sola domo maeret vacua stratisque relictis
> incubat, illum absens absentem auditque videtque.

> She grieves, alone in the empty house, throwing herself upon the deserted couches; parted from him, she sees and hears the one who has departed.

Like the Lucretian lover, Dido is also besieged by urgent, ineluctable images. Even when absent, the beloved is alive, and his impalpable features weigh heavily upon her. Whatever one might think of this passage, it must be admitted that Vergil's conception of love was (so to speak) distinctly un-Ovidian.

But in addition to these simulacra, Lucretius is obsessed with another type of image: the *dulce nomen,* the sweet name of the beloved, a sonorous image that obsesses the lover, ceaselessly resounding in his ears. The virtual presence of the absent beloved is thus hallucinated both as a simulacrum that is seen and as a name that is heard. The sound of the name "appears" to the ears, *obversatur,* as present and inescapable as the sight of an image appearing before one's eyes:[26] *illius et nomen dulce obversatur ad auris,* "even his sweet name appears to your ears." There is something very seductive about this theoretical explanation (simultaneously physical and psychological) of erotic agitation. These philosophical metaphors have an air of authenticity that makes us wonder if love might not really work this way after all. The absence of the beloved is felt as the presence of images and of shadows, with the simulacrum of the *dulce nomen* serving as yet another figure emanating from the beloved. Of course we have already seen that a name is able to evoke a person, that it is a powerful embodiment of that person's life and presence[27]—perhaps pronounced by the lover in solitude, or overheard (much to the lover's surprise) in the casual conversation of strangers, or even silently spoken in the privacy of his own thoughts. The sound is inaudible to the person who is not in love; without the metaphors and verbal tricks of the poets this sensation is not available for mass consumption.[28]

Therefore the Lucretian lover, when alone, is surrounded by simulacra of the beloved. More precisely, it is the emptiness *inside* the lover that naturally fills with simulacra, like liquid being poured into a jar. The ominous power of the beloved's image—both the physical image and the image of sound—thus begins to assert itself, and the situation becomes increasingly urgent; Lucretius insists that we must flee the images before it is too late, *fugitare decet simulacra.*[29] The only way to save ourselves is to avoid whatever nourishes love: we must direct our mind's attention elsewhere; the images of the beloved are malicious and destructive; it is best just to get rid of them. This is precisely the point at which Lucretius suggests the remedy of the *Venus volgivaga*—the lover should scatter his seed in any available body.[30] All images of the beloved person, visual images and also the sweet sound of the name, will be eliminated along with that seed (and of course it would be foolish to save it, expending it all on only one love).

Toys of Venus

Lucretius returns to the subject of erotic images a few lines later, but in a surprising new context. Indeed, they even seem a bit out of place at this point, but perhaps the strength of Lucretius's composition resides precisely in the fact that no one would have suspected to find the images here, in the midst of the lovers' battle. The corporeality and physical violence of the fight has now reached a point of extraordinary tension.[31] The wounds no longer come from Venus, or from Love, but from the lovers themselves, enthralled by an unstoppable dementia, "forcing themselves on the object of their desire," "digging their teeth into the other's lips," "inflicting kisses."[32] It is not purely a matter of pleasure; the lovers are actually "impelled by hidden stimuli to wound whatever has produced these sprouts of madness" in their minds.[33] In short, it is such a thoroughly physical encounter that one hardly expects the images to appear again here. But they do.

The impulses of Love are cruel, as Lucretius explains; the lover does not desire the good of the beloved, but instead wants the beloved to suffer. It is a violent possession, a devouring.[34] Even worse, such a desire can never be satisfied. With an exasperating philosophical lucidity, Lucretius insists on providing yet another "natural" explanation of this phenomenon:[35]

Nam cibus atque umor membris assumitur intus
quae quoniam certas possunt obsidere partis
hoc facile expletur laticum frugumque cupido.
Ex hominis vero facie pulchroque colore
nil datur in corpus praeter simulacra fruendum
tenuia: quae vento spes raptat saepe misella.
Ut bibere in somnis sitiens cum quaerit et umor
non datur, ardorem qui membris stinguere possit,
sed laticum simulacra petit frustraque laborat
in medioque sitit torrenti flumine potans,
sic in amore Venus simulacris ludit amantis
nec satiare queunt spectando corpora coram
nec manibus quicquam teneris abradere membris
possunt errantes incerti corpore toto.
Denique cum membris collatis flore fruuntur
aetatis, iam cum praesagit gaudia corpus
atque in eost Venus ut muliebria conserat arva,
adfigunt avide corpus iunguntque salivas
oris et inspirant pressantes dentibus ora,
nequiquam, quoniam nil inde abradere possunt
nec penetrare et abire in corpus corpore toto.
Nam facere interdum velle et certare videntur

.   .   .   .

usque adeo incerti tabescunt volnere caeco.

Food and drink can be taken into our bodies, and because they can occupy their assigned spaces, it is easy to satisfy the desire to drink and to eat. But a human face, with its lovely complexion, gives the body nothing to enjoy except an *insubstantial image,* a wretched hope which the wind often snatches away. Like someone who thirsts in a dream, and cannot find the liquid with which to extinguish the fire in his limbs, he craves what is merely an apparition of water, and strives in vain, and he thirsts even as he drinks in the very midst of the rushing river: so too Venus *toys with lovers in the game of love, deceiving them with images.* Lovers cannot find satisfaction by gazing at the bodies before them; they grope blindly but are not able to rub off anything from the tender limbs with their hands. And when at last, their limbs entwined, they enjoy the flower of youthfulness, when already the body anticipates the pleasure that is to come and Venus is on the point of sowing the woman's fields, greedily they grasp each other's bodies, saliva mingles, and their mouths fill with the other's breath as they press teeth to lips—but in vain, because they cannot rub anything off the surface, nor can they penetrate the other and lose themselves, though they want to do so; they seem locked in combat . . . until they waste away, confused, suffering from a hidden wound.

The lover grasps at simulacra; his desire is a mere mockery. More precisely, he is being toyed with by Venus who excites in him an empty craving for images. The lover wounds in order to feel; he gropes and squeezes, trying to possess something that—as an airy simulacrum—only recedes with the wind.

The Greek philosophical theory of images, of *eidōla,* has taken on an extraordinary emotional force here, becoming the concrete representation of an impossible love. One does not often find a philosophical category that can effortlessly detach itself from its own theoretical context (as has happened here) so as to express a new meaning that would not normally enter into a philosophical discussion. The result is a story of infernal torments, the lover transformed into a Tantalus trying to feed on a beloved who is hopelessly inaccessible or, to be more precise, a beloved who is hopelessly insubstantial. In the erotic rhetoric of the Greek novel, lovers are supposedly able to feed on the beloved image, finding satisfaction in the insubstantial visions of dreams.[36] But in Lucretius's poem, the comparison to dreams ("like one who thirsts in a dream," *ut in somnis sitiens*) relies on the same literary code for exactly the opposite purpose, reinforcing the conviction that these lovers can actually never be satisfied.[37] As we have seen, lovers left alone with a portrait of their beloved will often make an appeal to dreams, hoping that the pallid company of nocturnal shadows will provide a sort of solace. But these are lovers like Admetus, who has lost his Alcestis; lovers who are really and truly *separated* from the object of their love, which has vanished. In the cutting expanse of Lucretius's argument, on the other hand, the paradox is that even when the beloved is actually alive and *present,* the nature of love is still always a matter of dreams and empty simulacra.

In this alliance with Epicurean philosophy, our fundamental story thus undergoes an abrupt and unusual inversion. It is no longer the image that replaces the beloved, or that takes on the beloved's function: this time the beloved, the actual person, functions as an image. The various actors in the dramas of incredible love embraced figures as if they were living bodies, like that cruel painter who preferred the image to its model—but Lucretius goes even farther, proclaiming that *every lover* embraces nothing more than an image, even when he holds the object of his love in his arms. Each and every lover thus suffers from the same impotence as the fantastic lovers of images whose stories we considered earlier. Embracing the body of the beloved person, this lover (every lover) can enjoy only the same cold appearance that was enjoyed by Aristaenetus's painter, vainly making love to a painting in his bed. In Lucretius, the image is a relentless, haunting presence, arousing a desire that cannot be satisfied. If the beloved is far away, the image remains fixed in the lover's eyes, tormenting him; and even if the beloved is present, the lover nevertheless enjoys only an empty appearance.

It seems that there must be something more than Epicurean physics at work in Lucretius's bizarre account of love, given that Epicurus himself apparently limited his own moralistic admonitions against love to a few simple words, altogether neutral lines of reasoning without any spark of fancy—basically just a piece of good advice.[38] But after having finished with Lucretius's discussion of the subject, the reader is left with such a feeling of deep-seated despair that he might be ready to renounce love entirely. It is as if Lucretius's grim counsel secretly contained an instinctive and profound bitterness, a resentment that the philosopher's lucid and capable mind was able to transform into a theory of the insubstantiality of lovers, a madness that transforms the beloved into an image. Naturally, this tempts us to look behind the Lucretian theory of love to see if we can catch a glimpse of *him,* of Lucretius, and the life that he lived, for reasons that are both fully obvious and rather paradoxical at the same time. In reading this vehement and relentless condemnation of love, we cannot help but recall that the poet himself was supposedly one of love's victims: specifically, the victim of a love potion. But it is nevertheless paradoxical to seek the ultimate reason for this undeniably lucid product of a rational mind, this extraordinary Lucretian erotic theory, in the insubstantial gossip of Lucretius's biography. We possess only a few snippets of rather incredible information, the vagaries of the poet's life juxtaposed with the certainty of the poetic text.[39] Yet the impoverished lines of Lucretius's biography in fact sustained a story of such undeniable greatness that, like it or not, we cannot completely dismiss this paradoxical combination of philosophy and folly, this legend of the poet as the victim of a love potion. Whether it is the ingenuous creation of a biographer or of life itself, the story adds very much to the poem, and certainly takes nothing away from it.

The Lucretius of biographical legend was thus supposed to have committed suicide at the age of forty-four, tormented by the aftereffects of a love potion, a *poculum amatorium*.[40] The ancient sources tell us that he was driven mad as a result, and it was only in those brief moments, the *intervalla* of lucidity that he was able to compose the *De rerum natura*.[41] Reading the words and lines of this poem, we would thus be confronting the phantoms that populated the poet's intermittent presence—phantoms of hexameters, of philosophy, or of dazzling theory. If we put any faith in the biographical account and its implications, a curious question naturally arises: what sort of images besieged Lucretius's mind during his absences, during the far more frequent moments of his *insania?* If we might be so bold as to expand on the legend, adding some pages, equally fictitious, to Lucretius's biography, we could perhaps imagine him obsessed by images of a woman, her features, her body, her complexion—an endless gallery of simulacra filled with a thousand poses, scenes from inconsequential or unforgettable adventure, a long hallway through which the crazed poet drags himself, as he grasps at fleeting appearances, desperately seeking to satisfy his insatiable desire. Meanwhile, in the *intervalla* of respite from this insanity—which constitute, for us, the poem—each passing line still whispers to the poet: "There is nothing here you can hold on to. Remember the nature of the atoms: what you love is only a simulacrum, an image."

9

Narcissus and the Twin Images

Bent over the mirror of the fountain, Narcissus sees the reflected image of his face and is seized by a vain love, a desire that cannot be satisfied. Eventually he will lay his head down upon the grass, exhausted, and night will close his eyes, still filled with the beloved image. This, in a greatly abbreviated form, is the well-known story told by Ovid.[1] But such a summary must omit the most precious and what is perhaps the most profound part of the text: the intellectual play of reflections that manages to insinuate itself into the very language of Ovid's lines, intimately exploiting every possible reverberation. It is the triumph of grammar's incorporeal abstractions, as active and passive voices, antitheses, and figures of sound all assume the transparency of thought and—like the water in the magic fountain—inevitably return to the poet an inverted image of his own lines:[2]

> Cunctaque miratur quibus est mirabilis ipse.
> Se cupit imprudens et qui probat ipse probatur,
> dumque petit petitur pariterque accendit et ardet.

> And he admires everything for which he himself is admirable. Without realizing it he desires himself, and as he makes his appraisal, he is being appraised; while he yearns, he is yearned for; he equally burns and bursts into flames.

Ovid's Narcissus cannot exist without language. Even before the handsome hunter falls prey to his own reflection, it is Ovid's language that is smitten with itself.

The Mirror That Enchants and Disenchants

"You know the story," as Gide once remarked about the myth of Narcissus.[3] "Yet we will tell it once more. Everything has been said already, but since nobody listens, we must begin again": *il faut toujours recommencer*. But despite this elegant invitation to recommence, one must admit that the extraordinary popularity enjoyed by Narcissus (and by Ovid's Narcissus in particular) has turned the story of the boy infatuated with his own image into something so familiar that it begins to seem rather obvious—when in fact there is nothing at all obvious about this story, as we shall see. Of course, everyone vaguely knows something or other about Narcissus; to paraphrase a famous line, *cui non dictus Narcissus?*[4] In such a situation, we are naturally inclined to offer some versions of the story that are perhaps less well known, such as the Narcissus of Philostratus's *Imagines*. As he describes a painting that he saw of Narcissus, Philostratus ecstatically compares these two Narcissi, both equally images, and both equally fictive: one made of wax and pigment, and the other a reflection in the water.[5] The device of *ekphrasis* effortlessly allows Philostratus to let his observing eye linger on an image that actually contains another image of itself. He makes the paradox into an argument for the universal vanity of all things—and at this point the description becomes rather tiresome. Still, there is one statement here that surely merits our attention: "The gaze is indeed that of someone in love . . . and perhaps Narcissus thinks that he is loved in return, because the reflection [*skia*] gazes at him in the same way that he gazes at it." We will return again to this motif of love's gaze, and the gazes that lovers exchange with one another.[6]

We've heard it all before, of course (albeit in the vague distraction of an often repeated myth). Over the centuries, that sad young man, so tragically infatuated with himself, even became a figure of ridicule. For example, in the late antique collection of droll anecdotes called the *Philogelos*, we find the following story:[7] "The son of a professor was playing with a ball. The ball fell in a well, and the boy leaned down to pick it up. Seeing his reflection, he asked the reflection to give back the ball, but the reflection did not respond. Then the boy went crying to his father because he couldn't get what he wanted. The professor in turn leaned over the well, and seeing his image reflected there he said: 'Sir, could you please be so kind as to give back the ball?'" This foolish Narcissus in turn suggests the possibility of an ugly Narcissus, as in this ex-

ample from the *Greek Anthology:*[8] "Olympicus, be careful not to go to
the fountain with that ugly mug of yours, and don't look at yourself in
clear water. Like Narcissus, if you see your face reflected you will die . . .
from a fatal loathing of your own looks."

Joking aside, we can find an even less obvious story of Narcissus
in the animal world; at last, this might be a Narcissus we have not seen
or heard about before. Although it is rare, Columella informs us that
sometimes "this same madness [*rabies*] is also found among mares, such
that when they have seen their image in the water, they are seized by a
pointless love, which makes them completely forgetful of their food, so
that they perish, wasting away from infatuation. The signs of this madness are that they run around the pasture as if driven by some obsession,
turning their heads this way and that, apparently looking for something,
stricken by desire. This mistaken fantasy can be cured if you cut the
mare's mane at unequal lengths and lead her to water. When she has
seen her deformed image reflected in the water, her memory of the earlier image is erased."[9] In Greek and Roman folklore, the horse is supposedly an animal very close to man; moreover, horses are reputed to be
extremely passionate creatures.[10] It is thus not surprising to find Narcissus's vain reflection mirrored in the world of horses, where it again
results in a futile self-exhaustion. But the mares are more fortunate than
Narcissus: their peculiar madness, *rabies,* actually provides the means for
its own cure. When they see the reflection of their ugly deformity, the
mares are freed from the mirror's delusions. Such a remedy obviously
depends on the mirror's famous ability not only to enchant but also to
disenchant, turning aside the evil eye or other potential spells.[11] Just as
it can fascinate, the mirror also has the symmetrical power to free someone from enchantment.

This belief seems to have been well rooted in ancient folklore. Palladius, for example, describes a similar remedy for the prevention of hail-
storms:[12] "Sometimes when people see this disaster drawing near, they
hold up a mirror, which catches the image of the cloud. By means of this
remedy they manage to drive away the cloud, either because the cloud
is displeased by its own appearance, or because it yields to what it thinks
is another cloud." Like the mares seized by *rabies,* the clouds are not
pleased with their own appearance. The world evoked here is again that
of the ancient countryside; Columella and Palladius were both writing
agricultural handbooks, imbued with a rustic sensibility and stories that
convey the customs and beliefs of good, old-fashioned farmers. But
Narcissus, unlike the mares looking at themselves in the water and the

clouds reflected in the mirror, could not see himself as ugly. Instead, his beauty—and his tenacious sensation of that beauty—led inevitably to his demise.

The story of Narcissus appears again in the story of Eutelidas, one of the topics of conversation in Plutarch's *Quaestiones convivales*.[13] At a certain moment, the discussion turns to the powers of the evil eye and the paradox of people who accidentally cast the evil eye upon themselves. Soclarus, one of the guests at the table, quotes these lines of verse:[14] "Fair, too fair were the curls of Eutelidas. But seeing himself in the river's whirling water, the unlucky wretch cast the evil eye upon himself [*baskainen*] and suddenly fell strangely ill." Having seen his own beauty, Eutelidas fell so passionately in love with the image that he lost both his health and his good looks. According to Plutarch's Soclarus, this Eutelidas was actually the victim of his own eyes, that is, of the dangerous look that he cast upon himself.[15] Could it not also be the case that Narcissus is a myth of the Latin *fascinum*, the Greek *baskanon*, that malevolent power of an enchanting eye which in this paradoxical situation brings about its own destruction? In passing, Ovid himself remarks that Narcissus perished "on account of his eyes," *perque oculos perit ipse suos*.[16] It is indeed very tempting to interpret the story of Narcissus as an obscure, allusive warning about the danger of the amorous gaze, as a judgment upon the ruinous power that results when the selfsame person who casts the *fascinum* is struck by it. And perhaps such an interpretation would not be far from the truth.[17]

Narcissus the Twin

But rather than pursue this topic of the enchanting gaze any further, we should stop here and consider the narrative structure of this myth and the framework of its plot: that is, the story of a lover in love with an image—*his own*. If we align this story (whether the lover is Narcissus, or Eutelidas, or the infatuated mares of Columella) with the story of Pygmalion and those other deluded madmen, we see that Narcissus suddenly acquires an unexpected meaning. The stories of Narcissus are frighteningly similar to the stories of incredible love, sharing the same basic narrative pattern. At least in terms of the story's plot, there is little difference between a lover who is infatuated with a statue (or with a painted image) and a lover who is infatuated with himself. In both cases we are dealing with a love affair between a lover and an image that does not have a referent; the beloved is not absent, is not dead— the beloved is simply the image itself. Exactly as in the case of Pygmalion, for Narcissus the image *is already enough,* with no need at all for a real beloved of flesh and blood. But the Narcissus myth goes one step further, reducing the roster of pawns once again, and resulting in a complete short circuit: what began as a game of three players is now a game of solitaire. We started with a lover, a distant beloved, and a portrait: our fundamental story. Then we discovered that the lover and the image could play the game by themselves, dispensing altogether with the image's referent. And now we see that the image itself can simply be a reproduction of the *single* lover who is left in play, and the entire affair can be carried out between him and himself, with the fleeting assistance of the fountain's reflection.

But the only possible outcome of such a desperate match would have to be death. Simultaneously lover and beloved, portrait and referent, himself and the image of the other, Narcissus (like Eutelidas) is wasting away from a feverish, futile desire. Not even Pygmalion (Ovid's master craftsman and magician) could give life to that image—because, unfortunately, the image is *already alive.* As Ovid's Narcissus observes at a certain point, "I already have what I desire; and that having makes me hopeless," *quod cupio mecum est; inopem me copia facit.*[18] Unable to offer life to the beloved image, the lover instead accepts the one gift that this beloved can offer him: death.

But even when our fundamental story has been reduced in this way to a pure reflection of itself, an unexpected twist of the plot allows it to begin again, reopening the game between two lovers and an image. In a version of the Narcissus myth told by Pausanias, it turns out that the hero is not in love with himself at all; in fact, Pausanias dismisses that conventional version of the story as credulously simple minded.[19] There is, he says, another version of the story, one that is less well known but that is still repeated: Narcissus had a twin sister, absolutely identical to him—the same hair, the same clothes, everything. They used to go hunting together, and this Narcissus was in love with his twin. But the young woman died, which is when Narcissus went to stare into the fountain, knowing full well that he was only looking at his own reflection, but still finding in that image a consolation for his love.

The story of Narcissus and his twin thus continues our fundamental story (a lover, a beloved, a portrait), and deftly resumes the game by putting the shade of a referent back into play. Narcissus's eyes are no longer filled with a vain image of himself; the reflected image he sees is now also the portrait of his beloved twin sister. It is the story of a lover, an absent beloved, and a portrait, with the portrait once again serving as a substitute for that absent beloved, a cold consolation for the bereft and lonely lover. The scene reminds us of Petrarch, holding Laura's portrait in his hands—except that now the story involves a new motif, that of the twin. A story about twins continues the equivocation between loving an actual person and loving an image, while it also hints at a subject to which we will return shortly: incest.[20] Meanwhile, Narcissus's sexual doubling—his appearing as both male and female in the pair of twins—seems to be confirmed by the ancient iconographic tradition, in which Narcissus at the fountain is represented with decidedly feminine features (see Fig. 3).[21]

In any case, Narcissus's sister provided him with a portrait of himself. It sounds like an ancient version of "Wälsungenblut," Thomas Mann's tale of Siegmund and his twin sister Sieglind, spoiled, lonely scions of the Jewish bourgeoisie in Germany. This Siegmund also found in his twin sister "an *exact likeness* of himself, preciously adorned, obscurely lovable."[22] Narcissus and his twin/portrait are thus a literary pair, a stock conceit, whose singular innovation seems to consist in the way that the sister's image lingers in the presence of her brother, so that Narcissus, the remaining twin, becomes an effigy of the twin who has died. But Mann is not the only author to have played a game of twins; antiquity provides us with some other tales like this one.

For example, Malalas's *Chronographia* tells the following story about the twins Romulus and Remus:[23] after Romulus killed his twin brother Remus, Rome was no longer at peace. The very monarchy was shaken by internal warfare, until Romulus finally decided to consult the oracle at Delphi. The priestess informed him: "Unless you reinstall your brother on the throne by your side, Rome cannot stand; neither the people nor the wars will be calmed." So Romulus then copied Remus's features from an image of his brother's face and had a statue of his brother cast in gold. He then had the statue installed on the throne by his side. In this way he reigned ever after, together with the statue of Remus, thus bringing the civil wars to an end.

Thanks to the image, the twin pair is surreptitiously reconstituted, with the dead twin replaced by a portrait that resembles him. Without Remus, Romulus was not able to rule Rome; his royal status was painfully deficient. Deprived of his twin, the twin-king lost his identity as king, and the people rose up in rebellion. We can find something similar in Apollodorus's story of that famous statue of Athena known as the Palladium:[24]

They say that Athena, after she was born, was raised by Triton, who had a daughter of his own named Pallas. The two girls were schooling themselves in the arts of war, and one day they competed against one another. Pallas was about to strike Athena when Zeus, fearful for her, placed the aegis between them. Pallas was seized by wonder and turned her gaze upwards—at which point Athena managed to strike a fatal blow. Greatly distressed by her friend's death, Athena then had a simulacrum constructed that was similar to Pallas in every way, and she wrapped the aegis which had so terrified the girl around the breast of the image, which was then placed in a position of honor next to Zeus.

In this case, the story does not tell us that Athena and Pallas were twin sisters. But because the simulacrum of one of them is later regarded as a famous statue of the other, we can presume that these two foster sisters (or "milk-sisters") shared similar physical features.[25] Moreover, we know from other ancient sources that "milk-siblings" were often considered to be identical, like twins.[26] Thus, we find ourselves dealing with another ancient story about a twin (or a quasi-twin) who substitutes the deceased twin with an image, thus surreptitiously reconstituting the curtailed pair. And also as we have seen before, this image then becomes the recipient of conspicuous honors.

Late stories, marginal tales . . . We might even be tempted to dismiss them as useless—were they not so similar to the version of the Narcissus myth provided by Pausanias, and so insightfully analyzed in a masterful (and unexpected) ethnographic study by Krappe.[27] Krappe was in fact able to find repeated confirmation in diverse populations for this practice of consoling a surviving twin with an effigy, an image, or a doll that reproduces the features of the deceased twin. Moreover, the motivation is apparently the same in each case: to reconstitute the curtailed pair with an image that surreptitiously restores the element eradicated by death. It is as if twins must exist as a pair—"the twins are considered to be one body and one soul," as one of Krappe's South African sources explained.[28] When one of the twins dies, it is feared that the other might quickly follow, making it necessary to immediately replace the deceased twin with an image. But when this second twin eventually does die, something quite intriguing occurs: "The statue no longer serves any purpose, and can simply be discarded." The statue loses its meaning; the twins are two, or they are nothing.

Twins are undeniably exceptional creatures.[29] Born simultaneously, maturing in identical stages, their persons, while separate, are understood only in terms of one another. Their identity is not that of single persons, but of a pair. It is as if each twin wanted to make the singular

I agree with a plural verb, or the plural *we* agree with a verb in the singular. As the psychologist Zazzo observed:[30] "My twins always say *we* and hardly ever say *I* or *you,* as if they thought of themselves as a single person."[31] As is frequently the case with twins, they use doubled names to indicate themselves: "Each one says her name is Josette-Monique." A riddle to the community, a riddle to themselves—the pair of twins pose the continual question, "are we two, or one?" Because they are thought of in tandem, the death of a twin provokes a crisis, forcing their parents, the community, or the "spirit of the story" (as in the ancient tales recounted above) to find a replacement that can repair this unthinkable absence. The surviving twin, accustomed to read his own identity mirrored in the face of the other, seeks compensation in an image that is simultaneously an image of *himself* and an image of *the other*. Given this anthropological and psychological evidence (and its interpretation), all those extraordinary stories about the twins—Romulus and Remus, Athena and Pallas, Narcissus and his sister—unexpectedly begin to resemble a story from real life. Surely it is this fragility of the *I*—Zazzo's *fragilité du je*—that (at least in part) explains the story of that twin Narcissus who, deprived of his beloved sister, availed himself of the fountain's reflection.[32] His *I* needed to be *we;* by doubling his image, this twin Narcissus nourishes the illusion that everything is as it was before. Thanks to Pausanias (and his understandable if somewhat pedantic mistrust of the standard version of the story), we understand that Narcissus is not necessarily an example of incredible love, a man smitten with himself, the unwitting harbinger of "narcissism" for future generations of psychologists. Instead, Pausanias provides us with the equally precious story of a twin Narcissus who could find his identity only in a pair (just like the other twins we have seen). By looking at himself reflected in the fountain, the twin Narcissus was able to continually reconstitute that paired identity. And as Lucienne, another twin, explains: "Sometimes when I look at myself in the mirror, I suddenly see the image of my sister; but if I rub my eyes, then I see my own image again. . . . It is a quite bizarre sensation."[33]

Siblings in Love

And the lovers? And the portrait? Perhaps in speaking about the twins at such length, we might seem to be ignoring our subject, wandering far afield from our fundamental story—but this is not exactly the case. This unusual version of the Narcissus myth actually has a great deal to teach us about the portrait of the lover. As we have already seen in many examples, the absent beloved can also be replaced by an image, just like the missing twin. Petrarch consoled himself with a painting of Laura; Laodamia cherished an effigy of Protesilaus. Deprived of the beloved, the lover—like the curtailed twin—needs to surreptitiously restore the original pair by means of an image. This striking similarity between the behavior of twins and that of lovers suggests the following hypothesis: lovers also do not have individual identities, but exist only as a pair, as a couple, and as such they might need to reconstitute a curtailed pair with an effigy in exactly the same way that twins do. Like the twins, the lovers also make their *I* agree with a plural verb; they each think of themselves only as a reflex of the other. For both the pair of twins and the pair of lovers, as Zazzo again notes, there is a "fantasy of a single soul in two bodies," a need to say *we* as if it were *I*—or at least the illusion that it is possible to do so.[34] That is why a lover who disappears must be replaced, at least by an image. Our fundamental story functions like a piece of litmus paper, predictably displaying the same reaction to a pair of lovers as it does to a pair of twins.

But before confronting this parallel between the pair of twins and the pair of lovers, we should first try to determine what happens when the twins themselves happen to be in love with one another. Twinship is already a complementary relationship, a conjunction: fusion. In this sense twinship can also be a temptation. Being identical, the twins run the risk of being convinced that they were made for one another—for themselves, and no one else—and that they were therefore meant to love one another. Narcissus is in love with his dead sister, and is able to deceive the bitter *desiderium* of this love by looking at his image in the fountain; this is precisely what Pausanias tells us, even though he does not reveal the intimate details of their affair. But about Isis and Osiris, two twins who were also in love with one another, we are better informed: Plutarch tells us explicitly that "Isis and Osiris loved one another, and before their birth they coupled in the darkness of their mother's womb."[35] The twins, that perfectly matched pair, are attracted to one another, making it entirely plausible that they would be prone to incest. Byblis and Caunus were twins, so the story goes, and Byblis was seized by an uncontrollable desire for her brother.[36] Her kisses grew suspiciously passionate; she wanted Caunus to think she was beautiful, and her desires disclosed themselves in dreams, until at last she made an open declaration of her love in a letter. As usual, we are indebted to Ovid not only for some very elegant lines of verse but also for his ability to express the story's intricate complexities in extremely simple words:[37]

> Non hoc inimica precatur,
> sed quae, cum tibi sit iunctissima, iunctior esse
> expetit et vinclo tecum propiore ligari.

> It is not an enemy who implores you, but a woman who, although she is most closely related to you already [*iunctissima*], yearns to be even closer [*iunctior*], binding herself to you with even tighter ties.

The closest possible relationship begets a desire for a relationship that is even closer, and Ovid does not hesitate before the grammatical paradox of a superlative that is augmented still further by a comparative: *cum tibi sit iunctissima, iunctior esse / expetit.*

So when Narcissus consoles himself at the fountain by gazing at the image of his sister, he acts like a twin (like Romulus and Remus, or Athena and Pallas), like a lover (as in all the variations of our fundamental story, like Laodamia and Protesilaus, or Admetus and Alcestis), and also like a twin/lover (like the twins Isis and Osiris, Byblis and Caunus, predestined lovers who are inescapably attracted to one another). The story of Narcissus-the-twin thus appears as a coalescence of multiple models, pushing the schematic homology between the pair of twins and the pair of lovers to its structural limits. We can thus return to our earlier question: Do lovers, like twins, have the identity of a pair? Is the couple of lovers similar to a couple of twins?

Although lovers are not exactly twins, they are very similar to siblings. At least in Latin, lovers are able to call one another "brother" or "sister" in a way that seems to graze the very boundaries of incest (with ineffable delicacy), while somehow remaining untainted. For example, in a scene from Plautus's *Cistellaria,* the young man Alcesimarchus tries to placate his beloved Selenium with the following words:[38]

> *Alcesimarchus:* Germana mea sororcula!
> *Selenium:* Repudio te fraterculum!

> *Alcesimarchus:* My very own little sister!
> *Selenium:* I spurn you, my little brother!

Little sister/little brother. The very symmetry of the phrases, the equilibrium of diminutive suffixes, reveals a great deal about the figure of thought on which this relationship is modeled: it is a relationship of complementarity. We are dealing here with more than just a form of address: this kinship terminology is actually a way to imagine one's identity. Consider, for example, the Roman elegists, those passionate poets who—despite Augustus's antithetical regime—had the courage to put into verse (and perhaps also into practice) something extremely new: a paired association that was not matrimonial, a sexual and emotional relationship that was more than some fling with a dancing girl. The poet Propertius thus offered himself to Cynthia with the following words:[39]

> Cum tibi nec frater nec sit tibi filius ullus,
>   frater ego et tibi sim filius unus ego.

> Given that you do not have a brother or a son, I alone might be to you both brother and son.

Propertius was making a generic sort of declaration, but Lygdamus makes an even more specific claim to kinship when he asks the Muses to whisper this message in the ear of his beloved Neaera:[40]

> Haec tibi vir quondam nunc frater, casta Neaera,
>   mitti et accipias munera parva rogat,
> teque suis iurat caram magis esse medullis,
>   sive sibi coniunx, sive futura soror;
> sed potius coniunx; huius spem nominis illi
>   auferet extincto pallida Ditis aqua.

> The one who sends you these lines is someone who would be your husband [*vir*] one day, and now is your brother [*frater*], chaste Neaera; please accept this little gift from him. He swears that you are his heart's desire, whether you will be his wife [*coniunx*], or his sister [*soror*], but preferably [*potius*] his wife. The hope to call you by this name will be snatched from him only by the pale waters of Death.

Although Lygdamus's love affair with his lover and "sister" Neaera is not altogether clear in its details, he apparently wanted to make her into a proper *coniunx* according to the customary rituals of marriage.[41] And while we cannot be sure about the name of the (undeniably profound) bond that would always link him to Neaera in life, there is obviously a verbal game at work here that allows the poet to equate husband and brother, *frater* and *vir:* once again, the relationship between two lovers is comparable to that between siblings.[42]

Lygdamus's deft linguistic strategy leads us next to a passage from Seneca in which there is again a similar uncertainty of roles and emotional positions, featuring a strong verbal echo of the previous passage. Love-struck Phaedra is speaking to her stepson Hippolytus, who is naturally ignorant of the problematic passion that has seized his stepmother.[43] The chaste and ingenuous Hippolytus calls her *mater*, and Phaedra replies:

> Matris superbum est nomen et nimium potens:
> nostros humilius nomen affectus decet;
> me vel sororem, Hippolyte, vel famulam voca,
> famulamque potius.

"Mother" is a lofty name, and far too solemn. A more humble name is better suited to our affection. Call me sister, or slave girl, Hippolytus, but preferably [*potius*] slave girl.

Again, the sister makes her entrance as a disguised reference (simulating? insinuating?) to the more explicit designation of lover. In an effort to define themselves, the lovers look for names that best suit their situation. It is what we could call "the moment of *potius*": *famulam potius*, "preferably your slave girl," as Seneca's Phaedra explains; *potius coniunx*, "preferably my wife," in the words of Lygdamus. Love insistently demands that the lovers declare themselves, defining who they are in relationship to each other.

But Phaedra is rather too tragic, and Lygdamus is too serious (one might even call him a bit dull). But fortunately for us, there is also Petronius, a Latin author we cannot afford to neglect. In the *Satyricon*, Encolpius (disguised under the name Polyaenus) encounters the beautiful Circe in a little grove of plane trees. They do not get off to an auspicious start; Encolpius is cold and clumsy, and the conclusion, as we know, will be even more embarrassing for the hero's virility. But we join them at the moment when Circe has begun to laugh so sweetly that Polyaenus-Encolpius seems to see the full face of the moon rising from behind a cloud, and she speaks to him as follows:[44]

> Si non fastidis, inquit, feminam ornatam et hoc primum anno virum experta, concilio tibi, o iuvenis, sororem. Habes tu quidem et fratrem (neque enim me piguit inquirere); sed quid prohibet et sororem adoptare? Eodem gradu venio. Tu tantum dignare et meum osculum, cum libuerit, agnoscere.

Young man, if you will not disdain an attractive woman, one who has known a man for the very first time this year, then please consider me a sister [*soror*] to you. I know that you already have a brother [*frater*]; I was not ashamed to ask you about that. But what prevents you from also adopting a sister? The degree of kinship is the same. Only please acquaint yourself with my kiss too [*et meum osculum*], whenever you want to.

The brother to whom the presumptuous Circe alludes is none other than the boy Giton, Encolpius's lover. The game is highly amusing, and certainly more subtle than is often recognized by translators and commentators. As Circe insinuates, there is no difference in the degree of kinship between having a brother and having a sister; for Encolpius it would be one and the same. But if Encolpius were to accept Circe as his sister, then he would also have to test her kiss (*osculum*). And this kiss, in the kinship metaphor proposed by Circe, does not immediately refer to the kiss of love, but instead ironically invokes the *ius osculi,* the kiss of kinship, which according to an ancient custom, a Roman woman could receive from her male relatives up to and including the sixth degree of kinship—first and foremost from her brother.[45]

As for the insinuated relationship of brotherhood between Encolpius and his boyfriend Giton, Circe is merely availing herself of an appellation that Encolpius himself constantly uses in the *Satyricon* when he addresses Giton (and that Ascyltus also appropriates in similar circumstances).[46] Certainly neither Encolpius nor Giton seems to be ashamed at this form of address; indeed, they seem to find it a proper sort of designation, as when Encolpius presents Giton to Quartilla as *frater meus.*[47] It is a logical consequence of the system, after all: if a female lover becomes a sister, then the male lover cannot help but be thought of as a brother. Martial, for example, exploited the ironic acumen of an epigram in order to mock a certain Charmenion, who persisted in calling himself the poet's brother. We are so different from one another, Martial observes: we come from different countries, we have different appearances, we wear our hair differently, we speak differently.[48] Therefore, he says to Charmenion: *desine me vocare fratrem, / ne te, Charmenion, vocem sororem,* "stop calling me brother, Charmenion; otherwise I will have to call you sister!" With these words Martial perfidiously unmasks the true nature of his would-be brother, and reveals it to be feminine.

Of course, we cannot leave Martial without also citing one of his most clever linguistic games, an elaborate joke based on the kinship and the feelings that lovers pretend for each other:[49]

> O quam blandus es, Ammiane, matri!
> quam blanda est tibi mater, Ammiane!
> fratrem te vocat et soror vocatur.
> Cur vos nomina nequiora tangunt?
> Quare non iuvat hoc quod estis esse?
> Lusum creditis hoc iocumque? Non est:

matrem, quae cupit esse se sororem,
nec matrem iuvat esse nec sororem.

Ammianus, how sweet you are with your mother! And how sweet your mother is with you, Ammianus! She calls you brother, and she is called sister by you. Why do these naughty names attract you so? Why are you not pleased to be called what you are? Do you think this is a game, an amusement? It is not. A mother who wishes to be a sister is not pleased to be either mother or sister.

This general survey of Latin authors makes it clear that Roman lovers could hide behind the screen of being siblings. Even if the lovers are not actually twins, we can at least assert that they are brother and sister (or brother and brother). By making use of this admittedly paradoxical subterfuge, the love relationship finds a way to declare itself, to "speak itself," in words. To do so, it actually models itself on a relationship from which love—as passion, as desire—should be excluded by definition; indeed, from which it should be rejected with horror. But there is apparently nothing morbid, nothing incestuous, between these simulated siblings; it is an altogether social affair.

The reasons again appear to involve identity, and specifically identity as a pair. There is a problem to be solved, and it is not an easy one: how to provide the lovers with a codified model relevant to a paired relationship that is not in any way understood as the *coniunctio* of marriage (in both legal and family terms), and that actually aspires to radically distinguish itself from that kind of marriage. A married couple, husband and wife, obviously have an identity as a pair: they have reciprocal names by which they are designated (like the English "spouse," the Latin *coniunx* can be applied equally to both of them); they have family cults in common, a living space in common, children in common. But what about the lovers? What terminology can allow them to also "be spoken" reciprocally? It is a matter of producing *identity as a pair* within the realm of language, and thus in the realm of cultural representation. To define themselves as a pair, as a couple, the lovers make use of an already established model for this sort of paired identity: a pair of siblings.

This is a viable solution because siblings also share a name, kinship, physical resemblance, life experiences; they have the same ancestors, the same family cults; they respect and follow the same traditions. Each of them has a part of himself (or herself) in the other. Siblings are thus an outstanding emblem of togetherness; each one is seen in relation to the other; they each recall one another. Above all, a brother and sister love one another, and engage in displays of affection. They are authorized to do so, indeed, they are expected to do so . . . theirs is a complementary relationship. In order to find a natural basis for the ideal sibling relationship that he wants to describe in *De amore fraterno*, Plutarch can think of no better model than the perfect pairs visibly manifested in the design of the human body:[50] "Even in our anatomy, Nature has diligently arranged the greater part of the vital organs in pairs, like siblings, like twins: hands, feet, eyes, ears, nostrils." To be a sibling is thus to be involved in a homologous and complementary relationship, a unity of two identical and reflected halves. This is why the lovers—excluded from the model of marriage—are displaced onto this alternate model for a paired relationship, seeing themselves as siblings. Like a love relationship, fraternal affection is also constructed on the basis of likeness and conjunction; it too is a relationship that creates and entails participation in a paired identity.

Lovers as siblings, siblings as lovers, twins: such are the various terms that we can use to designate the protagonists in these often heartbreaking stories, all of which involve a desperate effort to reconstruct the unity of a lost pair (like Narcissus at the fountain seeking to regain his twin sister). But it is also possible to invoke this identity of the lovers—the two in one, the singular pair—with an occasional irony. In concluding this chapter, we cannot help but turn to the famous speech of Aristophanes from Plato's *Symposium,* and those primordial androgynous beings whom Zeus, in his cunning, decided to cut in half so as to render them harmless, slicing them right down the middle like sorb apples halved for pickling, or a hard-boiled egg cut in two by a single strand of hair.[51] We, of course, are the result of that mythical operation, inconsolable and awkward halves perpetually longing to be rejoined with our lost other half.[52] To fuse with the beloved, for the two to become one, reconstructing that primordial nature from the fabulous past: this is the fundamental impulse that leads to love. Aristophanes' story is thus an ironic version of the very subject of this chapter: that is, it provides a myth about the identity of the pair that characterizes, or perhaps haunts, the condition of the lovers—those lovers who want to replace *I* with *we.* Of course, it is already sufficiently difficult to stumble along the path of life with just these two legs and two arms (lacking the grace of our eight original limbs)—hence the need to double ourselves, reconstructing the earlier identity from which we were so sadly severed. But in the meantime, we can only hope that Zeus will be kind enough to refrain from his threat to further subdivide our already pathetic halves, splitting them in two yet again.

10

The Insult

Sextus Propertius had a dream one night, shortly after the funeral of his former mistress, Cynthia; once again, as in the past, the poet found himself deeply troubled on her account.[1] Of course, at the time of her death the fair days of their love, that elegiac affair, had probably vanished for both of them (based on the slight, ambiguous biography that emerges from Propertius's poems). Like so many loves supposed to endure forever, this one also seems to have failed, lasting even less than the span (also brief) of a human life.

In any case, Propertius was already working on his fourth book of elegies, filled with poems inspired by Rome, her grandeur, her legends—and by Augustus. In all likelihood, he was not enjoying himself very much, given that he was not really cut out for this sort of poetry. On the other hand, he was obviously worried about his literary fame and fortune, and thus wanted very much to write about something other than love. Meanwhile, there was now a new mistress, a *nova domina* living in Propertius's house, giving orders to Cynthia's faithful slaves. Was she also the *nova domina* of *perfidus* Propertius? Probably she was, although there is no trace of the poet's love for her anywhere in his elegiac couplets. This woman did not inspire Propertius to write poetry; his literary love came to an end with his love for Cynthia. Times had changed, and so had Sextus Propertius.

But on the night of her funeral he had a dream. Cynthia appeared to him as she must have looked at the moment of those funeral rites: the same hair, the same expression in her eyes—but her clothes were now singed, and the fire had damaged the beryl ring that she always wore on her finger. Cynthia chastised the poet: How could you, she said, have forgotten about us? After all the times I sneaked out through the window for you, and our impatient love more than once warmed the cold ground by the side of the road! But no, there was no sign of you there bowed with grief at my funeral, and only a few warm tears have stained your mourning robes. You ungrateful man, why didn't you summon the wind for my pyre? Why didn't you pour nard upon the flames? So Cynthia's implacable ghost proceeds with a long list of complaints; this is, after all, the ghost of a lover: she is expected to make reproaches.

It is decidedly eerie to listen to a lover as she rebukes her surviving partner for not having followed the rules at her funeral, but this is precisely what Cynthia does, launching into an extensive harangue that combines the feelings of a love betrayed with a precious inventory of Roman folklore.[2] This poem thus supplies yet another example (one of many) in which an ancient literary text clearly reveals its anthropological distance, the immense gap between its own cultural horizon and the cultural horizon of modern-day readers. But in the story of this love—an admittedly great literary love, so similar in many ways to modern affairs of the heart—we discover that Cynthia feels insulted because the rattles were not shaken at her deathbed,[3] because her head was placed on a *tegula curta,* a bit of broken tile,[4] and because she believes that she could have wrested one more day from the god of death if her faithless lover had been there to call her back. Not to mention the hissing viper, which she swears will coil itself around her bones if she ever betrayed their *fides;* or the ivy that Propertius is supposed to remove from her tomb, because ivy binds with its tangled foliage, impeding her freedom in the afterlife. So it happens that in the love of Cynthia and Sextus Propertius—as in any great love story—Eros is inevitably mingled with death. But what sort of death? Not death as we might imagine it; that much is clear. And, we must also ask, what sort of love? How can we be so sure that the love shared between Cynthia and Propertius was really similar to our own? Perhaps, as in the death that brings the love story to a close, the anthropological substance of this love, its adventures and its sentiments, might have been markedly different from the love that our modern experience unconsciously leads us to project into the text.

The *Imago* of the Lover and the Anxiety of the Mirror

Cynthia's shade, her *umbra,* is angry, and there is one thing above all that infuriates her: the other woman. A courtesan who until just yesterday was selling herself cheap on the streets—but who is now strutting about in fancy clothes, having set herself up as the mistress of the house, punishing the slave women with extra work if they so much as dare to mention Cynthia's beauty, even putting Petale in chains because the old woman brought flowers to Cynthia's tomb, and whipping Lalage because she had mentioned Cynthia's name as she begged for mercy! Even Propertius is behaving disgracefully:[5] *te patiente meae conflavit imaginis aurum / ardent<e> e nostro dotem habitura rogo,* "With your permission she melted down the gold of my image, so as to get her dowry from the flames of my funeral pyre." This is indeed a serious offense. The *nova domina,* as Cynthia calls her a few lines later, has destroyed Cynthia's effigy in order to extract the gold from which it was made. One has to admire the cutting elegance of the phrase: that shameless hussy has taken her dowry from the very flames of Cynthia's funeral pyre. It is a crime of outrageous ingenuity, and matchless economy.[6]

Of course, images are accustomed to this sort of abuse, especially when they fall into the hands of insolent heirs. Juvenal records the case of a wanton son who in great haste to raise a large sum of money (destined to be just as quickly spent) not only sells the household china but is ready to put "the shattered image of his own mother" up for sale.[7] Somewhat pedantically, the scholiast observes: "It means he would sell the image of his own mother if it were fashioned in gold or in silver."[8] Pliny also speaks despondently of people who show little interest in the subjects depicted in their ancestral portraits, but who are intent on accumulating such images for their sheer material value.[9] Yet there is probably something more at work in Cynthia's case. We have seen many examples of the care bestowed on the face, the *vultus,* of the vanished lover, making that portrait an object of veneration, of cultic devotion, even of erotic mania.[10] Propertius, on the other hand, is behaving in precisely the opposite way, allowing the image be converted into a dowry for his *nova domina.* It is hard to imagine that Allius would do such a thing, renouncing his plan to take the *imago* of Allia Potestas with him into the tomb, and instead melting it down on the day of her funeral.

Cynthia is thus humiliated in the one trace that remains of her, and the result is a new variation on our fundamental story: the insult to the portrait.[11] The hero of such a tale is that weak-willed or faithless lover who permits the act of destruction, goaded by a new paramour, someone we could rightfully describe as an adulterer who brazenly refuses to respect even the image of the former beloved. The deceased is not just replaced by a substitute: instead, she is held in contempt. With a highly symbolic gesture, the *nova domina* has destroyed the image of the woman who previously held her place. Cynthia is acutely aware of the act's implications, which she deplores in a bitter mixture of folklore and reproach. By behaving in this way the other woman has made a bold and explicit declaration: she is now the one in control. But in violating Cynthia's image, the *nova domina* can also be considered an adulterer precisely because the portrait of the lover is a sign of fidelity, a pledge, as we saw in an earlier chapter. The person who possesses a portrait of the lover has already filled the gap created by the loss of the beloved. The image ought to be enough for all time—but Propertius is apparently willing to sacrifice that image to the new love that has taken possession of his heart. Indeed, this is more than mere adultery: to commit adultery means only to slip like a sharp-edged knife between the lover and the beloved image; but when the image is also humiliated and destroyed, as in Cynthia's case, then we are dealing with an act of gratuitous and vicious depravity.[12]

For her part, the *nova domina* was well aware of what she was doing: to get rid of the beloved's portrait serves to eradicate her memory as well. Ovid, who was quite an expert in such matters, recommended exactly this strategy as an antidote to love's infatuations:[13] *Si potes et ceras remove: quid imagine muta / carperis? Hoc periit Laodamia modo,* "If you can, throw away the wax images too. Why pine away for a speechless portrait? That is how Laodamia met her death." And with a tone that is genuinely more sorrowful, Vergil's Dido will set about the same task, consigning the *effigies* of faithless Aeneas to the flames as she prepares for her own suicide.[14]

Of course, it is always risky for a woman to let her image out on the loose or, even worse, to entrust her image to the treacherous hands of another woman. Artemidorus tells the story of a woman who dreamed "that the maid assigned to do her hair borrowed her portrait painted on a tablet, along with some of her clothes, as if she wanted to take part in a procession. Not long afterwards that same maid stole the love of her mistress's husband."[15] Possessed of her mistress's image in a dream, she was able to disrupt her mistress's emotional world when awake—all because the mistress recklessly put her own image at the symbolic mercy of her maid.

The topic of images comes up frequently in Cynthia's complaints, perhaps because she herself is now confined to that world of insubstantial apparitions and shadowy figures. Later on her *lurida umbra* will make this specific request of Propertius:[16] *deliciaeque meae Latris . . . ne speculum dominae porrigat illa novae,* "do not let my darling Latris hold up a mirror for her new mistress." Lifted up in the hands of her favorite maid, the *speculum* should not reflect another woman's image. In the past, Latris was the servant who would hold up the mirror before her mistress, and each time Cynthia would smile, or nod, or bite her lip in annoyance . . .[17] How cruel it would be if this too were appropriated by the ambitious new mistress! That woman should not be allowed to take Cynthia's place even in the mirror, annihilating Cynthia's image over and over again.

The mirror—more precisely, the scene at the mirror, in which a woman holds up the mirror to herself, or when a maid carries out this task for her—is a symbol of love. The mirror clearly has this function in the context of Cynthia's offended sensibilities (her jealousy of the *nova domina* preening herself in Cynthia's mirror), and it is also found in the iconographic tradition, where the scene at the mirror serves as a concise indicator of amorous interest. In an Attic cup by the Berlin Painter, for example, we see Paris being received by Menelaus on his arrival at Sparta while Helen, seated, turns her face away from a mirror that a maid is holding up to her.[18] Love is about to blossom: this is what this scene at the mirror is meant to suggest. The presence of the mirror is also a presentiment of love for the bride as she prepares for her approaching nuptials, and Attic vase paintings frequently depict the bride seated in front of a mirror.[19] The tenacity of these specific iconographic elements is quite striking; even today, this scene at the mirror has a similarly symbolic function in modern photographic "myths" found in wedding albums or videotapes.[20] For that matter, the myth of Narcissus also suggests a strong symbolic link between the mirror and beauty, between the mirror and love.

But let us return to Cynthia's ghost. The two concerns that torment her—the destruction of her portrait, and her anxiety about the mirror—actually share a certain symmetry, inverting the opposite categories of empty and full. Respect for Cynthia's memory (for that scrap of survival which the survivor's love bestows on the absent beloved) would require that the golden effigy be kept full of her image, while the mirror, on the other hand, should remain strictly empty. Cynthia's concern for the empty mirror is more than a matter of vanity. In ancient folklore, the mirror was believed to have the power both to collect and to retain living images; therefore, the mirror must be kept empty of the *nova domina*'s image because it is still somehow full of Cynthia's image.[21] Similarly, in various popular traditions, the mirrors in a home are thought to retain the effigy of the master and mistress of the house, a belief that is certainly pertinent to Cynthia's situation.[22] As for the power of mirrors in general, Aristotle states that the shining surface of a mirror will cloud over if a menstruating woman looks into it, another sign that the mirror in some sense reacts to the image it is reflecting.[23] We find the same statement again in Pliny,[24] while Proclus[25] specifically argues that an image reflected in a mirror preserves many of the characteristics of the reflected person by means of *sympatheia*, just as shadow images also maintain a sympathetic connection with the person to whom they belong. (And Della Porta even maintains that a prostitute's shameless sexuality can be communicated to the mirror that she habitually uses and thus, by contagion, can infect anyone else who might later look into that same mirror.)[26] As an example of the mirror's ability to be deeply engaged with the person whose image is being reflected, and the related power it has to express or retain the most profound characteristics of that person by means of *sympatheia*, we can cite Paulus Silentiarius:[27] "They say that a man bitten and poisoned by a mad dog sees the image of the bestial creature reflected in water." The mirror thus expresses the deeper truth of things, the real nature of the person who is being reflected. On this basis Paulus Silentiarius very elegantly concludes that he has been bitten not by a rabid dog but instead by a rabid Eros, because every surface (the sea, the river, the cup from which he drinks his wine) reflects back to him the image of his beloved. When he looks in the mirror, the lover sees *the other;* he does not see himself any more. In the same way that the rabid dog possesses the person it bites, the beloved possesses the lover, and the lover no longer has an image of his own. The mirror expresses the lover's true identity—no longer himself, he is the image of the other.

We can find additional evidence of the mirror's power to retain images in a charming scene from a poem by Statius. The subject is Flavius Earinus, a favorite of the emperor, and more precisely the poem concerns the young boy's hair: Earinus's beauty has made such an impression on the goddess Venus that she apparently has taken charge of his clothes and coiffure. When the time arrives for him to have his first

haircut and to make a ritual offering of the shorn locks to the god Asclepius, Venus herself catches the hair as it falls. Standing nearby is another boy in the service of Venus, who happens to be carrying a beautiful mirror:[28]

> Tunc puer e turba, manibus qui forte supinis
> nobile gemmato speculum portaverat auro.
> "Hoc quoque demus," ait, "patriis nec gratius ullum
> munus erit templis ipsoque potentius auro.
> Tu modo fige aciem et vultus hic usque relinque."
> Sic ait et speculum reclusit imagine rapta.

> A young man emerged from the crowd, who happened to be carrying in
> his upturned hands a mirror resplendent with gold and gems. "Let us
> make an offering of this as well," he said, "as no gift could be more
> pleasing to the ancestral shrine; it is a gift more powerful than gold it-
> self! [He now addresses Flavius Earinus.] But turn your gaze in this di-
> rection, and leave your face [*vultus*] here forever." Having said this, he
> shut the mirror, capturing the image inside.

The mirror has the power to capture the image of the person reflected
there, thus realizing the ancient dream of freezing that shifting image.[29]
We might consider, by way of contrast, an example used by Umberto
Eco to describe the semiotic nature of mirrors, and the rigid dependence on the object that characterizes the sign produced in the mirror:
"Let us suppose I send a mirror in the mail to someone I love, after having 'reflected' myself in the mirror for a long time, hoping to leave a
memory of my appearance there. Even so, the other person would still
not be able to see my reflection in the mirror; she will only be able to
see herself."[30] This, then, is the objective truth, or the semiotic truth,
regarding the nature of the mirror: the mirror does not actually preserve
any images on its surface. But popular belief contradicts this diminished
notion of the mirror, insisting that once it has been trapped on the mirror's shining surface, the beloved image can in fact be kept there—snap
the mirror shut, and it's done!—so that later, when I open the mirror's
case, I will see my beloved there, and not just a reflection of myself.

In this sense, Cynthia's mirror is still full of her image, and she wants
it to stay that way; Propertius should not let her mirror be filled up by
anyone or anything else. Apuleius once noted that the image in the mirror is different from a sculpted or painted image not only because it is
closer to the original, but above all because it remains always *aequaeva*
to its original, a property that obviously does not apply in the case of
other types of figures.[31] The manufactured image thus tends to bring
time to a halt, a specific property of the image that has profound impli-

cations for the drama of our fundamental story. By keeping a portrait of the distant beloved, the lover arrests the flow of hours and days; the unchanging features of that face seem to say, "the whole world came to a halt when . . ."—and in this way the image is able to completely circumvent the beloved's absence. A mirror, on the other hand, not only gives free rein to time, but even explicitly tends to mark its passage. The reflected image is fixedly, obstinately *aequaeva* to its referent, as the hours run their course along with the image: the mirror holds up a mirror to time.[32] Cynthia is right to demand that her mirror remain empty of the *nova domina,* so that it can be filled with an image of the past. If the love of Propertius and Cynthia was a truly great love, then an image of that past, not the present, must be allowed to triumph.

The Portrait of a Roman *Matrona*

Proceeding through Book 4 of Propertius's elegies, a few poems later we find another speaking shade. Again it is the shade of a woman, but this time without the frame (or the contrivance) of a dream. Cornelia, the deceased wife of Paullus, addresses her husband directly in this so-called *regina elegiarum,* the queen of elegies.[33] "Enough, Paullus, I beg you, do not burden my tomb with your tears," *desine, Paulle, meum lacrimis urgere sepulchrum.* Cornelia speaks here as a wife, of course, a *matrona,* not a lover. Unlike Cynthia, Cornelia has not come to make reproaches, but rather to exhort and—within the limits imposed by the nobility of pagan resignation, which hopes for nothing— to console.

I am not sure if I would agree that this is the most beautiful of Propertius's elegies, as is often said (in fact, I rather think not). But in any case, we have here an opportunity to eavesdrop on the intimate conversation of a Roman *matrona* with her husband. It is an extraordinary occasion, given that these *matronae* were strictly prohibited from speaking with strangers, and were not even supposed to return the greeting of someone who inappropriately tried to make eye contact with them on the street.[34] Yet despite all that, Propertius agrees to escort us backstage (hidden behind the curtain of the page), where we find ourselves together with Paullus, still grief-stricken over his wife's recent death.

The brilliance of Cornelia's lineage, her marriage to Paullus, now count for nothing. Look at me, Cornelia says, reduced to ashes of so little weight that they can be easily lifted with one hand. But even though she died prematurely, Cornelia insists on the fact that she reached this threshold through no fault of her own. In fact, Cornelia is about to do something that no Roman *matrona* would ever actually have been able to do:[35] she is going to speak in her own defense, facing the tribunal of the Underworld. Her declamation then proceeds item by item through a precise and noble catalog of particulars ("I never violated the laws of the Censor; I never brought shame upon my house; I never wronged the dear person of my mother, Scribonia; I saw the honors of my family augmented," and so on)—until finally Cornelia reaches the subject of Paullus and their sons:[36]

> Oscula cum dederis tua flentibus adice matris:
>   tota domus coepit nunc onus esse tuom.
> Et si quid doliturus eris, sine testibus illis:
>   cum venient siccis oscula falle genis.
> Sat tibi sint noctes quas de me, Paulle, fatiges,
>   somniaque in faciem credita saepe meam.
> Atque ubi secreto nostra ad simulacra loqueris,
>   ut responsurae singula verba iace.
> Seu tamen adversum mutarit ianua lectum,
>   sederit et novo cauta noverca toro,
> coniugium, pueri, laudate et ferte paternum:
>   capta dabit vestris moribus illa manus.
> Nec matrem laudate nimis: collata priori
>   vertet in offensas libera verba suas.
> Seu memor ille mea contentus manserit umbra
>   et tanti cineres duxerit esse meos,
> discite venturam iam nunc lenire senectam.

When you will kiss them as they weep, add kisses from their mother; henceforward you will bear the burden of the whole household. And if you must grieve, do it far from them; when they come to you, dry your tears and deceive them with a kiss. Let the nights suffice, which you will wear out in mourning for me, Paullus, and the *dreams* that will often assume my features. And when, in secret, *you will speak with our portrait,* speak each word as if I could answer you. But if the door will witness a new marriage bed and a stepmother will sit cautiously upon the bedcovers, you, my boys, praise and support your father's marriage. She will give way, captured by your good manners. And do not praise your mother too much. Hearing herself compared to the first wife, she might be insulted by imprudent words. If instead your father remains mindful, and my shade will be enough for him, if he will esteem my ashes at so high a value, begin now to learn how to sweeten his coming old age.

Cornelia is an *umbra,* a shadow image, speaking about her image (her *simulacra,* and her *facies* as it will appear to Paullus in his dreams). In this sense, she is similar to Cynthia, that *lurida umbra* who was also much concerned with her image, her *effigies*. Ghosts love portraits, and maintain a close relationship with them, as we have seen.[37] We have also come to expect that the portrait of the absent person will be accompanied by the images of dreams, as we see again here in Cornelia's speech. But unlike Cynthia, Cornelia is not afraid that her simulacra will be subjected to insults. She is certain that her husband will preserve the cult that is owed to her image and that he will follow the usual practice of coming to speak with her (or with it, with the portrait).[38] Cornelia seems to have no fears that her *effigies* might suffer neglect or oblivion; she asks only that Paullus display the right attitude, observing a specific behavior in these colloquies with her simulacrum:[39] "Speak each word as if I could answer you," she says, *ut responsurae singula verba iace*. Cornelia's request is admittedly unusual. The portrait is inherently mute—yet she asks that her role in the dialogue be taken into consideration; indeed, that "each word" Paullus speaks to her should be subject to this discursive design: *ut responsurae*, he should speak as if to someone who is about to make a reply.

In this singular request made by his heroine, Propertius seems to have gone far beyond the typical dialogue motif that we have frequently seen associated with the solitary lover and his portrait of the absent beloved, as in the "sweet words" that Ovid's Laodamia addresses to the face, the *vultus,* of Protesilaus, or Petrarch's *ragionamenti* with Laura's portrait.[40] To communicate with a portrait means to communicate with a memory; the portrait is a creature of *desiderium,* a compensation for absence, an object that is welcomed precisely because it has the power to revive the memory of someone now absent.[41] But communication with memory is, by definition, communication with oneself, a contact established with a realm of experience that now abides only within the person who evokes it.[42] Dialogue with memory cannot be more than a *soliloquy.* The same is also true of the portrait, that materialization of memory: a person engaged in a dialogue with an image necessarily chooses to speak with himself. But against every rule of logic, Cornelia asks that Paullus's dialogue should involve (even by proxy) a speaking respondent, the living presence of a *reply.* Alive in memory, Cornelia's image also asks to be alive in language. The image rejects its muteness, the inertia that suddenly proclaims the image's lifelessness—but she does not demand the forced, Pygmalionesque fantasy of a speaking effigy. Cornelia's request lies between these two extremes. She wants the image to be conceived as an interlocutor speaking *within* the language of the survivor, responding by means of the manner in which the image is addressed.

Are we then to imagine that Paullus himself was supposed to pronounce Cornelia's silent replies, lending his voice to a mute person—and thus exercising a clever rhetorical strategy that bestows speech on someone without a voice? If this is what Cornelia had in mind, it would be a case of what ancient rhetoricians called *sermocinatio,* that figure of dialogism which comes into play when "one places in the mouth of a character words that are suited to his *dignitas*."[43] We do not know if Cornelia actually asked Paullus to go this far; but if she did, then we can be certain that the dialogue/soliloquy of this aristocratic speaker would have unconditionally respected Cornelia's *dignitas* as a noble Roman *matrona*.

Cornelia's *umbra* and Cynthia's shade clearly constitute a literary pair, but the tones and colors of their speeches are precisely inverted. Like Cynthia, Cornelia sees a connection between her image and the woman who might take her place beside the man she loved—but Cornelia is not threatened in any way by her replacement. She does not fear this hypothetical rival, who is only a *noverca* after all, a stepmother to her sons, not a *nova domina*. In this, Cornelia speaks as an *uxor,* a wife, not a lover. The stepmother will be cautious as she sits upon the new couch, and Paullus certainly would not associate with a gauche woman like Propertius's *nova domina,* who wants to make herself the mistress of the house at any cost. If there must be a *noverca,* she will be a woman whose noble status equals that of the family she is joining. What is more, the aristocratic education and *mores* of Cornelia's sons would be so outstanding that no thoughtless words would ever escape their lips; the stepmother will thus find herself quickly converted by the selfless nobility of her new family. Cornelia does not even want her sons to praise her, their mother; instead, she would even prefer to be forgotten rather than pose a risk to the continuation of the family line after she is gone. This is a carefully calculated gesture on Cornelia's part, given that a well-disposed stepmother would obviously be of greater value to her sons than their grief for her shade. One thinks of Thuria, another famous Roman *matrona,* who was unable to bear children, and who was thus praised in her *laudatio* for being willing to step aside so that a young wife might take her place, giving sons to her husband to carry on his family line.[44]

Unlike Cynthia, Cornelia is a wife, not a lover. She has not left behind a young poet, but instead an aristocratic Roman husband. Instead of sweet and unforgettable nights, they have shared something no less important: a family, a lineage—and this is what must carry on into the future. *Et serie fulcite genus,* urge your sons, she says, one after the other, to uphold this *nobile genus,* this noble family to which Cornelia was joined, bringing with her the honor of her own family and augmenting it with her own irreproachable conduct.[45] Perhaps from this we can conclude that when our fundamental story involves two elegiac lovers, it is easily entangled with the motif of the insulted image, but the motif of the insult is inappropriate when the story involves the simulacrum of an *uxor* from a noble family, one whose husband was an aristocrat, not a poet. But perhaps it would be more prudent just to say instead that Cynthia's fears did not suit the discourse of a Roman *matrona.*

11

Seduction and Vendetta

Ah, pobre honor! the king of Naples exclaimed, "Poor honor, if you are the soul of man, then why do we leave you in the hands of inconstant woman, who is frivolity incarnate?" This is the paradox that haunts honor-based societies (such as seventeenth-century Spain, as represented here by Tirso de Molina's story of Don Juan), and that to a greater or lesser degree affects any patrilineal society:[1] that is, any society in which one's name, one's goods, one's power, even one's physical features are supposed to be transmitted exclusively from the men of one generation to the next—except for the fact that each time it is a *woman* who must be relied upon to connect the chain.[2] As an irreplaceable instrument for male reproduction, women must therefore be kept as absolutely pure and neutral as possible. It is already difficult to tolerate their intrusion into the precious male lineage; how much more terrible if other men, by means of illicit and furtive contacts with the women, manage to pervert and contaminate that lineage's very identity.

The anxiety provoked by this paradox—a male society that cannot avoid involving women in its own reproduction—might result in an obvious and banal sort of misogyny. But it can also produce extravagant dreams of complete autonomy, utopian fantasies in which human offspring are finally removed from the monopoly of the female body. Hippolytus, in a famous passage from Euripides' play of the same name, reproaches Zeus for having chosen to accomplish the reproduction of the human species by means of women.[3] Would it not have been simpler, he adds, if men could receive the seeds of children directly in the temples of the gods, as a reward for their religious offerings? Meanwhile Lucian,

in his *True History,* imagines a world, the world of Selene, in which reproduction is entrusted directly to the men themselves, who conceive
in the knee and give birth through the calf.[4] But these are dreams. In
reality, women are required for men to generate sons. And this explains
the obsessive concern, in both ancient Rome and Don Juan's Madrid,
with the purity and decency of women.[5]

Woman, Image of the Man

Any illicit contact between a woman and a man immediately compromises the honor of some other man: this is one way to
define the problem. A man's honor can thus be compromised if his wife,
a woman he has "taken" for his own, engages in an illicit affair. But men
can also be compromised by the misbehavior of their daughters or sisters, women who are still "for the taking," as it were. The honor and
purity of these women corresponds to their potential to be offered, what
we could even call their "value." In addition, we must consider one
other important factor in this strict system of surveillance and acute hypersensitivity: the feeling of male jealousy. This potentially dangerous
emotion can be overcome (culturally and sociologically) when a woman
is given to some man as his wife, in accordance with the rules of exchange. But an uncontrollable jealousy can erupt in the event of un-
lawful love affairs or liaisons, which might also be termed "fruitless
loves." A young woman's brothers and father automatically become the
brothers-in-law and father-in-law of the man who *marries* the woman;
with its strategic (and linguistic) alliances, kinship is able to subdue these
feelings of jealousy, transforming them into familiarity, even into a sort
of concrete advantage. But when the woman is involved in an illicit
liaison, a fruitless contact, there is no kinship term that can straighten
things out—the man who has taken the woman is simply a rival, and the
woman's father or her brothers are seen as good-for-nothing failures
who cannot even manage to look after their own women.

The hypersensitivity of men regarding the purity of "their" women
involves more than just the amorous physical contact through which
women can become contaminated. Their preoccupation also extends to
contact by sight (better for those women not to be seen going out and
about), as well as to speech and conversation—not only the women's
own conversation, but even their entry as *an object of discourse* into any

conversation. In describing the Roman ideal of feminine purity, Seneca the Elder insists that women should not even come up in conversation, *in nullam incidisse fabulam*.[6] In some sense women are set aside, excluded—but this exclusion does not necessarily result in contempt. Indeed, it can sometimes lead to overvaluation. In the eyes of male culture, women carry out a precious function, a function that is so essential it is better to not even talk about it. Unfortunately, however, this function demands purity as an essential trait. Valuable merchandise, delicate, fragile—these women are made the object of regulations and taboos, and, like any irreplaceable organ of the social body, they also take on connotations of the sacred. Once again language proves a good witness for everything that occurs in a culture. There are thus an infinite number of forms of address used in conversation—*domina, madame, signora*—endless forms of courtesy, of distance, that have deepened the ambiguous veil of sacredness in which women are enveloped. Women are deified, both in the tumultuous cult of the elegiac lover and likewise in the ceremonial calm of the irreproachable husband. Both ethereal courtly love and romantic passion have been fueled by this male obsession with the sacredness of women. Water also immediately attracts a devotional cult, and so does the land. One adores whatever one makes use of, everything that is essential, and desperately irreplaceable.

In this type of society, the roles and positions of women closely recall those of an image. Like an image, a woman (in her social existence) does have an autonomous, self-contained meaning—but this meaning is sustainable only insofar as it points at the same time to something else or, more accurately, to *someone else,* to a man who expresses himself by means of her. Writing to the Corinthians, Saint Paul recommended that women should be veiled during church:[7] "The man is the image and the glory of God; the woman is the glory of man." Moreover, exactly like an image, a woman shares in the identity of her referent. To touch her, to treat her with disrespect, constitutes a direct blow to the man whom she "represents." Thus, better not to expose her to such a risk. Plutarch goes so far as to argue that a woman should be reserved and cautious even in exposing her voice.[8] Speaking, in fact, is a bit like disrobing, an act that she should blush at, and abstain from, in the company of strangers. Far better for her "to speak only to her husband, or by means of her husband," using another's tongue to speak just as a flute player relies on a flute to make music. In Roman culture, the rule of female silence had the habitual force of a law handed down from the remotest antiquity, as it was supposedly Numa himself who decreed that a woman "should not speak even of necessary matters when her husband happens to be absent."[9]

The men are apparently quite worried about the impression that their woman can make on other men, and so they surround her with admonitions or prohibitions. A man looks after his woman as if he were looking after himself; he supervises how the woman appears—the words that she uses, the greetings, the gazes—with the same concern that he displays for his *own* manner of walking, his *own* way of dressing or acting. These are serious matters, because it is in this way—through his own gestures or through the behavior of his woman—that a man communicates himself to those around him. It is a question both of his own way of walking, and the way his woman walks; his own personal prestige, and her reputation. It is always he, the man, who functions as the "signified," he is the meaning that this set of codified symbolic models communicates to the other members of the community. A woman is a person/sign, in the same way that the clothes that one chooses to wear (or one's characteristic gestures or gait) are a function/sign. A man *expresses himself* by means of a woman; she is for him one of the various cultural codes that allow him to communicate. This, then, is why what a woman says or does is immediately attributed to him, why it all refers back to the man.

In this patriarchal model, the woman thus always refers to someone else; she is an intermediary for "signifieds," a conveyor of messages. Her existence establishes a relationship between the man whom she represents and other men, his potential interlocutors. This is because patriarchal society has designated women as a means by which relationships are established; the social structure defines women in terms of linkages, a point of passage between groups that maintain a system of exchange based on women. These women are culturally destined to represent someone else for the same reason that they are destined to connect themselves and their men with other men and other groups of men. It is clear, in fact, that unlike the men of these societies, women are supposed to leave their paternal home in order to link their male group of origin to a new group. In their new home they once again begin to represent men, becoming the subject of new jealousies and new fears among this new group of men—the subject of another, ambiguous sacredness.

But what about the portrait of the lover? We are getting nearer to our story: after having been banished by the king of Spain, Don Juan is already making his way back to Madrid, traveling through hidden trails in the mountains. Finally he reaches the cemetery of San Antonio, and finds there an imposing tomb, with a statue on top: it is a statue of the Commendatore, his victim. But he is also struck by the beauty of a young woman, veiled in mourning, who pours forth her tears every day in front of that image—Donna Anna, of course. Despite Leporello's protests, the seducer cannot help himself. Dressed in the clothes of a poor hermit, Don Juan approaches the disconsolate widow.

This is the opening of Pushkin's *The Stone Guest*,[10] an unusual work in many respects,[11] and certainly the most successful of the author's "little tragedies."[12] But in terms of its plot, there is above all one innovation that strikes the reader: Donna Anna is no longer the Commendatore's daughter, but his *wife*. She is a widow, not an orphan. Pushkin's unusual modification of the original design has often been explained in terms of a strong autobiographical projection.[13] But in any case, Pushkin's invention has the virtue of exposing a profound feature of the story, something that might have remained only dimly perceptible in the traditional version. Thanks to the strong contrast provided by Pushkin's innovation, we can now clearly see that the plot requires a bond of possession, of belonging, between the violated woman and the murdered man—but the specific nature of this bond can be established by context or by personal choice.[14] Whether father or husband, what matters is that the Commendatore feel deprived of his honor if someone should seduce Donna Anna, and thus be ready to risk his life for her. The basic, irreducible feature of the plot is that the Commendatore must function as Donna Anna's possessor.[15] The myth of Don Juan seems more and more a story about responsibility or, more precisely, about relationships and about the woman who is a point of relation between men; a dispenser of honor and of shame, of risks and of precautions; a delicate relay around which there turns a universe of relationships in which the woman emerges as both protagonist and victim.

The Ancient Footsteps of the Commendatore

There is another motif of considerable interest in Pushkin's variation on the Don Juan story, one which pertains even more closely to our subject matter. Donna Anna, by having been transformed into the wife of the Commendatore, kneeling in front of the image of her dead husband, now joins the ranks of Laodamia, Charite, and all the other lovers we have seen. Once again, the absence of the beloved per-

son seems to be calmed by a cult of the portrait—even if the face of Protesilaus, his *vultus* shaped in wax, now assumes the unfamiliar form of a
massive marble statue. From this point of view, Donna Anna appears
highly reminiscent of Ovid's Dido, as she describes her situation in a letter addressed to the *perfidus* Aeneas: [16]

> Est mihi marmorea sacratus in aede Sychaeus
>   (oppositae frondes velleraque alba tegunt);
> hinc ego me sensi noto quater ore citari;
>   ipse sono tenui dixit, "Elissa, veni!"
> Nulla mora est, venio, venio tibi dedita coniunx.

> In a marble temple I have the consecrated image of Sychaeus (shaded
> by entwined leafy branches and fillets of white wool). Thence I have
> heard that familiar voice call to me four times, his own voice speaking
> faintly, "Come, Elissa!" Without delay, I come, I come to you, your
> rightful wife.

Thus the portrait of the lover, when it is transformed into a sepulchral
image, moves decidedly nearer to the deceased, establishing a much
closer contact with the person it represents. It is an image of the dead,
and at the same time it is a sign of his effective presence. In Carthage,
the portrait of Sychaeus certainly had nothing to fear from Aeneas, a
hero who was *perfidus* only in obedience to Fate, a seducer almost against
his will. But in Spain, as we know, things will develop rather differently.

"What a giant they have made of him!" exclaims Pushkin's Don Juan.
"What shoulders! Like some kind of Hercules! But the dear departed
was only a pipsqueak. If he were here now, standing on tiptoe, his hand
wouldn't even reach up to the nose. When we met behind the Escurial,
he ran himself through with my sword and died, like a dragonfly on a
pin. Yet he was proud and bold, and fierce in spirit. Ah, but here she
comes now!" [17] It is the widow Anna, who has arrived to pray at her husband's tomb: so the seduction begins. The impostor speaks with her,
implores her, even calls that cold marble happy because it receives the
warmth of her breath and is bathed in the tears of her love. This casts a
rather new light on our fundamental story: the adulterous pretender
now expresses *envy* for the portrait of the vanished lover. [18] At last the
beautiful widow relents a bit, leaving open a tiny gap of hope for the seducer, actually agreeing to meet him the following day, at her house.
For that matter, we know that she did not marry her husband for love.
The Petronian theme of the "Widow of Ephesus" subtly inserts itself
into the scaffolding of the story, winking at the reader discreetly (very

discreetly, thank goodness).[19] As soon as she has agreed to the meeting, Anna departs. It is the right moment for her to ask the name of the pretender; "Diego de Calvado," he replies.

The false Diego is exultant, and he now commits his last reckless, outrageous offense. Much to Leporello's terrified dismay, he plants himself in front of the statue and shouts, "Commander, I invite you to come stand guard at the door of your widow's house, where I myself will be received tomorrow. So, will you be there?" The statue nods its head. The rest is easy to imagine: the ponderous steps of the statue, its hand reaching out, and the death of Don Juan as his victim drags him down into the Inferno.

The taunting of the statue and the invitation to dinner take on a heavily sarcastic tone in this version of the story, as the deceased is invited to a ceremony that will celebrate his own disgrace, an observance of his definitive humiliation. The unpleasant task of being the custodian of one's own dishonor was the fate of other statues in the past—even the god Vulcan, for example, who stood planted outside a temple dedicated to Mars Ultor that also housed a statue of Venus. Ovid provides this malicious description of the scene:[20] *stat Venus Ultori iuncta, vir ante fores,* "Venus stands joined with Mars, while her husband waits outside." But there is an even more outrageous mockery, something closer to the impious words of the *burlador* Don Juan, in the speech that Perseus, recently married to fair Andromeda, makes to Phineus (Andromeda's former suitor who, in order to win her back again, had undertaken a bloody war with the famous hero). The victorious Perseus is now standing there, with the dreadful head of the Medusa in his hand, and in just a few moments Phineus will turn suddenly rigid, becoming a statue of stone. Perseus taunts his rival cruelly:[21]

> quin etiam mansura dabo monumenta per aevum,
> inque domo soceri semper spectabere nostri,
> ut mea se sponsi soletur imagine coniunx.

> I will grant you an eternal monument, and forever you will be on display in the house of my father-in-law, so that my wife may console herself with an image of her fiance!

To see the lover turned into stone, to see him actually become his own portrait, is an experience quite new to our fundamental story. And the way in which Perseus utters these words makes his riposte sound very much like a cruel dismissal of Laodamia and all the other lovers who found consolation in an image. This Ovidian figure manages to combine an extraordinary number of roles: as the assassin of his wife's fiance, Perseus is at the same time the author of her fiance's portrait—and, like Don Juan, he scornfully proceeds to mock this portrait of the lover in stone.

But for all their cruelty, Perseus's words still do not reach the brazen flippancy of Don Juan's taunts. This is because we are still in Greece (or, more precisely, in Ovid's Rome), and not yet in Spain, that country in which honor is sacred. The statue of the Commendatore is asked to play Leporello's usual role, keeping watch for Don Juan—but now it is his own wife on the other side of the door. At this point, the statue's vendetta is inevitable, and it will be as cruel and harsh as the insult that provoked it. A portrait knows how to rise up against traitors, how to enforce the pledge that its very existence embodies. Our fundamental story anticipates precisely this possibility: the image should naturally be able to vindicate itself when it is insulted. There was no need to wait for the story of "the stone guest" after all; already in many ancient stories we can hear the sinister thud of the statue's rigid footsteps.

In the story of Theagenes of Thasos, for example, we find a whole series of insults and vendettas involving statues.[22] As a child, Theagenes stole a statue from the agora (a crime that also demonstrated his precocious physical strength, of course). As an adult, Theagenes became an athlete of extraordinary valor, and was honored after his death with a statue—except that every night one of his enemies would come and whip the statue mercilessly. An offender of images who becomes in turn an offended image, Theagenes thus embraces the entire range of possibilities: his crime and punishment mirror one another. But the story continues: Theagenes' statue eventually fell on top of his assailant and killed him. The sons of the dead man were able to have the statue convicted for this crime because inanimate objects could be held legally responsible for a person's death. Theagenes' statue was accordingly thrown into the sea,[23] but the city was then afflicted by a dreadful plague. Emissaries were sent to Delphi, and the oracle enigmatically advised them to "recall the exiles." Of course, the citizens did not understand the response, and had to wait for the god to put things more clearly, explicitly inviting them to "remember mighty Theagenes." At this point they fished the statue out of the ocean, finally putting an end to the pestilence.

That persistent insult directed at the image of the great athlete had to be punished, and fatally. The retaliation that was then inflicted on the statue, while legally correct, was in fact unjust. This gives Theagenes' story an exemplary structure, involving both human and divine tribunals—tribunals whose judgments are in conflict until the final revelation. The insult and the image's vendetta constitute a dialectical pair, reflecting the two alternate possibilities of the plot. But one clear verdict is sanctioned both by the plague and then by the oracle's response: *an image should not be insulted.* The vendetta that such an insult provokes is not only possible, but legitimate.

The gods thus seem to extend their protection to statues, especially (as we have seen) to the statues of athletes. Euticles, another famous athlete, was unjustly accused of theft and imprisoned by the Locrians. Still not satisfied, they then wanted to insult Euticles' statue after his death. Although the image did not react directly, as in the more elaborate story of Theagenes' statue, the wrath of the gods once again broke out with comparable violence. Locris was ravaged by a terrible pestilence, and the citizens could find no relief until the oracle of Apollo intervened, explaining the cause of this tremendous destruction.[24] The statue of Euticles was then honored "equally with that of Zeus"[25] (similarly, it is worth noting that miraculous healing powers were also attributed to the statue of Theagenes[26]).

There is no such mythical profundity in the story of Pellicus of Corinth and his statue,[27] which apparently had the ability to detach itself from its pedestal at night in order to wander about people's houses and take baths. A foolhardy young man from Libya once dared to steal the offerings that grateful citizens had left in front of the statue; the statue happened to be absent at the moment, taking one of its nightly walks.[28] But as soon as it returned and realized that it had been robbed, the statue was infuriated, and punished the Libyan in exemplary fashion. The unlucky victim was seized by a strange sort of mania, which compelled him to wander all night long from house to house as if in a labyrinth. When the next day dawned he was caught, still carrying the stolen goods, and beaten with sticks by the angry citizens. But even this was not the end of it: the young man suffered mysterious beatings each and every night, until he finally died. Of course, this was a crime merely of theft and greed, not yet a matter of the highest honor (as it will be for the Commendatore's statue). But in any case the images are able to avenge themselves if they are insulted. They can either make use of the one, rigid movement that is within their power, falling upon their victim, or else they can delegate the matter to a very close substitute, the ghost.[29] And there is also a third possibility, even more terrifying than the other two.

In this case we are dealing with a story told by Philostratus, and it does in fact concern a question of the highest honor, even if wives and daughters are not actually involved.[30] A young Assyrian on a visit to Troy began to make insulting comments about Hector, reproaching the Trojan hero for having let himself be dragged around by Achilles, for having been almost toppled by Ajax's stone, and for having fled from Patroclus, leaving the Greek hero to be killed by somebody else. As if this were not yet enough, the young man finally insulted the statue of Hector that stood there at Troy, insisting that it was not really a statue of Hector at all, but a statue of Achilles (and he explained the statue's short hair by saying it showed Achilles at the moment when he had cut his hair in mourning for Patroclus). The young Assyrian then left the city. But along the road a stream—usually so dry and insignificant that it did not even merit a name—rose up and swelled into an indescribable torrent. A gigantic hoplite was marching in front of the wave, and with a raucous and booming voice he ordered the waters to overrun the road where the young man was passing in his chariot. As he was seized by the floodwaters and swept away, the horrified Assyrian recognized Hector in that gigantic hoplite. The young man's body was never recovered.

When his warrior's honor had been offended, Hector avenged himself. And in order to carry out this vendetta, the image became not only an animated statue, but one of explicitly gigantic dimensions.[31] As Pushkin's Don Juan said, looking at the statue of the Commendatore:[32] "What a giant they have made of him! What shoulders! Like some kind of Hercules!" The avenging simulacrum cannot be imagined as anything other than a giant statue, a creation endowed with extraordinary power. The legal force possessed by the "just" statue is expressed by means of the one cultural code that is available to inanimate objects: expansion. The statues of the Commendatore and the Trojan hero are able to communicate the enormity of the crime committed against them by means of their gigantic dimensions, proportionate to the justice of the punishment that they are about to inflict. One cannot escape a gigantic statue, just as the gigantic crime requires an equal punishment. The insults to Hector's statue were no less serious than the mockery to which the Commendatore was subjected. Not only was Hector's past honor as a hero impugned, but the honor of Hector's image was also insulted: and it is surely no small insult to disown a statue's referent, asserting instead that the statue belongs precisely to his mortal enemy, to the very man who murdered the person portrayed in the statue. To say to the image, "You are not the person you think you are" (indeed, to say, "You represent your own assassin")—even Don Juan does not go so far.

Those are words of pure and bitter malice, aimed right for the heart, striking at the image's essential identity.

This is because the image (which, as we know, forms a part of the person) tenaciously retains something of the character of its referent.[33] Hector was not the sort of person to let an insult go unpunished, nor was the Commendatore. We are dealing here with powerful men, deeply proud—a trait that is shared by their statues as well. In the cultural representation supplied by the story, the image reveals itself to be in extremely close proximity to its referent, able to convey and repeat his main characteristics. An epigram from the *Greek Anthology* recommends, "Stepsons, avoid even the tomb of your stepmother!"[34] The poem then tells the story (both amusing and uncomfortable) of a pious boy who decorated the stele of his stepmother with garlands, thinking that this external metamorphosis had also changed her character. But the stele of the stepmother fell on the boy and killed him: the image of the stepmother is a stepmother all the same. Once again the story insists on the *sympatheia,* the close contact, between the referent and his (or her) image.[35]

The Bond of the Ring

There is thus a long but fairly direct path leading from our ancient stories to that quintessential statue-as-justice, the Commendatore of Seville. To make our way from Theagenes of Thasos to the terrifying statue that punishes Don Juan, we would need only to review the medieval adventures of Julian the Apostate, the godless and brutal emperor who was punished by an image of Mercury (or Saint Mercury). But this stretch of the journey has already been well covered by Denise Paulme, and we do not need to retrace her steps at this point.[36] Instead, we will conclude with a final variant of our fundamental story: the tale of a young man's purely accidental liaison with a statue. When he later wanted to marry a living, actual woman, this statue—the image to which he had unwittingly bound himself—refused to let the marriage take place. As we will see, he is a frivolous and rather thoughtless young man, just what we should expect of a young Roman aristocrat as imagined in a popular medieval tale.[37]

On the day of his wedding, this young man decided to play a game of "catch" with his friends. So as to not lose or damage the wedding ring that his fiancee had given him, he placed it on the finger of a bronze statue which stood at the edge of the field. After the game was over, he went to take back the ring, but the finger of the statue had bent all the way down to its palm and no matter how hard he tried, the young man was not able to remove the ring. He did not breathe a word about this strange event to anyone, and later that night, after the party, he silently returned to the place where the statue stood. The finger had resumed its normal position, but the ring was gone. The young man attached no great importance to what had happened, and rejoined his wife in the bridal chamber. He lay down in the bed next to his bride, but quickly realized that a mysterious presence had insinuated itself between the two of them, a presence that was palpable but at the same time invisible. At last a voice spoke to him, saying, "Come lie next to me, my betrothed! I am that Venus on whose finger you placed the ring. Here it is; you see, I still have it."

It was a night filled with anxiety. Each time the young man approached his wife, the same scene repeated itself. The terrifying night finally ended, and the next day the groom told his parents about everything that had happened. They took him to a priest by the name of Palumbus, who had the reputation of being a sorcerer. He told the boy to wait until nightfall and then to go to the crossroads. He should stand there and wait until a great procession approached, a parade made up of young and old, men and women, mourners and revelers. Whatever happened, the young man was not to speak a single word. Finally he would see a man passing by who was taller than the others, seated on a cart. The young man was to give that man a letter that he had received from the mysterious priest. Our hero did as he was told, and the letter was punctually delivered. The devil (who was of course the one taller than the rest) cursed and swore, giving the boy a terrible look. Finally he burst out: "Do the heavens yet endure the wickedness of that priest Palumbus?" But in the end the devil could not resist the obscure powers of the priest, and ordered his servants to deliver the letter immediately to Venus. The goddess—or rather, the demon whose name happened to be Venus—put up a fight but finally gave in, and returned the wedding ring to its owner. From that moment on, the young man was able to consummate his marriage, joined at last with his true wife. But the priest Palumbus realized that his own time had come: the wretched priest asked that his body be dismembered as he confessed his sins to the pope contritely and commended his spirit to the Lord.

This tale of the jealous statue is the final variation that our fundamental story offers for our consideration. Like the Commendatore, this betrayed and humiliated statue also rushes to prevent a potential adultery, refusing to admit defeat: the vow contracted with a statue is inviolable. For that matter, we also know that the statue is fidelity incarnate; the statue is itself a pledge.[38] As a result, that pledge given to the statue, the pledge of the ring, becomes a pledge two times over. If someone breaks the vow that is made visible in the image (the sacralizing object), then the effective force of the sworn oath relentlessly pursues the traitor, mobilizing the very object in which it is embodied.[39] The bell of justice can be heard tolling in the faithful image's stiff, resounding footsteps.

There are also versions of Venus and her ring in which the goddess is replaced by an image of the Virgin Mary.[40] But the Virgin is equally possessive and jealous of her betrothed, even if in this case he is obviously a devout young man, and not a Roman noble. The story remains exactly the same, except that where the pagan goddess was defeated, the Virgin triumphs, and the devout young man is obliged to abandon his bride and shut himself away in a monastery, dedicating himself entirely to the cult of the Virgin. These are curious, even bizarre, cultural combinations—the result of playing games with the traditional tale, capriciously altering the characters' costumes and roles. We might also note here a humorous story in the *Capitulare de imaginibus* that provides further evidence of the dangerous proximity between the figures of Venus and the Virgin Mary.[41] The exemplum involves a painter who has created two identical images, one of the Virgin and one of Venus, but without any *superscriptio* to indicate the subjects of the pictures—and the poor canon Epiphanius cannot tell which is which.[42] Of course, the image of the Virgin should be honored, and the image of Venus should be destroyed—but how is Epiphanius to decide which image to revere and which to discard? The question is posed to the painter, who declares that "this one is Venus, that one there is the Virgin." So the one image is immediately honored, and the other is thrown away. But were they not originally identical? Does the mere addition of a name guarantee the sanctity of an object? Among its many interesting aspects, the story clearly shows that the identity of an image is a perilously delicate subject. The two extremes of Venus and the Virgin find themselves in fearful proximity simply as a result of the fact that these two particular figures (both so feminine, both so beautiful) can be encountered only as images.

As a pagan goddess, the statue of Venus cannot be fully vindicated. The statue is married, which gives her a certain claim, certain rights. But how could a pagan divinity exercise such binding power over a young

Christian man? No, her justice no longer has any foundation, and the young man must be released from his vow. But if she is converted into the Virgin Mary, then her image is able to assert and enforce her rights without reservation. For that matter, how else could such a variation of the story have possibly ended? If the image is itself a pledge, if the image is fidelity incarnate, then how much more true this must be in the case of Mary's *sacred* image.[43]

Venus or the Virgin Mary, the pagan demon or the compassionate madonna—this last version of our fundamental story suggests a sort of summary judgment: we now see that lovers can transfer their love to the image, fixing their desire in the rigid material of its features, dedicating themselves to a cult of the image (like Laodamia or Admetus); alternatively, they can dedicate themselves directly to the image by means of a ring, making a pledge that cannot easily be broken. In the stories we have looked at in this chapter—tales of the statue's vengeance, or stories about Venus/Mary and her ring—the images provoke a feeling of fear: somehow these images have the power to bind their human partners. The stories are thus almost a warning to keep the images at a distance, to not come too much into contact with them. In this sense, to marry a statue is not much different than to swear a vow of eternal fidelity to the absent beloved while embracing (with inordinate ecstasy) that person's image. Nor is it much different from inviting a statue to dinner or, even worse, inviting the statue to make itself an accomplice in a night of adulterous revelry. In each case a rapport is established with the image, involving the image in a mutual, reciprocal relationship that should clearly be reserved only for living creatures. As a result, the image itself may claim to be treated as a living creature, or may begin to behave as if it were alive. Moreover, the image can forcibly attach itself to the person who has entered into a binding relationship with it. So Venus and Mary refuse to agree to a divorce . . . while Laodamia and Charite (and also Don Juan) are dragged off to the Underworld. To treat the image as if it were an actual person apparently exceeds the limits allowed by the cultural code. If these stories are reformulated as a sort of metalanguage for the culture, we might say that they are teaching us about the need to confine the image to the role of an icon, a similarity, an analogy—and to not invest it with reality. Not everyone can enjoy the same (psychoanalytic) good luck of Norbert Hanold and his Gradiva. The image itself is a pledge, a promise to be true—but the other side of that faithful vow is the inexorable threat of punishment.

12

The Justice of Death
Standing Up

Among the many cultural values associated with the image, it is perhaps this last value that makes the greatest impression: the image as justice. Statues in particular appear to be endowed with the power to enforce laws or customs, intervening wherever someone has gone too far, as can surely be said of Don Juan. We can also add many examples from the ancient world, such as the statue of Theagenes, which killed its persecutor (as we saw in the previous chapter), and also a statue of Mitys, at Argos, that fell on top of the man who had killed Mitys, thus murdering the murderer in turn—indeed, the statue carried out its revenge while the assassin stood there staring at the effigy of his victim.[1] There is also the story about a statue of Eros that hurled itself on top of a cruel young man who had driven his lover to suicide by refusing to return his offers of affection.[2] Love demands to be reciprocated, and this story shows how dangerous it can be to refuse: the pledge—that pledge of love— is here enforced by its physical embodiment in an image, a statue of the god Eros himself.[3] Likewise, when Caesar was stabbed to death by his assassins, he fell at the feet of a statue of Pompey,[4] thus giving Pompey's image the satisfaction it had no doubt long awaited, while bringing Caesar's adventuresome career to a close—what a coincidence!—there at the feet of his enemy.[5]

The statue thus stands for what is right. When it rises up and pursues some mortal with its menacing steps, the statue is not a malignant force gone out of control: it is the incarnation of justice in the form of an image. We can thus attempt to formulate a hypothesis regarding this essentially moral power possessed by the statue: just as the statue is a pledge, the statue is also justice.[6] By its very nature, the statue embodies a pledge, a promise. Consequently, the statue is also endowed with the power to exact punishment if that pledge is violated—and to do so legally, as we saw in the story of Theagenes. The statue is a sacralizing object that is displayed in the swearing of an oath, and it is invoked in this way because it supposedly contains the power to punish any violation of that sworn oath.[7] As the symbolic proxy of the oath (or, more precisely, of the faithfulness that the oath expresses), the statue becomes the oath's guardian, enforcing the pledges and promises that regulate the lives of men. The statue is then transformed into a means of punishment when a person with whom the statue is connected suffers a serious injustice that has gone otherwise unpunished. In this way statues function much like the Erinyes, serving as a concrete trace of the crime that has been committed (so that it will not be forgotten) and also as a promise of inevitable vengeance.[8] When someone dies, it is still possible to leave behind a tangible, visible object that symbolically represents any crime committed against that person, and that also guarantees a punishment of the crime (sooner or later). Where human justice does not reach—either because it is ignorant, or because it is corrupted or otherwise inadequate—a superior justice can awaken in these rigid and inanimate objects, the statues that are the true guardians of our culture's boundaries.

But what could be the symbolic motivation of this incredible power possessed by the statue, its ability to shed its stony rigidity in order to move at will (almost) like a living person? What are the inherent structural assumptions that underlie this insidious metamorphosis? The statue that moves and walks is an admittedly frightening sight—but it is not inherently absurd. It is impossible, but at the same time seems somehow natural. It is surely not by chance that we possess so many stories about these statues on the move: this is a motif deeply embedded in our cultural horizon.

Perhaps we can begin by observing that the symbolic content of the statue develops along two principal axes, symmetrically opposed to one another. As a character in a story by E. T. A. Hoffmann explains:[9] "I always experienced a sense of overwhelming repugnance for those figures that do not imitate humanity but are rather a travesty of it, images like death standing up or mummified life. When I was little, I would always burst into tears and run away whenever they took me to visit the Wax Museum." It is a simple statement, but nevertheless quite profound. The simulacrum stands at the intersection of two equal and contrary axes, simultaneously defined in both directions: death standing up (death that has been brought to life), and mummified life (life that has become something dead). In a nutshell, Hoffmann's character has described what is now generally known as the uncanny, following the famous essay by Freud. More specifically, we see here what Jentsch identified as a key feature of the uncanny: [10] "the suspicion that something apparently alive might be dead and, vice versa, the suspicion that an apparently dead object might in fact be alive." The statue is an uncanny object precisely because in the statue there is something alive that seems dead, and something dead that seems alive. Moreover, the words of Hoffmann's fictional character closely anticipate Roman Jakobson's elaborate analysis of the poetic metamorphoses that a statue can undergo. "The immobile statue of a mobile being can be perceived in two different ways: either as a moving statue, or as a statue of an immobile being." Jakobson also describes the duality of the statue in terms of life and death: "The idea of life that is included in the meaning of a statue and the idea of duration that is furnished by its outer shape fuse into an image of *continuing life.*" [11] The statue's exterior form attempts to reproduce nothing less than the aspect of a human being (quite an ambitious task, after all): this pushes the statue in the direction of life, and even makes us suspect that it might really be alive. But at the same time, the statue is utterly rigid and immobile, despite having the appearance of an animate being: this is what pushes the statue with equal force in the direction of death. The statue has the same motionless, cold character of a corpse, with the exterior aspect of a living person.

This begins to suggest an underlying motivation for the many stories about the statue that rises up and begins to walk. Given that statues display the features of living people, it seems entirely possible that they are not inanimate objects after all, but a case of mummified life, fostering the uncanny suspicion that this "apparently dead object might in fact be alive." This is indeed one of the statue's two structural axes, one of the two possible ways of reading the statue. On the other hand, it is also clear why the statue (even in a rough, aniconic form) can function as a *kolossos,* as a perfect double and substitute for death: [12] the rigid material of the statue perfectly evokes the rigidity of death; it is death standing up, the immobile statue of an immobile being, the very image of death itself. The statue of the Commendatore that uncannily comes to life (mummified life) and the *kolossos* that functions as the double of death (death standing up) define the two ends of that symbolic range which these statues occupy in our cultural imagination.

Figure 1. Vatican sarcophagus representing Protesilaus as he returns from the Underworld, and showing his encounter with Laodamia. From C. Robert, *Die antike Sarkophagereliefs*, vol. 3, 423 (1969).

Figure 2. Head of the Aphrodite of Cnidos (ancient copy of Praxiteles' original dating to no later than 350 B.C.E.). Paris, Musée du Louvre.

Figure 3. Fresco depicting Narcissus at the fountain. Naples, Museo
Nazionale.

Figure 4. The woman in the window. Nimrud, eighth century
B.C.E. London, British Museum.

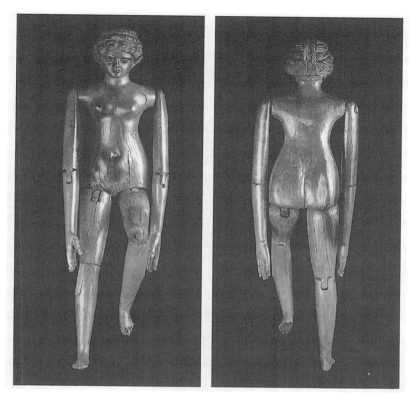

Figure 5. Crepereia Tryphaena, 150–60 C.E. Rome, Musei Capitolini.

Figure 6. Jean Léon Gérôme, *Pygmalion and Galatea,* 1880. New York, The Metropolitan Museum of Art, Gift of Louis C. Raegner, 1927. (27.200). Photograph (c) 1989 The Metropolitan Museum of Art.

PART 2

Other Adventures
of the Image

13

The Gaze

Impelled by curiosity, we might hope to enter into the heart of a statue: specifically, the heart of a statue who is in love. The resources of literary fantasy have already allowed us to enter into the heart of the other member of this pair, that incredible lover who is infatuated with an image—those somber artist-magicians like Pygmalion who captured and possessed the ghostly object of their desire in the form of a painting or a statue. But what about the feelings of the image itself? To answer that question we would have to see into the image's heart, yet this is a privilege that even literature cannot grant us. The heart of an image is too deeply hidden, made impenetrable by the essential requirement that the image must function as a shape, a form, a figure. This would be true even if an artist were to cleverly make an image with its heart revealed in the middle of its chest, like an ex-voto. Despite the artist's best efforts, the image can never really have a heart. But eyes: now that is a different matter entirely.

When Pygmalion's ivory statue finally thawed with life, she did not blush because she suddenly became aware of the kisses being pressed on her by her fortunate lover—rather, she blushed because she could see:[1] *sensit et erubuit timidumque ad lumina lumen / attollens pariter cum caelo vidit amantem,* "She became aware and blushed, timidly lifting her eyes toward the light; she saw the sky, and she saw her lover too." The eyes are the sign and window of life. So when Venus gives life to the statue, she opens her eyes: the statue is able to see. Once it is endowed with a gaze, the simulacrum abandons the rigid world of figures and rises up into the realm of humanity. And this, not surprisingly, might also be a cause for alarm.

The Life of the Gaze

The mysterious power of the gaze is a familiar topic in legends about artists and their creations. When the first images were made, there was no question of giving them eyes, although divine artists did possess extraordinary powers of invention: Hephaestus built for his own use "handmaids wrought in gold, with intelligence, speech, and strength like that of actual women"[2] while Athena devised "constructions similar to living creatures" that walked the streets of Rhodes.[3] But our Greek sources tell us that before Daedalus, the statues made by human artists always had feet that were welded together and, most importantly, eyes that were blind or closed.[4] Daedalus was the first to separate the feet, giving his statues the appearance of movement, and he also opened their eyes for the first time. But as he did so, Daedalus perhaps exceeded the limits of what was allowed. Once the feet of the statues were separated, they proved surprisingly reluctant to stay put, and there are many ancient stories about statues that had to be tied up to keep them from running away.[5] Ovid's Pygmalion, certainly a more humble craftsman than the bold Daedalus, experienced a feeling of *reverentia* at the thought of bestowing motion on his creation.[6] It was this *reverentia*, this fear of going too far, that imposed a limit on the powers of human artists.

But it was not only a matter of statues that could move. The statues of Daedalus also had eyes that were open and endowed with a gaze: these were figures that could see.[7] The verb used in our sources is very explicit in this regard: the statues of Daedalus were able to "look," *blepein*, they were able to "gaze at something."[8] What more did they need to qualify as living creatures? And this is precisely why they had to be tied up. The same problem is found in a Chinese legend about a painter who refused to make eyes for a portrait because that would turn the portrait into a person,[9] or another Chinese story about an artist who had painted a dragon without eyes—but when he added the eyes, his dragon ran away.[10] If the statue can see, it is no longer a statue. If something can move, it is somehow alive; the same apparently is true of anything that can see.[11]

Daedalus's statues were thus supposed to have the incredible ability to see, to be endowed with a gaze. Somewhat more modestly, the statues created by Daedalus's successors were reportedly able to meet the eyes of people who looked at them or, more precisely, to create the sensation of exchanging gazes in this way. Such an effect (even if it is only illusionary) makes a profound impression on the viewer, precisely because it associates the image with an attribute that by definition the image *cannot possess:* a directed gaze. For example, the Roman painter Famulus (a very stern fellow who indulged his art only a few hours a day, always dressed in his toga) painted a Minerva that reportedly could "look at every spectator from any angle whatsoever."[12] Many centuries later, Gerard d'Amiens would describe a painting of Dido whose eyes were similarly able to turn and meet the eyes of any person who looked at the painting.[13] The fact is that this act of looking, and above all the act of *returning* someone's gaze, is the quintessential social skill. To return the gaze is a kind of exchange, a form of reciprocity and contact; it is life in its most meaningful form: communication. This is why an image, that rigid creation, fundamentally lifeless, cannot really return anyone's gaze. But the images devised by myths and legends are able to see, they can look at the people around them: these fantastic images are able to communicate, participating in a network of social relations.

For the Romans, this act of turning and looking back—*respicere*—constitutes an immediate sign of contact and communication.[14] If a divinity turns and looks, if the god looks back—*respicit*—then it means he is favorably disposed: there is an open channel of contact with the god; he is looking right at us. But if the god doesn't turn toward us, doesn't look back, then the result is bound to be disappointing. For example, there was a statue of Mercury in Rome who was called Malivolus Mercurius because "he did not turn his gaze toward anyone's shop."[15] We can also compare the Roman practice of closing the eyes of the dead ("because it is not right for someone to see their eyes in their final moment") and then opening the eyes when the corpse was placed on the pyre, because "it would be wrong not to display them to the heavens."[16] It is precisely because the gaze is a form of contact that one should not look (back) at, *respicere,* anything dangerous or polluting, such as ghosts, infernal creatures, the dead, and so on. Orpheus lost his Eurydice forever because he turned and looked back at the world of the dead;[17] similarly, one of the *symbola* of Pythagoras forbids us to look back even when we leave our own home because we might see the Erinyes there on the threshold, divinities who are best left unseen.[18] In short, the act of returning the gaze is essentially equivalent to what Malinowski and Jakobson have termed the "phatic function" in language: a way to keep the channel of communication open so that information can be exchanged.[19]

Having finished our digression on the subject of *respicere,* we can now return to Pygmalion and his ivory beloved. The statue has just now awakened, and can see. More importantly, she can meet the eyes of her lover. This simple act is not only a sign of the life that Venus has recently bestowed on the statue: it is also a sign of *love.* Ancient erotic theory considered love to be a force emanating from and penetrating through the eyes. But there is something even more involved here: when looks are exchanged between lovers, love is reciprocated. A love relationship demands precisely this exchange of gazes.[20] The statue awakens and loves because she *returns* the gaze that is turned toward her. With the assistance of Venus, this master craftsman has not only roused the miracle of life, but that of love.

The Story of Anaxarete

But if we journey now to the island of Cyprus, we will find that the story told there takes a different turn entirely. In fact, we might say it takes an opposite turn, describing what happens when a woman refuses to meet her lover's gaze. As a result, the heroine of this story meets a fate exactly the reverse of Pygmalion's beloved: she is turned *into* a statue. In the previous story, Venus transformed a charming and flawless statue into an actual woman able to return the longing gaze of her lover. But in this case, the story involves a cruel young woman who refuses to return the gaze of her lover, even when he is on the verge of killing himself, desperate for her love. Venus will intervene in this affair as well, but now she is angry, and transforms the heartless woman into a statue. Once again, we owe the story to Ovid.[21]

Iphis, a young man of Cyprus from a humble family, has fallen in love with Anaxarete, a direct descendant of the hero Teucer, the legendary founder of Salamis. In Antoninus Liberalis's version of the story, this difference in the status of the two lovers is strongly emphasized: Iphis is specifically said to belong to the Phoenician population of Cyprus, thus making the wedding that he so desperately desires even more improbable.[22] But we will follow Ovid's version here, which is more concerned with the story itself than with its sociological undercurrents. Madly infatuated with Anaxarete, Iphis has lost his wits and his reason. He visits Anaxarete's house as a suppliant, adorning the threshold with garlands bathed in his own tears. He spends his nights stretched out on the steps in front of her house, cursing the locks and bolts on the door. But we should not be fooled by the elegiac behavior of this *exclusus amator*. Unlike Propertius or the Ovid we meet in the *Amores*—equally *exclusi*, equally dedicated to the *paraklausithyron* and its nocturnal maledictions—Iphis will not be able to console his heartsick melancholy by making it the subject of elegiac distichs, nor will he be able to drown his sorrows in carefree revels with other women. Iphis is really and truly afflicted with love. But Anaxarete is deaf to all his pleas, harder than iron, "more obdurate even than rock with roots of living stone," *durior . . . et saxo, quod adhuc vivum radice tenetur.* She scorns her devoted admirer, mocking him with proud and pitiless words that shatter the dearest possession of every lover: hope. This Iphis is no Propertius, much less an Ovid—rejected by his beloved, he intends in all seriousness to kill himself. Alone, outside the door of Anaxarete's house, he shouts the following words, which will prove to be his last:[23]

> "Vincis, Anaxarete, neque erunt tibi taedia tandem
> ulla ferenda mei. . . .
> Vincis enim, moriorque libens, age ferrea, gaude!
> certe aliquid laudare mei cogeris amoris,
> quo tibi sim gratus, meritumque fatebere nostrum.
> Non tamen ante tui cura excessisse memento
> quam vitam, geminaque simul mihi luce carendum est.
> Nec tibi fama mei ventura est nuntia leti;
> ipse ego, ne dubites, adero praesensque videbor,
> corpore ut exanimi crudelia lumina pascas.
> Si tamen, o superi, mortalia facta videtis,
> este mei memores. Nihil ultra lingua precari
> sustinet. . . ."
> Dixit et ad postes ornatos saepe coronis
> umentes oculos et pallida bracchia tollens
> cum foribus laqueis religaret vincla summis
> "haec tibi serta placent, crudelis et impia!" dixit
> inseruitque caput, sed tum quoque versus ad illam,
> atque onus infelix elisa fauce pependit.

"You have won, Anaxarete! At last you will no longer have to suffer the tedium that I inflict on you. . . . You have won, and I die gladly. Go on, heartless creature, rejoice in your victory! Yet you will have to admit that something in my love pleases you; you will have to confess that I have some merit. Remember, my love for you came to a stop only with my life, and thus I am deprived, simultaneously, of those two lights. And it will not be rumor that comes to you as a messenger of my death; I myself, you can be sure, I will be there, and you will see me

fully present so that you can sate your cruel eyes on my lifeless body.
O immortal gods, if truly you observe the deeds of men, do not forget me!" His tongue cannot manage to say more. . . . And turning his
weeping eyes and pale arms to the doorposts (so often decorated by his
garlands), he tied a noose to the top of the door and said, "O cruel and
wicked woman, are these the garlands that bring you pleasure?" Then,
having wound the noose around his neck, but always turning himself
in her direction, he hung there, strangled by the throat, a miserable
burden.

The macabre tolling of Iphis's feet against the wooden doorposts alerts
the servants to what has happened, and they come running to release
the desperate lover from his noose. But they are too late; Iphis is already dead.

The young man was fatherless, leaving only his mother to receive his
remains, after having lamented her misfortune as mothers are wont to
lament.[24] The bereft mother then sadly leads the funeral procession
slowly through the city streets. But this is all part of a story, of course,
and as chance would have it (*forte,* as Ovid says), the procession passes
near the house of Anaxarete, where the divine forces of vengeance are
already preparing the young woman's doom:[25]

> "Tamen videamus," ait, "miserabile funus,"
> et patulis scandit tectum sublime fenestris,
> vixque bene impositum lecto prospexerat Iphin,
> deriguere oculi, calidusque e corpore sanguis
> inducto pallore fugit, conataque retro
> ferre pedes haesit, conataque avertere vultus
> hoc quoque non potuit, paulatimque occupat artus
> quod fuit in duro iam pridem pectore saxum.

> "Let us observe," she said, "this pitiable funeral." And she went all the
> way upstairs, where the windows were open. But no sooner had she
> cast a glance [*prospicere*] at Iphis's body, arranged upon the bier, than
> her eyes grew stiff, and the warm blood departed from her pale limbs.
> She tried to turn back, but her feet were stuck; she tried to turn her
> face aside, but could not even do that. And gradually her limbs were
> taken over by that stone which had long lodged in her hardened heart.

As Ovid himself tells us, this is the *aition* of the Venus Prospiciens of
Salamis: a statue that casts a glance, that looks into the distance as the
Latin epithet tells us.[26] This Venus Prospiciens glances into the distance,
and the goddess is always depicted (as we will see shortly) gazing from
the window that frames this enigmatic scene.[27] In Ovid's poem, Anaxa-

rete is also caught in the frame of the house's open window (*patulis fe-nestris*), as she glances at the unfortunate Iphis (*prospicit Iphin*). The Ovidian metamorphosis thus involves the woman as the story imagines her, but also as she is represented in the iconographic tradition: the *aition* is absolutely precise and the image unfolds appropriately.

But in Greek descriptions of this woman's gaze (or rather, the gaze of this goddess of Cyprus), we find a quite curious word used in place of the Latin *prospiciens:* the Greek Aphrodite of Salamis is specifically said to be *parakyptousa*.[28] Likewise, when Antoninus Liberalis tells the story of the cruel young woman's metamorphosis into the goddess, he uses a related word: *ekkyptousa*.[29] The meaning of the Greek verb *para-kyptein* is to "peek" or "wink" at something, and *ekkyptein* also means to "peek." So in Antoninus Liberalis, the young woman (and likewise the statue of Aphrodite produced by the woman's petrification) does not "cast a glance at Iphis," *prospicit Iphin,* as we read in Ovid; instead, she "peeks," she "sneaks a look," as if she were a spy. To make things worse, she acts out of arrogance, *hybris,* wanting only to take a peek at the corpse of her infatuated victim, heedlessly satisfying her cruel curiosity.[30] But even though Ovid uses a different verb, his Anaxarete acts in much the same way: she decides to look at her unfortunate lover only when there is nothing left of him but a corpse, a *miserabile funus.* Her glance, *prospiciens,* encompasses him as he lies on the bier, *bene imposi-tum lecto.*[31] It is only the funeral parade, and the wretched young man's remains, that (finally) attract her scornful attention.

The fact is that this heartless woman never looked at her admirer before; she never returned his imploring gaze, refusing to have any contact with him whatsoever. She looks at him only in death, and even then she only peeks at him, casting a quick and furtive glance. In every way, this is the opposite of love.

It is also the opposite of Iphis, who, as Ovid tells us, passionately longed for that gaze. Indeed, this is what Iphis says about himself, as he insistently tells Anaxarete that his death will be "present." It will not come in the form of a messenger's speech telling of his suicide, as we might find in a tragedy, for example. No, Iphis exclaims, "I myself, you can be sure, I will be there," and in this way Anaxarete will be able to sate "her cruel eyes" upon the sight of his lifeless body. The lover has tied his last hope to a completely desperate strategy: although he could not get Anaxarete to look at him while he was alive, he will at least manage to do so in death. Suicide is the price for obtaining her gaze—and it is a price that Iphis is willing to pay. So when he winds that noose around his neck, he "turns himself in her direction," still hoping for that gaze, if only at the moment of his death. The lover still longs for his gaze to be returned, so he keeps his *lumina* always turned toward the beloved. Admittedly, his eyes will be empty when she finally looks in his direction, but this does not matter. The myth of Iphis is a *myth of the gaze*, a story of the gaze of love.

But Anaxarete has aroused Venus's wrath; this disdainful woman has gone too far. She does not return her lover's gaze even when he is ready to sacrifice his life in return for that favor. Prompted by *hybris,* Anaxarete does finally "peek," she "casts a glance" from the window to see the funeral, "looking out" at the moment when her lover, now dead, is utterly unable to meet her gaze. Then she wants to turn her eyes aside, but she suddenly cannot. She is unable to turn aside; she has to look, her eyes are locked in place. Her feet have also taken root on the spot, frozen in place; she can no longer back away from the window. Anaxarete, in short, has become a statue. The fixed gaze and fixed feet are exactly the opposite of Daedalus's mythical creations, those statues that could both look around and run away. The cruel young woman who refused the reciprocity of the gaze of love has finally acquired the fixed gaze of a marble statue.

Of course, it is often the case that ancient stories are even more ancient than they appear to be, and the creases of their past history can conceal adventures, turmoil, and all sorts of sundry circumstances, as well as unexpected ironies. Indeed, Anaxarete's story has this air of irony about it, as we will see if we consider it somewhat more closely. Given its eastern location, the island of Cyprus was no stranger to the so-called "woman at the window," a type of iconographic representation connected with the cult of Astarte, in which a woman with an elegant coiffure and large eyes is shown *en face,* enclosed in a frame shaped like a window (see Fig. 4). Only her face is visible; the rest of her body is hidden by a balustrade of wrought columns.[32] Thus, the Venus Prospiciens of Ovid, and the Aphrodite Parakyptousa of the Greek sources, should be situated in this wider religious horizon. This Graeco-Roman goddess is not the aetiological product of a single story, but is actually a manifestation (one of many) derived from a profoundly influential and widespread Near Eastern cult.[33] But there is something even more curious. This cult of the goddess at the window was apparently connected to the practice of sacred prostitution.[34] And in effect, if we leave aside the Ovidian terminology (the *prospicere* of his Anaxarete at the window, and the resulting Venus Prospiciens),[35] our Greek sources apparently reinforce this connection to sacred prostitution, given that *parakyptein* (as in the Aphrodite Parakyptousa of Salamis) is precisely the word used in Greek to describe the inviting wink, the alluring gaze that the prostitute uses to draw a man toward her.[36] Moreover, the iconographic representations that we possess of this "woman at the window" make it easy to imagine how she might strongly attract the observer's attention with her flirtatious wink, that look of someone who wants to see and be seen. Thus, before being cast as a cruel and disdainful mortal, Ovid's Anaxarete in the window was once affiliated with a powerful love goddess: not someone who would *refuse* the gaze of love (deigning to look only upon the corpse of her admirer), but a sacred prostitute who would wink at her admirer, returning his gaze and even actively making contact with him, initiating that reciprocal gaze of amorous seduction. This is the sort of surprising irony that ancient stories can unwittingly conceal. Ovid's Iphis died for a woman who, in another time, and in another civilization, would not only have been delighted to return his gaze but who would have been the first to wink at him, a sign that she wanted to share her gaze with him, and her love.

But how did it happen that this prostitute, so lavish with her gazes, later acquired the role of a disdainful young woman? How was the seductive wink of Astarte's priestess transformed into that supreme act of *hybris,* that furtive and cruel glance at the funeral of a man who had killed himself for the sake of her love? The question is difficult to answer, and the hypotheses previously advanced by various scholars do not appear to be very helpful.[37] We would probably have to ask the Venus Prospiciens herself to account for the shifting beliefs that her enigmatic appearance in the window frame provoked as the centuries passed. Somehow over the course of time, that unchanging image was able to produce a new type of story. Those who contemplated, or worshipped, this depiction of the goddess eventually found themselves facing a figure that lacked any plot or motivation. But such a lack is bound to prompt a story sooner or later, leading to the invention of Anaxarete and her Iphis.

But we should stick to the one story that we do possess: that is, the story of Anaxarete and the gaze that was denied when it should have been returned, the gaze cast from the window when it would have been better not to look out from the window at all. This is the gaze that, in Ovid's version, remains permanently turned outward, looking forever into the distance: Venus Prospiciens. Anaxarete has by now become a statue that wants to turn its gaze elsewhere ("she tried to turn her face aside") but finds herself unable to do so.[38] She is frozen there, *prospiciens*, because the stone has locked even her eyes in place, and she can no longer refuse her gaze to anyone. As we said earlier, the Ovidian myth of Iphis and Anaxarete is a myth of the gaze. But why this casting glance, this looking into the distance, this Latin *prospicere*? It is scarcely credible that Ovid chose this word as a merely mechanical (and, for that matter, mistaken) translation of the Greek epithet *parakyptousa*.[39] If Ovid had wanted to speak of a Latin Aphrodite who peeps or who winks, he would have had at his disposal all the necessary linguistic means to do so.[40] But Ovid chose differently, and instead made his Anaxarete/Venus glance into the distance, her gaze turned outwards, forward, *prospiciens*. In Ovid the myth has become purely a story in which the reciprocity of love is denied, gazes are not exchanged, and instead the woman who looks into the distance is finally turned into a statue, all for refusing to meet her lover's eyes. We should probably look for the sense of this odd Latin *prospiciens* in the immeasurably great distance that divided the ancient cult of Astarte from the new meaning that the story assumes in Ovid's *Metamorphoses*.

We cannot ever hope to enter the heart of a statue, of course, but we might now be better able to understand something about its eyes. We already know that the marvelous creations of Daedalus were actually able to see; the statues of no other artist possessed a similar ability. But thanks to the imagination of paradoxical lovers (especially those paradoxical lovers infected with rhetoric, as we saw in Aristaenetus and Onomarchus), it was possible for an image to have a seductive gaze—although Pygmalion was the only one such lover who was lucky enough to exchange gazes with his beloved.[41] This is because, as a rule, statues cannot look back, they cannot *respicere*, returning the observer's gaze: this is something only living creatures can do.[42] And the inevitable fixedness that characterizes the eyes of a statue was such a natural and obvious feature of the image that it acquired a paradigmatic force. Thus, when Xenophon wanted to describe the incredible reserve that characterized the behavior of the young Spartan men who never returned the loving gazes turned in their direction, he compared them to statues: "It would be easier to attract the gaze of a bronze statue than to attract the gaze of those Spartans."[43] These young men famously refuse any form of contact, they cannot *respicere*, and in this, as Xenophon observes, they are no different from statues.

This, I think, is precisely why Ovid's Venus is described as *prospiciens*. The statue of the goddess of Cyprus has a gaze, but it is fixed, turned forwards, looking into the distance. The cruel Anaxarete, who did not want to *respicere* her lover when he was alive, and who only agreed to look at him when the light of his eyes was forever extinguished, now has the gaze of a statue: a fixed gaze, *prospiciens.* Ovid's Anaxarete / Venus—a character in a story, an image made out of words—is a figure of myth but also of language. Created by grammar and linguistic morphology, she relies on an elegant game of verbal prefixes, the substitution of a *pro-* for a *re-.* If the gaze of Anaxarete had been *re-spiciens,* for even just one moment, Iphis would not have had to die—but that of course would have put an end to the story.

14

Respect

In his oration concerning the statues of Rhodes, Dio
Chrysostom asks (not without sarcasm) why it is that the statues of
great men are not simply made of clay, an inexpensive material and
easier to work with than marble or bronze.[1] The answer, of course,
is that the statues are meant "not only as a sign of respect, but also
so that the honors awarded to great men will last forever, if possible." But, as the orator further explains, the statues of Rhodes are
even less durable than statues made of wax—not because they melt in
the sun, but because the citizens of Rhodes are always seeking to
flatter or placate someone or other. A magistrate has only to find it
convenient to get rid of someone's memory . . . and lo and behold,
the great men of the past cease to exist. But the citizens of Rhodes
nevertheless keep on dedicating statues in much the same way as
fathers continue to buy dolls for their children, knowing full well
that there will be something to cry over when those dolls eventually
break.

The poor images. After they have been manufactured and consigned
to the flux of material things, they suddenly become the subjects
of human caprice. Like dolls in the hands of small children, sooner or
later they end up in pieces, carelessly shattered or, even worse, dis-
graced.[2] A sad situation, as one can imagine, sometimes even worth crying over.

The Image Touches the Person

This is why the images must be treated with respect, which is exactly what Lysias demands in his oration *Against Andocides,* attacking that infamous Athenian orator for his role in the smashing of the herms.[3] "Something must be done!" Lysias insists. "After all, when a person wounds another person in some part of his body—in the head or the face, the hands or the feet—the laws of the Areopagus compel that man to leave the city of his victim and to pay for his crime by death if he ever dares to return. What then if someone injures the statues of the gods? Should we not exclude him from their sanctuaries and punish him for his crime?"[4] Justice for the images. As material that has been shaped in human form (or for that matter, in the form of a god), the images are effectively involved in legal relationships, with corresponding rights and obligations; the images have a legal status.[5] But instead of discussing institutions, we will begin with the behavior of some exemplary individuals who—out of actual respect, or madness, or superstition—were willing to defend the images' dignity, and to insist that others do so as well.

Tiberius, for example, was known to prosecute crimes of lèse-majesté with extraordinary severity; for example, it was considered a punishable offense "to take a coin or a ring bearing Augustus's image inside a brothel or latrine."[6] Tiberius here displays a clear awareness of the bond between an image and its referent: even the tiny image on a coin was still closely linked to the person of the deceased emperor, which meant that to take this image inside an impure place was insulting to Augustus, and to his successor Tiberius as well. There are many other bizarre anecdotes about Tiberius's concern with the possible defilement of images, such as the story of a praetor named Paulus, who once arrived at a banquet wearing a large ring adorned with a cameo of Tiberius. But at a certain moment he needed to make use of the chamber pot (Seneca, our source for this story, says that it would be ridiculous to speak about the facts of life with euphemisms, and rightfully so)[7]—but when Paulus lifted that chamber pot up off the ground, a certain Maro, one of the most notorious informers of the time, did not fail to notice the gesture. He immediately turned to the other guests at the banquet and announced that "the image of the emperor had been put next to something indecent," *admotam esse imaginem obscaenis.*[8] It would have been certain doom for poor Paulus, if not for the fact that this ill-fated gesture had also attracted the attention of his faithful servant, who managed to slip the ring off his master's finger immediately before his hand grasped the indecent object. Paulus was thus able to show that the contamination of the image—the fearful *obscenis admoveri*—had luckily not taken place after all.[9]

In his biography of the emperor, Suetonius provides various other examples of Tiberius's odd esteem for the images.[10] Woe to the person who removed a head from a statue of Augustus in order to replace it with another one; woe to the person who disrobed or changed clothes where the statue could see him, or who stripped and flogged a slave in view of the statue. The perpetrators of these and similar crimes were guilty of lèse-majesté, much like the person condemned for defiling the *effigies* of Augustus (in the form of a ring, or a coin) by taking it inside some unclean place. In Tiberius's mind, the image of Augustus commanded the same respect as its referent.

Augustus's successor was apparently somewhat obsessed in this regard, and there is often a brute physicality, a vaguely offensive whiff of the repressed that seems to pervade the stories about Tiberius and the images. The brothel, the latrine, or the chamber pot; the nudity of the person changing his clothes, or the sadistic violence of the person whipping his slave's naked body . . . these are the sorts of things that Tiberius did not want to so much as *touch* his image or the image of Augustus. But how to account for Tiberius's squeamishness in these matters? And what might have caused him to imagine precisely these particular combinations, with their elements arrayed in such prescriptive detail? Moreover, we should not forget that this is the same Tiberius who fell madly in love with Parrhasius's painting of an Archigallus (that is, one of the chiefs of the Galli, those lascivious devotees of Cybele), paying a price of six million sesterces for that work of art which he then kept locked away in the privacy of his bedroom.[11] Another painting by Parrhasius also ended up in Tiberius's bedroom: a study of the passion of Meleager and Atalanta drawn in such remarkably lurid detail that the wealthy Roman to whom the painting originally belonged was afraid Tiberius would find the work offensive (indeed, this timid citizen even anticipated in his will that the emperor might prefer to receive a bequest of one million sesterces in place of that obscene work of art).[12] The accumulation of pornography in Tiberius's bedroom is a fitting prelude, of course, to the debaucheries of his *secessus Caprensis,* when the old emperor, now utterly ravaged by lust and insanity, retired to Capri. There Tiberius busied himself with multiplying the number of bedrooms and decorating them with licentious works of art, while out of doors his erotic fantasies invented various "places of Venus" scattered among the villa's grounds, where young boys and girls dressed as Satyrs and Nymphs would prostitute themselves in the caves and grottoes.[13] Eros thus became a subject for images and set design, while Tiberius's fervor was aroused by (or perhaps required?) the presence of these effigies and figures.

But this topic brings us dangerously close to entering the twisted labyrinths of Tiberius's mind—so we will come to a halt here *in limine,* because that is certainly not a subject we want to consider too closely. Tiberius was perhaps a madman or a neurotic (at least, this is the impression left by the literary persona transmitted in the ancient sources). But in his idiosyncratic regard for the images—his maniacal terror about their possible defilement or violation—there is a profound principle at work, which is not necessarily neurotic at all. Indeed, Tiberius's behavior involves some fundamental elements of the anthropological code, and the meaning that was attributed to the image in its ancient cultural representation. For example, there are a variety of Pythagorean *symbola* that are strangely reminiscent of Tiberius's own prohibitions: "Don't carry the likeness of a god on your finger,"[14] "Don't carry images to a funeral or into any other unclean place,"[15] "Don't expose an image to any possible contamination."[16] The similarity between these precepts and Tiberius's own personal obsessions is so specific as to be almost disconcerting. The Pythagorean maxims even have the same *contents* as the emperor's idiosyncrasies—providing yet further confirmation of the way in which peculiar mannerisms, nervous tics, and other quite private neuroses are often reproduced in common superstitions and folk beliefs. In any case, what is important for our purposes here is the message, the basic admonition, underlying each of these examples: one must always treat the images with respect.

The motivation for the protective aura surrounding the images seems to depend on the implicit or explicit conviction that there is a strong and intimate bond between the image and its referent. Dio Chrysostom (as we saw earlier) compared the relationship between an image and its referent to that between a wife and her husband.[17] Obviously, a wife deserves respect, and if she is insulted, her husband is insulted too.

But in addition to respect for other people's images, a complementary behavior is also involved: a concern for the image of oneself. Scribonius Largus, a doctor of the first century C.E., wrote a dedicatory letter for his *Compositiones* in which he complains that very little attention is ever paid to the selection of a doctor, whereas a portrait painter is chosen only after long and careful deliberation:[18] "It happens only rarely that people diligently consider the doctor's capabilities before entrusting themselves or their loved ones to his care, but no one entrusts his image to a painter without having first put that painter to the test several times before commissioning a work from him." To be reproduced in an image is a serious matter, and each person selects his painter with considerable care and attention. With his scientific assumptions, Scribonius finds it hard to understand why people would be more diligent in choosing a painter than in choosing a doctor, but such behavior makes perfect sense in the context of our fundamental story. The portrait *exposes* its referent; it replicates the person and puts his features into circulation even in his absence: no wonder he wants to find an artist who will carry out this delicate operation in the best possible way.[19]

But despite his medical prejudices, it is nevertheless interesting that Scribonius chose to describe the search for the ideal doctor in terms of the ideal portrait painter. The *medium comparationis,* although not explicit, is fully obvious: in both cases, we are dealing with a decision to make someone else the master of our person. Whether as the subject of a painting, or the victim of an illness, the client gives the painter/ doctor a certain control over his body, putting his "self" in someone else's hands. For Scribonius, the painter is only a lesser sort of doctor, the master of physical appearance, but not of the body in all its vitality. Yet if we pause to consider the situation, it is clear that the painter's power should not be taken lightly—especially if one believes in the forces of analogical magic (that is, the power to wound the body of a person by means of that person's image), or if any credit is given to the story of Poe's cruel painter.[20] In either case, the artist, that doctor-of-images, is endowed with a mastery that is even more absolute, and more dangerous, than that enjoyed by the doctor of science.

This close connection between the image and its referent means that images need to be respected, cared for, and protected from all possible insults, as we have seen.[21] Taken one step farther, this connection can actually produce a *solidarity* between the sign and its object, a fundamental awareness that the image is never entirely detached from the person it represents.[22] It is this solidarity between the image and its referent that explains why the eyes of Hiero's statue fell to the ground just before Hiero himself fell at Leuctra, and why Lysander's statue was covered by grass and moss after the battle of Aegospotami.[23] On the Ides of March, an image of Caesar standing in the vestibule of his house spontaneously fell to the ground and shattered just as he was leaving for the Senate.[24] Likewise, when Vitellius marched against his rival Otho, there was a sign that Vitellius's victory would not be long-lived: "The equestrian statues that had been erected in Vitellius's honor in various places suddenly collapsed at the same time, their legs broken."[25] As for the savage Domitian, we know that for several months toward the end of his reign an extraordinarily large number of thunderbolts fell from the sky, signs of an angry Jupiter. Domitian himself finally remarked, "let him strike whom he likes," *feriat iam quem volet!* Domitian's own bedroom was then struck, and the force of the gale blew away an inscription on one of his triumphal statues, depositing it on top of a nearby tomb.[26] This list of prodigies and warnings is potentially endless, of course, without necessarily saying anything new. But what is clear is that the image was thought to represent the person in a fuller and more profound sense than its merely iconic meaning would suggest: the effigy adheres to its referent.[27]

As a substitute, or a close relation, of its referent, the image can also find itself having to suffer the negative aspects of this condition: if the person does not merit respect but instead merits condemnation, then the image can also find itself the victim of taunts and abuse. We saw earlier that the statue of Theagenes was whipped by Theagenes' infuriated rival.[28] Likewise, the statues of the tyrants of Syracuse were forced to appear as defendants in a court of law.[29] A decree from Chios explains that the tyrants of that island were afraid to knock down the statue of the tyrannicide Phylites, but as a precautionary measure they took away his sword (in the same way that they disarmed citizens of Chios whom they considered to pose a threat to their rule).[30] In a manner that is more sophisticated (but substantially still the same), this privileged relationship between the image and the person makes it possible to play a symbolic game with the images, communicating particular meanings or specific messages by manipulating the image's absence (or presence). In a tacit triangulation with the person evoked in the image, the contexts and situations constructed around the image can assume the force of a warning sign, like an alarm or signal. Once again the sheer abundance of examples makes it difficult to choose which ones to cite; because of their elegant symmetry, we can take two examples involving the emperors Galba and Otho. When Galba was on the verge of seizing the empire (but before he learned of Nero's death), he "mounted the tribunal, having assembled in front of it as many portraits as he could find of people condemned or killed by Nero."[31] At the moment of a decisive undertaking, one seeks justification from the images. By being present (if only in effigy), Nero's unfortunate victims were able to provide a guarantee, an incentive, perhaps even a sort of protection for his successor. Otho, on the other hand—a highly suspect figure—agreed at the start of his reign to let the populace address him as Nero, and showed no sign whatsoever of wanting to refuse the appellation. Moreover, he was said to have added the name of Nero to his own cognomen in certain official acts. Worst of all, he "reinstalled the statues and portraits of Nero" that had been previously removed.[32] Otho and Galba thus behaved in exactly opposite ways: for Otho, it was not the victims but the executioner— again in effigy—who gave his auspicious nod to the new regime. The fact that Otho's symbolic game also appropriated Nero's name in addition to his images should come as no surprise; we have already seen several examples of the close connection that unites the name and the image together with their common referent.[33]

Suetonius is obviously an inexhaustible gold mine for these sorts of anecdotes, so much so that it would be tedious to report them all. But in terms of a profound dialogue with the images, in which they are made to convey highly significant and unambiguous messages, surely no one outdid Caligula, who even had a temple erected to the cult of his own divinity: "Inside the temple there was a life-size simulacrum of the emperor made of gold, which every day was dressed in clothes that matched exactly the clothes Caligula was wearing."[34] Making the image and referent exist in simultaneity, Caligula must have felt himself to be not only the emperor, but an actual god. Those clothes, changed every day in conformity with the emperor's apparel, made his living person into a homology of the god, while turning the image into a living statue. The secret relationship of reciprocity between the image and its referent could not be expressed more clearly. Between the person and the statue there is a daily dialogue; moreover, we know that Caligula was in the habit of conferring with the gods on a regular basis: "Each day he spoke in confidence with Jupiter Capitolinus, sometimes whispering in the ear of the god and offering him his own ear in return, sometimes shouting at him, and even insulting him. One time he actually made threats against Jupiter, screaming at him: 'Either you get rid of me, or I'll get rid of you!'"[35] It was a very learned threat, taking the form of a quotation from Homer: but a threat nevertheless.

Indeed, Caligula considered himself to be the master of every image, and thus had "the statues of famous men that Augustus had placed in the Field of Mars knocked down and destroyed, after which he commanded that no images were to be erected in the honor of any living person without his express permission."[36] Caligula clearly recognized the powerful meanings that images could convey, comprehending the deeper significance of their cultural function. (Does it perhaps take a maniacal emperor like Caligula or the debauched Tiberius to fathom the nature of these figures?) Caligula's actions reveal that it is better to have as few statues as possible in circulation; above all, the emperor wanted to decide for himself whether or not a person deserved to be reproduced in this form. Images augment the presence of their referent, whether living or dead, and thus contribute to a fame that Caligula apparently felt should be his alone to enjoy. After this attack on the statues, it was then but a small step to decide that Vergil's and Livy's portraits (along with their books, of course) should be removed from the libraries; Caligula claimed to not like their style.[37]

When the Tyrannicide Is a Woman

But let us resume our discussion of the respect owed to the images. Having finished with the emperors' eccentric (and sometimes profound) follies, we can now turn to the subtleties of ancient Roman rhetoric. Quintilian, in order to illustrate the embarrassing case of two laws that conflict with one another, posed the following dilemma:[38] "The image of a tyrannicide should be placed in the gymnasium; the image of a woman should not be placed in the gymnasium; a woman killed a tyrant." Quintilian then explains the nature of the dilemma: "On no account could the image of a woman be placed in a gymnasium, and on no account could the image of a tyrannicide be removed from the gymnasium." If the statues of tyrannicides are placed in the gymnasium, but the figures of women are not placed there, what is to be done when a woman kills the tyrant? It is clearly a subtle case; as we have seen before, the schools of rhetoric can imagine situations that far surpass the inventions of reality itself.[39] But more than the solution, it is the very structure of this dilemma that interests us here. Just why is it that a woman's image is not to be placed in the gymnasium, *mulieris imago in gymnasio ne ponatur*? What assumptions underlie this unusual prohibition, thus causing such trouble for the rhetorician when the tyrannicide is a woman?

The gymnasium, of course, was considered to be the most exemplary male space. In Plutarch's *Amatorius,* the ironic exhortation to create an upside-down world is expressed in seemingly proverbial terms:[40] "Let's hand the gymnasium and the city council over to the women!" We know, of course, that the gymnasium was adorned with nude statues of spear-bearing ephebes,[41] as well as with statues of athletes.[42] In this exclusively male realm, there was obviously no room for a woman. Indeed, there was no room even for the image of a woman, but this is a somewhat less obvious point. By being placed in the gymnasium, that woman's image would represent something more than a monument; it would introduce into the men's little kingdom a female presence that would be indisputably out of place.

This in turn suggests a very interesting hypothesis: the opposition between the sexes—that archetypal cultural model, whose branches even extend into the gendering of language, with its masculine and feminine pronouns—must also be respected in its manifestation as an image. Perhaps the effigy of a woman placed in the gymnasium might feel insulted by what was taking place in her presence, or perhaps the men would be embarrassed to exercise in front of her. Whatever the case, the prohibition forbids not only the image of one particular woman, but any image of a woman. The whole female group is apparently implicated; the personal dignity of an entire sex would be compromised by any image (the image of any woman) that stands as its representative (a representative whose actual status is, as we have seen, always somewhat enigmatic and mysterious). The prohibition against female images in the gymnasium thus reveals something noteworthy, perhaps even unexpected: the image, understood in terms of its cultural significance, does not involve only a single individual; it can in fact stand for an entire group, an entire social category, embodied in the form of a "person." The image does not function only as a proper noun with a unique identity (Poppaea's effigy, Alcestis's simulacrum) but can serve as a common noun referring to an entire class or group (the statue of a woman, *mulieris imago*).

This sexual prohibition against female images in a male environment also has a counterpart in the Roman cult of the Bona Dea. The rituals of this goddess were rigidly and exclusively reserved for women. No male (human or animal) was allowed to enter into her temple or to be present (even purely by accident) when her *sacra* were being conducted.[43] Needless to say, it caused quite a scandal when Clodius boldly infiltrated Caesar's house during the rites of the Bona Dea, dressed as a woman and intending to commit adultery with Pompeia, the wife of the *paterfamilias*.[44] These anti-male prohibitions were deeply rooted in the cult of this goddess, whose name (as Lactantius explains, citing Varro) could not even be spoken in public.[45] The goddess was not to be seen by men; indeed, she had never been seen by any man at any time. This was the reason why men were not allowed to enter her temple. In short, it was at the sacred rituals of the Bona Dea that *castitas* celebrated its triumph as the quintessential feminine virtue, meaning that any possible male presence had to be avoided. In this context, Juvenal provides some very valuable testimony, explaining that during the rituals of Bona Dea, "any painting that depicted someone of the opposite sex had to be covered with a veil."[46] Seneca confirms this aspect of the cult's exclusively female orientation.[47] "Men are excluded from the sacred grounds with such great severity that all pictures representing male creatures are carefully covered." The presence of men even in the form of an image was prohibited. Once again, an entire sex could violate the social "person" of the opposite sex merely by inserting its own image (his or hers, as the case might be) in a context where the flesh and blood representatives of that same gender were also forbidden.

But it can also be the case that women—those cultural creations whose modesty could be violated even in the form of an image, a figure—might actually turn out to be the greatest possible threat to their own symbolic representations.[48] At least, this is the contention of Juvenal's rabidly misogynistic sixth satire, in which it is the women themselves who make the most offensive possible assault on the goddess of modesty, Pudicitia, the very image that embodies the virtues that were (supposedly) most coveted by the women of Rome. In lurid detail, Juvenal describes two perverse Roman *matronae* as they drunkenly make their way home from a banquet that has lasted long into the night. They pass in front of an ancient altar to the goddess Pudicitia where they order their stretcher bearers to come to a halt. The two women then get down and, in the dark of night,[49]

> Micturiunt hic
> effigiemque deae longis siphonibus implent,
> inque vices equitant ac luna teste moventur,
> inde domos abeunt: tu calcas luce reversa
> coniugis urinam magnos visurus amicos.

> They urinate there, soaking the effigy of the Goddess with long streams of piss. Then they ride one another, moving under the gaze of the moon, and finally arrive home. When the next day dawns, you walk the trail of your wife's piss as you go to visit your powerful friends.

Despite its crudity, there is an important symbolic significance to this little incident. The *pudicitia* of the *matronae,* their feminine modesty, has become so degraded that they insult the very *imago* of that virtue in the most vulgar way imaginable.[50] The disrespect shown to the image is fully explicit, and becomes even more striking if we consider the ancient precept declaring that merely to disrobe in a sacred place is *nefas,* strictly forbidden.[51] Of course, Juvenal was hardly famous for his good taste — and the same can be said of his nefarious Roman *matronae.*

15

Premonition

Chaerea is a lucky young fellow, in the prime of life, vigorous and high-spirited. But imagine him hiding inside someone else's house, draped in robes that are hardly his usual attire, cautious, wary. He has managed to infiltrate the women's quarters, and now he stands there, watching attentively as the slave girls prepare a bath for a beautiful young girl, just sixteen years old, "a very flower," *flos ipsus*, who (naturally enough) shows no sign of shame or embarrassment. Chaerea has in fact been assigned to keep watch over the girl, "staying alone with her while she is alone," *solus cum sola*. Upon receiving such delightful orders, Chaerea realized that it would make a good impression if he lowered his eyes at just that moment, modestly looking down at the ground. Our hero is not only vigorous and high-spirited, but quick-witted as well. No, that is not quite right: we would do better to say that he is assisted by a quick-witted slave whose name says it all—Parmeno, "Old Reliable." When Parmeno saw Chaerea's predicament, he did just what we would expect: the quick-witted slave came to his young master's rescue. Don't you worry, Parmeno promised him, I'll find a way to get you inside that house so that you can visit your sweetheart (the sixteen-year-old girl, that "flower" of youth). In fact, Parmeno continued, they happen to be delivering a new slave to that house this very day and, even better, he's a eunuch; so all you have to do is take his place, wearing the appropriate disguise, and you will effortlessly reach the very heart of the fortress without having had to strike so much as a blow.

Two Stories from Roman Comedy

And just as effortlessly, we have reached the very heart of
the plot: it is Terence's *Eunuchus,* of course, which is surely one of the
poet's most appealing comedies. In this case Terence's inclination to
sentimental refinement and philosophizing cannot obscure the vivid romantic fiction of a recognizably Plautine plot. The resulting text is filled
with life: so let us return to our hero Chaerea, the false *eunuchus* of the
play's title, now ensconced in the very bedroom of the lovely girl, giving orders to the slaves, telling them to get on with their tasks and finish
as quickly as possible. Chaerea later confides the details of his adventure
to another young man, his friend Antipho: [1]

> Dum adparatur, virgo in conclavi sedet
> suspectans tabulam quandam pictam: ibi inerat pictura haec, Iovem
> quo pacto Danaen misisse aiunt quondam in gremium imbrem aureum.
> Egomet quoque id spectare coepi, et quia consimilem luserat
> iam olim ille ludum, impendio magis animus gaudebat mihi,
> deum sese in hominem convortisse atque in alienas tegulas
> venisse clanculum per impluvium fucum factum mulieri.
> At quem deum! "qui templa caeli summa sonitu concutit."
> ego homuncio hoc non facerem? ego illud vero ita feci—ac lubens.

While they are getting her ready, the girl sits in her room looking up at
a painting, a picture of Jupiter, when he sent that golden shower into
Danae's lap. I also began to look at it, and because he had played such
a trick long ago, my spirit rejoiced all the more: a god had changed
himself into a man and had secretly climbed up on someone else's roof,
making his way along the gutter, with the intention of seducing a
woman. And what a god! "He shakes the lofty heights of heaven with
his thunderbolt!" [*qui templa caeli summa sonitu concutit*]. And should
I, a miniscule human, not do the same? Indeed, I had done exactly that,
and gladly.

Like an emblem or narrative symbol, the picture is fixed upon the bedroom wall, and its depiction of the god's cunning trickery reflects the
amorous episode that is now taking place there in the very same bedroom. This figurative ricochet is both ironic and amusing. The literary
irony is actually very specific: this lofty adulterer is described with words
(also undeniably lofty) that have been lifted from a tragedy by Ennius,
that *pater* of Roman poetry who never would have expected to find
himself implicated in such a risqué affair.[2] But Ennius can rest in peace,
so to speak, because the comedy will of course come to a happy and

honest conclusion, a final resolution that arrives with the reassuring punctuality that is characteristic of Roman Comedy in general. Even though Chaerea's trick comes close to violating the rules of sexual conduct, this amorous mise-en-scène will not end in a sexual crime: the girl will in fact be recognized as an Athenian citizen, and thus able to marry her lover Chaerea.[3] But for the time being, Chaerea is understandably encouraged by the painting of Jupiter's sexual prowess: the painting, daubed with splendid colors, supplies the young man with a painted premonition of his own expectations of the future. Even before Chaerea arrived on the scene, his love story was already unfolding right there on the bedroom wall.

If we turn to Plautus's *Mostellaria,* another example of the light-hearted world of Roman Comedy, we find a young man again in difficult straits, more strictly economic than erotic: Philolaches has frittered away the family fortune during the absence of his father, Theopropides, and it is now time to pay back the money he had to borrow from a loan shark. But all of a sudden Theopropides comes back home: a hopeless situation. Except that Tranio, Philolaches' faithful and quick-witted slave, instantaneously invents a fantastic explanation. We borrowed the money to buy the house next door, he says, the one belonging to Simo (an old man, a *senex,* like Theopropides), a bargain at twice the price. So Tranio is busily spouting whole heaps of nonsense to Theopropides on the one hand and to Simo on the other; the beauty of it is that he is telling entirely different stories (both of them utter fictions) to each of the old men simultaneously. So Tranio tells Theopropides that they have purchased Simo's house at an unbeatable price, and now he is about to give Theopropides a guided tour of his property; meanwhile, to justify this tour of the house, he tells Simo that Theopropides is so impressed by the design of his neighbor's house that he wants to remodel his own house to look exactly like it, if Simo will be so kind as to let them take a closer look around. So there they are, the three of them, standing in front of Simo's house, each of Tranio's victims believing his own false version of the truth, with Tranio the master of them both. But simply to trick the old men is too easy: Tranio wants to reveal himself, to make a show of his own cunning virtuosity. But even as he discloses the real truth of the story, he does so with such artfully crafted metaphors that the foolish old men still understand nothing at all—thus making them appear doubly ridiculous.

"The more I look around," Theopropides says, "the more I like it." He is very satisfied with his supposed purchase. But he still has not seen the best part of all:[4]

TH.: Ut quidquid magis contemplo, tanto magis placet.

TR.: Viden pictum ubi ludificat una cornix volturios duos?

TH.: Non edepol video.

TR.: At ego video; nam inter volturios duos cornix astat, ea volturios duo vicissim vellicat. Quaeso, huc ad me specta, cornicem ut conspicere possies. Iam vides?

TH.: Profecto nullam equidem illam cornicem intuor.

TR.: At tu isto ad vos optuere, quoniam cornicem nequis conspicari, si volturios forte possis contui.

TH.: Omnino, ut te absolvam, nullam pictam conspicio hic avem.

TR.: Age, iam mitto; ignosco; aetate non quis optuerier.

> *Theo.:* The more I look around, the more I like it.
>
> *Tranio:* And do you see the picture there, where a crow is playing a trick [*ludificat*] on two vultures?
>
> *Theo.:* No, by Pollux, I don't see it.
>
> *Tranio:* But I see it. There is a crow standing between two vultures, plucking the two vultures in turn. Come on, look in my direction if you want to see the crow. Do you see it now?
>
> *Theo.:* No, indeed, I do not see any crow at all.
>
> *Tranio:* Then look that way, in your direction, if you cannot see the crow, at least you might see the vultures.
>
> *Theo.:* Honestly, I do not see any painted bird.
>
> *Tranio:* Well, that's too bad, but I forgive you: it's your age that prevents you from seeing it.

Naturally this painting, a verbal picture created by the inventive slave, does not exist, which makes the deception all the more pitiless. The trick by itself is not enough; a premonition is also required. In the very house that the *senex* Theopropides thinks he has bought (and that the *senex* Simo has no knowledge whatsoever of having sold), right there on the wall—in Tranio's words—it was already possible to see everything that was going to happen: the two old vultures deceived by the cunning crow.[5] The trick was prefigured, foreshadowed . . . and inescapable. In the absence of a real premonition, Plautus simply invents one, painted in Tranio's words at a moment's notice.

The Image as Perfection

The painted image thus has the force of a revelation; it discloses something that would otherwise remain hidden. The painter Apelles and the Egyptian king Ptolemy were not on the best of terms, but a storm at sea (with its wicked sense of humor) once compelled the famous artist to seek refuge in the port of Alexandria.[6] Apelles was immediately approached by Ptolemy's court jester, who pretended to deliver an official invitation to dinner at the palace (but this false messenger had been suborned, in fact, by the great painter's enemies). When Apelles arrived, Ptolemy was indignant and asked him to point out which servant assigned to deliver the invitations had given him the message. Of course, the jester was nowhere to be seen, but this did not trouble Apelles. Having asked for a piece of coal, he began to draw on a wall a sketch of the trickster who had lured him into this trap. Apelles made quick work of it, and after just a few deft strokes of the charcoal, Ptolemy recognized his jester. Ctesicles found himself in a similar situation when he was very rudely received by Queen Stratonice and, like Apelles, he found in his exceptional artistic talent a perfect means of revenge.[7] The offended Ctesicles decided to paint the queen's tryst with a fisherman (said to have been her lover), and to then have the painting prominently exhibited in the port of Ephesus while he himself boarded a ship that swiftly carried him away to safety.[8] But because Ctesicles' painting was so well executed, and the likeness of the figures depicted there was so extraordinary, Stratonice ordered that the painting should remain on display, securing a double victory for the painter's vendetta.

But there is more at stake here than the realistic accuracy of these painters' efforts.[9] These sorts of stories suggest that the painted image is actually endowed with the power to reveal how things really are; in an elegant paradox, the painted image itself tears aside the veil of fiction. This is because, in a more general sense, the image is an embodiment of perfection, possessed of an indisputable certainty (moral or physical); it is therefore no surprise to discover that truth—the real truth, a truth above and beyond the dissembling tricks and fictions practiced by mankind—is to be found there in the image, rather than in the banal appearance of reality. Returning to the world of Roman Comedy, we can find many other examples of the truth value of the image, especially the painted image. This is because Plautus, in marked contrast with Plato's rejection of the figurative arts, was convinced that images could be more true and perfect than truth itself (for better or worse, Plautus was blissfully ignorant of Plato). So, if a young woman is beautiful, absolutely beautiful, Plautus observes: "Isn't it like looking at a beautifully painted picture?"[10] And if there is someone who has the exact appearance of an *amator*, unmistakably so, then Plautus remarks: "If you have ever seen a picture of a lover, then you know exactly what he looks like!"[11] But it is not only a matter of external appearance; it is even possible for moral perfection, a perfection of feeling, to take the form of a picture in Plautus. At the end of the *Poenulus,* for example, when Agorastocles experiences the heartwarming recognition that finally resolves the intricacies of the complicated plot, he joyfully exclaims:[12]

> O Apelle, o Zeuxis pictor,
> cur numero estis mortui, hoc exemplo ut pingeretis?
> Nam alios pictores nihil moror huiusmodi tractare exempla.

> O Apelles, O Zeuxis the painter, why did you both die before being able to paint this subject? Because I would not have any other painters treat a subject of this sort.

To depict a recognition, and above all the feeling of well-merited justice that it provokes, is no easy task, and would require the talents of a Zeuxis or an Apelles.[13] But Plautus not only considers such a scene to be completely "paintable," he even insists that it *should* be painted, precisely because it is so moral and just. The picture is not a bad imitation of reality: quite the opposite. It is manifest perfection, rendering the truth even more worthy of being true.

With its metaphors and similes, Plautus's language itself provides additional evidence for this popular philosophy of painting as it develops in Roman Comedy. Plautus makes frequent use of one word in particular, and in a distinctively Plautine way: the adjective *graphicus,* and its adverbial form, *graphice.*[14] The basic meaning of this Graecism should be "having to do with painting" or "pictorial," but in Plautus it never has this meaning. Instead, Plautus uses these two words with a rather sly nuance, to indicate everything that appears (in this world of tricksters and happy scoundrels) to be perfect, right on the mark, or to describe someone who is cocksure and completely confident in whatever he does. If somebody is going to get tricked, it needs to be done *graphice;*[15] if an old man pulls off a good stunt, he is *graphicus,*[16] as is the slave who lives up to his roguish responsibilities.[17] And a thief able to steal the rug right out from under your feet is a *graphicus fur.*[18] *Graphicus,* "(as if) painted," indicates perfection, exactly the kind of perfection required by the carefree comic world of the Roman *palliata.* If we recall Tranio's ingenious invention[19]—his painted crow plucking the two vultures— we now see that the trick he has played on the old men here is precisely *graphice* or, to borrow a phrase used elsewhere in Plautus, Tranio *graphice ludificabat.*[20] The linguistic metaphor is conjoined with actual fact: it was a perfect trick on Tranio's part to simulate that painting, *graphice* in every sense of the word.[21] Plato and his aesthetic misgivings are thus completely alien to the *graphicus* design of Roman Comedy.[22] Despite the quibbles of philosophers, the image clearly *is* perfection in the world of Plautus and Terence, and also in the world of artists' anecdotes. The image is able to represent reality in its fullest form; moreover, the image can also function as a premonition, anticipating or prefiguring a reality that has yet to unfold. One would naturally expect that these two aspects of the image must be related to one another: precisely because it contains the truest, most perfect part of the represented subject, the image is contextually able to access this same dimension of truth as it exists in the future. To get a better sense of this effect, we can consider some further examples of the precursory power possessed by the image.

In some cases, for instance, the premonition disclosed by an image can be as solid as rock: when Galba was building fortifications around his base camp (just on the verge of seizing control of the empire), a ring was unearthed, "of ancient make, with an engraved stone that showed Victory bearing a trophy."[23] This image from the past was sending a message to the present, providing a reflection of current events. Galba will win; it is revealed in the image. On the eve of Vespasian's triumph over Judaea (and his conquest of the empire) we find an even stranger example of the premonitory image: at exactly the same period of time, a sacred site at Tegea in Arcadia was being excavated as ordered by the soothsayers, "and some ancient vases were discovered there, one of which depicted an image greatly resembling Vespasian."[24] In the iconographic heritage of the world, Vespasian was already there, and this forecast in the form of an image reinforced his destiny, bestowing the power of the past on the future that awaited him. An artist, at some unknown time, had already depicted the advent of the emperor; he had somehow seen it all, in advance. In the form of images, both people and events can supposedly exist somewhere else before they come to be as they are now, before they actually happen. Such a belief clearly parallels the conviction that the images, before they have been sculpted or created, can already exist, fully formed inside the material in which they are lodged. Pliny, for example, tells the story of a little statue of Silenus that was discovered inside a block of stone when it was split with a wedge.[25] The images that surround us are even more numerous than we suspected, and they are often trying to warn us of something, the harbingers of a sinister fate.

On the occasion of Pompey's third triumph, for example, a head of the great leader made entirely of pearls was put on parade, which Pliny thought was a disagreeable extravagance:[26] "Great Pompey, how could you have your face [*voltus*] rendered in pearls, which are ridiculously expensive and set aside for women, and which, moreover, it would be wrong for you to wear yourself?" That head of pearls was a serious disgrace, "if indeed it should not be considered a cruel sign revealing the wrath of the gods: Pompey's head had already been put on display without the rest of his body, surrounded with oriental splendor." Pliny's meaning is clear: that triumphal parade anticipated Pompey's beheading, a premonition—in the form of an image—of his eventual beheading in Egypt. But Pompey, alas, did not recognize the warning in time.

With its rigid perfection, the image is envisioned as a prototype, the outline of an event (or of a fact of life) that sooner or later will actually take shape in reality. Employing a metaphor that would prove very dear to the language of Christian writers, we could say that the image foreshadows the future, that it is a "shadow of things to come," an *umbra futuri*,[27] as when Augustine says that Solomon *per umbram futuri* foretold the coming of Christ.[28] Like the long shadow (with its imprecise, unfocused image) of an event that as yet eludes our gaze, the image anticipates in a figural form what is about to take place—or having been retrojected backwards in a vortex of time (perhaps over thousands of years), the *umbra futuri* may anticipate something that is happening right before our eyes, an ancient prefiguration of current events. This seems to be the reason why mirrors are able to adumbrate the image of future events. In the mirror's reflection, the image of an event comes before the event itself—a reduplication (in the form of an image or a reflection) is seen as an anticipation. But the elaborate Greek science of *katoptromanteia* and the related magical powers of the mirror would lead us too far astray from the subject with which we began this discussion.[29]

Fame in Images, Fame in Words

Let us return, then, to the fictions of literature. Chaerea was encouraged by what he saw in the painting of Zeus and Danae. Invited to observe the crow and the vultures, the two old men understood nothing, but Tranio enjoyed himself immensely, laughing along with the audience. But it is not always this way: in another time and place, someone reading a scene painted on a wall found himself subject to completely opposite emotions, and he wept many tears. But these are strange tears, obscure, so difficult to understand in their literal form as to suggest that we are dealing here with an unfinished text—or with an acknowledgment of the sorrows of this world, so heartfelt that it simply cannot find a conclusion.

We have left the happy world of Roman Comedy far behind. The terrible storm at sea has subsided, and Aeneas finds himself on the coast of Carthage. Together with Achates he enters the grove where the Phoenicians—other refugees cast upon these shores by the ocean's gales—had excavated the sign indicated by Juno: a horse's skull. Queen Dido then erected a splendid temple on the sacred spot, dedicated to the goddess:[30]

> Hoc primum in luco nova res oblata timorem
> leniit, hic primum Aeneas sperare salutem
> ausus et adflictis melius confidere rebus.
> Namque sub ingenti lustrat dum singula templum
> reginam opperiens, dum, quae fortuna sit urbi,
> artificumque manus intra se operumque laborem
> miratur, videt Iliacas ex ordine pugnas
> bellaque iam fama totum vulgata per orbem,
> Atridas Priamumque et saevum ambobus Achillem,
> constitit et lacrimans: "Quis iam locus," inquit, "Achate,
> quae regio in terris nostri non plena laboris?
> En Priamus. Sunt hic etiam sua praemia laudi,
> sunt lacrimae rerum et mentis mortalia tangunt."

In this grove, an unexpected event lessened his fear. For the first time Aeneas dared to hope for safety, and to take heart in difficult straits. While he is observing everything in the great temple, waiting for the queen, and while he admires the wealth of the city, the hands of the craftsmen in competition and the industry of their works, he sees the battles around Troy in order, and the war that fame had now spread throughout the whole world—the sons of Atreus, and Priam, and Achilles brutal to both sides. Aeneas halted, and weeping he said, "Achates, what place, what region of the earth is not filled with our suffering? Look, there is Priam! Even here glory has its reward; there are tears for things, and mortal things touch the soul."

Any translation of that famous Vergilian phrase—*sunt lacrimae rerum*—is doomed to fail.[31] But fortunately the translation of this phrase is not our main concern here; what matters is that as he stands in front of those pictures (his "soul feeding on the empty painting"), Aeneas weeps and takes heart.[32] The entire Trojan War was actually there in the temple, depicted on its walls. The white tents of Rhesus, Diomedes who razed them, Troilus—and "he recognized himself among the throng of Argive princes."[33] In some sense, Aeneas *was already there*. His painted image—like a shadow escaped from its owner, a wandering *eidōlon* driven by fame—preceded him in the land of Carthage. Let us try to imagine his amazement (which would have been at least equal to ours): Vergil's invention is indeed very striking. Aeneas sees himself; he discovers that, in the form of a picture, his presence has arrived before him. His premonition was already there, in Carthage.

Somewhat later, when he is hidden in Venus's cloud, Aeneas listens, unseen, to the conversation between his companions and Queen Dido, and hears her speak these words:[34]

> Solvite corde metum Teucri, secludite curas.
> . . . .
> Quis genus Aeneadum, quis Troiae nesciat urbem,
> virtutesque virosque aut tanti incendia belli?
>
> Loose the fear from your hearts, O Trojans; set aside your worries. . . .
> Who does not know Aeneas's people, the city of Troy, the valor, the heroes, and the conflagration of that great war?

Aeneas's men are thus already known, preceded by their reputation, and Dido finally exclaims, "If only Aeneas were here, driven by the same South Wind!"[35] They are expecting him there, the great hero, the king. But we should not forget that the presence of Aeneas has already been announced, fixed there on the wall of the temple. Aeneas's arrival has been declared in advance by means of a *figure* painted on the wall of the temple. The image flies more swiftly than the person to whom it belongs, and it waits there, suggesting the arrival of the person it has announced in advance.

But we should pause here for a moment. Standing in front of those pictures in the temple, the ones that tell the story of Troy, Aeneas *weeps*. It is a powerful scene—and a famous one, a central moment in the literary tradition. And as we know, especially in the ancient world, great texts always emerge one on top of the other, like blossoming branches that grow from the same trunk. Thus we cannot help but think of the *Odyssey*, and the scene in which Odysseus, seated at the table of Alcinous, listens to Demodocus as he sings an account of the Trojan War. Odysseus, also unrecognized, *weeps*.[36] In other words, we cannot help but think of Vergil's model, although that would be a cold and analytical way to enter into this later text. We should therefore try to have more respect for the spirit of literature than for the rules and usual practices of modern literary criticism. Let us instead simply reflect on the fact that Aeneas is there in the temple at Carthage, while at more or less the same moment, in some other part of the vast and endless ocean, another wandering hero, another survivor returning from the same war, is likewise suffering the revived emotions of that war and its remembrance. And he also weeps. Somewhere else, in another palace, Odysseus is undergoing the same experience as Aeneas; together they form part of the same story (a "superstory"? An "archestory"?—but these are ponderous words, and probably not very useful).

The experiences lived in literary simultaneity by these two heroes are extremely similar, but very different nevertheless. The resemblance between Vergil's text and the Homeric passage is clear. In both cases, the mise-en-scène and the plot of the event are the same. Even the topic of the hero's double presence repeats itself, because not only is Odysseus there, in disguise, but at a certain point he asks the bard to sing about himself, about Odysseus, who is already there:[37] "Come now, change the subject, and sing the stratagem of the wooden horse, which Epeus built with Athena's help, and which godlike Odysseus led by a trick into the city, having filled it with the heroes who would demolish Troy." Odysseus, as usual, is very clever. He himself puts a question about himself to someone who is ignorant of the fact that it is he, Odysseus, who is asking. It is the sort of trick of which Odysseus is very fond. Such antics would be unthinkable in the case of a stern and rigid hero like Aeneas. But the real difference lies elsewhere. In Homer, fame comes in the form of a story; it is the *word* that has come flying in advance of the hero, and has prefigured his presence.[38] In Vergil, fame is first of all a painted image.[39] Odysseus, unrecognized, discovers that a verbal image of himself was already in circulation among the Phaeacians, in the form of a song that told his story; Aeneas, unrecognized, discovers that his effigy already exists in Carthage, in the form of his painted figure. And now the sorrows of Troy, which make both heroes weep, are no longer told as formally styled hexameters but are shown instead as figures. Those obscure "tears for things" are effigies stretching along a wall, a simple fact that nevertheless marks an immense difference, of time and of culture, between these two great texts of ancient literature.

Galleries of Premonition

The image prefigures, and thus anticipates. To look upon the image is sometimes reassuring and encouraging, as in Aeneas's case, but at other times the image can instead suggest something disquieting.

A picture selects one possible future and, in a reality strangely emptied of time, it suggests that somehow, someone already knew what would happen—the alarming sensation that what is happening now has happened once before.

Abandoned by Giton, betrayed by his friend Ascyltus, Encolpius enters a picture gallery. He is deeply distressed. A short while ago he had finally tried a bold maneuver, taking up his sword to prowl the arcades of the city with a menacing expression on his face. But a real soldier unmasked him in quick order, much to his embarrassment. So our humiliated lover, this would-be adventurer, struggles in vain within the magnetic field created by his author's irony. But Encolpius is nothing if not the prey of passion:[40] "So I went into a picture gallery remarkable for the variety of paintings that it contained. I was able to see the work of Zeuxis there, not yet ravaged by time, and sketches by Protogenes, which vied with the very truthfulness of nature itself. Touching them, I could not help but tremble. And then I paid homage to the figure by Apelles that the Greeks call *Monoknēmos*, the 'One-Legged.' The contours of the images were designed with such stupendous subtlety that you would have said they were a picture of the soul itself. In one there was an eagle lifting Ganymede up high into the sky, while in another fair Hylas tried in vain to repulse the brazen Naiad. Apollo was cursing his murderous hands, and wreathing his unstrung lyre with the newly born flower. And amidst the faces of these painted lovers, I shouted as if in a deserted place, 'So love strikes even the gods themselves!'" The unhappy love story of Encolpius and—what a coincidence—Ganymede, Hylas, Hyacinth: the unhappy love stories of doomed young men, stories just like his own.

Greatly distressed at having lost his beloved young boyfriend, the infatuated Encolpius thus happens to find himself in a picture gallery where exact fragments of his own story reappear on painted tablets, and he realizes that love strikes even the gods themselves . . . It is a far less fortunate situation than Chaerea's encounter with the painting of Jupiter. In Encolpius's case the mythological paintings do not relay the propitious joys of the lofty Adulterer. Instead, they depict the piteous stories of lost young men. And the suggestive power of these melancholy paintings is so strong that at a certain point Encolpius imagines himself there in nature's solitary haunts (as is required, after all, in certain heartbreaking circumstances), and he exclaims, "I stood contending with the winds . . ." God only knows where those winds came from, there inside the picture gallery. Perhaps from the pictures themselves, which stood there before him, reflecting his own story, as in a mirror? The heavens opening up for Ganymede, the tragic fountain in the woods where Hylas met his doom, the meadow where Apollo is grieving for Hyacinth, as that dire flower begins to blossom. The painting already says it all—Encolpius's lovelorn melancholy has been prefigured, with the pathos of the scene bursting out in a perfect lament of elegiac love. He thus resembles Propertius, also lost in the solitude of nature, who shouts his complaints to the lonely halcyons, lamenting the injustice and agony of his love.[41] But as luck would have it, a white-haired old man, remarkable for his profoundly tormented expression, but wearing rather shabby clothes, is about to enter the gallery and take his place beside Encolpius. The old man's pompous chattering (he is, of course, the poet Eumolpus) quickly distracts the abandoned lover from his anguish. This is the work of Petronius, after all, who takes nothing too seriously, not even the disquieting game of mirrors that, for a moment, was being played out in this gallery of pictures.

Petronius has now steered us toward that literary realm in which the premonitory image enjoys its greatest privileges: the Greek novel and, in particular, the stories of *Leucippe and Clitophon* recorded by Achilles Tatius. As the book opens, the author in fact tells of having come to Sidon during a violent storm at sea. And there, among the votive offerings in the temple of Astarte where he had gone to make a sacrifice, he sees a painting of the rape of Europa. But the background shows "the Phoenician sea, and the land of Sidon. There is a meadow and a troop of maidens standing on the ground, while on the sea a bull swims along, with a beautiful young girl seated upon his back."[42] The description goes on a good while longer, as Achilles Tatius contemplates the scene, until finally he is approached by a young man who overheard his comment about the tiny Eros leading the bull ("Look how the little tyke is able to govern the sky, the land, and the sea!").[43] The young man then tells our author that he also has had some experience of that little god, and of the sufferings that Eros so capably inflicts. Thus we make the acquaintance of Clitophon, who begins to tell us the story of his love affair with Leucippe.[44]

The romance thus opens with the long *ekphrasis* of a painting,[45] a type of description frequently found in Greek novels.[46] In fact, there was one author who outdid even Achilles Tatius in this regard: the pastoral loves of Daphnis and Chloe were imagined by their author Longus precisely as the endless *ekphrasis* of a painting whose amorous contents he had the good fortune to observe at Lesbos, in a grove sacred to the nymphs. As Longus explains, he admired the painting so much that he was seized by a desire to reproduce the picture in the form of a romance.[47] But we should return to the love story of Leucippe and Clitophon, where we will find that the subject of painted images is so closely entwined with the events of the plot that images can be justifiably considered not only as characters in the novel, but as a narrative category of the tale itself.

The painting of the bull's rape of Europa that opens the text perfectly prefigures this story about the sea and young women stolen away across the sea, and about lovers who, from the land side, desperately contemplate the ineluctable vanishing of their beloved, as if in a painting. But that is not all. When Clitophon (as he himself explains) sees Leucippe for the first time, it is just like a vision seen in a painting, the sight of something already seen before:[48] "A girl appeared on my left, and her face dazzled my eyes. She was like a painting I had seen of Europa on the bull: her eyes fierce but enchanting, and her golden hair set in golden curls."[49] Even before he encountered her, Leucippe *had been there.* In the form of an image, Clitophon had (unwittingly) met his beloved; again, the image is a premonition.

What is more, the lover has not only seen his beloved, but he has seen her depicted in terms of a precise subject, the rape of Europa (the same scene that opens the novel itself, in the form of an *ekphrasis*). This is significant. It is not only the beloved's physical features that were already there; rather, that picture of violence showed the entire story of the two lovers in emblematic form. Leucippe will really and truly be abducted, and will have to wander far and wide over the sea. The painted Europa foretold not only the entry of Clitophon's beloved Leucippe into the story, but also the nature of the story itself, and the ensuing vicissitudes of their love.

As we continue reading in Achilles Tatius, we discover that so-called reality, the scenario of the novel, does look increasingly like the painting—like *that* painting—and a new, dense premonition of danger enters into the play of events. A wedding party is being readied at Tyre; there are young maidens, flowers, enticing odors, sacrificial offerings in abundance, and, most conspicuous of all, Egyptian bulls. The narrator praises the solemn beauty of one bull in particular, who "walks with his head held high as if to show that he is the king of the other cattle. If the myth of Europa is a true story, Zeus surely must have taken the form of an Egyptian bull."[50] So once again there is a nod toward the mythological abduction, and in a context whose scenographic details and arrangement are disconcertingly similar (except that it is not a scene of grief) to the description of the pictorial *ekphrasis* that opens the novel. But all of a sudden the scenic serenity of these nuptials is unexpectedly disturbed by the arrival of a troop of men hired by Callisthenes, who is also in love with Leucippe, but without ever having actually set eyes on her; the mere reputation of her beauty has won his heart. As a result, when the pirates abruptly descend upon the women, they do not abduct Leucippe (whose actual appearance is unknown to Callisthenes), but instead seize Calligone, Clitophon's sister. Of course, this case of mistaken identity (a common event in the novels) can elude the workings of fate only temporarily. For now, at least, Clitophon's beloved Leucippe is safe, but the machinations of painted symbols (the bull, the rape) are already at work; the fog of premonition grows ever more dense.

And so we move from one painting to the next. The story develops, other events take place, and now in the rear chamber of the temple of Zeus Casius at Pelusium, Leucippe and Clitophon contemplate a painting that shows two images: "There were Andromeda and Prometheus, both of them in chains (I believe this was why the painter placed the two of them together). Because of other coincidences these images were akin to one another. In both, there were chains attached to a rock, with wild beasts as the executioners; his came from the air, and hers from the sea."[51] The continuation of the comparison is rather pedantic (as is also the long description of the painting itself that provokes the discussion), but the prophecy is clear: a man and a woman, in chains, will be joined together in a common fate, in the same way that they are placed together in a single painting. Very shortly, as a matter of fact, an Egyptian vessel will seize the two lovers, and they will indeed be put in chains; the painting has already said as much. But the story continues.

Rescued from these further disasters (by the usual, obsessive reversal of fortune that characterizes the plots of Greek novels), the two lovers confront another test, and again it is depicted in advance. We are now in Alexandria, and a newfound friend, Chaereas, is proposing a trip to the island of Pharos. But Chaereas is also secretly in love with Leucippe, and the trip provides a likely opportunity for betrayal. "Just as we had gone out the door, an evil omen befell us: in pursuit of a swallow, a hawk bumped his wing against Leucippe's head. Disturbed by this I turned my gaze to the sky and said, 'O Zeus, why do you reveal this sign? If truly this bird belongs to you, let us see another augury that is more clear!' Then when I turned around (by chance I had stopped next to a painter's shop), I saw a painting on display, which in an enigmatic way offered an analogy with the present situation.[52] The painting in fact showed the rape of Philomela, Tereus's violent attack, and the cutting out of her tongue."[53] Again, the chance happenings of literature: Clitophon finds himself standing beside a painter's shop . . . and reality is again very close to what is painted on the canvas. A real swallow pursued by a hawk is immediately reflected in the swallow/Philomela, raped by Tereus, all of which just happens to be the subject of the painting. But it is not only a reflection: that canvas also anticipates what is going to happen (or what could happen) to Leucippe/swallow/Philomela. Clitophon apparently has no doubts about this whatsoever; he recognizes that what is said enigmatically in the painting is a riddle suited to his own situation.

Menelaus, his faithful friend, finds this deeply disturbing:[54] "It seems to me that we should give up on this trip to Pharos, for we have now had two bad signs [*symbola*], as you yourself have seen: the wing of that bird turned against us and the threatening danger depicted in the painting. Interpreters [*exēgētai*] of such signs advise us to pay attention to the subjects of the images that we happen to see as we depart on some sort of business, and *to deduce by analogy the future unfolding of events through the meaning of the story that is shown.*[55] So you can see what sort of misfortunes pervade that painting: illicit love, shameless adultery, women beset by disaster. This is why I implore you to abandon your plans for this journey."

But the voyage will in fact be made, and Leucippe will indeed be abducted. More reversals of fortune ensue; the novel must go on, after all, but we will come to a halt here. The ancient soothsayers, the interpreters of symbols, recognized the premonitions revealed by effigies. The image had a prophetic value; it was acknowledged that—*in figuris*—images could reflect and foretell future events. There is a rather striking analogy here with the dream image, which was also an *eidōlon,* a simulacrum, an autonomous precursor of coming events. The image in the dream and the manufactured image both contained a symbolic message that had to be interpreted. Moreover, the interpretation of images and the interpretation of symbolic dreams explicitly based their procedures on the possible analogies to be found between the elements of the image on the one hand and the present situation on the other.[56] The ancient science of dream interpretation assumed that, like an image, an allegorical dream was enigmatic,[57] demanding a specific interpretation provided by an *exēgētēs* skilled in analogy.[58]

The world thus teems with premonitory images (figures, dreams) that can convey an ulterior meaning beyond what their visible layer of

meaning—their representation of a specific subject, or of a person—
would lead us to think. In addition to signifying themselves, manufactured images or oneiric visions are able to contain much broader meanings, which are entwined with the destinies of the people who look at
or perceive them. But from this point of view, images and words find
themselves once again in perfect harmony, as likewise in the case of fame
discussed above.[59] In addition to teeming with figures that are full of
meaning, the world also teems with premonitory *words*, words that do
not seem to be addressed directly to the person who hears them but that
in reality do have a deep connection to that person's destiny, containing a sense beyond their immediate significance. These premonitory
words or phrases—Latin *omen*, or Greek *klēdōn*—are abundantly attested in antiquity.[60] Crassus, for example, on the eve of his disastrous
expedition against the Parthians, heard the shout of a passing vendor of
figs, as he cried out, *Cauneas!* ("Figs from Caunus!"). Someone able to
read beneath the surface of the words would have easily understood the
profound truth revealed in that cry: *Cav(e) ne eas!* "Do not go!"[61] But
at the time no one understood this meaning; the unwitting fig vendor
tried in vain to deliver a direct message from Fate. Words, like images,
can contain a false bottom, a secret compartment that expands their
natural communicative function. People communicate with one another in their everyday lives by means of words and images, exchanging
messages according to the ordinary rules of language or of art; but by
means of these same words and images people can also communicate directly with their destinies, provided that they possess the skill to deci-
pher the words and images in this way.

We should be grateful to Clitophon's friend Menelaus for having explicitly told us that the premonitory force of the images was recognized
in daily practice, showing that its observance was recommended as a
prudent practice when going out of the house to attend to some business.[62] Once again (as so many other times before), we realize to what
an extent ancient literature derives its sources, designs, and metaphors,
from anthropological models that are also at work *outside* the realm of
literature. It is not merely a matter of literary forms: it is a matter of culture. And it is in the context of this specific culture—not in the ancient
rules of literary composition—that we should seek the reasons behind
the Trojan story painted on the temple at Carthage, the portents deduced by means of images, or the picture gallery in which Encolpius was
able to see himself mirrored in the paintings of the ancient masters. We
know, of course, that the genre of Latin epic poetry was much inclined
to describing works of art (perhaps following Naevius in this regard?),

so much so that finally even Petrarch felt compelled to do the same in his *Africa*. So too we know that Suetonius had a taste (often criticized) for omens, and that Petronius was very fond of picture galleries and descriptions of paintings (as were the other writers of ancient novels). But even so we should not neglect the interpreters of divinatory signs, those experts in images, and the advice they might once have offered at the outset of any serious enterprise.

16

Resemblance

Augustine listened carefully to the arguments of Reason. "We speak of a false tree when we see a painting of a tree," Reason began, "and we say that a face reflected in a mirror is also false, and the movement of towers and the bending of oars that voyagers at sea think they observe: we also say that these things are false, because they only resemble what is true." Augustine conceded that it must be so, and Reason then continued his argument. "In the same way, we are deceived by twins, by eggs, by the seals made from the same signet ring, and so on." "That is all quite correct," said Augustine; "I must admit you are right." "It is therefore the case," Reason concluded, "that the resemblance we see with our eyes is actually the mother of falseness [*mater est falsitatis*]." Augustine had no choice but to agree.

In the course of Augustine's *Soliloquia*, this theory of resemblance is developed in further detail, until we reach what is one of the most interesting points in this dialogue between Augustine and himself, between *Augustinus* and *Ratio*.[1] Reason explains that all this material can be divided into two distinct types: some resemblances (that is, some kinds of "falseness") are a type of "equal" resemblance, what Augustine calls *in aequalibus,* while others are a type of "worsened" resemblance, *in deterioribus.* There is resemblance *in aequalibus* when one can say that "this resembles that as much as that resembles this, as with twins, or seals made from the same signet ring." Resemblance *in aequalibus* therefore does not involve a model and its copy; there is no before and after in hierarchical or temporal terms: the resemblance is reciprocal and works both ways. Resemblance *in deterioribus,* on the other hand, applies when one can say that "something that is inferior to some other thing resembles that other, better thing. If a man looks at himself in the mirror, surely he would say that the image there resembles him, and not that he resembles the image." Therefore, resemblance *in deterioribus* means that we know exactly what is imitating and what is being imitated: what resembles and what, so to speak, "is resembled." Augustine seems to have been quite fond of this distinction, as he makes use of it again in his *De trinitate:* [2] "when the image perfectly reproduces the object of which it is the image, then the image is in accordance with its object; it is not the object that is in accordance with its image."

It is this second type of resemblance—resemblance *in deterioribus*—that fascinates the philosopher (and that is also the far more common type, of course). Reason therefore proceeds to make a further subdivision, distinguishing two different types of resemblance *in deterioribus:* one involving sensory perceptions (optical illusions, nocturnal visions), and another involving actual things. These resemblances involving actual things are then further subdivided into resemblances produced by nature, and those produced by animate beings: "Nature produces resemblances *in deterioribus* by generation or by reflection—by generation, as when children are born who resemble their parents, and by reflection, as in any sort of mirror." Under the heading of resemblances *in deterioribus* that are produced by animate beings, Reason includes "paintings and all manner of depictions."

At this point we will leave Augustine and Reason to continue their dialogue, as the bifurcations among the branches of this logical tree begin to multiply at an alarming rate. What matters for our purposes here is that pictures and other effigies created by animate beings, together with reflected images produced by nature, all belong to the same class of objects that are "worsened" or "inadequate," resemblances *in deterioribus.* As a result, they are marked by an undesirable element of *falsitas,* "falseness." [3] But what is even more interesting is that family resemblance—the likeness of parents and children—is also considered a form of inadequacy, of falseness. Therefore, if Catullus's "little Torquatus" resembles his father, Manlius Torquatus (to take a quite famous example), does that then imply that he is an inadequate Torquatus, an impoverished copy of the original? Are we to conclude that he is in fact a *false* Torquatus? The question merits our careful attention, particularly since this chapter will pursue the subject of family resemblances at some length before we return (by a perhaps unexpected shortcut) to the subject of images in general. Of course, it is reassuring that Augustine himself chose to group painted images and family resemblances under the same heading, assigning them both to that unusual category of things that apparently have no intrinsic value, but are of interest only because they recall some other thing, which they resemble. In a spontaneous moment, or in some ritual circumstance, a recognition takes place ("Doesn't that remind you of . . . ?"), and we realize that something derives its meaning, its scope, even its very identity from the discreet and irresistible power of resemblance.

From Father to Son

We will begin precisely with Catullus's "little Torquatus." At a certain point in his epithalamium for the marriage of Manlius Torquatus and Vinia Aurunculeia, the poet invokes the offspring expected to result from their union. This is, after all, a *nomen*, a lineage, which must by definition produce descendants in order to survive:[4]

> Torquatus volo parvulus
> matris e gremio suae
> porrigens teneras manus
>   dulce rideat ad patrem
>   semihiante labello.
>
> Sit suo similis patri
> Manlio et facile insciis
> noscitetur ab omnibus,
>   et pudicitiam suae
>   matris indicet ore.
>
> Talis illius a bona
> matre laus genus adprobet,
> qualis unica ab optima
>   matre Telemacho manet
>   fama Penelopeo.

I wish for a little Torquatus, reaching out his tender hands from his mother's lap, who will laugh sweetly at his father, his lips half parted. Let him resemble his father, Manlius, and be easily recognized by everyone [*noscitetur ab omnibus*], even those who do not know, and let him declare by the features of his face his mother's sense of decency. May such praise, thanks to his good mother, approve his descent, as the unequaled reputation from his noble mother comes to Telemachus, son of Penelope.

Catullus's text is extremely informative. The way in which the boy will turn to his father and laugh is reminiscent of the laughter that the mysterious *puer* of Vergil's Fourth Eclogue is said to direct toward his mother as a sign of recognition.[5] Such laughter is the first instance of contact, and it has a ritual significance; despite the tender sweetness of the display, it is actually a very solemn moment. As Servius notes in his commentary on Vergil: "In the same way that adults recognize one another by means of speech [*sermone*], little children show that they recognize their parents by means of laughter [*risu*]."[6]

And then there is the resemblance: the poet hopes that the young couple will be blessed with a baby boy who resembles his father so closely that he will be recognized as "little Torquatus" even by people who do not know anything about his identity. Resemblance thus indicates "belonging," a sign of membership in a group. These tokens of resemblance allow the disconcerting uniqueness of an individual to be safely elevated to a more general category: "For goodness' sake, doesn't he remind you of Manlius Torquatus?" Because it relates one thing to another, resemblance is a sign of identification, a guarantee that the individual belongs to a group. Needless to say, the group is male: Roman society was profoundly patrilineal, and Roman resemblances, as we will see, adhered closely to this male cultural model.[7]

In a letter addressed to the perfidious Jason, Hypsipyle (in Ovid's imagination) uses these words to describe their twin sons:[8]

Si quaeris cui sint similes, cognosceris illis:
    fallere non norunt, cetera patris habent.

If you ask whom they resemble, you will recognize yourself [*cognosceris*] in them: they do not know how to deceive, but in everything else they are their father's sons.

To know these boys is to recognize—to identify—their father Jason. The sons are his faithful mirror; we might even call them his portrait. Ovid expresses a similar idea in some lines from the *Tristia,* when he writes to a friend:[9]

Sic iuvenis similisque tibi sit natus, et illum
    moribus agnoscat quilibet esse tuum.

Thus may your young son be similar to you, so that anyone would recognize [*agnoscat*] by his behavior that he is yours.

In this case it is a matter of moral, not physical, resemblance, but the point is essentially the same.[10] The son is defined in terms of his resemblance to his father; this is what gives him his identity and makes him a member of the group. *Noscitetur ab omnibus,* as Catullus says of the little Torquatus; *cognosceris,* as Ovid's Hypsipyle explains to Jason; *agnoscat quilibet,* as we read in the *Tristia.* Such linguistic repetitions and lexical reiterations are themselves a source of meaning: *noscitetur, cognosceris, agnoscat.* In cases of family resemblance there is clearly an insistent emphasis on knowing and recognizing—but who precisely is recognized, and by whom?

The answer to this question is also self-evident: the person is recognized by somebody, by anybody, *agnoscat quilibet.* It is the others, the strangers, who recognize the child as a member of the family, and thus acknowledge his identity. This act of recognition is central to the cultural code, and it is the community—the "others"—who serve as its trustees (whether or not they are conscious of this role). Resemblance is a display, a demonstration of genuineness that is directed toward an onlooker, whose very presence constitutes a sanctioning judgment. The onlooker can be anybody, *quilibet;* even a person who does not know anything at all about the situation will have no doubts whatsoever about little Torquatus: *facile insciis noscitetur ab omnibus.* But why, one might ask, should there be any doubt to begin with?

The fact is that this male obsession with *agnatio*—this awareness of kinship along the male line of descent that characterizes any patrilineal society (including Rome)—always nourishes the fear that something alien might insinuate itself into the net of family relations, disturbing the blood that maintains the enduring ties of kinship by being passed from father to son.[11] Any society that is strongly governed by *agnatio* is marked by this paradox: the family name, its cults, its lineage all descend from male to male, but in each instance this descent depends on the intervention of a woman.[12] The result is a constant risk of contamination, of an adultery that might "adulterate" the family line. The son's resemblance to the father thus functions as a sort of guarantee of authenticity, a family trademark: a baby boy's resemblance to his father perpetuates the fantasy, which demands that no interloper be allowed to disrupt the established relations between male family members. Indeed, as Apuleius tells us, fathers love most of all the sons who look like themselves: *filiorum cariores esse qui similes videntur.*[13]

This is why it doesn't seem to have mattered very much whether children resembled their mother.[14] The result is a kind of cultural paradox (described quite elegantly by Catullus) according to which a child recalls his mother most when his features do not recall her: *pudicitiam suae matris indicet ore,* "let him declare by the features of his face his mother's sense of decency." It is by resembling his father, Manlius, that the little Torquatus *indicates* his mother, Vinia Aurunculeia. The maternal element has been erased from his appearance, and he is stamped exclusively with paternal traits. The little boy thus invokes his mother in the way that best defines and represents her in the eyes of a patrilineal culture: as evidence of her propriety and chastity. The male fantasy is reaffirmed by the transparent, perfectly neutral intervention of women in the line of descent—or, to put things more drastically, by the women's invisibility. In contrast, it is interesting to see what happens when a child perfectly resembles both his father and his mother, as in this example from Ovid: [15]

> Cuius erat facies, in qua materque paterque
> cognosci possent; nomen quoque traxit ab illis.

> In his face both mother and father could be recognized [*cognosci possent*]; he also took his name from the two of them.

The problem, of course, is that we are talking here about baby Hermaphroditus. The combined inheritance of features from both parents in a single countenance thus seems to presuppose some kind of irregularity, a dubious uncertainty. It is as if this atypical resemblance to the mother also carried with it the appropriate gender of that resemblance, which in this case is oddly mixed with paternal resemblance, given that sons cannot help but resemble their fathers.

Praising Augustus's restoration of ancient customs, Horace used these words to describe the honorable status of Roman mothers: [16]

> Nullis polluitur casta domus stupris,
> mos et lex maculosum edomuit nefas,
> laudantur simili prole puerperae.

> The home is pure, and is not polluted by sexual crime; custom and law have stamped out the blemish of sin; new mothers are praised for their similar offspring.

Simile prole, similar offspring: but offspring similar to whom? The ellipsis is transparently obvious: to the father. Language can apparently tolerate such looseness precisely because of the compensating force (or violence) wielded by culture itself.[17] Since Augustus revived the moral principles of ancient times, Roman sons once again resemble their fathers; the reign of justice triumphs. This is why the new mothers should be praised (as Horace praises them): they have produced sons who attest to the caliber of their lineage, sons who display an appropriate, undeniable, patrilineal resemblance free from any other determining elements. In this regard, we can return to Catullus's "little Torquatus":[18] the poet hopes that the young bride will receive the praise bestowed by a good mother, *a bona matre laus,* which sustains and confirms the family lineage, *genus adprobet.* It is something to be openly acknowledged; indeed, there is a need for visible proof.

"You have a daughter," writes Martial, "whose face is marked by the image of her father: the girl is a witness to her mother's sense of decency [*testis maternae pudicitiae*]."[19] Such family resemblance is like an affidavit submitted in a court of law: a witness (*testis*) is required, because the line of descent is hardly self-evident. In this seemingly endless trial, the signs, marks, and allusions of resemblance must bear the burden of proof. The process attributes to each person his proper identity, and secures the respectability and prestige of the entire lineage.[20] As Seneca's Andromache says of her son Astyanax:[21]

> O nate, magni certa progenies patris, . . .
> veteris . . . suboles sanguinis nimium inclita
> nimiumque patris similis. Hos vultus meus
> habebat Hector, talis incessu fuit
> habituque talis, sic tulit fortis manus,
> sic celsus umeris, fronte sic torva minax
> cervice fusam dissipans iacta comam.

> O my son, certain offspring of a great father, . . . too famous offspring of an ancient bloodline, and too much like your father. My Hector had such a face, such was his gait and bearing, so he carried his mighty hands, so he towered with his shoulders, and such was the intimidating look of his stern brow when he shook his head and tossed his flowing locks of hair.

Because he is Hector's *certa progenies,* his certain offspring, Astyanax reproduces the ancient blood of his family line. Just as we would expect, the boy bears a perfect resemblance to his father, and this time Seneca even provides a detailed inventory of the traits and characteristics through which this likeness is established—an inventory that includes not only the boy's facial features but even the form of his body, along with his gestures and attitudes.[22] When confronted by doubt or by the need to recognize someone, these are the traits that can identify the person in question, attesting to his membership in a group. The forehead was a site of resemblance;[23] it was considered a very meaningful element of the face, in which all sorts of interior qualities were revealed, a sort of gateway for the soul.[24] Resemblance of the hands could also serve as a clear sign of recognition, as could the feet. Indeed, as we saw earlier, Electra was convinced that her brother Orestes had come to the tomb of their father Agamemnon when she saw footprints pressed into the ground that were identical in every way to her own.[25] Such resemblance through the feet apparently extended to other cultures as well; the *Mahabharata,* for example, describes Yudhisthira's remorse for not having recognized his half-brother Karna by the resemblance of his feet to the feet of their mother, Kunti.[26]

Of course, when Andromache declares Astyanax to be Hector's sure offspring, his *certa progenies,* she is praising the boy, but her words are also a veiled encomium of her own virtue. The son who resembles his father does honor to his mother, whereas the alternative was a potential pitfall for every woman: if a son did not resemble his father, this might be taken as proof of her infidelity. In each case, the mechanism of certainty or suspicion depends on resemblance. So, for example, Theocritus describes the woman "without love" in the following terms:[27] "The mind of the woman without love is always turned toward another man. She gives birth easily, but the children do not resemble their father." Pliny records the similarly embarrassing case of a woman who "gave birth to twins, one of whom resembled her husband and the other who resembled her lover."[28] Martial likewise describes each of the seven children whom Cinna believed he had by his wife Marulla, but who were actually seven different witnesses to seven different fathers other than Cinna, as evidenced by their various physical defects or facial features:[29]

Hic qui retorto crine Maurus incedit
subolem fatetur esse se coci Santrae;
at ille sima nare, turgidis labris
ipsa est imago Pannychi palaestritae.
Pistoris esse tertium quis ignorat,
quicumque lippum novit et videt Damam?
Quartus cinaeda fronte, candido vultu
ex concubino natus est tibi Lygdo:
percide, si vis, filium: nefas non est.
Hunc vero acuto capite et auribus longis
quae sic moventur ut solent asellorum,
quis morionis filium negat Cyrtae?
Duae sorores, illa nigra et haec rufa,
Croti choraulae vilicique sunt Carpi.

This one, who goes about like a Moor with curly hair, confesses himself to be the son of the cook Santra. That one with the pug nose and the fat lips is the very image [*ipsa est imago*] of Pannychus the wrestling trainer. Who would not recognize the third as the son of Dama the baker when he sees and knows those runny eyes? The fourth, with the forehead of a catamite and pallid face, was born to you from your own lover Lygdus. Screw your son, if you want: no incest here. And who could deny that this one is the son of that fool Cyrta, with his pointed head and long ears that move like donkey ears? As for the two sisters, one black, the other red, they belong to Crotus the flute player and Carpus the bailiff.

Epigrams are attracted to paradox, as in the case here of Lygdus, Cinna's *cinaedus* and *concubinus*, who had also committed adultery with the shameless Marulla—except that the result was a boy like himself, a *cinaedus* and potential *concubinus* for his putative father, Cinna (without even the threat of incest: *percide, si vis, filium: nefas non est*). In each and every case, the children reveal the preeminence of male, paternal characteristics (real or metaphorical)—those specifically masculine traits that, in one pregnancy after another, were imprinted on Marulla's children as if the adulterous mother were nothing more than a layer of wax on which figures were continually impressed by the signet rings of her lovers. Even in the disorder of adultery a certain kind of order still prevails. When the blood has been adulterated, the father's traits obviously cannot emerge as dominant, but it is nevertheless a male who leaves his mark on the child.

For that matter, the general rule that males play a dominant role in the procreation of life (and that the male is logically the initiator of this process) holds true not only in literary caricatures and the assumptions of everyday life, but also in ancient scientific theory. According to Aristotle, for example, when the active principle of the male seed prevails (as it logically should) over the material substance that the woman has at her disposal, then the conception will be "male, not female, resembling the father, not the mother."[30] But with the gradual reduction of male prevalence by an incremental process of "deviation," the resulting birth can consist of girls rather than boys, or boys who resemble their mother rather than their father, and so on. The birth of sons who resemble their father is the norm, while the rest is all deviance, even if it is admittedly "required by nature."[31]

Occasionally, these Roman resemblances were able to traverse vast stretches of time, referring back to models from the ancestral archives. In the last years of the Republic, some members of the Iunii Bruti boasted of their resemblance to a statue of Brutus that stood on the Capitoline. At least in their eyes, this resemblance was sufficient proof with which to refute the suspicion that they were not actually descendants of Rome's great liberator.[32] The statue, in short, guaranteed the certainty of their lineage, their identity as members of a group. These atavistic resemblances, projected from the distant past, are surely related to the cult of the *imagines* practiced by the Roman aristocracy, who diligently preserved the funeral masks of their ancestors in special cabinets located in the atrium of the house. When a member of the family died, these masks would be removed from their shrine and carried in the funeral procession. The *imagines* were put on parade according to a prearranged order, such that the masks were worn by those living family members who physically resembled the ancestor whose features they were assuming; they would also wear the clothes appropriate to the honors that their ancestor had acquired in his lifetime. But among the many cultural functions of the *imagines,* what is most important for our discussion here is that they constituted a monumental archive of family iconography. By means of these reproductions the Romans possessed (or believed that they possessed) the very faces of their ancestors: the *imagines* transformed the memory of family resemblances into a fixed, objective form.[33]

Lucretius speaks at great length about the topic of family resemblances, seeking to explain them in scientific terms:[34]

> Fit quoque ut interdum similes esistere avorum
> possint et referant proavorum saepe figuras
> propterea quia multa modis primordia multis
> mixta suo celant in corpore saepe parentes,
> quae patribus patres tradunt a stirpe profecta;
> inde Venus varias producit sorte figuras
> maiorumque refert voltus vocesque comasque.

> It also happens that children may arise who can resemble their grandfathers and reproduce the appearance of their great-grandparents, because parents often conceal in their bodies many basic elements [*primordia*] mixed in many different ways, and these things arising in the lineage are passed down from fathers to fathers [*patribus patres*]. Thus by means of chance arrangements Venus yields assorted forms and reproduces the faces and voices and hair of the ancestors.

The section of Lucretius's poem that deals with "genetics" seems surprisingly modern, but we should not allow ourselves to lose sight of the cultural prejudices on which the entire discussion depends. These prejudices serve as a kind of anthropological observation post, a keyhole through which we can directly glimpse the cultural assumptions of the person behind the discourse.[35] The *primordia,* Lucretius says, are combined in many ways in the bodies of the parents, and they are repro-

duced along the line of descent. But he speaks only of fathers who transmit these elements to other fathers, *patres patribus,* with no mention at
all of the mothers, *matres matribus.* This is somewhat odd, because only
a few lines earlier Lucretius explicitly speculates about the various possible combinations between maternal and paternal seed, explaining how
when one prevails over the other the result is a child who resembles the
father or the mother, whereas a perfect parity between the seeds produces a balanced blend of resemblance.[36] This particular scenario thus
includes mothers in the theory of combinations, and on an equal playing field with the fathers. But when Lucretius speaks about the resemblance of the lineage—the evocation of the ancestors (hair, voices, faces)
in their descendants—the mothers unexpectedly vanish, as if they had
never existed. It is the fathers who, at the outset of the lineage, transmit the genetic message of the *primordia.* Genealogical awareness thus
supercedes scientific speculation, and the model of *agnatio*—kinship
through the male line of descent, *patres patribus*—supplants the theory
of genetic combination, warping its basic coherence.

We might call it a mere oversight, of course, just another ellipsis like
the *simile prole* that we saw earlier in Horace.[37] It is as if the resources
of language itself stood in the way of a more balanced and comprehensive theory. Think of how much trouble it would be to supplement
the phrase *patres patribus* with *matres matribus,* along with even more
phrases to further specify that the elements can pass from a father to a
future mother, from a mother to a future father, *matres patribus* and *patres matribus,* following the winding threads of *agnatio* and *cognatio*
along both the male and female lines of descent. It seems so much easier to prune and reduce these various scenarios. Indeed, it is not easier
to do so, but *it just seems to happen that way*—as if language itself were
able to do the pruning and reducing, so that the male component is
finally able to express the entire panoply of relations.[38] Once again we
find ourselves dealing with a series of linguistic suppositions that are the
product of very precise and deep-seated cultural prejudices.[39]

But let us return to Augustine's theory of resemblance and our earlier questions. Does a son who resembles his father actually recall him
in deterioribus? Is the little Torquatus only an inadequate copy, a false
Torquatus (as we originally proposed by way of paradox)? In some
sense, this turns out to be true. Augustine's theory of resemblance and
its tight logical design can actually be extrapolated and applied *tout
court* to the analysis of culture, so that little Torquatus can be seen as
"tending" in his father's direction; in the initial moments of his exis-

tence, he is a meaningful object of interest precisely because he is the image of Manlius, his father, and not of anyone else. As Augustine said, when a person stands in front of a mirror, he would never say that he resembles the image in the mirror; it is instead the image that resembles him. Likewise, we could say that Manlius, standing in front of his little Torquatus, would never say that he resembles his son, but only that the son resembles him. The culture imposes a vector, defining a hierarchy in which the son is the image of his father, but never the other way around. Cassius Dio has Augustus make the following speech to an audience of Roman men:[40] "The son is the image of the body and the image of the soul. When he grows up, the father realizes another 'himself' [*heteros autos*] in his son." The son, in short, is a sort of a false father, an approximation, a resemblance. Needless to say, such a situation can easily become the stuff of psychological tragedy.[41] But within this falseness, this deficiency, it is also possible to create and explore: indeed, it is absolutely essential to do so. In his dissimilarity and inadequacy, the son is able to carve out a life of his own. He becomes his own "self," while still remaining similar to others. Within Augustine's falseness, within the *falsitas* of resemblance *in deterioribus,* personal identity and group identity confront one another: and the result is precisely what we would call a person.

The Powers of Resemblance

Pliny concedes that "there are an immense number of things that can be said on the subject of resemblance, because it involves so many chance elements, such as sight, hearing, memory, and the images that are perceived at the moment of conception. A simple thought that crosses the mind of either one of the two lovers is supposed to be able to produce likenesses, or to mix them up. This is why the differences among human beings are so much more numerous than in other animals. The swiftness of thought, the rapidity of the mind, and the variety of innate human character create the widest possible diversity of signs. The minds of other animals are inflexible, and such animals thus resemble one another simply according to their kind."[42] This is why children cannot help but resemble their fathers, or their parents: the mind is so swift, and the substance of its thoughts is so impalpable! It is thus the excellence of humanity in and of itself that explains the multiplicity of human faces and features. Aetius refers to a similar belief, which he attributes to Empedocles:[43] "Empedocles maintained that children acquire their form from the woman's imagination [*phantasia*] at the moment of conception, and it often happens that when women are seized by a passion for images or for statues, they give birth to children who resemble those images or statues.[44] The Stoics, on the other hand," Aetius explains, "contend that resemblances are produced not by images [*eidōla*] but rather by sympathies of thought transmitted through penetrating fluxes and rays."[45]

Of course, it is not only a question of theories, but also of stories. In Heliodorus's *Ethiopica,* the king and queen of Ethiopia, Hydaspes and Persinna, finally recognize the young woman Chariclea as their long-lost daughter.[46] She has already shown them her indisputable tokens of recognition, but there is still one remaining obstacle, which King Hydaspes thinks is insurmountable: the color of her skin. Chariclea is white, so how could she be the child of two black Ethiopians? But on the swaddling clothes that Chariclea has offered as proof of her identity the solution has already been written out, and in Ethiopian letters:[47] "Persinna hereby swears that she absorbed certain images [*eidōla*] and visual forms [*phantasia*] of resemblance from the painting of Androm-eda that she looked at while in your embrace. If you wish to assure yourself that this is the case, you have the model [*archetypon*] at your disposal: look at the figure of Andromeda that is shown in the paint-ing and you will see the girl's features faithfully reproduced."[48] The painting was brought in, and everyone was amazed by the extraordinary resemblance.

The story provides an example of how one of the many principles of resemblance described by Pliny might operate in the framework of a novel: specifically, it is a case of resemblance produced by images per-ceived at the moment of conception. Putting our faith in Empedocles rather than the Stoics, we are supposed to believe that painted figures can exert a determining influence on the shape of reality. Indeed, it was very lucky for Chariclea that her mother found herself staring at a mythological image of extreme beauty, because otherwise she might have ended up like a young woman from the environs of Pisa whom Montaigne describes as "all rough and hairy, which her mother said was a result of the fact that there had been a picture of Saint John the Bap-tist hanging above the bed in which she was conceived."[49] Apparently that poor mother from Pisa could find nothing better to occupy her at-tention while in her husband's embrace. We can find additional evidence for this belief in the writings of Jerome[50] (who also provides a curious citation from Quintilian).[51] Jerome begins by explaining that women "can conceive according to what they see or imagine during the moment of amorous climax, giving birth to offspring that resemble those images." But it is not only women who are subject to this sort of external influence: Jerome tells us that the same is also true of Spanish mares.[52] Finally, Jerome concludes his discussion with a *controversia* of Quintilian that is a perfect inversion of Persinna's situation in Heliodorus's novel: in this case, a Roman *matrona* is accused of having given birth to an Ethiopian, and defends herself with the argument that she had conceived such a child as a result of external influences acting on her at the moment of conception.[53] The existence of a white child among the Ethiopians, like the existence of a black child among the Romans, causes a disturbance in the rules of culture: as if in a game of colored mirrors, the whites in Ethiopia and the blacks in Rome demand a symmetrical explanation, and in both cases it is to be found in the power of perceived images.

But it is not always necessary to have recourse to the *eidōla* of thought in order to account for a confused transmission of resemblances. As the philosopher Favorinus explains, "while the force and the nature of the seed work to create likenesses in both body and spirit, it is also true that a no less powerful influence is exerted by the qualities and properties of breast milk. This can be observed not only in human beings, but also in animals. If kids are suckled by sheep or if lambs are suckled by goats, one can be sure that the kids will have a softer coat, and that the lambs will have stiffer wool." The philosopher then goes on to explain that this is why he considers it thoroughly reprehensible that Roman mothers refuse to nurse their children and instead entrust them to wet nurses: "By Hercules, this is exactly why one is so often surprised to meet children of otherwise chaste women who completely fail to resemble their parents, both in body and spirit."[54] In order to guarantee the proper functioning of resemblance, it is not enough for the woman to be chaste and faithful: she must be a devoted mother willing to nurse her own children. The milk conveys resemblances; therefore, if some woman other than the mother nurses the child, it is possible that her milk will transmit features to the child that have their origin somewhere else. But where would those alien resemblances come from? Does that milk simply convey the wet nurse's features? Or does the trail lead even farther back?

It is a pivotal question, and the only possible response appears to be the following: the resemblances follow the nature of the milk, and therefore have their origin *where the woman's milk itself originates.* Fortunately, Favorinus is very explicit in this regard: "From the beginning, the nature of the milk is *imbued with the concretion of the paternal seed* and also shapes the newborn's personality by drawing from the body and the spirit of the mother." The mother's milk thus seems to have a strongly paternal inflection. By means of the milk the woman communicates not only her own body to the child, but also the body of the man who has made her conceive, imbuing the woman's milk with his own "concretion."[55] By means of a quite complicated logic of body fluids, even the mother's milk leads back again to the subject of paternal dominance and male prevalence in the creation of resemblance. Pliny also has some similar observations about mother's milk, citing Nigidius Figulus:[56] "The milk of the recently delivered woman who is nursing her child will not go bad [*corrumpi*] if the woman conceived the child with her own husband." Such testimony clearly implies that if the nursing woman conceived from a man who was not her husband, her milk would go bad. The woman's milk is unequivocally stamped by the male, and as a result the milk cannot help but go bad if it is exposed to a second conception and a second stamp from another man. This bad milk from the second conception with another man greatly resembles the confused blood of the woman who has sexual relations with another man after having already been impregnated by her husband.[57] The fluids—milk or blood—must not be disturbed or confused; otherwise, everything is thrown into uncertainty, as we will soon see in the case of Faustina's confused blood. But before turning to Faustina's story, there is one last conclusion we can draw from the paternal "concretions" of maternal milk. If, as it seems, the mother's milk also conveys paternal resemblances (derived from the milk that is imbued with the concretion of paternal seed), then the male stamp upon the features of the child is effectively doubled: first in the seed and the conception, and then once again in the milk and the nursing.

In other cases, the external influences upon resemblance are exercised by powers far more disturbing and shadowy than those of the milk, crossing over into the realm of magic, but still obeying this "logic of the body fluids." One of the writers of the *Historia Augusta* tells the story of how Faustina, the wife of Marcus Aurelius, fell madly in love with a gladiator.[58] Her passion showed no signs of abating, and Faustina at last confessed everything to her husband. The emperor then consulted the Chaldaeans, who advised him to cut the gladiator's throat and to sprinkle the queen with the gladiator's blood before going to bed with her. Marcus Aurelius did as he was told. As a result, Faustina was freed from her passion, and that night in the royal bed the future emperor Commodus was conceived—that same Commodus who later played at being a gladiator, making frequent appearances in the arena before crowds of spectators. The alien blood sprinkled on the body of the empress thus produced an effect analogous to that of the alien milk with which a baby is nursed: in both cases, the paternal resemblance is disturbed and confused. Just as lambs suckled by a goat consequently have stiffer wool, so too the son of the emperor, conceived in the blood of a gladiator, was drawn to the arena. Julius Capitolinus, to whom we (allegedly) owe this rather gruesome tale, was fully convinced that Commodus had to be the fruit of an adulterous relationship, even if he considered this story of the gladiator and the blood sprinkled on the empress's body to be an old wives' tale, a *fabella anilis* concocted out of common gossip. Be that as it may, it is clearly evident that Commodus bore little resemblance to his father the philosopher.[59]

There is still one more episode we can add to Faustina's story, something that leads in a different direction from the incredible *fabella* of the gladiator—but that will later return us to the same story by a different route. Commodus had a twin brother, Antoninus Geminus, who died in infancy.[60] In a letter to Marcus Aurelius, Fronto described his encounter with this tender and august pair of imperial twins:[61]

> I saw your little chicks, and it was one of the most pleasing spectacles I have ever beheld in my life; they are so similar to you in their appearance that I cannot imagine anything more similar. . . . It was not just that you seemed to stand before me, but—more abundantly!—I was able to see you both to the left and to the right. . . . One of the boys was holding a piece of white bread, as befits a scion of imperial stock, and the other held a piece of plain brown bread, as befits a philosopher. May the gods bless the sower, the seed, and the harvest that yields such resemblance [*sit salvus sator, salva sint sata, salva seges sit, quae tam similes procreat*]. I also heard their little voices, so sweet and lovely that in their chirping I recognized (but I know not how) the limpid and elegant sounds of your own speech.

Fronto had no doubts about the patrilineal resemblance that was perfectly revealed in the features, the personalities (the king together with the philosopher), and even the voices of the twins: hence his blessing upon that seed and that harvest in which the controlled order of nature is perpetuated with such remarkable resemblance! The resemblance plays a double role here, constituted by two images refracted in a single mirror. The boys are similar to their father, and they also recall one another. To meet them is to meet a twofold version of their father, a "more abundant" Marcus Aurelius, the product of a vertical resemblance (the lineage itself) having been crossed with the horizontal resemblance of twins. The dual nature of Marcus Aurelius—philosopher and king—is expressed in the resemblance of the twins. Indeed, Fronto seems to suggest that Marcus Aurelius somehow had to have twins in order to be adequately reflected in his offspring. This emperor required a double progeny, two simultaneous sons.

Yet while Fronto seeks to assure his illustrious disciple about the favorable course of his family affairs and the perfection of his descendants, we also know that the conception of those twins was surrounded by a veil of suspicion. Whether the story about the gladiator's blood and the Chaldaeans is true or not, there were certainly many people who suspected that the offspring of Faustina and Marcus Aurelius had adulterous origins. But these contradictory reactions are hardly surprising in the case of twins. Some doubts about the twins' paternity can probably be attributed to the fact that Commodus turned out differently from his father (and hence the need to explain that difference), but there are also a number of further contradictions intrinsically connected with the birth of twins that might have provoked some misgivings right from the start. According to both ancient and medieval beliefs, the birth of twins often aroused suspicions of adultery. It is as if twins could not possibly be conceived in the normal and correct fashion, but must necessarily be the result of their mother's superimposed encounters with a variety of men.[62] As the mother of twins, and the mother of a monster like Commodus, Faustina was inevitably a subject of gossip. And perhaps Fronto insisted a bit too much on the quality of the sower, the seed, and the harvest: indeed, those twins may have produced as much embarrassment as delight.

Doubles and Stand-ins

But let us continue with Pliny, who provides us with many curious stories about capricious resemblances.[63] For example, Vibius, a plebeian, and even Publicius, who was only a freedman, were both said to have had an incredible resemblance to Pompey the Great: the same noble face, the same austere forehead. But according to Valerius Maximus, it was not merely a trick of fate: this seemingly chance *ludibrium* was actually an embarrassing sort of family tradition.[64] Pompey's father, who had originally been called Pompeius Strabo, "Pompey the Cross-Eyed" (because of a defect in his eyes that, as it happens, he shared with one of his slaves), at a certain point acquired the cognomen Menogenes because of his physical resemblance to the household cook, who was called by that name. And there was nothing to be done: he was stuck with this sordid surname, despite being a man of fiery spirit and extraordinary martial valor! Scipio Nasica likewise inherited the cognomen Serapio from the lowly slave of a pig dealer. And Valerius Maximus, who was greatly concerned with the respectability of these Roman nobles, observes that neither the honorable character of this particular Scipio, nor the respect owed to the *imagines* of such a family, was able to save him from this affront. One might be tempted to describe it as strife among the resemblances, in which the severe faces of the ancestors, the archive of the family features, must confront the insistent, ignoble presence of that Serapio, whose image is displayed as if in a mirror—coarse, but perfect: a slave whose appearance let him get the better of those *imagines.*

Later, another Scipio of the same family took his cognomen, Salutio, from a mime. Similarly, Spinther and Pamphilus, two rather modest actors, gave their names to the consuls Lentulus and Metellus, which was all the more embarrassing because it meant that the public seemed to be watching their two consuls perform on the stage. Resemblance, in short, insidiously insinuates itself, mixing servants and masters, powerful men and commoners, magistrates and actors, leaving an impermeable mark in the mischievous Roman cognomina, creating unexpected, Saturnalian family regroupings among men who actually have nothing in common—or do they? This repressed suspicion can erupt in contemptuous aggression or, not surprisingly, in a well-aimed joke, like the anecdote that Valerius Maximus tells about the Sicilian proconsul (Pliny gives his name as Sura)[65] who found himself standing face to face with a fisherman who perfectly resembled him.[66] (Pliny adds that the fisherman made a characteristic face when he spoke, and that he stuttered and stammered just as the proconsul did.) In a haughty tone the proconsul declared that he was amazed by the extraordinary resemblance between himself and the fisherman, given that his father had never been to that province. "But my father," the fisherman replied, "was often in Rome."[67]

And there are still more examples. The orator Lucius Plancus gave his cognomen to the actor Rubrius, while the elder Curio received his name from Burbuleius, an actor, and Marcus Messala took his from Menogenes, another actor. Theater actors, as we can see, are irreplaceable partners in this dense exchange of cognomina. Life and the stage are reflected in one another; the theater—a mirror of the city—is filled with its faces and names. For example, Cassius Severus, the famous orator, was taunted for his unseemly resemblance to a gladiator, Armentarius. This is a Rome peopled with stand-ins, each aristocrat apparently ensnared by his plebeian or servile double. Features are exchanged like actors' masks as the cognomina circulate, shamelessly attaching themselves to new owners. The caprices of resemblance assign roles and parts in the great urban performance; its absurd powers—like the commands of the Saturnalian king—are inescapable.[68] The world suddenly seems to have two bottoms, or two tops: everything on high is found also below. Apuleius observed that "there is nothing a man is happier to look at than an image of himself."[69] But Apuleius was referring to a man's image in the mirror, not to another man who is his living double.

What is most striking about Pliny's foray into the realm of capricious resemblances is precisely this relentless net of similarities binding illustrious Roman personages on the one hand with actors and mimes on the other. We have seen no fewer than six cases of such connections, or even seven.[70] It may be possible to explain this unusual relationship in terms of the elaborate funeral rituals of the Roman nobility.[71] Describing the funeral for Lucius Aemilius Paulus, Diodorus Siculus provides some precious testimony in this regard: "Among the Romans, those with the highest noble status or the most famous ancestors are portrayed at their funeral in figures with lifelike features that show their whole bodily appearance, for they are accompanied throughout their life by actors [*mimētai*], who carefully study their behavior and the peculiarities of their appearance."[72] This statement by Diodorus seems to be confirmed by a source (and an event) that is admittedly much later than the Rome of Lucius Aemilius Paulus, but nevertheless worthy of our attention. Suetonius explains that at the funeral of Vespasian, "in keeping with the traditional custom [*ut est mos*] an *archimimus* bearing the emperor's mask [*persona*] imitated the deeds and words of the living emperor."[73] Suetonius explicitly says that this was not a singular invention, but was instead a traditional part of the ritual. The *archimimus* described here by Suetonius strongly recalls the *mimētai* in Diodorus, those "doubles" who accompanied the Roman aristocrats in life so that after their death they could enjoy a funeral ritual much like the one staged for the emperor Vespasian.

Roman funeral practices thus apparently relied on the participation of *mimētai,* actors or mimes who accompanied Roman noblemen throughout their lives in order to study their characteristic behaviors and mannerisms. If we consider this *mos* in terms of the relentless net of resemblances described by Pliny, those onomastic ties between the Roman nobles and the actors and mimes, then we can hypothesize that these unusual *similitudines* might have involved precisely those *mimētai* who accompanied the aristocrats in order to study their comportment and peculiarities of expression. The migration of cognomina from the one to the other would be the result of the fact that one member of the pair actually served as the other's alter ego: a man who resembles a Roman aristocrat, and who is able to use the actor's art to heighten and exploit this natural contiguity, is attracted into the other man's orbit to such a degree that he becomes something like that other man's double or stand-in.

Meanwhile: tragic events have separated a young couple, and our heroine is bewailing the death (or so she thinks) of her beloved. We find her on board a ship, sailing a sea that swarms with tempests and pirates, pervaded by premonitions, signals, coincidences—the sea of Greek romance. Callirhoe has been captured by pirates; in the throes of despair she is beating her breast with her fist when suddenly "she glimpses the little ring bearing Chaereas's portrait, kisses it, and begins to speak, 'Chaereas, truly I am now lost to you.'"[74] This portrait of Chaereas—the ring and the image it bears—will prove to be closely involved in the plot of this story, and we will glimpse them once again when Callirhoe (now the wife of Dionysius) erects a cenotaph to the lover whom she supposes to be dead, and stages a solemn funeral procession in which "an effigy [*eidōlon*] of Chaereas is borne aloft, modeled on the image set in the seal of Callirhoe's ring."[75] The image of the absent lover appears and reappears, refracted from one end of the story to the other.

But let us return to Callirhoe's earlier adventures, as she is deciding whether to marry Dionysius. She already knows that she is pregnant with Chaereas's child when Dionysius, an Ionian citizen of some importance, declares his love for her and proposes marriage. It is a true dilemma. Should Callirhoe remain faithful to Chaereas by committing suicide—but bringing about the death of their child? Or should she choose life for the child's sake, persuading Dionysius that the child is his—thus betraying the fidelity she had pledged to Chaereas?[76] Callirhoe realizes that she needs some advice:[77]

> So she goes upstairs and shuts the door, and presses the image of Chaereas to her womb, saying: "Here we are, all three of us, husband, wife, and son. For myself, I want to die as the wife of Chaereas alone. To not know a second husband is more dear to me than my own parents, than

my country and my son. And you, my child, what do you choose for yourself? To die from poison before seeing the sun, or to live and have two fathers? Once you have grown up, you will be easily recognized by your relatives, because I am convinced that I will give birth to you in the likeness of your father. And what do you, the father, have to say? But the father has already spoken. He appeared to me in a dream and said, 'I entrust our son to your care.' I call you as witness, Chaereas: it is you who give me as a bride to Dionysius."

A lover, and his son in the mother's womb—as the portrait of the lover is pressed against that womb. There is also a dream, another familiar feature of our fundamental story: the portrait of the lover is once again accompanied by fleeting oneiric images.[78] But most striking of all is the fact that Callirhoe is certain that the child will be a boy, and that he will be similar to his father, so similar, in fact, that his relatives will recognize the boy as soon as they see him. But there is something very intriguing about this scene: in addition to Callirhoe's absolute fidelity, the cultural requirements of male domination, and the obvious demands of the plot, it also seems that Chaereas's image—tightly pressed against the womb in a moment of great solemnity—might also be contributing to the future resemblance between father and son, thanks to the powerful influence that we know can be exercised by images at such critical junctures.

Callirhoe gives in. The child will live, and she will marry Dionysius, swearing that he is the child's father. But after the wedding (and after the birth of her child), Callirhoe finds herself alone in the temple of Aphrodite. She picks the little boy up in her arms, lifting him toward the goddess as she says: "For his sake, O mistress, I am grateful to you; as for myself, I do not know. I would add my own gratitude if you had preserved the life of my Chaereas. Although at least you have given me this image of the man who is most dear to me; you have not taken Chaereas from me entirely."[79] The resemblance has turned out well in every sense of the word. Chaereas's little son is the portrait of his father, and the bereft lover can console herself with the image of the beloved that she sees in their son. Chaereas has not been taken away from her entirely; a part of him remains in his son, his living image. What was a story of family resemblance has unexpectedly become a portrait of the lover. But we must immediately proceed to Dido's palace in Carthage; there is, in fact, no time to lose.

Having fallen madly in love with Aeneas, Dido now finds herself alone in the palace; all the guests have departed, and the queen is tossing and turning on the empty couches:[80]

Sola . . .
. . . illum absens absentem auditque videtque
aut gremio Ascanium, genitoris imagine capta
detinet, infandum si fallere possit amorem.

Alone, . . . parted from him, she sees and hears the one who has departed, or she takes Ascanius in her lap, overcome by the image of his
father, as if to deceive her unspeakable love.

Haunted by the mental image of the beloved who assails her senses even
in his absence, the queen finds a certain comfort (or its illusion) in Ascanius: the boy's face recalls his father's features, perhaps allowing her
to think that it is Aeneas she is embracing.

Resemblance can thus function as a surrogate; a person can be val-
ued precisely for his resemblance to someone else ("Doesn't he remind
you of . . . ?"). When Hippolytus asks his stepmother whether her ar-
dor is due to a chaste love for his father Theseus, Seneca's Phaedra declares:[81] "The fact is that I love Theseus's face, that same face he had
when he was a boy." Hippolytus displays to her the image of a young
Theseus; what Phaedra loves (or what she says she loves) is the image of
her husband's past reflected in his son's face, a resemblance that is somehow able to justify her unspeakable passion. One thinks of Perseus's
mirror: no one could withstand the direct sight of Medusa, but when the
horror was reflected—when it was doubled—it also became dimmed.[82]
In this game of extras and stand-ins, resemblance is apparently able to
refract and soften the sharp edges of inconceivable desires. If ques-
tioned by the voice of Sychaeus, Dido can claim that she was only amusing herself with a small child; accused by her husband, Phaedra can
defend herself by saying that Hippolytus is simply a young Theseus,
Theseus *puer*. It is enough to displace the object of one's desires onto
something else, playing a game of doubles and reflected images. The
compromise is both effective and strategic: if you do not look it straight
in the eye, even the horror of incest becomes less riveting. For example,
Nero supposedly lusted for his mother and accordingly "found a prostitute who was said to greatly resemble Agrippina and chose her to be
one of his concubines."[83] In similar fashion, Commodus bestowed his
mother's name on one of his concubines.[84] It is the stand-ins, of course,
who must play the most dangerous parts.

But let us return to Dido's palace at Carthage. The queen's passion
yearns to look upon Aeneas's face, but the hero has abandoned her. She
desperately desires a substitute for that face, so that she might glimpse

Aeneas in another human being, a living portrait of the beloved she has lost. The brief period of their happiness is now over (that brief interval during which she possessed him, her beloved, and not just a surrogate of his form); the last good-byes have been said. Dido is left with nothing, and she reproaches Aeneas bitterly:[85]

> Saltem si qua mihi de te suscepta fuisset
> ante fugam suboles; siquis mihi parvulus aula
> luderet Aeneas, qui te tamen ore referret
> non equidem omnino capta ac deserta viderer.

> If only I had conceived a child of yours before your flight; if only there were a little Aeneas who would play here in my halls, who might reproduce you in the features of his face—then I would not seem so entirely overcome and abandoned.

A little Aeneas would have been his father's portrait: Dido wants a *parvulus Aeneas*. Commenting on this passage, Servius notes that Dido talks like a lover—*sic dixit quasi amatrix*—not like a queen or a wife. Her desire for a child has nothing to do with maternal or domestic instincts, or her recognition of the need to carry on the royal lineage; this little Aeneas would simply be a mirror of love, the equivalent of Laodamia's simulacrum, or the shadow traced on the wall by Butades' daughter. Although in this case, it would be a portrait of the lover generated by Dido herself, without the mediation of art.

From the Portrait to the Mirror

But let us finally rejoin our original topic: Augustine's theory of resemblance. "Nature," as Augustine was saying, "produces resemblances *in deterioribus* by generation or by reflection: by generation, as when children are born who resemble their parents, and by reflection, as in any sort of mirror." In addition, there are those resemblances *in deterioribus* that are produced by animate beings, such as "paintings and all manner of depictions."[86] Reflected images, family resemblances, and artistic reproductions thus all belong to the same type of *similitudo;* they are all resemblances *in deterioribus,* which means that in every case we can confidently distinguish the model from the copy, the person who resembles from the person who is resembled. Augustine's philosophical observations, which assemble these various types of resemblance into a single category, seem to correspond closely to the speculations of literature: as in the case of Dido, who wants a son, a little Aeneas, who will be a living reproduction of the father who conceived him; or the story of Callirhoe, who places a portrait of her beloved Chaereas next to the son she is still carrying in her womb, the son who will be the portrait of his father. There is also a close correspondence between Augustine's theory and the metaphors and spontaneous exclamations of everyday life: "That boy is the living image of his father," or "his father's spit and image," and so on. But it is in the symbolic system of dreams and dream interpretation that this metaphorical association displays its greatest productivity; the science of dream interpretation is actually able to assemble and combine elements belonging to almost all of the cultural models that we have considered in this survey of resemblances.

According to Artemidorus, "to dream about a portrait indicates sons, . . . because sons and portraits are similar to one another." [87] This means that "what happens to the portrait in the dream is what will happen to the sons of the dreamer." In the science of dream interpretation, sons and portraits recall one another, and it is the shared element of resemblance (a man's son resembles him as does his portrait) that effectively links these two otherwise disparate phenomena. Of course, we saw earlier that sons and portraits could be linked not only in dreams, but also in the belief that resemblances could be produced by looking at images, or in the fictional plot that united Callirhoe, her son, and Chaereas's portrait. But in the symbolic system of dream interpretation another element is added to the array of sons and portraits: the mirror. Artemidorus explains that "to be reflected and to see one's own image reproduced faithfully in the mirror is a good sign for someone who wants to marry, whether the dreamer is a man or a woman. The mirror indicates the wife (in the case of a man) or the husband (in the case of a woman) since *the mirror reproduces their faces in the same way that their faces are reproduced in their children*." [88] The mirror (that quintessential source of doubles and resemblances) is a symbol of reproduction and procreation, much like that curious legend we encountered in an earlier chapter: [89] "whoever enters the birthplace of Zeus at Parrhasia simultaneously loses his shadow and his fertility." Both the image reflected in the mirror and a person's shadow are able to double the person. Moreover, these reflections and shadows symbolize the fundamental and far more consequential way in which human beings are able to double themselves: producing children. In one of his *Sonnets* (if they are in fact his), Shakespeare offers the following advice to the hand-some man who inspired those poems, urging him to give up his single status:[90]

> Look in thy glass, and tell the face thou viewest
> Now is the time that face should form another;
> Whose fresh repair if now thou not renewest,
> Thou dost beguile the world, unbless some mother.
>
> . . . .
>
> But if thou live, remember'd not to be,
> Die single, and thine image dies with thee.

But there is more. Artemidorus also explains that "if the dreamer sees someone else's image in the mirror, it is a sign that the dreamer will be called the father of bastard sons, or of other men's sons."[91] The mirror is thus a reliable symbol not only of family resemblance, but also of the dreaded dissimilarity between fathers and sons. If the reflecting surface sends back an image that does not resemble the father, then the moth-er's chastity is placed in doubt. In dream interpretation, the mirror is able to encompass all the various outcomes, anticipating every possible variety of reproduction—faithful, unfaithful, and even partially faithful, as in the following example:[92]

> Someone dreamed that he was holding a barber's mirror as he stood in the road near the market, and he attached great importance to looking at himself in that mirror. When he was able to do so, he saw that his face was all covered with spots. This man was in love with a courtesan, and had taken her by force to live with him illicitly. The child she bore him had various defects from birth, and was cross-eyed. The barber's mirror symbolized the woman, who was publicly available and at every man's disposal, and whom the man had gained possession of only with diffi-culty, because there had actually been an attempt to prevent him from taking the woman to live with him. And because he had seen his image in the mirror, he had a son who resembled him; but that son was not with-out defects, because his face in the mirror had been covered with spots.

In this long and complicated dream, the symbolic connections that we have already observed (the mirror, the image, the son) expand to in-clude a further combination of relationships. The son of the courtesan was not an adulterous son—the man looking in the mirror saw a true image of himself reflected there—but the image was spotted, an omen of the son's future defects. The courtesan (the barber's mirror) was available to all, inevitably retaining traces of those who had previously been mirrored in her (much like the other examples we have seen in which *sympatheia* causes images to be conserved by the reflecting surface).[93] The dreamer thus could not help but have an impure and distorted son with such a woman. The reflected image, Augustine says, is inevitably inferior to the original—so what can one expect of the reflection that appears on the surface of a second-rate mirror?

17

The Doll

On the tenth of May in 1889, during excavations for the construction of the Palace of Justice in Rome, two sarcophagi were unearthed, both belonging to members of the same family, and inscribed respectively with the names CREPEREIUS EUHODUS and CREPEREIA TRYPHAENA. The sarcophagus of CREPEREIUS EUHODUS was smooth and plain, without any ornamentation, but the sarcophagus of CREPEREIA TRYPHAENA was decorated with a quite intense scene of funereal grief: we can see a small female figure stretched out on a bed in the center of the scene, with another female figure, her head covered by a veil, sitting on a cushion at the foot of the bed, and a man standing at the head of the bed, dressed in a chlamys, captured in a moment of grief, resting his head in the crook of his arm. At the moment of the discovery, it was immediately obvious that Crepereia's sarcophagus had become filled with water, so: [1]

> it was decided to break the seals . . . by which the lid was attached, in order to empty the box and carefully gather whatever happened to be preserved inside. . . . They lifted the lid of the sarcophagus and let their gaze fall on the corpse, which they saw through the clear and limpid water. The skull had a surprising appearance, as it seemed to be covered with long and thick hair waving back and forth in the water. The news of this miraculous discovery quickly gathered a crowd of curious onlookers from the neighboring Prati district, so that Crepereia's exhumation was carried out with honors of surpassing solemnity, and was long remembered in the neighborhood's local legends. The phenomenon of Crepereia's hair was quickly explained: when the water flowed into the sarcophagus, it apparently brought with it the bulbs of an aquatic plant that

produces extremely long jet-black filaments; this plant had rooted in the skull of the corpse. The skull itself was slightly turned in the direction of the left shoulder, where a charming little doll had been carefully placed.

Along with the doll (see Fig. 5), the sarcophagus contained many opulent funeral goods, including jewelry with which Crepereia had been adorned for her funeral, along with a crown of myrtle leaves. There were also two tiny little mirrors found in the sarcophagus, and some pieces of "grown-up" jewelry, including a gold ring with an inscription in red jasper, spelling out the name FILETUS.

The archeologists were deeply moved by this exceptional discovery, and they gathered around the girl's sarcophagus, accompanied by a crowd of curious onlookers. But there was someone else lurking in the shadows, an invisible presence, lost in memories of things that had happened long ago:[2]

> In nigros circum taciturna lucos
> fugerat cornix, repetebat urbis
> turba corvorum memorum quadratae
>   saxa Palati,
> Cum solum Tuscum decimo die te
> reddidit Maio, Crepereia, soli
> pronubam post innumera induentem
>   saecula gemmam.
> Vitrea virgo sub aqua latebas,
> at comans summis adiantus undis
> nabat. An nocti dederas opacae
>   spargere crinis?
> Sed quid antiquis oculi videnti
> nunc mihi effeti lacrimis madescunt?
> Quas premo curas alioque eundem
>   corde dolorem?

A silent crow fled into the surrounding dark groves, while a flock of ravens, mindful of the squared city, were returning again to the stones of the Palatine; there, on the tenth of May, the Tuscan earth restored you to the light, after countless years still wearing the engagement gem on your finger. A girl hidden beneath the crystal waters, but with maidenhair floating on the rippling surface—or had you let the dark night scatter your hair? But why are my tired eyes bathed with ancient tears at the sight of you? What are these anxieties that trouble me, what fear shared with another's heart?

This obscure ghost from the distant past was none other than Crepereia's fiance hovering near the sarcophagus—or rather, it was the spirit of a poet, Giovanni Pascoli, who crafted one of his Latin *carmina* around the news of this discovery. According to the archaeologists' report, the exhumation had taken place on the tenth of May. But Pascoli (with his auspicious education in the classics) was well aware that the ancient Romans celebrated the festival of the Lemuria on the eve of the eleventh of May. This was a sacred and somber holiday of the dead, marking the moment when the shades of the deceased ancestors would return from the Underworld, tearing aside the veil that separates life from death, filling the house with their ephemeral presence, and rousing the emotions of the living family members.[3] It was thus an easy matter for Pascoli (tentatively, gradually, in a spiraling process of identification tinged with anxiety) to assume the identity of Crepereia's beloved fiancé, who must have been (as Pascoli supposed) the FILETUS whose name was inscribed on Crepereia's ring.[4] And Giovanni-Filetus knew what he had to do: on that sacred night, in its darkest hour, when "the birds of various colors and the dogs have fallen silent," he must remove his shoes and throw a handful of beans over his shoulder, pronouncing the formula of the ancient ritual nine times: "with these beans, I ransom me and mine, O shades of Crepereia," *his fabis manes redimo Tryphaenae meque meosque*. But contrary to all the rites of the Lemuria, Giovanni-Filetus will not ring the bronze gong to drive the ghosts away. Instead, he will turn around and look at the shades and the ghosts, the *lemures*. Rather than freeing himself and his relatives from the burden of the family's ghosts (which was the purpose of the ancient ritual), Giovanni-Filetus wants to follow the ghosts, and to accompany them on their journey. Above all, he wants to see the pale shade of Crepereia coming to him from the Underworld; he wants to remember the sad day of her funeral—until finally a vortex of silence seizes his soul, dragging him into the abyss from which there can be no return, where he will hear his mother as she hopelessly cries out his name, the name of his poetic persona: "Filetus!"

Absences, funerals, familiar ghosts—and the mesmerizing spell, the *envoûtement* of death. Crepereia, that archaeological find from the Prati district of Rome, has become a full-blooded character in Pascoli's poetry, a ghost of erudition quivering with nostalgia. The archaeologists had prosaically defined her hair as the filaments of some aquatic plant, but Pascoli uses instead a technical-poetic name: *comans adiantus,* the plant called "Venus-hair" (*capelvenere*) in Italian, "maiden-hair" in English.[5] But about the doll, Pascoli has little to say, neglecting even to mention that Crepereia's head had been turned toward her toy. Instead, he mentions only later in the poem that this doll had been denied to

Venus: *Veneri pupa negata*. This is because Crepereia did not live long enough to dedicate her doll to Venus on the eve of her wedding, a practice followed by Roman girls (and not unknown to Pascoli).[6] But that is all he says about the doll. Strange, given that they buried Crepereia with her head turned carefully in the direction of that charming little doll. Indeed, how can we resist its fascination?

The Girl in the Eye and *Neurospaston*

So, with no further assistance from Pascoli (or from Filetus), we will have to proceed on our own. The doll is 23 centimeters tall, and for some time it was thought to be made of wood but, as was discovered later, the doll is actually made of ivory.[7] It has articulated joints at the shoulders, at the elbows, and at the hips and knees. The body is carved with visible breasts and nipples, and the belly is gently rounded (not flat), with a visible belly-button. The hair is carved in an elaborate style reflecting the fashions of the second century C.E., and the eyes are wide and large, with irises and pupils that are distinctly formed. The hands and feet are carved in perfect detail. The doll thus has the figure of a maturing young girl. No doubt many people, hearing the name "Crepereia Tryphaena," consciously or unconsciously associate the dead girl with the features of her doll; or, seeing the photograph of this famous doll (the most famous doll from antiquity), they automatically call the doll by the name of the girl, Crepereia. Such confusion is understandable; in fact, as we will see, there is a profound meaning at work here in the ambiguous relationship between that girl and her doll.

Antiquity has been rather generous with its dolls, and we have archaeological evidence dating as far back as the third millennium B.C.E. in ancient Egypt, followed later by Greek dolls from various regions of the Mediterranean, and then by Roman dolls.[8] Crepereia's doll is surely the most beautiful, although there are admittedly many similar dolls from the beginning of the millennium until the Christian period. There is one particular feature about these dolls that immediately catches the modern viewer's attention: these dolls have the features of young girls; they are not baby dolls.[9] Therefore, the game that the dolls' owners played with them (finally admitting that impossibly difficult word into our discussion: "play") could not have been a game of simulated maternity.[10] Instead, this kind of doll was a miniature simulation of a companion for her owner (the word "owner" being another awkward phrase we will have to reconsider later). The doll-companion enters the game as a full and equal partner, not someone to protect and care for like an infant.

Ancient Greek and Latin vocabulary also makes it clear that dolls were regarded as young girls, not babies. We will return to this vocabulary in detail later on, but for now it is worth noting that in Latin the doll is called *pupa*, a word that can also mean "little girl"; the same is true of the Greek word for doll, *korē*, which is also the standard word for "girl."[11] Another Greek word for the doll—*plangōn*—is found as a proper name in Greek New Comedy (something like the English "Dolly"). Thus, as defined in Greek and Latin, the doll is like a tiny mirror that reflects the world at large. This mirror is not simply a metaphor: the words *pupa* and *korē* were also both used to mean the "pupil" of the eye, and more specifically the miniaturized image captured in the mirror of someone else's pupil when we look into the eye of the person who is looking at us.

Of course, this topic of the "girl in the eye" greatly exceeds the bounds of our discussion.[12] We will have to be content with the observation that this particular linguistic and metaphorical game involving the pupil, the girl, and the doll seems to have emerged very far back in time, and can be seen already in the Homeric use of the word *glēnē*:[13] when Hector wants to insult Diomedes for having retreated in combat, he first accuses him of acting like a woman and then adds: *erre, kakē glēnē*, "away with you, you stupid doll," apparently mocking Diomedes by comparing him to a girl or a doll.[14] Ancient Greek lexicons also tell us that the word *glēnē* was a synonym of *korē* or of *korokosmion*, another word for "doll."[15] It thus appears that the Homeric Greek word, *glēnē*, could be used to mean both "pupil" and "girl." Given that the primary meaning of *glēnē* seems to have been a "precious object" (or perhaps something "brilliant"),[16] it might appear that in this case the metaphorical process has taken an unexpected path.[17] That is, we might expect that *glēnē* originally meant "girl/doll" and later came to be associated with the pupil of the eye; but apparently the process began with the pupil (that brilliant little mirror, the precious light of the eyes) and was then transferred to the girl/doll. The pupil and the girl/doll thus seem to be completely interchangeable creatures: we can reach the one from the other, and vice versa. But before leaving this topic, there is one other important vocabulary item that must be noted. Literary evidence tells us that in Greek the pupil, the *korē*, could also be called *parthenos*, "virgin," a true and proper girl defined in terms of her most relevant cultural characteristic, her virginity. Moreover, the girl in the eye was also supposed to be chaste (like any good girl or virgin).[18] With these lexical parallels in mind, we can now return to the ancient girl who plays with her doll: the two Greek *korai*, the Latin *pupae,* who share a single name in the game that binds one to the other.

As we said before, the doll is like a tiny mirror that reflects the world at large. In this sense, dolls can be included among the other miniaturized objects deposited in tombs, objects that constitute the doll's accoutrements and context. For example, a doll excavated at the temple of Venus in Anxur was accompanied by a tiny table and chair, candlesticks, plates, and cooking utensils. Similarly, a doll found in the tomb of Julia Graphis came equipped with a miniature table and chair, along with a little bucket and copper pot.[19] Crepereia's sarcophagus also contained tiny mirrors and combs, and the doll itself was wearing a little gold ring with a key.[20] The doll is not alone: she lives inside an actual little house, a simulated *kosmos* in which the *korē* resides.

There is another distinctive difference between the doll and the other votive figurines and dedicatory offerings: the doll has jointed limbs, which are capable of movement.[21] These dolls actually possessed various types of articulated joints, with a greater or lesser degree of refinement, ranging from a simple articulation of stiff legs beneath a torso elongated to simulate a dress, rigid arms joined at the shoulders, and finally the marvelous engineering of Crepereia's doll. To give the doll articulated joints offers her the possibility of movement; as opposed to other types of simulacra, the doll appears naturally predisposed to sustain the illusion (or better: the fiction) of her body's articulated movement. Moreover, some ancient dolls held cymbals or castanets in their hands,[22] and they sometimes had pierced ears, allowing them to wear earrings,[23] as is precisely the case with Crepereia's doll.[24] The dolls were often designed as nude figures, which means that they could be dressed up,[25] wearing doll clothes like those that a girl named Timarete dedicated to the goddess Artemis (as we read in an epigram from the *Greek Anthology*).[26] In addition, lines drawn on the feet simulated the presence of shoes,[27] while the top of the head was sometimes adorned with actual hair, whose strands were attached to the scalp by means of tiny wooden pegs.[28]

The doll is therefore a kind of image: but what kind of image exactly? We possess a rather detailed inventory of the doll's features, which may allow us to draw some conclusions. First of all, we are dealing with the figure of a girl, an image that simulates—as much as possible—the features of a real person. The limbs are jointed, which suggests movement, and the castanets and the cymbals can jingle, simulating the presence of sound. In addition, the doll has two surfaces, just like a real person: she can be nude (a nudity that is marked by breasts and other anatomical features), and she can also be dressed, wearing tiny clothes that change her aspect and function. This gives the doll an inside and an outside, making her distinctively different from the other images that we looked at earlier.[29] By being nude and dressable, the doll explicitly shows that she possesses a body—a body that can be hidden and also adorned, a body that makes her a "person" able to change her external appearance according to the conventions or necessities imposed by the rules of the culture. This is quite unlike the images—the other images—that do not seem to possess a distinct body apart from their exterior aspect.

As a matter of fact, all these characteristics combine to push the *pupa* more toward mobility and life, and away from the fixedness of an icon. Her nude body can be dressed, she can wear earrings in her pierced ears, her tapered fingers allow her to wear rings, and her real hair requires an array of little combs.[30] In short, the doll seems increasingly alive, unlike the immobile simulacrum of a live person who is strongly distinguished from his or her inanimate representation (as happens in the case of a painting or a sculpted portrait). The doll is an image/nonimage living on the margins of a world of movement and sound, ready to participate in that world if she should ever choose to do so. As such, the doll admits—indeed, she requires—a range of activities; she is defined precisely in terms of the possibility of being dressed or wearing earrings, of having her hair combed, or taking a few steps (perhaps halting, perhaps bold and confident) guided by a little girl's hands. The doll interacts with the person who owns her—indeed, she allows or even requires that manipulation.[31] This sort of doll, equipped with an array of personal items, furniture, and furnishings, can only be understood as an object that exists in order to be manipulated at the hands of the person who plays with her.

This, then, is the essential point: the doll suggests a specific style of behavior—interactive behavior—that is entirely different from the behaviors expected by statues or other types of simulacra. It is not only that the doll has additional exterior features (mobile joints, real hair, a trousseau, and so on). Rather, the doll is transformed into a different type of iconic object because this difference in technical features implies a different model of behavior; one responds to the doll differently than one responds to a statue or a painting. This means, strangely enough, that any sort of image could be transformed into a *pupa,* without giving it mobile joints or pierced ears: all that is required is to treat the image in an interactive way. An unexpected source—the Christian writer Lactantius—confirms precisely this possibility, although Lactantius is exploiting the paradox in order to polemicize with the pagans, and also with pagan images of the gods. The discussion opens with a passage from Persius, which we will later consider in some detail: [32]

> In sancto quid facit aurum?
> Nempe hoc quod Veneri donatae a virgine pupae.

> What is the use of gold inside a holy place? It is about as useful as those dolls that a girl dedicates to Venus [*Veneri donatae a virgine pupae*].

Commenting on these lines, Lactantius argues: [33]

> Perhaps the poet spoke dismissively of the dolls because of their small size. But did he not see that even the simulacra and images of the gods made in gold and ivory by such artists as Phidias, Euphranor, or Polyclitus are nothing other than big dolls? Of course, they are dedicated not by little girls (whose games we can forgive) but by full-grown men with beards. And these men give to these toys of theirs, to their big fancy dolls, offerings of balm, incense, and perfume, sacrificing to them victims that are rich and fat (even though, while they have mouths, they have no teeth), giving them cloaks and precious clothing when they have no need to be dressed, and presenting them with gold and silver that is not so much the property of those who receive it as it is of those who offer it.

Lactantius then rubs salt into the wound with a famous exemplum about Dionysius of Syracuse who reportedly took back a golden robe belonging to a statue of Jupiter. He replaced the golden robe with a cloak of wool, capping his sacrilege with sarcasm: "Gold is so heavy in the summer and retains the cold in winter, but woolen clothes are good to wear all year round." [34]

While Dionysius gladly plays the skeptic, compounding theft with mockery, Lactantius instead plays the honest and amazed traveler—an Uzbek in Paris, an Anacharsis visiting Greece for the first time. But someone who believes in only one god is already a man of a different culture, with a different perspective, a gaze "from afar." Lactantius, the Christian, evokes a pagan ceremony and focuses all his attention on those self-important men who make offerings of perfumes and unguents to the simulacra of the gods, consecrating robes and even preparing food for the toothless images. Lactantius makes the unavoidable comparison: those full-grown, bearded men are no different from little girls playing with their dolls.

The fact is that one behaves in a certain way only with dolls, and not with statues. Moreover, as Lucilius already observed, children are indeed prone to mistake images for living creatures:[35]

> Ut pueri infantes credunt signa omnia aena
> vivere et esse homines: sic istic omnia ficta
> vera putant, credunt signis cor inesse in aenis.
> Pergula pictorum, veri nihil, omnia ficta.

> As small children believe that all bronze statues are living people, so too they think that all fictions are true, and believe that there is a heart in the bronze statues. But it is all a picture gallery, nothing true, everything fiction.

Yet at this point we must ask once again what distinguishes the doll from other images; or, to put the question another way, what other sort of image (painted, sculpted, or carved) exists as an object for manipulation—as an object of private ownership, changing its clothes and accessories, changing its context and function according to the game being played? (There it is again, that impossible word: play!) At this point, we might try to confront these questions in terms of the iconic object and its referent.

First of all, can the doll actually be said to have a referent? That is, does there exist something or someone that the doll—thanks to her basic and intrinsic qualities—reproduces by means of similarity? In one sense, the doll can be said to have a referent in that the *pupa* represents a female person with the features of a young girl; that is, the doll is marked as belonging to a specific gender and a specific age group. But in the relationship that the doll reproduces with regard to this referent—in terms of the doll's actual substance as a sign—we find many features that are not associated with other types of images: mobile limbs, a nude body that can be dressed, the possibility of emitting sounds, and so on, an entire series of elements that combine to create an impression of reality, an active life, "real life." In other words, it is as if the doll is able to appropriate a kind of "life" from her referent in order to acquire for herself (as much as possible) the living nature of the object that she reproduces by similarity. The doll is a sign that aspires to autoreference; this is an image that tends to escape from the closed and fixed world of the icons in order to journey into the domain of reality. The doll is a simulacrum of a girl, but at the same time the doll pretends *to be* a girl. Moreover, thanks to the game that the little girl plays with her doll, the doll can succeed in being a girl: a docile little girl subjected to the capricious preferences of the owner who manipulates her, an image that is simultaneously inclined toward autoreference and to submission.

But if the doll in some sense comes to life in the game played by her owner, she can become even more alive, become a girl even more fully, in the game of literature—until finally the fantasy of the story is able to overturn the last and most stubborn barrier that stands between the doll and reality. E. T. A. Hoffmann's "The Sandman," for example, is the story of how a doll was endowed with true movement by her "father," the morally ambiguous Spalanzini, aided by the decidedly sinister Coppelius-Coppola. The product of their experiments, the doll/girl Olympia, receives guests in good German bourgeois fashion; she can sing, dance, entertain, and enchant. But despite its fantastic extravagance and Romantic obsessions, "The Sandman" is simply another variation on an illusion that has existed for millennia, and that is in some sense intrinsic to the cultural characteristics of the object itself.[36] The doll, by its very nature, is inclined toward movement and toward life. The uncanny effect reaches its extreme when that semiotic equivalence unexpectedly becomes reality itself: when the image/doll peremptorily dismisses her referent, strips her of the privileges enjoyed by living creatures and then slowly takes her first independent steps into a ballroom that is gradually filling with guests.[37]

The mechanical science dramatized in Hoffmann's story is an admittedly exaggerated example of Romantic fantasy. But there was also an actual science of *technē mēchanikē* that seriously attempted to simulate movement in inanimate objects long before Hoffmann invented his automaton Olympia. Heron[38] and Vitruvius[39] provide us with some famous ancient evidence for figurines (*sigilla*) that operated by hydraulic pressure and thus seemed able to drink, or were able to imitate blackbirds chirping, and other equally marvelous creations. As later in the European Baroque, the Hellenistic age of Greece was fascinated by automatons. The masterpiece of this form of art, described to us again by Heron, was apparently a miniature theater that operated entirely by mechanical devices.[40] At the beginning and end of every scene tiny doors opened automatically to reveal the whole history of Nauplion dramatized by little painted figures endowed with mechanical movement: the Danaids sailing in their ship, the dolphins, and so on.

But it seems we have lost sight of the doll. The art of the automaton can offer only figurines that run around the stage pulled by ribbons, or *sigilla* that at regular intervals gulp water when they reach the top of a water clock. Such machines cannot compare to the subtle movements and delicate gestures of a marionette, or *neurospasma*. A puppet pulled by strings is really able to move and gesticulate in various ways like a human being, unlike the mechanical *sigillum,* which remains chained to a fixed course that it endlessly repeats. The marionette's gestures are not limited to the rigid reiteration of a single gesture, as monotonous as the turning of a gear. Therefore, given that a doll has articulated limbs, it would seem possible simply to attach strings to those limbs, and to pro-duce the apparent miracle of movement. The *technē neurospastikē* could thus replace the contribution made by the little girl's imagination, or by the overexcited fantasy of the storyteller. In the pseudo-Aristotelian *De mundo,* the puppeteer's art actually becomes a metaphor used to de-scribe the economical way in which divine energy intervenes to impart movement to the things of the world:[41] "The puppeteer needs only to pull the strings, and the puppet's head (or its hand, eyes, shoulders) will move, giving the impression that all its members are participating in a certain harmonious motion."[42]

But the puppeteer's art is often judged much more harshly, and the metaphors prompted by the marionette are not always so positive as in the *De mundo.*[43] In fact, it is often quite the opposite. Instead of em-phasizing the unity, the *eurhythmia* of the puppet's movement, ancient authors frequently call attention to the puppet's awkwardness. Above all, the movement of the *neurospasma* is determined by someone else, controlled from the outside—a characteristic that was essential to the metaphor in the *De mundo* as well, of course. For example, Plato con-siders the marionette to be a paradigm that is the perfect opposite of hu-manity:[44] the marionette is moved by others, and thus expresses the to-tal absence of freedom. When a person succumbs to his passions, he is reduced to the status of a puppet; the origin of his movements is out-side himself, and eludes his control. This Platonic metaphor went on to enjoy an enduring popularity. "You give me orders," Horace observes, "but in fact you are the slave of someone else, a wretched creature who is moved about like a piece of wood obeying the strings that someone else is pulling."[45] Aulus Gellius applied the metaphor to someone with an excessive faith in astrology: to put too much trust in the stars de-prives a man of his privileged endowment of *logos,* as if human beings were only "silly, ridiculous puppets."[46] The marionette is an object of mockery and derision: it moves, but only because its strings are pulled.

When mechanical principles aspire to take the place of fantasy and attempt to make the doll move as a matter of fact, the result is inevitably ridiculous.[47]

In attempting to imitate life mechanically, technology paradoxically succeeds in doing just the opposite: it calls attention to the inanimate, dead character of the thing that is supposed to be alive. Surely it was no coincidence that Trimalchio owned a silver skeleton, a flexible marionette "crafted in such a way that the articulation of its limbs and vertebrae could be twisted in any direction."[48] At a certain point during that famous dinner a slave brings the object to Trimalchio, who "throws it down on the table several times, and the mobility of its structure thus makes it assume a variety of positions."

The Friendly Double

But let us return to the doll. As we were saying before, to play with the doll means to imagine that the doll is a sign that aspires to a kind of autoreference, an image on the verge of making itself into a person. This is precisely why the doll, unlike any other sort of image, suggests to the human world the possibility of interacting with it (of playing with her, with the doll). The doll is able to cross the boundary separating signs from objects (copies from originals) because the doll is not just something to look at or observe: she is meant to be manipulated. The girl who plays a game with her doll thus translates into practical terms the extremely unusual semiotic character of the object that she holds in her hands. But now we must try to determine what sort of game is being played here, a question that brings us back to where we began: the *pupa*.

When Crepereia was interred, that veiled woman and that grief-stricken man (his head leaning in the crook of his arm) carefully turned the girl's face in the direction of that charming little doll. The game played between that girl and her doll must have been very important if it became part of such a serious decision at the moment of Crepereia's funeral. It recalls a similarly intimate and profound game suggested by the discovery of a doll in the tomb of a fully adult Vestal Virgin, Cossinia of Tivoli:[49] the doll was her one funerary object; she took nothing else with her. What did that doll remind her of? What meaning did it have for her, and for the people who wanted to inter her together with that doll? We will never know exactly how Crepereia amused herself with her doll (but it is easy enough to imagine, given the combs, the earrings, the little table with its chair . . .). What we do know for certain is that these games would have come to an abrupt end even if an early death had not suddenly cut short Crepereia's life: indeed, we can even be fairly sure that this end of the game would have constituted one of its most important moments.

The ancient sources[50] tell us that both Greek and Roman virgins consecrated their dolls to the goddess on the eve of their wedding,[51] what we would call a typical rite of separation.[52] This final act (when the days of the little girls playing with their dolls finally must come to a close) signals the profound difference between the function of the doll in ancient culture and the function of the doll in modern European culture, a difference we cannot emphasize too much, given the fact that the dolls are similar in so many other ways. Lactantius has already cited for us a passage from Persius which refers to this ritual offering of the *pupa* or *korē* by the girl who is about to get married:[53]

> In sancto quid facit aurum?
> Nempe hoc quod Veneri donatae a virgine pupae.

> What is the use of gold inside a holy place? It is about as useful as those dolls that a girl dedicates to Venus [*Veneri donatae a virgine pupae*].

The scholiast to Persius (relying on the authoritative support of Varro) comments:[54] "Riches are as worthless to the gods as are the dolls that are given to Venus by the virgins who are getting married." It was in fact customary for virgins to consecrate to Venus certain gifts of their virginity before they got married.[55] In an epigram from the *Greek Anthology* (also cited earlier), the virgin Timarete addresses the following prayer to Artemis:[56] "Before her wedding, Timarete offers to you, Limnatis, her tambourine, her favorite ball, the cap that protects her hair, and also her dolls (as it befits a virgin to give them to you, the virgin goddess), along with the doll's clothes, O Artemis!" The translation inevitably ruins the play on words, which is not only elegant but above all provides precious evidence for the cultural meaning of this offering: "she who is a *korē* offers her *korai* to you, who are a *korē*." The Greek noun *korē* plays out all three of its meanings here: doll, girl, virgin (both the one who makes the offering and the goddess to whom it is made). In some sense, therefore, the girl Timarete offers to the goddess (who shares with her the trait of virginity) another *korē* able to represent them both: the doll.

The symbolic relationship that exists between the doll and the girl's virginity is given an understandable emphasis here.[57] The consecration of objects similar to the divinity, precisely on the eve of a wedding, makes a very clear statement: the doll is virginity. Surely this link between the doll and virginity can help to explain the presence of the doll found with the Vestal Virgin Cossinia, a *pupa* in the tomb of a grown woman who was nevertheless still a virgin. In this case, the doll almost seems to mean that for this woman the state of girlhood was prolonged even until the day of her death; Cossinia certainly never made that famous offering to Venus.[58] We should also add that the ancient sources often refer explicitly to the virginity of the girls who possessed or who were dedicating dolls.[59] We can thus now reconsider what we said earlier about the terminology of the Latin *pupa* and the Greek *korē*.[60] The doll already carries the name of "girl"; the same word is used to indicate both the girl and the doll. But by translating—or analyzing—the term, we end up positing two sides to something that in ancient culture had only one.

From this point of view, the other names of the doll take on a particular significance. As we said earlier, the noun *plangōn* is found in Greek New Comedy as a girl's name ("Dolly")—a sign that the girl and the doll can be classed in exactly the same group.[61] There are actually many different Greek words for "doll," and almost all of them point in the direction of "girl," such as the words *nymphē* and *korokosmion*, which is even more complicated and curious. In the explanation of one scholiast, *korokosmion* is "the puppet with which girls adorn themselves."[62] We are probably dealing here with a false etymology[63] (and perhaps a better interpretation could be supplied[64]), but even etymologies that are apparently false in strictly linguistic terms can nevertheless prove to be true in terms of the language's culture and the perceptions of its speakers. In short, we cannot exclude the possibility that the anonymous scholar who glossed the word *korokosmion* as a "puppet that adorns girls" did so with some good reason: that is, because the doll was felt to be closely connected with the girl's *kosmos,* with her private array of identifying objects—those virginal objects that, as we know, she was destined to consecrate when she crossed the threshold of matrimony.

We can now resume the thread of our earlier discussion. From a symbolic point of view, the ancient doll represents the condition of a virgin. But she is also a girl in a linguistic sense (as we have seen), and she even has the form and appearance of a girl, with her tiny breasts and her slender but shapely body. This girl/doll is then offered by her owner to a divinity who is supposed to preserve in votive form this thing that will cease to exist when the virgin girl is married.[65] The conclusion appears quite clear: the ancient doll is not only a girl but, so to speak, *it is the girl,* the actual girl who owns the doll and who offers her to the goddess when she gets married. The *pupa* functions as a cultural symbol, protecting the girl, constituting her virginal equivalent.[66] As an object on the boundaries of life, an image that pretends to take its place among the living, the doll has no difficulty in functioning as the double of someone with whom she shares the same basic features. Among the possibilities available to someone (or to something) that is half alive, there is precisely the option of duplicating a life that belongs to someone else.

In any case, there is no doubt that ancient cultural practices located the doll within a precise framework of meaning, which assigned specific functions to the doll. The doll meant virginity; by its very existence, the *pupa* indicated a precise age group, acting as that group's representative in its interactions with its owner. The doll was a sign, and the meaning that it conveyed was absolutely specific, and endowed with extraordinary cultural force. This meaning is so precise and distinct, in fact, that when the girl abandons her virginal state in order to marry, the doll can no longer properly remain in her company. The doll would communicate the wrong message; it would be out of place: by giving up her doll, her own virginal double, the ancient girl peeled away a layer of her identity, shedding a part of herself that had ceased to exist.

With its eventual dedication in the temple, consecrated to the divinity, the *pupa* or the *korē* became the simulacrum of a time (or of a person) that had vanished over the farthest horizon—the one remaining piece of evidence from a world made up of tiny tables and household goods reproduced and reduced as if by a pantograph, tiny clothes that can be put on and taken off, hair that is styled with elaborate care or tousled impatience. All these imaginary occasions and pretend activities were played out over and over again until the moment when this entire world of little mirrors was obliterated in an elaborate social ceremony (this time a real ceremony). The wedding ritual ended this game of "pretend," and there was no longer room for the doll, for this friendly double of the young, unmarried girl. The *pupa* finally became a simulacrum of absence; the girl lost her virginal identity and the doll became her *kolossos,* that rough sculpture which in ancient Greek culture was able to reproduce the absence of life, capturing the elusive lightness of the *psychē* in the coldness of stone.[67] The doll abandoned in the temple stood for the rigid equivalent of a lost age (physical and cultural) that could never return. It is an object full of the past (because we know, of course, that the past is still with us, hidden away somewhere). But now we look again at the doll and see that her eyes have been hopelessly stilled: and they are filled with melancholy sadness.

Image, Mirror, and *Homo Suus*

All lovers are not created equal. Some are ardent, others are lukewarm; some are reasonable, others are out of their minds; some are chaste, others are shameless. Hostius Quadra was one of those shameless lovers, so shameless that perhaps he ought not to be counted among the lovers at all: we could say instead that he suffered from a monstrous libido. Oddly enough, it is Seneca who tells us Hostius's story,[1] for which he was curtly rebuked by a seventeenth-century commentator:[2] "You ought to have kept quiet about this, Seneca! I am ashamed to read and comment on such things, so I will proceed quickly, closing my eyes." But the philosopher might have answered his censor with these words (borrowed from another seventeenth-century author):[3] "If mere knowledge of lusts and vices made one lustful and vicious, then the mind of God would be the worst of all." The fact of the matter is that moralists, if they want to correct and guide the habits of others, have no choice but to speak about vices. If they keep silent, how can they explain what they are warning us against?

Hostius Quadra apparently enjoyed both sexes equally, and his immense wealth meant that he could satisfy himself in whatever way and however much he wanted. As Seneca explains, his particular perversity consisted in a desire to watch his own debauched performances. Hostius therefore "surrounded himself with mirrors, by means of which he was able to distinguish and orchestrate all his degenerate acts."[4] These mirrors magnified the anatomical details that most aroused his interest, reflecting Hostius himself, revealing all the body parts and positions that (for various practical reasons) are normally hidden from view. This notorious Roman voyeur thus realized the dream of autoscopy: the ability to have a vision of one's own body, replicated externally.[5] A depraved variant of Narcissus, Hostius Quadra managed to make himself into his own object of pleasure, with those longing gazes at the fountain's reflection now accompanied by shameless gasps of pleasure. If we wanted to gossip about the greats of history, we might mention that this very same vice was also attributed to the poet Horace by his biographer.[6] But let us listen instead to what Seneca has to say. Not wanting to sully himself with this lurid subject matter, Seneca makes Hostius Quadra speak about himself, in a quite grandiloquent style: "Let my eyes also take part in this lust, becoming its witnesses and executors; let this device reveal aspects of our body that its position hides from view, so that no one may suspect that I am ignorant of what I am doing."[7] In the end, Hostius was murdered by his own slaves, and, at least according to Seneca, "they ought to have immolated him in front of his own mirror."[8] But when the philosopher reaches the climax of his exemplum, he suddenly turns to the reader and asks: "Do you think perhaps he might not have wanted to have his portrait painted in such a pose?"[9] As we will see, this is a far from obvious assumption.

Apuleius also had some trouble with mirrors when he was formally accused of witchcraft.[10] Pudens, his adversary, charged him with possessing a mirror (*habet speculum philosophus, possidet speculum philosophus!*), which seems to have been taken seriously as evidence of sorcery. The rhetorician, of course, rebuked his accuser in admirable fashion. Since when is it a crime to own a mirror? Don't you know that there is nothing a person likes to look at more than his own image? And what's wrong with looking at images in a mirror, after all, when there is nothing wrong with looking at painted or sculpted images—indeed, when such images are even bestowed on worthy citizens as a public honor? Moreover, images reproduced in painting or sculpture can never equal the mirror's perfection:[11]

> Clay lacks vigor, stone lacks color, painting lacks solidity, and all of them lack motion, . . . but the image in the mirror is a perfect reproduction, full of motion, exactly obedient to the least gesture of the person it reflects [*ad omnem nutum hominis sui morigera*]. The mirror matches the age of everyone who looks at it, from earliest infancy to extreme old age, assuming the entire span of life; it shares the full array of bodily postures, and all the possible faces that a person may have, ranging from joy to sorrow. Meanwhile what is molded in clay, or cast in bronze, or chiseled in

stone, or impressed in wax, or daubed in paint, or imitated with any other form of the artist's work soon ceases to resemble its subject, and becomes like a corpse, whose face cannot move and never changes.

Despite the symmetries and verbal parallels crammed into this passage, or perhaps precisely because of them, the argument is very cogent. The image of the mirror changes with us, while other types of images (by whatever means they are made) are fixed, frozen—dead.[12] That is why we cannot be so sure that Hostius Quadra, as he looked at his image reflected in the mirror, would have wanted it to be painted in such a pose after all.

But carried away by his rhetorical zeal, Apuleius happens to have omitted an important virtue of manufactured images. True, they are lifeless and immobilized: but it also means that they "stay put," so to speak. Images reflected in mirrors, on the other hand—although they are alive and obedient, perfectly *aequaevae* to the reflected person— actually suffer from an extraordinary weakness: they come and go with the person who produces them. If Hostius Quadra were to agree to be painted, his autoscopy would indeed be less opulent; the portrait would be only an impoverished and paralyzed copy, something altogether different from a *spectaculum*—but it would at least be there afterwards: the image would be able to endure.

In this sense, the image in the mirror is only the illusion of an image; it is not really anything other than its referent. As a result, when its referent moves away, the image in the mirror disappears as well. Ovid was well aware of this, as we can see in his description of the reflected image whose vanity was so enticing to Narcissus:[13] "It has nothing of its own: it comes with you, with you it remains, and with you it will depart." The image in the mirror is its own referent, and nothing more; this is why it is so obedient and sensitive, so fully alive and *aequaeva* to the reflected person. As Augustine observed in his discussion of mirrors and *similitudines,* there is a special relationship between the reflected image and the person who projects that image: "Doesn't it seem to you as if your image in the mirror somehow wants to be you yourself?"[14] The *imago* tends toward the person, actually aspiring to be its referent. This is what produces the perfection of the mirror image—and also its utter nonexistence. Precisely because it tends toward the person, because it wants to identify itself with that person, the reflected image cannot exist on its own. Always perfect, the mirror image is consumed in an instant because it dances in step with that same swift rhythm—the tempo of Time—according to which *homo suus* also moves (thanks to a shortage of terminology, Apuleius coined this term—*homo suus,* "its person"—in order to define the referent of the mirror image).[15] The image in the mirror is not even a sign; it does not stand in the place of some other thing:[16] it is something that is not there, or rather, it is something that is there already—too much so, one might say. This is what Ovid's Narcissus tells us, as he stares in fascination at the fountain:[17] "I already have what I desire; and that having makes me hopeless," *quod cupio mecum est; inopem me copia facit.* But this is not a problem for the icon, the little sister of the reflected image: although it is lifeless, insensible, with only the most tenuous resemblance to its referent, the icon does not vanish. It "stays put." This gives the icon the advantage of being independent of its referent, of being able to last, even in the absence of that referent. The world of creation is governed by an ironclad law: life is fleeting; death is permanent. The same is true of the world of images.

Gazing at his reflection in the fountain, Narcissus thought he could address that reflection as *you.* But he was wrong. Narcissus had to say *I* to that image: what he saw before him was simply another "himself." A person looking in a mirror cannot help but say *I*—at most he might have recourse to a trick of language and say *it,* meaning the image. But that is indeed just a trick, a pretense, because as soon as the *I* disappears, *it* likewise vanishes. The person who is reflected is a person who says *I;* each *homo* is inevitably the *homo suus* of his reflected image. When the slave Sosia finds himself facing another "himself" (in that famous scene from Plautus's *Amphitruo*), he can't believe his eyes. Then, slowly, he starts to understand, resigning himself to the facts:[18]

> Certe edepol, quom illum contemplo et formam cognosco meam,
> quem ad modum ego sum (saepe in speculum inspexi), nimis
>   similest mei.

> By Pollux, surely when I look at him, I recognize my own appearance,
> in the same way that I am (for I've often seen myself in the mirror); he
> is even overly similar to me.

When forced to explain the whole absurd story to his master Amphitruo, Sosia provides a funny, but nevertheless profound, description of the dilemma:[19]

> Formam una abstulit cum nomine.
> Neque lac lactis magis est simile quam ille ego similest mei.

> He stole my appearance along with my name. And there is no milk
> more like milk than that *I* over there [*ille ego*] is just like me!

When referring to his double, Sosia has no choice but to call him *ego:* "that *I* over there," he says, *ille ego*. Faced with this duplicated image of himself, Sosia still calls him *I*. Neither the mirror nor the double can create anything other than the *ego*, the *I:* when I look at my reflected image, I cannot help but call it *I*.

But what is the situation with the manufactured image? Could a person say *I* in speaking about his own painted or sculpted image? Apparently not: it would be impossible to speak about *it* in the first person. When a person is reproduced, even though his *I* takes the form of an image, the person somehow stops saying *I* about that image of himself. His *I* has now taken the form of an object. This means his *I* can become an object of interest—something to look at, something to talk about—for other people, even in his absence (or even especially in his absence). The person who allows his image to be reproduced does not say *I* about this image: he says *me, myself*. This linguistic phenomenon becomes more clear if we imagine how other people would describe this relationship between the referent and his painted image: it is a question of that person and a painting of him, that man and himself. There is a good example of this sense of "himself" in a famous passage from Pliny the Elder, who is complaining that the people of his day no longer have any interest in passing down their likenesses and features to posterity. Bronze shields engraved with silver are all the rage, but they bear figures that are poorly cast and barely identifiable; people do not even hesitate to switch the heads on statues, and there is no longer any interest in recording human figures or reproducing people's actual features: "Each person wants the value of the raw material to be noticed more than he wants *himself* to be recognized." [20]

In this sense, we can decline the images just like personal pronouns: first of all, we can put the mirror image in that noble but desperate category of the nominative case—always on top, at the start of the sentence—the mirror image is *I*. Meanwhile, all the manufactured images (paintings, sculptures, etc.) would go in the subordinate but more adventuresome slot of the accusative case: the manufactured image is *me, her, him,* and so on. Once they have been produced, the manufactured images become detached from their referents (the ones who say *I*), and they follow the path of their syntax, objects governed by a dependence on something else, on someone else. Along the threads of speech, or of stories, or of life, these images are a person in the accusative—they can be made into something: they can be made into sentences.

Given this paradigm, let us consider once again the intricate and complicated relationship that exists between the image and the referent.

How does the image form a part of the person, of his identity? To what degree is it able to represent him? We might say that the image forms a part of the person precisely insofar as it is an *I* in the accusative, an *I* in the form of an object—a *me*—that has entered into the circulation of facts and things, susceptible to (unlimited) linguistic production. In the image, a person is grammatically declined: as the referent exits the stage, his image enters, playing his part in the discourse of culture. Any person, any object (regardless of whether they actually exist or not) can be made into an image, and thus become a cultural artifact.

It seems, in fact, that the manufactured image is defined as such precisely in the absence of its referent. When an *I* enters into the discourse of culture as an image, the subject becomes an object: the *I* is supposed to exit the stage, agreeing to his declension in order to make room for a representative who takes his place. But it sometimes happens that the *I* and his self (*I* and *me*) suddenly find themselves face to face, simultaneously: it is as if the mirror image were being passed off as a manufactured image, making the *homo suus* confront a reflection that unexpectedly pretends to be detached from him, and to constitute an autonomous object of discourse.

But this does not bode well for the *homo suus*. This is not simply an image of the person, but that person's double. Between the *I* and his *him* (or her *her*), there is an acceptable rapport, often a necessary one: but the rapport between two of the same *I*, between an *ego* and its double, is dangerous. When Narcissus met his double at the fountain, he came to a tragic end, a fatal victim of his own error. Sosia's troubles in the *Amphitruo* were the fault of that *ille ego* (or alter ego) who challenged Sosia and stole his identity: with the result that Sosia thought he might accidentally have died without even realizing it, meeting his own funeral image, his *imago funebris,* as the result of a fatal magic spell.[21] The *I* can be declined (a subject made into an object), but not divided (one subject becoming two subjects). If the *I* is divided, it ends up inevitably having to confront itself: the double wages war against its *I*. After having buried Icarus, the son of Daedalus, on an island (the future Icaria), Heracles was given a statue that Daedalus made with his own hands. The mythical craftsman constructed this statue with his customary astounding skill: it was Heracles. Heracles happened to run into the statue in the dark one night and struck it with a stone, thinking that it was a living person.[22] It is already rather bizarre to think about a referent who stones his own image: but even more odd is a variant of the story in which the statue suddenly turns around and attacks Heracles, returning blow for blow.[23]

The image is supposed to be a replacement, not a double. With this in mind, let us go back now to the very origins of the image, to the story of Butades' daughter and her absent lover, and to the father in the Wisdom of Solomon who lost his son.[24] The cultural roots of the image reside in *pothos, desiderium,* that irreparable absence of the beloved person, an emptiness that the image is meant to fill. In such circumstances, it is an act of devotion, of love, to replace the beloved with an image, a way to console the *pothos* of the solitary lover. But to double someone who is still there is a different matter entirely. If the image that is supposed to be a replacement is placed in the presence of its own referent, then that image—the double—tends to replace its referent, manifesting or provoking the death of the *I* whom it confronts. This is why the double is inevitably a signal of death.[25] There is a dialectic between the replacement and the double, between the manufactured image and the mirror—between a justification for the image, and its condemnation.

But let us return to the good image, the image of the person who becomes an effigy only at the moment when that person is ready to depart the stage. The *I* is thus declined, not divided, while there continues to be a strong relationship between him and his representation, between *he* and *himself.* But even this has its risks. Once a self-image, a *me,* is created within the discourse of culture, what then happens to the *ego*-referent, to the *I?*

In a famous passage from Plato's *Phaedrus* about the risks and defects of writing, we might find a way to answer this question.[26] Plato explains that "writing [*graphē*] has a strange quality similar to painting [*zōgraphia:* pictures of living creatures]. This is because things produced in this way are like living things [*zōnta*], but if you question them, they maintain a solemn silence. This is also the case for written words [*logoi*].[27] You might expect them to speak as if endowed with intelligence, but if you question them, wishing to understand what they are saying, they mean only one thing, and it is always the same." Written words are therefore fictions that only simulate the presence of intelligence: just as pictures of living beings only simulate the presence of real life; the painted image and the graphic sign are brought together in the familiar Platonic condemnation of things that poorly produce what is true.[28] But let us consider the other side of the problem: the risks involved in this sort of imitation, and the way that images are able to threaten the living beings that they reproduce. "Once it is written, the word is tossed about, both by those who understand and by those who have no interest in the word at all; it doesn't know to whom it should speak, and to whom it should not speak.[29] When it is unjustly slandered and offended, it always needs its father to help it, because it is unable to protect or help itself. . . . Should we not therefore want to direct our attention to that other type of word, the legitimate brother of this one, in order to see in what way it is created and how much better it is than the other? . . . That is, the word that is written with wisdom in the mind of the learner, which is able to defend itself, and which knows to whom it should speak and before whom it should be silent?" And Phaedrus responds: "You mean the living and breathing word of the one who knows, of which the written word can properly be called the image [*eidōlon*]?"

Promiscuous coming and going, the threat of being offended, and the inability to defend itself: these are the risks to which the life of discourse is exposed by writing. Reproduced in its written image (*eidōlon*), true discourse not only loses its capacity to reply to questions that it is asked (and therefore to mean something beyond what it strictly contains), but it also exposes its own vital substance to all the dangers of abandonment and absence. At this point, extending Plato's analogy between writing and painting—the *zōgraphia* that is so similar to written discourse, and written discourse that is itself but an *eidōlon* of living discourse—we could say that there are analogous risks involved for the person who is represented in a manufactured image. Made into an independent creation, separate from the father whom it reproduces, the image now passes from hand to hand, unable to distinguish the dignity and worth of those to whom it is offered, becoming a possible object of either slander or scorn. The image "divulges" its own referent: the surface of the *homo suus* that it exposes to danger is now potentially unlimited. These are precisely the terms in which Favorinus explained why Agesilaus, as he was dying, did not want to leave any images of himself behind:[30] "One ought not to extend the fortunes of men, nor expose one's body either in stone or bronze to any kind of risk."[31] Images expand the dangerous possibilities to which our person is already exposed. This is the reason why one needs to protect the images from any possible abuse, to defend the matrimonial rapport that binds them to their referent,[32] to castigate the lustful (or incestuous) madness of the various Pygmalions,[33] to prescribe rules requiring that images be respected:[34] or, in the realm of fantastic stories, to imagine a world in which the image has the unexpected power to defend itself from the provocations of a young Assyrian or from the sneers of Don Giovanni.[35] There are many stories about images, but comparatively few stories about writing. Yet if writing were able to become a character in stories and myths, we could imagine (by analogy) a plot in which written words would finally acquire the power of speech, and become able to counter, measure for measure, all the misinterpretations to which they are subjected.

Images can therefore be manipulated, just like written discourse. The father, as Plato calls him, is absent, and cannot intervene to defend the products of his own creation. This aspect of the image is obvious to us, living as we do besieged on every side by living images (images far more alive, more illusionistic, than anything Plato could have imagined—and that he would have surely loathed). Each of the infinite *I*'s that populate the real life of the world can at any moment become a *her*, a *him*, and so enter into the endless discourse of images that continually occupy our daily experience. Are these images all reliable productions of the *homo suus*, faithful copies of the *I* that they represent? No, very often this is not the case. But there is nothing that the *I* can do about it. The father, the *homo suus*, is unsuspecting, far away; often he has disappeared entirely. Perhaps the Platonic aversion to manufactured images (useless replicas of things that already exist, third-order imitations[36]) also warns us about the dangers faced by any heedless and conceited society (like our own) that wilfully proceeds to surround itself with images.

Notes

For each secondary source mentioned, the author, title, and year of publication are provided in the note. This should allow the reader to match each item to the complete reference in the *Works Cited* that follows these notes. For primary sources, the relevant book/chapter/line numbers are provided in the notes. Primary sources are included in the *Works Cited* only if the source is not a standard item in one of the widely available series of classical texts, such as the Teubner or Oxford Classical Texts. In these cases, the notes will refer to the name of the edition (e.g., *Carmina Latina epigraphica, Corpus inscriptionum Latinarum*) or the editor (e.g., Vahlen, Abel, Marx, Pfeiffer, Jahn, Ribbeck), and additional bibliographical information is provided under that editor's name in the *Works Cited*. The standard classical dictionaries and encyclopedias are also referred to in an abbreviated form (e.g., Pauly-Wissowa, Daremberg-Saglio), with complete bibliographical information appearing in the *Works Cited*.

Introduction

1. For a study of Petrarch and the visual arts, see M. Bettini, "Fra Plinio e S. Agostino: Francesco Petrarca sulle arti figurative" (1984). Petrarch was actually a very serious student of the lute; see L. Chiovenda, "Die Zeichnungen Petrarcas" (1933).

2. Petrarch, *Canzoniere* 78. See p. 4–6.

Chapter 1.   The Fundamental Story

1. Ovid, *Metamorphoses* 10.245 ff. See pp. 147–50.
2. For Laura's image appearing, see Petrarch, *Epystole metrice* 1.6.

Chapter 2.   A Potter Who Was Not Jealous

1. Pliny, *Naturalis historia* 35.151. On the possible source of the story (Xenocrates of Samos), see F. Münzer, "Zur Kunstgeschichte des Plinius" (1895), especially p. 509; E. Sellers, *The Elder Pliny's Chapters on the History of Art* (1896 = 1967), pp. xxxivf.; and S. Ferri, *Plinio il vecchio e la storia delle arti antiche* (1946), pp. 208f.

2. According to the commonly accepted interpretation, the contemporary mention of the two cities of Sicyon and Corinth (a potter of Sicyon who worked in Corinth) would indicate that both of these cities had claimed the discovery of *plastice,* giving rise to a story that is meant to reconcile the claims of both cities. See C. Smith in "Pictura" (1890) and E. Sellers, *The Elder Pliny's Chapters on the History of Art* (1896 = 1967), p. 120 for a discussion of this passage in Pliny (*Naturalis historia* 35.151). See also S. Ferri, *Plinio il vecchio e la storia delle arti antiche* (1946), pp. 208f. and G. Brunn, *Geschichte der griechischen Künstler* (1889), vol. 1, pp. 18f. and p. 283.

3. Athenagoras, *Legatio pro Christianis* 17.2; see M. Marcovich, *Athenagoras: Legatio pro Christianis* (1990), pp. 53f. Marcovich gives a rather improbable explanation according to which the story would have originated simply from a paretymology, i.e., the first person who made *korai* was a *korē.* But this seems to be a dubious sort of hypothesis. On the general subject of Athenagoras's version of the story, which seems better substantiated from a technical point of view, see S. Ferri, *Plinio il vecchio e la storia delle arti antiche* (1946), p. 209.

4. Pliny adds a different account of the origin of *plastice* in *Naturalis historia* 35.152, the chapter immediately following the story of Butades (although he returns to the subject of Butades again at the close of 35.152).

5. See p. 40.

6. It is interesting that Nietzsche also felt the shadow to be something hollow: "so dünn, schwärzlich, *hohle*" ("so thin, blackish, *hollow*"), he says in *Also sprach Zarathustra* (1968), p. 335.

7. For the powers of the shadow, see pp. 42–48. The same conception of the shadow as "a potential design that is only waiting to be filled in" likewise recurs in Mongolian and Tibetan legends about the origin of the image of the Buddha, as discussed in E. Kris and O. Kurz, *Die Legende vom Künstler: Ein historischer Versuch* (1934 = *Legend, Myth, and Magic* [1979]).

8. Pliny, *Naturalis historia* 34.35.

9. Ibid., 35.156: *Pasitelen qui plasticen matrem caelaturae et statuariae scalpturaeque dixit,* "Pasiteles, who said that *plastice* was the mother of engraving, statuary, and sculpture."

10. Ibid., 35.15: *Graeci autem alii in Sicyone, alii apud Corinthios repertam [picturam adfirmant], omnes umbra hominis lineis circumducta.* See also Quintilian, *Institutio oratoria* 10.2.7 (speaking about painting in its primitive state): "painting was but the tracing of the outlines of a shadow cast by bodies in the light of the sun," *non esset pictura nisi quae lineas modo extremas umbrae, quam corpora in sole fecissent, circumscriberet.* See also Athenagoras, *Legatio pro Christianis* 17.2. The question of the origins of painting in Pliny is naturally quite complex (also because Pliny himself does not seem to have been much con-

cerned with reconciling his sources). On this topic, see the general discussion in the notes by J. M. Croisille to *Pline l'ancien: Histoire naturelle, livre XXXV* (1985), pp. 139 f.

11. Pliny, *Naturalis historia* 35.151, describes the actions of the daughter of Butades as follows: "she made an outline of the shadow of his face," *umbram ex facie eius . . . lineis circumscripsit*. In *Naturalis historia* 35.15, Pliny says that painting began "with tracing the outline of a man's shadow," *umbra hominis lineis circumducta*.

12. C. Lévi-Strauss, *La potière jalouse* (1985), pp. 35 ff.

13. I am using "passage" here in the sense elaborated by A. Van Gennep, *Les rites de passage* (1909).

14. See the scholia to Aelius Aristides in Dindorf, vol. 3, pp. 671 f., where the plot of Euripides' lost *Protesilaus* is succinctly told (the fragments can be found in Nauck; see H. J. Mette, "Protesilaus (Euripides)" [1982]). A lengthy attempt to reconstruct the tragedy can be found in F. Jouan, *Euripide et les légendes des chants cypriens* (1966), pp. 317 ff., which provides abundant materials and bibliography, even if its final conclusions appear somewhat dubious. See Hyginus, *Fabulae* 103; Servius *ad Aeneidem* 6.447; etc. In addition, Propertius (*Elegiae* 1.19.7 ff.) tells the story of how the *umbra* of Protesilaus left Hades in order to come visit his wife, and says that he too in the afterlife will never forget his Cynthia (*illic quidquid ero, semper tua dicar imago: / traicit et fati litora magnus amor*, "whatever I will be there, even as a shade [*imago*] I will always be called yours; a great love can cross even the shores of fate"); in point of fact, things turned out otherwise for Propertius and Cynthia (see pp. 109–16).

15. Hyginus, *Fabulae* 104; Apollodorus, *Epitoma Vaticana* 3.30. On the folkloric background of this myth, see S. Trenkner, *The Greek Novella in the Classical Period* (1958 = 1987), pp. 66 ff.

16. I am reading *simulacrum cereum*, and not *aereum* (as in H. J. Rose's *Hygini fabulae* [1963], p. 77, following the manuscript tradition). It would sound odd if Laodamia had a statue of her lover made in bronze (?), and even more odd if her father, to destroy it, ordered it to be burnt (*comburi*). The hypothesis was already suggested by J. Scheffer (see B. Bunte's *Hygini fabulae* [1856], p. 92). See also p. 27.

17. Hyginus, *Fabulae* 104; Apollodorus, *Epitoma Vaticana* 3.30. Admetus, in the *Alcestis* of Euripides, also uses rather ambiguous expressions to describe his behavior with the statue that will lie in his bed in place of his dead wife (see pp. 18–22). On the subject of incredible loves for statues or images, see pp. 59–74.

18. In the lost *Protesilaus* of Euripides, Laodamia defended her love for the simulacrum of her husband with these words: "I would not abandon my lover, even if he lacks life" (frag. 655 in Nauck; based on the way in which the citation appears in Dio Chrysostom, it can be clearly deduced that Laodamia is referring to the statue that she has in her possession).

19. Thomas, *Roman de Tristan* 942 ff. Tristan possesses a portrait of Yseut that he adorns with jewels, a little box of perfumes on her breast, an automaton in the shape of a bird on its scepter, etc. Indeed, he also keeps a portrait of her beloved servant Brangien as well. By speaking with these statues, the smitten

lover is able to relieve his jealousies and emotional distress. For a discussion, see V. Bertolucci Pizzorusso, "La clergie di Thomas: L'intertesto agiografico-religioso" (1996).

20. Ovid, *Heroides* 13. The letter and the portrait, as we know, recall one another. As Danceny wrote to the Marquise de Merteuil (letter 150 in Laclos, *Les liaisons dangeureses*): "La nuit j'aurais encore quelque plaisir à toucher ton portrait—Ton portrait, ai-je-dit? Mais une Lettre est le portrait de l'âme. Elle n'a pas, comme une froide image, cette stagnance si éloignée de l'amour; elle se prête à tous nos mouvements: tour à tour elle s'anime, elle jouit, elle se repose." ("At night I still enjoy touching your portrait. Portrait, did I say? But a Letter is the portrait of the soul. It is not like a cold picture, that inertia which is so far from love; the Letter reflects all our motions: it is able to be lively, to rejoice, and to rest in turn.") In some sense, the letter *is alive*. This passage is apparently opposed in every way to that famous Platonic assertion (*Phaedrus* 275 ff., for a discussion, see pp. 234–35) that written discourse is hopelessly dead and unable to interact with the reader. The same basic idea expressed here by Danceny can already be found in Seneca, *Epistulae ad Lucilium* 40.1.

21. Ovid, *Heroides* 10. In any case, Ovid's invention is highly successful. But this is what we should expect: the merely probable has little literary value, while the powers of the improbable are much greater—especially when the author effortlessly mixes pathos with irony, combining love and literary conceits. Ovid, in short, is bound to succeed. The resulting epistolary form becomes an exaltation of literature itself, by relying on the fiction of a character who is actually writing about herself and her emotions, the author (that is, Ovid, the actual writer) is spared the struggle of making his readers forget that they are reading a written story of love. In a sense, the literature of love is best served by a world in which love becomes a *letter* at every opportunity, no matter how unthinkable. We are lucky enough to possess some precious manuscripts of the *Heroides* filled with lovely ladies, seated with pen and paper in hand; some fine examples can be found in P. Durrieu and J. J. Marquet de Vasselot, "Les manuscrits à miniatures des Héroïdes d'Ovide traduites par Saint-Gelais, et un grand miniaturiste français du XVIᶜ siècle [Robinet Testard]" (1894).

22. Various interpreters have noted with a certain amazement that Ovid's Laodamia, unlike the heroine of other versions, possessed "a waxen image of her absent lord and fondled it even in his lifetime" (J. G. Frazer, *Apollodorus: The Library* [1922], vol. 2, p. 200). Similar observations can also be found in U. Wilamowitz, "Sepulchri Portuensis imagines" (1937), especially p. 527, and W. Schmid and O. Stählin, *Geschichte der griechischen Literatur* (1940), volume 3-1, p. 353 n. 9. But to justify Ovid's variation on the story, it is enough to recall that in every version the form frequently affects the contents: if in Ovid's *Heroides*, Laodamia is going to write a letter to her husband, she obviously could not have done so knowing he was already dead—and at the same time it would be impossible for Ovid to simply omit the portrait of Protesilaus from her story: hence the presence of the portrait while Protesilaus is still alive.

23. In other accounts we also find that the portrait of the lover is constructed of wax. Examples include *Anthologia Palatina* 12.183 (Strato), in which the cold kiss of Heliodorus is compared to what the lover, at home, could receive from "the simulacrum in wax" that he has in his possession, and also Ovid, *Remedia*

amoris 723f. For a discussion, see E. Pellizer, "Narciso e le figure della dualità" (1991). On this use of wax, see the entry for "Cera" (Saglio) in Daremberg-Saglio (vol. 1-2, pp. 1019ff.) and also W. Brückner, "Cera—Cera Virgo—Cera Virginea" (1963). For a further discussion, see p. 27.

24. Ovid, *Heroides* 13.149ff.

25. The importance of this Ovidian text was emphasized by J. Babelon, "Protésilas à Scioné" (1951), p. 6: "These lines are noteworthy for the insight they offer into what one could call the emotional history of the portrait, in terms of its plastic conception as well as its psychological framework."

26. It goes without saying that among these lost texts, Euripides' *Protesilaus* is the most regrettable. For some comments on this lost tragedy, see p. 239n. 14.

27. Eustathius, *Commentarii ad Homeri Iliadem* 2.701 in Dindorf, p. 325.26, fuses the two variants of the story: after he has died, Protesilaus continues to love his wife madly and obtains the privilege of returning to see her—but finds her embracing his image. According to Apollodorus (*Epitoma Vaticana* 3.30), the shade also returns from the Underworld after Laodamia has had her husband's portrait made; in Hyginus (*Fabulae* 104), the episode of the return of the shade is instead placed before that of the portrait, which Laodamia then uses to console herself *after* the shade has abandoned her.

28. The drawing of this sarcophagus (reproduced in Fig. 1) is taken from C. Robert, *Die antiken Sarkophagreliefs* (1969), vol. 3, p. 3.423. For a discussion, see B. Andreae, *Studien zum römischen Grabkunst* (1963), pp. 39ff.; and P. Blome, *Zur Umgestaltung griechischen Mythe in der römischen Sepulkralkunst: Alkestis-, Protesilaus- und Proserpinasarkophage* (1978), pp. 435ff.

29. For additional discussion of this topic, see p. 27.

30. The cameo is now housed in the Bibliothèque Nationale of Paris; see E. Babelon, *Catalogue de camées de la Bibliothèque Nationale* (1897), n. 150. For a discussion, see A. David Le Suffleur, "Le camées de la collection de Luynes" (1926), and the interpretation provided by J. Babelon, "Protésilas à Scioné" (1951).

31. For Eustathius's version of the story, see p. 241n. 27: Protesilaus returns from the Underworld and discovers his wife embracing his portrait.

32. J. P. Vernant, "Figuration de l'invisible et catégorie psychologique du double: Le colossos" (1966). For other important observations regarding the ancient Greek *kolossos,* see U. Wilamowitz's comments in S. Ferri, "Alcune iscrizioni di Cirene" (1925), p. 39 and (1927), p. 169; P. Chantraine, "Grec kolossos" (1931); E. Benveniste, "Le sens du mot kolossos et les mots grecs de la statue" (1932); G. Roux, "Qu'est-ce qu'un kolossos?" (1960); K. Kerényi, *Griechische Grundbegriffe* (1964), pp. 37ff. It is worth noting also the Roman practice of replacing the corpse at the moment of the funeral rites with an *effigies* in wax, as mentioned by Cassius Dio, *Historia Romana* 56.34, Appian, *Historia Romana* 2.17; Herodianus, *Historiae imperii post Marcum* 4.2, etc. Other examples of replacing the corpse with an image can be found in L. Radermacher, *Hippolytos und Tekla* (1916), pp. 98ff. (but Radermacher's general conclusions should be treated cautiously). The practice of replacing the corpse "durch einen Stein" is also recorded among the Bulgarians and Ostyaks (J. Von Negelein, "Bild, Spiegel und Schatten im Volksglauben" [1902], pp. 2 and 5).

33. But it should be noted that *skia* is often used to indicate the shade of the deceased. Examples include Homer, *Odyssey* 10.495; Aeschylus, *Seven Against Thebes* 992; etc.

34. J. P. Vernant, "Figuration de l'invisible et catégorie psychologique du double: Le colossos" (1966). See also the story of the *kolossos* of Alcmene in Antoninus Liberalis, *Metamorphoses* 33, and similar examples in Plutarch, *Vita Romuli* 28.7 and Pausanias, *Graeciae descriptio* 9.16.17.

35. Ovid, *Heroides* 13.105 ff.

36. On the various meanings of *eidōlon*, see pp. 21–22. On the *imago* as an artistic image, see R. Daut, *Imago: Untersuchungen zum Bildbegriff der Römer* (1975) and G. Pucci, "La statua, la maschera, il segno" (1991).

37. Aeschylus, *Agamemnon* 408 ff.

38. G. Hermann already thought that it was a question not of Helen's portraits but of "columns in the house and perhaps even statues," *columnae in domo et fortasse etiam statuae* (in *Aeschyli tragoediae,* edited by M. Haupt [1852], p. 402). On the other hand, C. Picard's "Le cénotaphe de Midéa et les 'colosses' de Ménélas" (1933) argues that the reference is in fact to statues of Helen, based on the documented Greek practice of replacing absent persons with *kolossoi.* (For more information on this use of the *kolossos,* see p. 241n. 32.) For an exegesis of Aeschylus's text, see above all the observations of E. Fraenkel, *Aeschylus: Agamemnon* (1962), vol. 2, pp. 218 f. Fraenkel is resolutely opposed to the hypothesis of Picard, insisting instead that these *kolossoi* are simply the traditional *korai* that decorated the royal palace: "every statue of a beautiful woman is more than the deserted husband can bear, for it reminds him of her whom he has lost." Fraenkel also rejects a parallel between these statues and the statues that function as substitutes for the absent beloved in Euripides' *Alcestis* and *Protesilaus* (see pp. 18–22). Fraenkel seems to regard these as two separate issues, but the cultural meaning of the archaic Greek *kolossos* cannot be separated from the literary motifs of Greek tragedy; such a rigid discrimination between literary text and cultural context is bound to result in an incomplete interpretation. See also J. Bollack and P. Judet de la Combe, *L'Agamemnon d'Eschyle: Le texte et ses interprétations* (1981), pp. 432 ff.; as well as the elegant observations of C. Brillante in "Metamorfosi di un'immagine: Le statue animate e il sogno" (1988), especially pp. 25 ff.

39. J. P. Vernant, *Figures, idoles, masques* (1990), pp. 41 ff. For a further discussion, see also p. 242n. 38.

40. A. W. V. Verrall, *The Agamemnon of Aeschylus* (1889), p. 53, does not seem to have had any doubt that the passage involves impressions left on the nuptial bed ("the husband's bed yet printed with her embrace"). G. Devereux was also a convinced champion of this interpretation in his *Dreams in Greek Tragedy: An Ethno-Psychoanalytical Study* (1976), pp. 82 ff. But as R. H. Klausen already observed (in *Aeschyli Agamemnon,* edited by R. Enger [1863], p. 155), *stibos* should mean a step, *gressus,* or a footprint, *gressus vestigium.* This appears to be the principal difficulty confronting those who want to see in this passage an allusion to the bodily imprint that Helen left behind in the marriage bed. One might also add a comparison with the *Homeric Hymn to Mercury* 352 ff. For a discussion of this passage, see E. Fraenkel, *Aeschylus: Agamemnon* (1962), vol. 2, p. 215. Materials for the history of the exegesis can be found in J. Bollack

and P. Judet de la Combe, *L'Agamemnon d'Eschyle: Le texte et ses interpretations* (1981), pp. 427 f. For additional observations and recent bibliography, see C. Brillante, "Metamorfosi di un'immagine: Le statue animate e il sogno" (1988).

41. See the preceding note.

42. In "Metamorfosi di un'immagine: Le statue animate e il sogno" (1988), p. 32 n. 36, C. Brillante cites the following examples: Ovid, *Heroides* 15.147 ff.; Propertius, *Elegiae* 2.29.35; Petronius, *Satyricon* 97.6; Aristaenetus, *Epistulae* 2.22, among others. In cases like this, the imprint left behind by the beloved is able to recall by means of metonymy the love relationship that has been interrupted. See, for example, pseudo-Quintilian, *Declamationes* 338: "The new bride was brought to the bed still warm with the impression [*vestigium*] of the former wife," *in torum uxoris prioris vestigio calentem adducta est nova nupta.* It is also worth mentioning Dido's pathetic kiss "pressed upon the bed" immediately before her suicide in that same bed (*Aeneid* 4.659: *os impressa toro*). See also Euripides, *Alcestis* 175 and Apollonius of Rhodes, *Argonautica* 4.26. See also Ovid, *Heroides* 10.51 ff., and the comments of F. Verducci, *Ovid's Toyshop of the Heart* (1985), p. 265 and B. Lier, *Ad topica carminum amatorium symbolae* (1973), pp. 45–46.

43. Frag. 34 in Boehm pp. 40 f., as reported in Iamblichus, *Protrepticus* 29. The footprint plays an important role in various Pythagorean symbols (and one can also compare frag. 35 in Boehm, regarding the need to erase the print left in the ashes by the cooking pot). On the nature and significance of these precepts, to which we will make additional references in the course of this book, see W. Burkert, *Weisheit und Wissenschaft* (1962), pp. 76 ff. and also M. Detienne, *Homère, Hésiode et Pythagore* (1962). The commentary of A. LeBoulluec in his *Clémente d'Alexandrie: Les Stromates* (1981), vol. 5, pp. 114 ff. is especially rich and well informed.

44. Aristophanes, *The Clouds* 973 ff.

45. *Hēbē,* "youth," stands here for "genitals," as discussed in the scholia ad loc. Commentators generally fail to mention the comparison of this passage from Aristophanes with the Pythagorean *symbolon,* but F. H. M. Blaydes, *Aristophanis Nubes* (1890), p. 465, does provide some observations on this subject.

46. But in the Pythagorean precepts it is instead a matter of an "impression," *typos,* or a "trace," *ichnos,* rather than an "image," *eidōlon;* see also pp. 21–22.

47. J. G. Frazer, "Some Popular Superstitions of the Ancients" (1931). See also F. Boehm, "De symbolis Pythagoreis" (1905).

48. On the powers of the shadow, see pp. 42–48.

49. See J. G. Frazer, *The Golden Bough* (1922), vol. 1, pp. 210 ff.

50. The text is not collected in Boehm but is listed as number 25 in Mullach, vol I, p. 510 (*Pythagoraeorum symbola quaedam et praecepta mystica e codicibus manu exaratis petita et a Lil. Gyraldo Latine conversa*). See J. G. Frazer's comment in "Some Popular Superstitions of the Ancients" (1931), p. 138.

51. See M. M. Sassi, *La scienza dell'uomo nella Grecia antica* (1988), pp. 70 ff. (along with the bibliography that is cited there). On resemblance in the feet, see pp. 193–94.

52. Aeschylus, *Choephori* 205 ff. (Electra is speaking): "Behold a second sign, footprints [*stiboi*] similar and analogous to mine; . . . the heels and the outline of the tendons, if you measure them carefully, correspond to my own foot-

prints" (compare also Euripides, *Helen* 534 ff.). For a discussion, see M. M. Sassi, *La scienza dell'uomo nella Grecia antica* (1988), pp. 70 ff.

53. Aeschylus, *Agamemnon* 414: "a phantom will reign in the palace!"

Chapter 3.   The Story of Admetus, and the True Portrait of the Lover

1. Euripides, *Alcestis* 132 ff.

2. The basic form of this myth seems to presuppose a sort of family economy of life, almost as if the surviving family members could take advantage of the portion of the "life not lived" that is left behind by the person who dies prematurely. Similarly, the Roman *matrona* Cornelia, in a speech to her sons from beyond the grave says (Propertius, *Elegiae* 4.11.95): "Let what has been taken from me be added to your years," *quod mihi detractum est, vestros accedat ad annos*. We are surely dealing here with a very general way of thinking about life and death, such as can be found again and again in many contexts and cultures. For example, it is worth noting that the very same concept is seen again among the Winnebago of North America. In the story "Two Friends Who Became Reincarnated" (in P. Radin, *The Culture of the Winnebago: As Described by Themselves* [1949], pp. 12 ff.), after the death of the chief's son, his surviving relatives then recite this prayer: "That portion of his life that he has left unused behind him, may we be permitted to make use of it. . . . Here is what you have left unutilized. . . . Assuredly, you intended it for those you left behind, your relatives, to use" (p. 28). Radin also informs us that the Winnebago have "a theory that to every individual belongs a specific quota of years of life . . . and that if a person dies before his time his relatives can ask the spirits to distribute among them what he had failed to make use of. This is the persistent content of all the prayers at the Four Nights' Wake and the Medicine Rite" (p. 41). For an analysis of these Winnebago stories, see also C. Lévi-Strauss, "Four Winnebago Myths" (1960).

3. With specific regard to Euripidean tragedy, see U. Schmidt-Berger, *Philia: Typologie der Freundschaft und Verwandtschaft bei Euripides* (1973), especially pp. 68–83, for a useful but somewhat disappointing collection of materials. There are interesting suggestions (especially on the subject of the failed exchange with the parents) in G. A. Seeck, *Unaristotelische Untersuchungen zu Euripides* (1985), pp. 92 ff. On the myth and its relationship to stories from folklore, see above all A. Lesky, *Alkestis: Der Mythus und das Drama* (1925) and also S. Trenkner, *The Greek Novella in the Classical Period* (1958 = 1987), pp. 69 ff. Other interesting observations (including some Turkish folklore) are found in R. S. P. Beekes, "You Can Get New Children" (1986). For a discussion of the myth (and the supposed characteristics of its reformulation on the part of Euripides), see D. J. Conacher, *Euripidean Drama: Myth, Theme and Structure* (1967), pp. 327 ff.; by the same author, see also the more recent *Euripides: Alcestis* (1988).

4. Euripides, *Alcestis* 392.

5. Ibid., 328 ff. See the commentary by C. Franco, "Una statua per Admeto (Euripides, *Alcestis* 348–354)" (1984). A singular modern parallel for the story of Admetus and the simulacrum of Alcestis, taken from the English news of

the time, is noted by H. J. Rose, "Euripides, *Alcestis* 340 ff." (1927), p. 58: "His name was Michael Kallosy, and he was a Hungarian of good family. Being refused marriage by the parents of a remarkably beautiful Jewess, he had a lifelike wax figure of her made, and for some time kept it in his flat and talked to it, until he was induced to take it with him into an asylum. Admetos, half-mad with grief and incipient remorse at the impending death of his wife, is represented as intending to do what Kallosy actually did in a rage of disappointed love."

6. See J. P. Vernant, "Figuration de l'invisible et catégorie psychologique du double: Le colossos" (1966), regarding the *kolossos:* "unusual and ambiguous presence that is at the same time the sign of an absence."

7. On the topic of the statue as animated death, or as immobilized life, see pp. 135–37.

8. Euripides, *Helen* 31 ff.

9. Ibid., 35 f.; compare *Alcestis* 352.

10. C. Brillante, "Metamorfosi di un'immagine: Le statue animate e il sogno" (1988).

11. Artemidorus, *Oneirocritica* 2.35 and 2.40; Plutarch, *De Iside et Osiride* 28; Tacitus, *Historiae* 4.83 ff.

12. Suidas s.v. *Domninos* in Adler 1355.

13. C. Brillante, "Metamorfosi di un'immagine: Le statue animate e il sogno" (1988), p. 18.

14. On the relationship with the body's shadow, see pp. 42–48.

15. For the understanding of all these various phenomena in terms of *eidōla*, see J. P. Vernant, "Figuration de l'invisible et catégorie psychologique du double: Le colossos" (1966); "Psyche: Simulacro del corpo o immagine del divino?" (1991). On the history and meaning of *eidōlon*, see S. Saïd, "EIDOLON: Du simulacre à l'idole" (1990).

16. Stesichorus 192 in Page.

17. The question is rather complicated, and does not directly concern us here; see C. M. Bowra, *Greek Lyric Poetry* (1961); and especially B. Gentili, *Poesia e pubblico nella grecia antica* (1989), pp. 166 f. See also the fundamental work by W. A. Prost, "The EIDOLON of Helen: Diachronic Edition of a Myth" (1977).

18. Scholia to Aelius Aristides in Dindorf, vol. 3, p. 150. The version that interests us is A–C; in B–D there is no mention of the painted image but only of a generic *eidōlon* that Alexander received in Pharos. J. Vürtheim, however, confused the two versions in his *Stesichoros' Fragmente und Biographie* (1919), pp. 65 f. That this scholium is not *fide dignum* for the reconstruction of Stesichorus's text is of course clear (see T. Bergk, *Poetae lyrici Graeci* [1878–82], vol. 3, p. 218; see also C. M. Bowra, *Greek Lyric Poetry* [1961]).

19. As described by Euripides, *Helen* 34.

20. There does not seem to be much doubt about the fact that, in the matter of Alcestis's statue, Admetus expresses himself in a way that evokes a sort of erotic relationship: the statue "will lie in his bed," (*ektathēsetai*), Admetus will "fall" upon it (*prospesoumai*), and "embrace it" (*periptyssōn cheras*), thinking that he has his dear wife in his arms (*tēn philēn en ankalais doxō gynaika . . . echein*)," and thereby obtaining "a cold delight" (*psychran . . . terpsin*).

21. On Admetus's invocation, see C. Brillante, "Metamorfosi di un'imma-

gine: Le statue animate e il sogno" (1988), p. 29 and n. 47, for some extremely interesting observations regarding this scene of the drama.

22. Propertius, *Elegiae* 4.7.24: *unum impetrassem te revocante diem,* "if you had called me back, I would have been able to obtain one more day." On these lines of Propertius, see R. Dimundo, *Properzio 4.7* (1990), pp. 128 ff.

23. Statius, *Silvae* 2.7.120 ff.: *vocante Polla, / unum, quaeso, diem deos silentum / exores,* "called by Polla, may you beseech the gods of the silent places for one more day." See pp. 32–33. This invocation of the name of the dead surely has some connection to the ritual *conclamatio* of the deceased at the moment of burial (Vergil, *Aeneid* 6.220; Livy, 4.40.3; Propertius, *Elegiae* 2.13.28; Servius, *ad Aeneidem* 6.218, etc., and already in Homer, *Odyssey* 9.64).

24. See, for example, Tacitus, *Annales* 11.38: the *nomen* and the *effigies* of Messalina were removed from private and public places. On the practice of smearing mud on the *tituli* placed on the statues of tyrants, see Scriptores Historiae Augustae (Aelius Lampridius), *Vita Antonini Heliogabali* 13.7 and 14.2.

25. See pp. 88–89.

26. Thomas, *Roman de Tristan* 250 ff.: Tristan approaches Yseut of the White Hands only because "she is called Yseut / and the name makes her beautiful," (see also Gottfried von Strassburg, *Tristan* 18969 ff.). Yseut of the White Hands, by sharing the same name as Yseut the Beautiful, therefore plays the role of an *image,* a substitute for her homonym. In this sense the name resembles the statue of Yseut, another substitute that Tristan has erected in her memory. For a discussion, see p. 10.

27. See Plautus, *Amphitruo* 305 ff., and M. Bettini, "Sosia e il suo sosia: Pensare il doppio a Roma" (1991). For another change of name and identity in Plautus, see *Asinaria* 374: *ne hodie malo cum auspicio nomen commutaveris,* "lest you have changed your name today under the sign of a bad omen."

28. See "Magia" (Hubert) in Daremberg-Saglio (vol. 3-2, pp. 1494 ff.). It is interesting that in Ovid, *Amores* 3.7.29 the magic *defixio,* which normally is made over an image of the person in wax (Vergil, *Eclogae* 8.80; Horace, *Sermones* 1.8.30 f.; Ovid, *Heroides* 6.91, etc.), is instead done over the name of the person, equally fixed in the wax: "or did a witch put a curse on my name in red wax?" *sagave poenicea defixit nomina cera?* On the name and its relationship with the person, see J. G. Frazer, *The Golden Bough* (1922), vol. 3, pp. 318 ff.; and for many observations about the name and the ancient world, see M. Salvadore, *Il nome e la persona* (1987).

29. This notion of a "crisis of presence" follows de Martino's brilliant *Morte e pianto rituale nel mondo antico* (1958 = 1975).

30. On the topic of fidelity in the *Alcestis* (and its function in this tragedy and in other Euripidean texts) see G. A. Seeck, *Unaristotelische Untersuchungen zu Euripides* (1985), pp. 54 ff.

31. See pp. 9–10.

32. See pp. 50–58.

33. *Carmina Latina epigraphica* 1988.44 ff. (= *Corpus inscriptionum Latinarum* VI 3795). This famous epitaph for Allia Potestas, discovered in 1912 (see G. Mancini, "Anno 1912" [1912] for a report of its discovery), became the object of a large number of studies. There is a commentary with bibliography in

N. Horsfall, "CIL VI 3795 = CLE 1988 (Epitaph of Allia Potestas): A Commentary" (1985).

34. See pp. 9–10.

35. W. Kroll, in fact, correctly supposed it was a small image; see his "Die Grabschrift der Allia Potestas" (1914), especially p. 287.

36. Ovid, *Heroides* 13.151: *quae referat vultus est mihi cera tuos,* "I have a waxen image that reproduces your face."

37. Statius, *Silvae* 2.7.129: *vultus . . . simili notatus auro,* "a face that is carved in gold resembling [you]." See pp. 32–33.

38. See pp. 28–29.

39. See p. 12.

40. See p. 12 and fig. 1.

41. On the strongly Dionysiac character of this representation, see pp. 32–33.

42. *Carmina Latina epigraphica* 480 (= *Corpus inscriptionum Latinarum* VIII 434). The word *labium* is difficult to interpret definitively (see Flury in *Thesaurus linguae Latinae,* VII-2, pp. 775.46 ff., who takes it as the equivalent of *osculum,* in the sense of *pignus amoris,* a "pledge of love," but Flury also records the interpretation, advanced by Buecheler, of *labium* as a genitive plural; both interpretations appear possible). J. A. Tolman, *A Study of the Sepulchral Inscriptions in Buecheler's Carmina Latina Epigraphica* (1910), p. 92, in a chapter dedicated to the means of consolation to which epigraphic poetry commonly appeals, commented: "the method of consolation in 480 is unique." (The epigram of Allia Potestas was in fact published in 1912.) For additional observations, see E. Galletier, *Étude sur la poésie funéraire latine* (1922), p. 21.

43. Given the plural *vultus,* the possibility cannot be excluded that Cornelia Galla had also had her own face sculpted next to that of her husband.

44. See, for example, the famous passage in Tacitus, *Agricola* 46.3: "The images of the face are weak and mortal, the effigy of mind is eternal" (*simulacra vultus imbecilla ac mortalia sunt, forma mentis aeterna*). The motif is fully discussed by F. Vollmer, *P. Papini Stati Silvarum liber* (1898), p. 498.

Chapter 4. A Plaster Dionysus

1. See Apuleius, *Metamorphoses* 4.22 ff.

2. Apuleius, *Metamorphoses* 8.1 ff. We are not directly concerned here with the problem of the possible sources for this episode (although the story of Camma [Plutarch, *Mulierum virtutes* 20 and *Amatorius* 22] along with the myth of Protesilaus and Laodamia appear to be the closest parallels to Apuleius's story). A discussion of the texts and of the various possibilities is provided in C. Roeder Wohlers, *A Commentary on Apuleius' Metamorphoses Book VIII* (1986), pp. 341 ff. An ample discussion of the episode can also be found in B. L. Hijmans, Jr., et al., *Apuleius Madaurensis: Metamorphoses Book VIII* (1985).

3. Apuleius, *Metamorphoses* 8.7.7: *diesque totos totasque noctes insumebat luctuoso desiderio, et imagines defuncti, quas ad habitum dei Liberi formaverat, adfixo servitio divinis percolens honoribus ipso se solacio cruciabat.* This passage is

carefully analyzed by B. L. Hijmans, Jr., "Charite Worships Tlepolemus-Liber" (1986).

4. Apuleius, *Metamorphoses* 8.13.5: *iam tempus est ut isto gladio deorsus ad meum Tlepolemum viam quaeram.*

5. Ibid., 8.14.4 ff.

6. See pp. 121–31.

7. "Audacious, arrogant, rash" is in fact the meaning of the Greek adjective *thrasys.* See Apuleius, *Metamorphoses* 8.8.1: *Thrasyllus . . . ipso nomine temerarius,* "in his very name, Thrasyllus was a rash man." See B. L. Hijmans, Jr., et al., *Apuleius Madaurensis: Metamorphoses Book VIII* (1985), p. 85, which includes bibliography.

8. On the subject of Don Juan, see pp. 121–27.

9. M. Mayer, "Der Protesilaos der Euripides" (1885), especially pp. 126–29; C. Buonamici, *La leggenda di Protesilao e Laodamia* (1902), pp. 79 ff.; L. Radermacher, *Hippolytos und Tekla* (1916), pp. 98 ff.; U. Wilamowitz, "Sepulchri Portuensis imagines" (1937), especially pp. 526 ff.

10. See pp. 9–10.

11. Philostratus, *Imagines* 2.9.5: "[Pantheia] abandons the world not like the wife of Protesilaus, bound with garlands of the Bacchic rites that she was celebrating."

12. Statius, *Silvae* 2.7.120 ff.

13. For a discussion of this passage see the note by H. J. Van Dam, *P. Papinius Statius, Silvae Book II* (1984), pp. 502 ff.

14. See pp. 11–13.

15. See U. Wilamowitz, "Sepulchri Portuensis imagines" (1937); H. Wrede, *Consecratio in formam deorum* (1981), especially pp. 116 ff.

16. See Statius, *Silvae* 5.1.231 ff.; Suetonius, *Vita Caligulae* 7; etc.; H. J. Van Dam, *P. Papinius Statius, Silvae Book II* (1984). For a discussion, see H. Wrede, *Consecratio in formam deorum* (1981).

17. On this question, see U. Wilamowitz, "Sepulchri Portuensis imagines" (1937). On the diffusion of the Bacchic cult at Rome, see the résumé provided by L. Foucher, "Le culte de Bacchus sous l'empire romain" (1981). B. L. Hijmans, Jr., in "Charite Worships Tlepolemus-Liber" (1986), suggests in Charite's case a double motivation for this particular type of cult: one internal to the text along with an external reason in accordance with its "contemporary readership."

18. In this cycle of stories, elements from the Dionysian mysteries are combined with Orphic and Pythagorean features (with the complication that many of these texts have reached us filtered through the speculations of philosophers). At a minimum, see I. M. Linforth, *The Arts of Orpheus* (1941), especially pp. 291 ff. and pp. 307 ff. where Linforth provides a very careful study of the fragments pertaining to the myth of the infant god's dismemberment and his rebirth. See also H. Jeanmaire, *Dionysos: Histoire du culte de Bacchus* (1951 = 1978).

19. Firmicus Maternus, *De errore profanarum religionum* 6.1 ff. (= frag. 214 in Kern).

20. Ibid., 6.4: *Tunc quia diutius pater ferre lugentis animi tormenta non poterat et quia labor ex orbitate veniens nullis solaciis mitigabatur, imaginem eius ex gypso plastico opere perfecit et cor p<ue>ri . . . in ea parte plastes collocat qua pec-*

toris fuerant lineamenta formata. Post haec pro tumulo exstruxit templum et paedagogum pueri constituit sacerdotem.

21. The possibility that these characters were originally something other than the notorious enemies of Zeus is already discussed in Pausanias, *Graeciae descriptio* 8.37.5 (in which Onomacritus would have been the first to take from Homer the name of "Titans" and to associate them with the murderers of Dionysus).

22. The preservation of Dionysus's heart is attested in many sources, as discussed in I. M. Linforth, *The Arts of Orpheus* (1941), pp. 313f. On the precise reason why this part of the body would be preserved as the germ for the god's future rebirth, see P. Boyancé, "L'Apollon solaire" (1966), and especially M. Detienne, *Dionysos mis à mort* (1977), pp. 163ff.

23. At a minimum, see Plutarch, *De Iside et Osiride* 35 and *De EI apud Delphos* 9; J. Harrison, *Themis* (1927), pp. 14ff.; A. Loisy, *Les mystères païens et le mystère chrétien* (1914), p. 33; and especially I. M. Linforth, *The Arts of Orpheus* (1941), pp. 314ff.; and also H. Jeanmaire, *Dionysos: Histoire du culte de Bacchus* (1951 = 1978). There is a discussion of the relationship between this story told by Firmicus and other Christian authors who take up euhemerizing theories in A. Pastorino, *Iuli Firmici Materni: De errore profanarum religionum* (1956), pp. 80ff. (see also pp. 41–42).

24. See pp. 12–13.

25. See pp. 31–33.

26. See pp. 45–46.

27. Pausanias, *Graeciae descriptio* 1.40.4 (for the head of the statue of Zeus Olympicus made by Theocosmus of Megara); Arnobius, *Adversus nationes* 6.14; Prudentius, *Apotheosis* 458; Tertullian, *De idolatria* 3, etc.

28. *Anecdota Graeca* 31 in Bekker, vol. 1, p. 272; *Etymologicum magnum* 530.11; Suidas s.v. *koroplathoi*, etc. (the makers of plaster or terra cotta dolls were also called *koroplathoi*).

29. See the entry for "Gypsum" (Blümner) in Pauly-Wissowa (vol. 7, col. 2099), which assembles the main evidence.

30. Herodotus 3.24.

31. Frag. 205 in Kern; see Nonnus, *Dionysiaca* 6.169f. R. Turcan, in his *Firmicus Maternus: L'erreure des religions païennes* (1982), p. 222, strangely interprets these two texts as if the Titans had spread gypsum not on themselves, but on Dionysus. On the religious value of *apomattō/perimattō* ("spread"), see A. Dieterich, "Ueber eine Scene der aristophanischen Wolken" (1893).

32. Frag. 205 in Kern. See Nonnus, *Dionysiaca* 27.205, 27.228f., 30.122, and 34.144. Interpretations can be found in A. Loisy, *Les mystères païens et le mystère chrétien* (1914), p. 33 note 2; H. Jeanmaire, *Dionysos: Histoire du culte de Bacchus* (1951 = 1978). Many important suggestions can be found in M. Detienne, *Dionysos mis à mort* (1977), pp. 163ff.

33. Eustathius, *Commentarii ad Homeri Iliadem* 2.735, in Van der Valk p. 519.

34. For the precise meaning of this term (commonly used to designate lime but already an ancient synonym of *gypsos*), see the entry for "Gypsum" (Blümner) in Pauly-Wissowa (vol. 7, col. 2091f.).

35. Frag. 220 in Kern.

36. See frag. 224 in Kern. Concerning this aspect of the myth, see I. M. Linforth, *The Arts of Orpheus* (1941), pp. 326 ff.

37. Frag. 220 in Kern.

38. *Etymologicum magnum* 565.32.

39. Eustathius, *Commentarii ad Homeri Iliadem* 2.735, in Van der Valk p. 519: "*titanos* properly refers to the lime (or gypsum), which we commonly call *asbestos*, that is, the white powder that is obtained from burnt stones."

40. Paraphrasing frag. 220 in Kern, Linforth states that men "are made of the soot from the Titans" (*The Arts of Orpheus* [1941], p. 327), which is not entirely accurate. In this context *aithalē* indicates something much more specific than generic "soot," and should be strictly connected with the notion of "gypsum." On the other hand, a paraphrase such as that provided by A. Lobeck, *Aglaophamus* (1829), p. 565 ("and from these 'Titanic' ashes they say man was born," *et ex hoc Titanio cinere genus humanum ortum praedicant*, etc.), or Marsilio Ficino (as cited by Lobeck, "men were born from that conflagration," *homines ex illorum incendio genitos*) turns out to be excessively generic. I would suspect, in fact, that the choice of *aithalē* as a material of rebirth might have been suggested by its assonance with the adjective *aeithalēs* "ever-flowering, eternal" (the contracted form *aithalēs* is found in an Orphic Hymn to Helios, 8.13 in Abel).

Chapter 5.   The Sign Stained by Reality

1. See pp. 7–17.

2. See pp. 14–15 (regarding Menelaus). For the meaning of *pothos*, see Plato, *Cratylus* 420a–b: *himeros* is the desire for that which is present; *pothos* is desire which is directed toward that which is absent. See J. P. Vernant, "Figures féminines de la mort en Grèce" (1989), and *Figures, idoles, masques* (1990), pp. 41 ff. An analogous story connecting the origin of painting with regret for the death of a beloved person is told about Brahma and a brahmin whose son had died: see E. Kris and O. Kurz, *Die Legende vom Künstler: Ein historischer Versuch* (1934 = *Legend, Myth, and Magic* [1979]) where some more recent stories are also reported.

3. Pseudo-Quintilian, *Declamationes maiores* 10.11.

4. Seneca, *Epistulae ad Lucilium* 40.1: *imagines nobis amicorum absentium iucundae sunt quae memoriam renovant et desiderium falso atque inani solacio levant*. See also Seneca, *Epistulae ad Lucilium* 84.8.

5. Pliny, *Naturalis historia* 35.9: *pariuntque desideria non traditos vultus, sicut in Homero evenit*.

6. Wisdom of Solomon, 14.15 ff. For the historical context, see S. R. Price, *Rituals and Power: The Roman Imperial Cult in Asia Minor* (1984), pp. 200 ff. and A. Momigliano, "How Roman Emperors Became Gods" (1986).

7. See J. D. Cooke, "Euhemerism: A Medieval Interpretation of Classical Paganism" (1927); A. Beltrami, "Clemente Alessandrino nell'Ottavio di Minucio Felice" (1920); G. W. Clarke, *The Octavius of Minucius Felix* (1974),

pp. 274 f.; J. Seznec, *La survivance des dieux antiques* (1980 = *The Survival of the Pagan Gods* [1953]).

8. Minucius Felix, *Octavius* 20.5.

9. Lactantius, *Divinae institutiones* 1.14 ff. See also R. Pichon, *Lactance* (1901), pp. 73 ff. See also Augustine, *Contra Faustum Manichaeum* 22.17.

10. Minucius Felix, *Octavius* 20.5: *dum reges suos colunt religiose, dum defunctos eos desiderant in imaginibus videre, dum gestiunt eorum memoriam in statuis detinere, sacra facta sunt quae fuerant adsumpta solacia.* The most ample catalog of parallels to this famous passage in Minucius is the one provided by M. Pellegrino, *M. Minucii Felicis Octavius* (1947), pp. 160 f.

11. Isidore, *Etymologiae* 8.11. A study of the sources and a commentary on this text can be found in K. N. MacFarlane, "Isidore of Seville on the Pagan Gods" (1980). For the historical fortunes of this topic in medieval iconography, see M. Camille, *The Gothic Idol* (1989), pp. 50 ff.

12. Fulgentius, *Mythologiarum libri* 1.1 in Helm, p. 16: *dumque tristitiae remedium quaerit, seminarium potius doloris invenit nesciens quod sola sit medicina miseriarum oblivio. Fecerat enim ille unde luctus resurrectiones in dies adquireret, non in quo luctus solatium inveniret. Denique idolum dictum est, id est idos dolu, quod nos Latine speciem doloris dicimus.* See also *Mythographi Vaticani*, proem. 3.

13. Also in Apuleius, *Metamorphoses* 8.7.7.

14. Isidore of Seville refers to other defective interpretations of this type in *Etymologiae* 8.11.14, when he takes to task those *Latini* who because they are "ignorant of Greek, naively say that 'idol' is derived from *dolus*" (*ignorantes Graece imperite dicunt idolum ex dolo sumpsisse nomen*). By some oversight, M. Camille, *The Gothic Idol* (1989), p. 50, instead states that Isidore himself derives "idol" from *dolus*.

15. See pp. 99–102.

16. Proclus, *In Platonis Rempublicam commentarii XII*, in Kroll, p. 290. Proclus attributes the same virtues also to the images that are created in the mirror: see p. 114. See also A. J. Festugière, *Proclus: Commentaire sur la République* (1970), pp. 98 f.

17. Pliny, *Naturalis historia* 28.69: *Magi vetant . . . umbram cuiusquam ab ipso respergi* (following the interpretation of A. Ernout, *Pline l'ancien: Histoire naturelle, livre XXVII* [1962], p. 43). See also Pliny, *Naturalis historia* 30.17.

18. Frag. 48 ff. in Boehm; see also Diogenes Laertius, *De clarorum philosophorum vitis* 8.17. The *resegmina* of the body are often an object of numerous warnings, insofar as they preserve a close connection with the person. See J. G. Frazer, *The Golden Bough* (1922), vol. 3, pp. 281 ff.

19. Aelian, *Historia animalium* 6.15; Pliny, *Naturalis historia* 8.106. Compare also Ad-Damiri in his *Hayat al-hayawan* (1908), p. 206: "If a hyena treads over the shadow of a dog in moonlight, even if the dog be on the top of a house, it falls down, and the hyena eats it."

20. Proclus, *In Platonis Rempublicam commentarii XII*, in Kroll p. 290; see also pseudo-Aristotle, *De mirabilibus auscultationibus* 145. On the shadow of the hyena, other materials can be found in A. J. Festugière, *Proclus: Commentaire sur la République* (1970), pp. 98 ff.; see also F. T. Elworthy, *The Evil Eye* (1895), pp. 66 f.

21. Acts 5:15. See J. Novakova, *Umbra: Ein Beitrag zur dichterischen Semantik* (1964), pp. 68f. On beliefs regarding the shadow in the ancient world, there are some observations in A. Delatte, *La catoptromancie grecque et ses dérivés* (1932), pp. 148ff. and R. Caillois, *Les démons de midi* (1991).

22. Ennius, *Scenica* 349 in Vahlen. On the subject of contamination and the transmission of impurity, see G. Guastella, *La contaminazione e il parassita* (1989).

23. On the entire complex of rituals and beliefs concerning this sanctuary, see the extremely learned pages of A. B. Cook, *Zeus: A Study in Ancient Religion* (1914), vol. 1, pp. 66ff., along with the observation of W. Burkert, *Homo necans: Interpretationen altgriechischer Opferriten und Mythen* (1972 = *Homo necans: The Anthropology of Ancient Greek Sacrificial Ritual and Myth* [1983]). On the loss of the shadow, see especially W. H. Roscher, "Die Schattenlosigkeit des Zeus-Abatons auf dem Lykaion" (1892).

24. Pausanias, *Graeciae descriptio* 8.38.6.

25. Scholia to Callimachus, *Hymnus in Jovem* 13 (in Pfeiffer 42).

26. Luke 1:35.

27. The absence of the shadow is interpreted in the psychoanalytic literature in terms of impotence. See, for example, O. Rank, *Der Doppelgänger* (1914 = *The Double* [1971]).

28. Plutarch, *Quaestiones Graecae* 39; see W. R. Halliday, *The Greek Questions of Plutarch* (1928), p. 173; G. Méautis, *Recherches sur le pythagorisme* (1922), pp. 34f.

29. Plutarch, *De sera numinis vindicta* 24; see also *De Iside et Osiride* 47. Dante also states that the dead cannot project a shadow (*Purgatorio* 3.25ff.). See also Porphyry, *Sententiae* 29.

30. There is obviously a vast literature about the shadow in cultures beyond the ancient Greek and Roman world. Many materials can be found in J. G. Frazer, *The Golden Bough* (1922), vol. 1, pp. 141ff.; J. von Negelein, "Bild, Spiegel und Schatten im Volksglauben" (1902); O. Rank, *Der Doppelgänger* (1914); S. Sinisi, *Le figure dell'ombra* (1982). See also M. Bettini, "Sosia e il suo sosia: Pensare il doppio a Roma" (1991), p. 18.

31. See pp. 34–35.

32. Xenophon of Ephesus, *Ephesiaca* 5.1.9.

33. See p. 25 regarding Laodamia and Admetus. On the portrait as a possibility of rebirth, see the Indian legend of the origin of painting in E. Kris and O. Kurz, *Die Legende vom Künstler: Ein historischer Versuch* (1934 = *Legend, Myth, and Magic* [1979]), along with the two authors' observations.

34. Statius, *Silvae* 5.1.7ff.

35. See M. Bettini, *Antropologia e cultura Romana* (1986), pp. 228ff.

36. Homer, *Iliad* 23.103. See J. P. Vernant, "Psyche: Simulacro del corpo o immagine del divino?" (1991); *Figures, idoles, masques* (1990).

37. On the relationship between the image and the person, see also pp. 228–36.

38. Published by R. Roca-Puig, *Alcestis: Hexámetres llatins* (1982).

39. *Alcestis Barcinonensis* 87ff., in M. Marcovich, *Alcestis Barcinonensis* (1989): *in gremio cineres nostros dignare tenere / nec timida tractare manu.*

40. It is not clear on what basis M. Marcovich (*Alcestis Barcinonensis* [1989],

p. 77) rejects a literal reading of the ashes: "*cineres* is a poetic metaphor here standing for an effigy of Alcestis."

41. See pp. 40–42.

42. See pp. 221–22.

43. C. S. Peirce, "Speculative Grammar" (1931–35).

44. Ibid.

45. U. Eco, *Sugli specchi e altri saggi* (1985), pp. 32f.

46. Hyginus, *Fabulae* 104. See pp. 9–10.

47. *Anthologia Palatina* 5.166; see also 12.183. On this text of Meleager, there are some splendid observations in E. K. Borthwick, "Meleager's Lament: A Note on Anth. Pal. 5.166" (1969).

48. In the case of Petrarch (the poet with whom we began our fundamental story), it must be admitted that he was not completely faithful to Laura, even though he had a portrait of her. But this does not matter: in his poetry he was faithful to her, and that is probably the part of himself he would consider to be the most important. The rest were trifles, sorry concessions to the flesh to be recorded with sorrow and regret on the flyleaf of a manuscript containing the letters of Eloise and Abelard (the actual codex is *Par.* 2193). See P. de Nolhac, "Les mémoriaux intimes de Pétrarque" (1907).

49. E. Benveniste, "L'expression du sarment dans la Grèce ancienne" (1948), reprinted in *Le vocabulaire des institutions indo-européennes* (1969 = *Indo-European Language and Society* [1973]).

50. Ibid. But see also R. Lazzeroni, "Per l'etimologia di horkos: Una testimonianza ittita" (1989).

51. E. Benveniste, "L'expression du sarment dans la Grèce ancienne" (1948), reprinted in *Le vocabulaire des institutions indo-européennes* (1969 = *Indo-European Language and Society* [1973]).

52. *Supplementum epigraphicum Graecum* 9.3. See L. Gernet, "Droit et prédroit en Grèce ancienne" (1976). For a discussion of this and related topics involving the *kolossos,* see J. P. Vernant, "Figuration de l'invisible et catégorie psychologique du double: Le colossos" (1966), pp. 254f.

53. *Supplementum epigraphicum Graecum* 9.72. See J. Servais, "Les suppliants dans la loi de Cyrène" (1960).

54. D. Paulme, "La statue du Commandeur" (1958), pp. 34ff.

55. See also Pausanias, *Graeciae descriptio* 8.15.2, for a discussion of swearing upon the *Petrōma,* two large rocks connected to one another that stood inside the temple of Demeter Eleusinia at Pheneus in Arcadia. In the Roman world, we can compare the swearing of the *fetiales* on the *Iuppiter lapis* (Jupiter stone), as reported in Servius (auctus) *ad Aeneidem* 8.641. In addition, stones were used as conventional boundary markers where the people sanctioned the limits of their territories with solemn oaths (see the thorough study in R. Oniga, *Il confine conteso* [1990], pp. 102ff.).

56. See pp. 18–25.

57. Tacitus, *Annales* 14.61: *exim laeti Capitolium scandunt deosque tandem venerantur. Effigies Poppeae proruunt, Octaviae imagines gestant umeris, spargunt floribus foroque ac templis statuunt.*

58. Ibid., 3.76: *sed praefulgebant Cassius atque Brutus, eo ipso quod effigies eorum non visebantur.*

59. Suetonius, *Vita Neronis* 37.1: *quod in vetere gentili stemmate C. Cassi percussoris Caesaris effigiem retinuisset.* According to Tacitus, *Annales* 16.7, Nero had accused Cassius because, "he also kept the effigy of Gaius Cassius among the images of his ancestors [*imagines maiorum*]." See Diodorus Siculus, *Bibliotheca historica* 62.27.2.

60. On this topic, see also pp. 64–65.

61. See pp. 48–49.

62. See pp. 128–31.

63. We are referring here in general to the model of linguistic functions proposed by K. Bühler, *Sprachtheorie: Die Darstellungsfunktion der Sprache* (1934), and reworked by R. Jakobson, "Closing Statements: Linguistics and Poetics" (1960), and then further reworked by narratologists with successive modifications in the terminology, as in A. J. Greimas, *Sémantique structurale* (1966).

64. Dio Chrysostom, *Orationes* 31. Several topics treated by Dio Chrysostom in this oration are found also in Favorinus, *Corinthiaca* 95 in Barigazzi.

65. Ibid., 31.12: the Greek word used is *parabainein.*

66. Ibid., 31.27.

67. Ibid., 31.33.

68. Ibid., 31.155.

69. Ibid., 31.36: *adikōs poiein to pantōn dikaiotaton,* "to do unjustly that thing which is most just of all."

70. Ibid., 31.152f.

71. Ibid., 31.59.

72. Ibid., 31.47.

73. Ibid., 31.115.

74. Ibid., 31.154.

75. Ibid.

76. In the ancient world, such a crime was considered to be especially serious: consider, for example, the entire system of custody and supervision that Roman culture connected with the pregnant widow's childbirth (*Edictum perpetuum* 118), precisely to avoid the possibility that sons would be substituted. See Y. Thomas, "Roma: Padri cittadini e città dei padri" (1986).

77. Dio Chrysostom, *Orationes* 31.42. We can recall, for example, the famous case of Marcia, the wife of Cato, who was requested from her husband by Hortensius and then given to him: Plutarch, *Vita Catonis minoris* 25 and 52; Strabo, *Geographica* 11.9, etc. See M. Salvadore, *Due donne romane* (1990), pp. 13ff.

78. I am using here the terminology employed by C. Lévi-Strauss, *Les structures élémentaires de la parenté* (1968).

Chapter 6.   Incredible Loves

1. Petrarch, *Canzoniere* 78; see pp. 4–6.

2. Ovid, *Metamorphoses* 10.243ff. Obviously, there is an immensely rich bibliography on the story of Pygmalion (myth, literary topos, iconography, etc.). See, for example, W. Fauth, *Aphrodite Parakyptousa* (1966), pp. 366ff.; H. Dörrie, *Pygmalion: Ein Impuls Ovids und seine Wirkungen bis in die Gegenwart* (1974); G. Rosati, *Narciso e Pigmalione* (1983), pp. 51ff. A comparative sketch

that includes stories from various cultures can be found in the entry for "Pygmalion" (Türk) in Roscher (vol. 3-2, pp. 3317 ff.), and in S. Trenkner, *The Greek Novella in the Classical Period* (1958 = 1987), p. 67. Several modern variations can be found in G. Ponnau, "Pygmalion" (1990). For the medieval fortunes of the iconography of Narcissus, see M. Camille, *The Gothic Idol* (1989), pp. 316 ff. On the subject of arousal by image, D. Freedberg has written some very elegant pages in *The Power of Images* (1989), pp. 317 ff. Oscar Wilde was known to have an interest in the love of statues, and he wrote an ambitious poetic composition on this subject, entitled "Charmides" (1913). On this topic, see B. Fehr, *Studien zur Oscar Wildes Gedichten* (1918) pp. 133 ff. It is also interesting that Wilde was inspired by a passage in Walter Pater describing Winckelmann "handling . . . pagan marbles with no sense of shame" (see R. Ellmann, *Oscar Wilde* [1988], pp. 134 f.). A topic such as this naturally did not escape the attention of M. Praz, and is discussed in his "L'amore delle statue" (1982).

3. Arnobius, *Adversus nationes* 6.22; see also Clement of Alexandria, *Protrepticus ad Hellenos* 4.57, where it is specifically stated that the statue was made of ivory (for the source, see Philostephanus 13, in Müller, vol. 3, p. 31). See J. Overbeck, *Die antiken Schriftquellen zur Geschichte der bildenden Künste bei den Griechen* (1868 = 1971), n. 1227 ff. and 1263. The subject of this chapter is also treated in E. Kris and O. Kurz, *Die Legende vom Künstler: Ein historischer Versuch* (1934 = *Legend, Myth, and Magic* [1979]), including the stories of more modern artists. See also T. Birt, *Laienurteil über bildende Kunst bei den Alten* (1902), p. 40; and the useful observations in S. Trenkner, *The Greek Novella in the Classical Period* (1958 = 1987), p. 67.

4. Pliny, *Naturalis historia* 36.12 f. (and also 7.127). See also Valerius Maximus, *Facta et dicta memorabilia* 8.11 ext. 4; Arnobius, *Adversus nationes* 6.22; Lucian, *Imagines* 4; Tzetzes, *Historiarum variarum chiliades* 8.375; Clement of Alexandria, *Protrepticus ad Hellenos* 4.57; Philostratus, *Vita Apollonii* 6.40, etc. For the source, see Posidippus 1, in Müller, vol. 4, p. 482.

5. Arnobius, *Adversus nationes* 6.22.

6. Pliny, *Naturalis historia* 36.22 f.

7. Lucian, *Amores* 15 ff. (see also *Imagines* 4). There are serious doubts regarding the authenticity of Lucian's *Amores;* see E. Degani's introduction to *Luciano: Questioni d'amore* (1991). According to R. Bloch, *De Pseudo-Luciani Amoribus* (1907), pp. 44 f., the source for (pseudo-)Lucian would be the *Kainē historia* of Ptolemy Chennus, on which Degani also has some observations, p. 18 and n. 8.

8. W. R. Halliday, *Greek Divination* (1913 = 1967), pp. 205 ff. The story of an actual game of dice played between Hercules and the guardian of his temple can be found in the Roman myth of Acca Laurentia (Macrobius, *Saturnalia* 1.10.17 ff.; Augustine, *De civitate dei* 6.7).

9. In the game of knucklebones, the highest throw was called the throw of Venus: see Plautus, *Asinaria* 905; Propertius, *Elegiae* 4.8.85; etc., and also the entry for "Alea" (Hubert) in Daremberg-Saglio (vol. 1, pp. 179 ff.).

10. On the impulse to dedicate, vowing each and every thing to the beloved, see R. Barthes, *Fragments d'un discours amoureux* (1977).

11. Needless to say, the Roman punishment for incest was to leap from the Tarpeian Rock (see, for example, Tacitus, *Annales* 6.19 and 6.49). The presence

of this motif in Seneca the Elder, *Controversiae* 1.3 and Quintilian, *Institutio oratoria* 7.8.3 ff. shows that the leap of someone who committed incest eventually became a subject for *controversia*. Regarding the Tarpeian Rock, see E. Pais, *Ancient Legends of Roman History* (1906), pp. 109 ff.; G. Franciosi, *Clan gentilizio e strutture monogamiche a Roma* (1978). As for the quintessential perpetrator of incest, Sophocles' Oedipus exclaims at the moment of realizing his guilt (*Oedipus rex* 1411 ff.): "Kill me, throw me into the sea, in a place where none of you will ever see me again." If we consider Oedipus's story in further detail, we will find a quite unusual (and perhaps less well-known) piece of evidence for the way in which incest and the leap from a cliff are closely associated in traditional Greek and Roman culture: in order to describe the death of Oedipus, the *Iliad* (23.679) makes use of an extremely unusual expression, *dedoupotos Oidipodao*. The verb apparently means "fallen" or also "fallen in battle" (see W. Leaf, *The Iliad* [1900], vol. 2, p. 519), but the scholia ad loc. suggest as one possible reading: "he threw himself down from a cliff" (*katekrēmnise heauton;* see also Eustathius, *Commentarii ad Homeri Iliadem* 23.679). The association between incest and leaping from a cliff was thus apparently common enough that it could be used—albeit incorrectly—to explain an unclear expression in Homer. The same was said about horses (those lascivious animals), who reportedly would hurl themselves into a ravine if they were forced to commit incest: for examples, see Aristotle, *De historia animalium* 576a; Aelian, *Historia animalium* 4.8 (see also p. 96).

12. See pp. 101-8.

13. Aelian, *Varia historia* 9.39.

14. More generally on this topic, see also Aelian, *Varia historia* 2.14; the anecdote is also found in Herodotus, 7.34, and other comical loves of this type are discussed in Athenaeus, *Deipnosophistae* 13.606b ff.

15. Plutarch, *Amatorius* 8.

16. See pp. 150-57.

17. Athenaeus, *Deipnosophistae* 13.605f ff.

18. A work by Ctesicles, according to Athenaeus, *Deipnosophistae* 13.605f ff. (who cites as his source the *Peri agalmatopoiōn* of Adaeus of Mitylene).

19. As Athenaeus himself tells us, Alexis, the writer of comedies, made a reference to this episode in his work entitled *Graphē* (frag. 40 in Kock), as did Philemon (frag. 139 in Kock). By comparing the title of Alexis's comedy, *Graphē*, with the text of the fragment ("Another example of the same thing happened at Samos: a man fell in love with a female statue, and shut himself up in her temple"), A. Meineke reached the conclusion that the subject of the comedy must have been the love of a man for the painting of a woman (*Fragmenta poetarum comoediae mediae* [1840], p. 402). I think that his hypothesis must be the source for an otherwise cryptic and hasty assertion in E. Kris and O. Kurz, *Die Legende vom Künstler: Ein historischer Versuch* (1934 = *Legend, Myth, and Magic* [1979]) that Attic comedy quite quickly adapted the subject of the infatuated young man who shuts himself up in a house with the portrait of his beloved. (They refer to T. Birt, *Laienurteil über bildende Kunst bei den Alten* [1902], which does not appear to be pertinent, and must refer to something else.)

20. Aristaenetus, *Epistulae* 2.10.

21. Clement of Alexandria also alludes to the story of a girl who fell in love with a painting in his *Protrepticus ad Hellenos* 4.57, but see p. 258n. 56.

22. Libanius, *Ethopoeiae* 27 in Forster, vol. 8, p. 435ff.

23. Jacques Ferrand, *Traité de l'essence et guérison de l'amour ou mélancolie érotique* (1610), chapter XI. See also D. Beecher and M. Ciavolella, *J. Ferrand: A Treatise on Lovesickness* (1990), p. 260. In this treatise, the love of statues is situated in a paragraph devoted to various types of love that are blind or foolish, and therefore a source of amorous melancholy.

24. Aristotle, *Magna moralia* 2.7.1208b; *Ethica Nicomachea* 8.2.1155b.

25. Philostratus, *Vitae sophistarum*, 2.18 in Kayser, p. 101.

26. The passage is reported by Philostratus, *Vitae sophistarum*, 2.18 in Kayser, p. 101.

27. Pliny, *Naturalis historia* 34.48; Martial, 9.48.

28. Pliny, *Naturalis historia* 34.48 and 34.82 (*eucnemon*). See also S. Reinach, *Cultes, mythes et religions* (1912), vol. 4, pp. 388ff.

29. Pliny, *Naturalis historia* 35.18: *Gaius princeps tollere eas conatus est, libidine accensus, si tectorii natura permisisset.*

30. Pliny, *Naturalis historia* 34.62: *non quivit temperare sibi in eo, quamquam imperiosus sui inter initia principatus, transtulitque in cubiculum alio signo substituto, cum quidem tanta populi Romani contumacia fuit, ut theatri clamoribus reponi apoxyomenon flagitaverit princepsque, quamquam adamatum, reposuerit.*

31. Pliny, *Naturalis historia* 35.70; Suetonius, *Vita Tiberii* 44. See p. 160.

32. Pliny, *Naturalis historia* 34.82: [Strongylion] *fecit puerum quem amando Brutus Philippiensis cognomine suo inlustravit.* The *puer Bruti*, "Brutus's boy," enjoyed a proverbial fame: see Martial 2.77, 9.50, and 14.51.

33. See entry for "Iunii" (Münzer) in Pauly-Wissowa (vol. 10, col. 967).

34. See O. Salomies, *Die römische Vornamen* (1987), pp. 277ff.

35. Clement of Alexandria, *Protrepticus ad Hellenos* 4.57.5.

36. Philostratus, *Vita Apollonii* 6.40.

37. S. Freud, "Der Wahn und die Träume in Wilhelm Jensens 'Gradiva'" (1960). Regarding the cultural and symbolic framework in which the "Gradiva" can be located, S. Settis makes some splendid observations in his "Presentazione" to the Italian translation of J. Seznec's *La sopravvivenza degli antichi dei* (1981). As we know, Jensen was rather dissatisfied with Freud's analysis, insisting that it had distorted his story; see E. Kris, *Psychoanalytic Explorations in Art* (1952). On a comic note, a story absolutely similar to that of the "Gradiva" (involving a young man who, in love with an antique statue, did not want to pursue any kind of marriage with real women) had already been dramatized in N. T. Barthe's *Amateur,* a comedy first staged in 1764 and published as *L'amateur: Comédie en vers* in 1870.

38. The images' *foot* seems to be a privileged place on which the attention of "incredible love" tends to focus. In Balzac's story "Le chef-d'oeuvre inconnu" (1965), the painter Frenhofer was consumed by a passion that he cherished for a woman whom he tried to bring to life in a painting that he kept jealously hidden. At last he decided to show his work to two of his colleagues,

Porbus and Poussin, but it turned out to be a "wall of paint" in which the only thing that could be clearly seen was *a woman's foot,* the only result of that impossible "masterpiece."

39. On the subject of the *daemon meridianus,* the spirit that appears at noon, see E. Rohde, *Psyche* (1890–94 = *Psyche* [English translation, 1972]), and also R. Caillois, *Les démons de midi* (1991).

40. S. Freud, "Der Wahn und die Träume in Wilhelm Jensens 'Gradiva'" (1960). In his *Fragments d'un discours amoureux* (1977), R. Barthes proposes an elegant phenomenology of the delirium with which Hanold is afflicted.

41. S. Freud, "Der Wahn und die Träume in Wilhelm Jensens 'Gradiva'" (1960).

42. Ovid, *Metamorphoses* 10.243 ff.

43. See pp. 63–64.

44. See pp. 48–49.

45. V. J. Propp, *Morfologija skazki* (1928 = *Morphology of the Folktale* [1968]).

46. See pp. 60–61.

47. Incest constitutes a strong model, a paradigm that can be put forward (as an effective scare tactic) whenever one wants to vehemently forbid some possible sexual relation. An example can be found in Xenophon, *Respublica Lacedaemoniorum* 2, which states that in Sparta "the lovers abstain from sexual relations with beloved young boys no less than parents abstain from sexual relations with their children, or brothers with their sisters. "

48. L. Gernet has written a famous sociological analysis of this phenomenon in ancient Greece, entitled "Mariages de tyrans" (1976).

49. Scriptores Historiae Augustae (Aelius Spartianus), *Vita Caracallae* 10: *An nescis te imperatorem esse et leges dare, non accipere?*

50. See p. 208.

51. Suetonius, *Vita Caligulae* 24.

52. See pp. 97–98.

53. See pp. 98–101.

54. See p. 96. For the horses who fall in love with the image of another horse, the bronze mare of Olympia, see Aelian, *Historia animalium* 14.18.

55. In this regard, we should recall Dio Chrysostom's speech about the statues of Rhodes; see pp. 54–58.

56. There appears to be evidence for only one case of a woman subjected to an incredible love, but we know almost nothing about this "girl who fell in love with an image," as mentioned by Clement of Alexandria, *Protrepticus ad Hellenos* 4.57 (it is even possible that Clement is referring here to the story of Butades and his daughter; see pp. 7–8). As for Laodamia, who in some versions of the myth did "have relations" with the statue (see pp. 9–10), the image in that case is not autonomous, but simply a *substitute* for her true and proper lover, Protesilaus.

57. M. Foucault, *L'usage des plaisirs* (1984 = *The Use of Pleasure* [1988]).

58. Ibid.

59. On the sexual arousal of images, see especially D. Freedberg, *The Power of Images* (1989), pp. 317 ff.

60. See P. Klossowski, *La rassomiglianza* (1987), pp. 75 f. and 81 ff. R. Barthes (*Fragments d'un discours amoureux,* 1977, p. 16) observes: "many surprising co-

incidences and chance associations were required to find the Image that, among the many thousands of images, was suited to my desire."

61. P. Klossowski, *La rassomiglianza* (1987), pp. 75f.

62. J. W. Goethe, *Leiden des jungen Werthers* (1987), letter dated June 16.

63. R. Barthes, *Fragments d'un discours amoureux* (1977), p. 227: "nous aimons d'abord *un tableau* . . . et, de tous les arrangements d'objects, c'est le tableau qui semble le mieux se voir pour la première fois: un rideau se déchire: ce qui n'avait été encore jamais vu est découvert dans son entier, et dès lors dévoré des yeux."

64. In Achilles Tatius's *Leucippe and Clitophon* (1.4.3), Clitophon describes his first, fatal encounter with Leucippe: "A girl appeared on my left, and her face dazzled my eyes. She was like the *painting* I had seen of Europa on the bull." The fatal vision corresponds to that vision already encountered in a painting. See pp. 181–86.

65. See p. 62.

66. Horace, *De arte poetica* 9f.: *pictoribus atque poetis / quidlibet audendi semper fuit aequa potestas.* Lucian, *Pro imaginibus* 18, cites the same expression as "an ancient saying."

67. Antoninus Liberalis, *Metamorphoses* 41.10.

68. The scene truly has a dreamlike, hallucinatory quality, as in Homer, *Iliad* 22.199f.: "in a dream . . . the person who flees does not succeed in his flight, he who pursues does not succeed in his pursuit."

Chapter 7.   The Story of the Cruel Painter

1. It seems in fact that the creator ought not to entertain great expectations that the image that he has created will reciprocate his love. In his essay "Of the Affection of Fathers for Their Children," Montaigne proposed an "Aristotelian principle" according to which "every artist loves his own work far more than he would be loved by it, if the work were able to feel" (*Essais* [1933] = *Essays* [1958]).

2. Plutarch, *Vita Cimonis* 6.

3. Pliny, *Naturalis historia* 35.87. Athenaeus, *Deipnosophistae* 13.590f, on the other hand, speaks of Phryne as the model for the Anadyomene; the *Anthologia Palatina* 16.179 refers to a vision that he had of the goddess.

4. Pliny, *Naturalis historia* 35.125.

5. Ibid.

6. Plato, *Respublica* 10.2.597ff.

7. Pliny, *Naturalis historia* 35.119: *fuit et Arellius Romae celeber paulo ante divum Augustum, ni flagitio insigni corrupisset artem, semper ei lenocinans, feminae cuius amore flagraret, et ob id deas pingens, sed dilectarum imagine. Itaque in pictura eius scorta numerabantur.* Regarding the artist who depicts the beloved in his work, see also Pliny, *Naturalis historia* 35.141; Pausanias, *Graeciae descriptio* 6.10.6; Clement of Alexandria, *Protrepticus ad Hellenos* 53.4 (and the relevant scholia); Athenaeus, *Deipnosophistae* 13.588e; Aelian, *Varia historia* 12.34., etc.

8. M. Proust, *La fugitive* (1954), p. 440. "Le mot de l'énigme est proféré,

vous avez efin sous les yeux ces lèvres que le vulgaire n'a jamais aperçues dans cette femme, ce nez que personne ne lui a connu, cette allure insoupçonnée. Le portrait dit: 'Ce que j'ai aimé, ce qui m'a fait souffrir, ce que j'ai sans cesse vu, c'est ceci.' "

9. E. A. Poe, "The Oval Portrait" (1902); see also T. Ziolkowski, *Disenchanted Images* (1977), pp. 122 ff.

10. E. A. Poe, "Marginalia" (1902), vol. 16, p. 164 (number 86).

Chapter 8.   Lucretius

1. See pp. 54–58.

2. Lucretius, *De rerum natura* 4.1030 ff. For a commentary on this section of Book 4 of Lucretius, see the invaluable observations of A. Traina in his "Sul linguaggio lucreziano dell'eros" (1981), beginning with his exegesis of the expression *dira libido*, 4.1046, as "sinister" or "inhuman" pleasure (pp. 11 ff.). In the preface to his study, Traina rightly calls attention to the comparative critical neglect of this section of poem with respect to the other parts, perhaps out of embarrassment, or out of moralistic prejudice. But we can now profit from the extremely useful assistance of R. D. Brown's *Lucretius on Love and Sex* (1987). For the section dealing with erotic dreams (4.1030 ff.), see also J. Pigeaud, "Il sogno erotico nell'antichità greca e romana" (1988).

3. Lucretius, *De rerum natura* 4.1049 ff.

4. Ibid., 4.1058 ff.

5. Ibid., 4.1145 ff.

6. Ibid., 4.1174 ff. *nempe eadem facit, et scimus facere, omnia turpi, / et miseram taetris se suffit odoribus ipsam / quam famulae longe fugitant furtimque cachinnant. / at lacrimans exclusus amator limina saepe / floribus et sertis operit postisque superbos / unguit amaracino et foribus miser oscula figit; / quem si, iam admissum, venientem offenderit aura / una modo, causas abeundi quaerat honestas, / et meditata diu cadat alte sumpta querella, / stultitiaque ibi se damnet, tribuisse quod illi / plus videat quam mortali concedere par est.* "For she does (and we know that she does) all the same things as the ugly woman does, fumigating her wretched self with foul odors while her maids keep their distance and laugh at her behind her back. But the lover kept outside [*exclusus amator*] weeps and often covers the threshold with flowers and wreaths, anointing the proud doorposts with marjoram oil, wretchedly planting kisses on the doors; yet if he is then let inside, and but one breeze should strike him as he is coming, he would seek some good excuse for taking his leave, and the complaint so long rehearsed and so deeply felt would fall silent, and he would then and there curse his stupidity, once he sees that he has attributed to her more than is right to grant a mere mortal."

7. Ovid, *Remedia amoris* 437 ff. The comparison with Ovid (which is not included in R. D. Brown's extensive discussion in *Lucretius on Love and Sex* [1987], pp. 296 ff.) might make one suspect that Lucretius was alluding not to the medical practice of fumigations on the fair lady's part, but to a much more banal bodily function. In his poem "The Lady's Dressing Room" (1937; first published in 1732), Jonathan Swift obviously took no account of Ovid's warn-

ing, and the result is one of the most disgusting misogynist poems ever written. In any case, Lucretius and Ovid certainly deserve to be more carefully considered as part of the intertextual horizon of Swift's poem as, for example, in the description of the wretched Strephon as he flees from the bedroom: "Thus finishing his grand Survey, / Disgusted Strephon stole away / Repeating in his amorous Fits, / Oh! Celia, Celia, Celia shits! / But Vengeance, Goddess never sleeping, / Soon punish'd Strephon for his Peeping; / His foul Imagination links / Each Dame he sees with all her Stinks."

8. Ovid, *Remedia amoris* 513; see also 211 ff.: *Aut his aut aliis, donec dediscis amare, / ipse tibi furtim decipiendus eris,* "with these or other means, until you will have unlearned how to love, you ought secretly to fool yourself." Ovid provides a quite unusual pedagogy based not on learning but on unlearning (*dediscere*), advising his reader to "fool your own judgment" (326: *iudicium . . . falle tuum;* see also 297 and 503 f.). See also the observations of P. Pinotti, *P. Ovidio Nasone: Remedia amoris* (1988), pp. 218 ff.

9. Lucretius, *De rerum natura* 4.1068 f. For the violent substitution of the word *ulcus* in place of the more customary word for "wound," *volnus,* see Traina, "Sul linguaggio lucreziano dell'eros" (1981), p. 24. Meanwhile, it is worth noting the quite discrete and measured Ovidian imitation of these lines in his *Remedia amoris* 101 f. and 105 f.

10. Lucretius, *De rerum natura* 6.1145 ff., about the plague at Athens. The expressions used by Lucretius to describe the plague's victims actually seem to recall the famous fragment of Sappho (fragment 31 in Lobel-Page; also in a translation by Catullus, *Carmina* 51). For an analysis of these lines of Lucretius and their connection to Sappho, see C. Segal, *Lucretius on Death and Anxiety* (1990), pp. 84 ff.

11. Lucretius, *De rerum natura* 4.1063 ff. Regarding these lines, see once again the commentary by R. D. Brown in *Lucretius on Love and Sex* (1987), pp. 208 ff.

12. As recommended also by Horace in the *Sermones,* 1.2.116 ff. As a partisan of the *Venus facilis atque parabilis,* love that is easy and available, Horace preferred to vent his turgidity on a maid, or a male slave in the household, or a boy (*ancilla, verna,* or *puer*), if only to avoid the dalliances and caprices of a woman. See also Cercidas, *Meliambi* ("The Aphrodite of the Agora") in Powell, p. 207, and R. D. Brown's *Lucretius on Love and Sex* (1987), p. 215. Montaigne, who shows himself to be a convinced champion of a similar remedy, invoked these same lines of Lucretius in support of his argument in an essay entitled "On Diversion": "If violent passion in love overcomes you . . . you must weaken it, divide and divert it in order to bring it to a halt so that it will not dominate and tyrannize you" (*Essais* [1933] = *Essays* [1958]).

13. *Volgivagus* seems to be used only in Lucretius, and the poet was obviously fond of this type of construction: compare *montivagus* at 1.404, 2.597, and 2.1081; *noctivagus* at 4.582 and 5.1191; it is also worth noting that Varro used *Venerivagus* in his *Menippea,* frag. 275 in Buecheler. The word is generally understood to refer to a Latin *Venus* equivalent to the Greek *Aphroditē pandēmos.* In 5.932 *volgivagus* is used to describe the *mos ferarum,* the customary behavior of wild beasts that the human species also obeyed at the beginning of its history. Regarding these Latin compounds and the rules for their formation, see the re-

cent study by R. Oniga, *I composti nominali latini: Una morfologia generativa* (1988). H. A. J. Munro, *T. Lucreti Cari De rerum natura libri sex* (1928), vol. 2, p. 274, noted a fine comparison with Seneca (or pseudo-Seneca), *Hercules Oetaeus* 364: *adice quot nuptas prius, quot virgines dilexit: erravit vagus,* "not to mention all the women, all the young maids whom he loved; he was a 'roving rambler.'" But if we keep in mind the features that Horace attributes to his *Venus facilis atque parabilis* (see the preceding footnote), one might imagine loves that are even more *vagi* and indiscriminate than the seduction of virgins and married women.

14. See also Lucretius, *De rerum natura* 4.1262 ff. In these lines we find an explicit sanction (for physiological reasons) of the Roman belief that the wife, the *uxor,* should under no circumstances augment her husband's pleasure during the sexual act. According to R. D. Brown in *Lucretius on Love and Sex* (1987), p. 361, this Lucretian theory has no explicit parallel or precedent, and can accordingly be attributed to popular wisdom. See also A. E. Hanson, "The Medical Writers' Woman" (1990). Brown has some observations regarding Lucretius's views on marriage in general (pp. 87 ff.). In his essay entitled "On Some Lines of Virgil," Montaigne takes up once again the opinion of the "doctors" who maintain that "an exceedingly hot, voluptuous, and assiduous pleasure can corrupt the semen and impede conception" (*Essais* [1933] = *Essays* [1958]). On good amorous relations between Roman spouses (in which an excess of love and voluptuousness could transform the marriage into adultery), see M. Bettini, "Il sistema della parentela e la struttura della famiglia" (1992).

15. Lucretius, *De rerum natura* 4.1137 ff. I actually do not think that Lucretius, in order to describe the jealousy of the man and the flirtatiousness of the young woman, would have needed to be influenced by Plautus's *Asinaria,* as R. D. Brown supposes in *Lucretius on Love and Sex* (1987), pp. 267 f.

16. See L. Perelli, *Lucrezio poeta dell'angoscia* (1969), pp. 32 ff.

17. On the subject of *respicere* as contact, see pp. 147–57. There is a famous example in Naevius's *Tarentilla* (75 ff. in Ribbeck), that "little courtesan from Tarentum" who, among her innumerable charms and infinite allures (all put into play simultaneously, which is what makes the passage so remarkable), naturally knew how to throw glances: *alii adnutat, alii adnictat, alium amat, alium tenet,* "nodding at one, winking at another, loving one, embracing another." Paulus-Festus (26 in Lindsay) glosses *adnictat* precisely as *saepe et leviter oculo annuit,* "to wink often and delicately." On this famous "fragment of the coquette," see M. Barchiesi, *La Tarentilla rivisitata* (1978).

18. Lucretius, *De rerum natura* 4.1160 ff. See also Horace, *Sermones* 1.3.38 ff.; and L. Canali, *Orazio: Anni fuggiaschi e stabilità di regime* (1988), pp. 26 ff. On the Platonic origins of this topic, see the fine observations in R. D. Brown's *Lucretius on Love and Sex* (1987), pp. 128 ff. On the Graecisms in these lines, see C. Barone, "Le spese e le illusioni degli amanti (Lucrezio IV.1123–1130, IV.1160–1169)" (1978).

19. "È la grande maestosa, la piccina ancor vezzosa," "the large woman is majestic, and the petite one is also pretty." L. Da Ponte, "Don Giovanni" (1956), p. 210.

20. Ovid, *Remedia amoris* 325 ff.: *qua potes, in peius dotes deflecte puellae /*

iudiciumque brevi limite falle tuum. / 'Turgida' si plena est, si fusca est, 'nigra'
vocetur; / in gracili 'macies' crimen habere potest. / Et poterit dici 'petulans' quae
rustica non est; / et poterit dici 'rustica' si qua proba est. "Whenever you can,
turn your girl's good qualities into something worse, and fool your judgment
[*iudicium falle tuum*] by the slightest margin. If she's full-figured, call her
bloated, if she's dark, call her black, if you change lithesome to emaciated it
sounds like a fault. If she is sophisticated, she can be called insolent; and if she
is demure, she can be called unsophisticated." See J. Shulman, "Te quoque falle
tamen: Ovid's anti-Lucretian Didactics" (1981). See also P. Pinotti, *P. Ovidio
Nasone: Remedia amoris* (1988), pp. 188f.

21. Horace, *Sermones* 1.3.107f.: *nam fuit ante Helenam cunnus taeterrima
belli causa / sed ignotis perierunt mortibus illi,* "even before Helen, some slut
was the ruinous cause of war, but those men died unknown deaths." These
lines would appear to provide a precise parallel (admittedly crude, and perhaps
ironic) to the other famous lines of Horace, in his *Carmina* 4.9.25f.: *vixere
fortes ante Agamemnona / multi sed omnes inlacrimabiles / urgentur ignotique
longa / nocte, carent quia vate sacro,* "many heroes lived before Agamemnon,
but unwept and unknown they are buried in a perpetual night, because they did
not have a divine poet, a *vates.*"

22. Lucretius, *De rerum natura* 4.1061f.

23. Epicurus, *Sententiae Vaticanae* 18. See the note ad loc. by C. Bailey,
Lucreti De rerum natura libri sex (1947), vol. 3, p. 1304. R. D. Brown provides
an extensive commentary in his *Lucretius on Love and Sex* (1987), p. 198, where
he is not inclined to see any major contradiction here between Epicurean theory and the theory of Lucretius.

24. Vergil, *Aeneid* 4.1ff. We are dealing here only with the beginning of her
passion for Aeneas, but this is a love that is filled with pain right from the start,
and is immediately marked by the motif of absence.

25. Ibid., 4.82ff.

26. Lucretius, *De rerum natura* 4.1062. On the use of *obversatur* (a visual,
not auditory, term), see A. Traina, "Sul linguaggio lucreziano dell'eros" (1981),
p. 22.

27. See pp. 23–34.

28. Petrarch comes to mind once again, and the obsessive diligence with
which he managed to insert the name of Laura everywhere imaginable, like a
goldsmith's filigree: by inserting her name into his poetry, he makes everything
speak of her; everything would be written only about her. The name is a substitute that is extremely close to its object, creating a kind of amorous metonymy;
this sweetness of the beloved name—like a game of reassuring anagrams—bestows sense on any sort of speech: hidden in the depths of the words, it is *there.*

29. Lucretius, *De rerum natura* 4.1061ff.

30. See pp. 85–86.

31. Lucretius, *De rerum natura* 4.1079ff.

32. Ibid.: *quod petiere premunt arte faciuntque dolorem, / corporis et dentis
inlidunt saepe labellis / osculaque adfligunt, quia non est pura voluptas. / Et stimuli subsunt qui instigant laedere id ipsum / quodcumque est, rabies unde illaec
germina surgunt,* "they force themselves on the object of their desire, and cause

pain to the body, digging their teeth into the other's lips, inflicting kisses, because this is not an unsullied pleasure. And there are lurking stimuli that prompt them to wound the very thing, whatever it may be, from which those sprouts of madness arise." See A. Traina, "Sul linguaggio lucreziano dell'eros" (1981), pp. 22 ff.

33. See C. Segal, *Lucretius on Death and Anxiety* (1990), pp. 23 ff., regarding these and other similar metaphors that imply the presence of "something dark and hurtful *beneath* the surface," pointing toward "Lucretius's grasp of something that we would call the unconscious."

34. Ibid., pp. 136 f. for the metaphorical use of oral engulfment in Lucretius.

35. Lucretius, *De rerum natura* 4.1091 f. For the sense of *abradere*, see A. Traina, "Sul linguaggio lucreziano dell'eros" (1981), pp. 25 f.

36. The young Clitophon (Achilles Tatius, *Leucippe and Clitophon* 1.5) remembers his first meeting with Leucippe: "As to the food I was eating, I swear I have no idea. I seemed to eat the way people do in dreams. With my elbow propped on the couch, and turned slightly to the side, I had eyes only for her, but not staring openly: that, then, was my meal."

37. On the function of simulacra in this section of Book 4, and on the close connection between dreams and love (both dominated by the presence of simulacra), see R. D. Brown's *Lucretius on Love and Sex* (1987), pp. 69 ff. and J. Pigeaud, "Il sogno erotico nell'antichità greca e romana" (1988).

38. The evidence is collected in C. Bailey, *Lucreti De rerum natura libri sex* (1947), vol. 2, p. 1303.

39. Of course, this was not the only fate recorded for the poet; in fact, we rarely ever possess a true biography for ancient writers. In Benedetto Croce's opinion, this lack of biography was actually a stroke of good luck: see, for example, his *Ariosto, Shakespeare e Corneille* (1929), p. 85, and *La poesia* (1930), p. 145, where he argues that it is Shakespeare's good fortune that we know almost nothing of his biography.

40. The Victorian Lucretius was supposed to have been offered the love potion not by his mistress but by his wife who wanted to rekindle the love of her cold master: Lucretius, it seems, paid very little attention to kissing his wife when returning home. In a poem simply entitled "Lucretius" (1929), p. 253, Tennyson explained the poet's distracted behavior as a result of being lost "in some weightier argument / or fancy-borne perhaps upon the rise / and long roll of the Hexameter." Tennyson's poem exercised a considerable influence on his contemporaries, and marked the beginning of a specifically English approach to Lucretius and his philosophy; see F. M. Turner, "Lucretius among the Victorians" (1973).

41. St. Jerome, *Chronicon* 1–3, for the years 96–94 B.C.E. It would be superfluous to take up again the question of the authenticity of this information, or its lack thereof (a question that is often confused with the question of the authenticity of the source from which it is taken). A useful analysis is provided by A. Dalzell, "A Bibliography of Work on Lucretius: 1945–1972" (1972–73). This aspect of Lucretius's biography is also the subject of M. Bollack's (sometimes fascinating) bibliographical and interpretive study, *La raison de Lucrèce* (1978), pp. 75 ff.

Chapter 9.   Narcissus and the Twin Images

1. Ovid, *Metamorphoses* 3.407 ff.

2. Ibid., 3.424 ff.

3. A. Gide, *Le traité du Narcisse* (1946).

4. On this subject (which is not central to the particulars of our study), there is of course a vast bibliography: above all, see L. Vinge, *The Narcissus Theme in Western European Literature* (1967) and G. Rosati, *Narciso e Pigmalione* (1983). For a history of the iconography of Narcissus, see P. Zanker's valuable contribution, "*Iste ego sum:* Der naive und der bewusste Narcissus" (1966), pp. 152 ff. Beginning with the myth of Narcissus, R. Brilliant has developed some interesting considerations about the portrait and its identity in *Portraiture* (1991), pp. 46 ff.

5. Philostratus, *Imagines* 1.23. See F. Frontisi-Ducroux, "Du simple au double" (1980).

6. See pp. 147–57.

7. *Philogelos* 33, in B. Baldwin, *The Philogelos or Laughter Lover* (1983) (regarding the meaning of *scholastikos* in this text, see pp. 52 f.). On the topic of speaking to oneself in a mirror as a sign of stupidity, see p. 266 n. 17.

8. *Anthologia Palatina,* 11.76 (Lucilius).

9. Columella, *De re rustica,* 6.35: *Rara quidem, sed et haec equarum nota rabies, ut cum in aqua imaginem suam viderint, amore inani capiantur, et per hunc oblitae pabuli, tabe cupidinis intereant. Eius vesaniae signa sunt, cum per pascua veluti extimulatae concursant, subinde ut circumspicientes requirere ac desiderare aliquid videantur. Mentis error discutitur, si decidas inaequaliter comas equae et eam deducas ad aquam. Tum demum speculata deformitatem suam, pristinae imaginis abolet memoriam.*

10. For horses who commit incest and parricide, see Aelian, *Historia animalium* 4.11; Columella, *De re rustica* 6.27; *Anthologia Palatina* 9.302 (Antipater) and 9.548 (Bianor); Pliny, *Naturalis historia* 11.60. Even the hippopotamus, the "river horse," is also supposed to commit incest and parricide, as reported in Plutarch, *De Iside et Osiride* 32 (compare also Horapollo, *Hieroglyphica* 1.56).

11. J. Touchmann, "Le fascinés, 4" (1898–99), p. 79; S. Seligmann, *Der böse Blick und Verwandtes* (1910), vol. 2, pp. 276 ff.; W. Deonna, *Le symbolisme de l'oeil* (1965), pp. 290 ff. In addition to the powers of the mirror, the cutting of the mane plays an important role in curing the mares, which is hardly surprising. From other sources we know that this procedure is able to curtail the mare's pride (so much so that the mare can be induced to let an ass mount her, as reported in Plutarch, *Amatorius* 9; Xenophon, *De equitandi ratione* 5.8; Pliny, *Naturalis historia* 10.180). In general, the procedure is able to eliminate her *libido* (Pliny, *Naturalis historia* 8.164; Aelian, *Historia animalium* 6.35).

12. Palladius, 1.25.14: *Nonnulli, ubi instare malum viderint, oblato speculo imaginis nubem accipiunt et hoc remedio nubem, seu ut sibi obiecta displiceat seu ut tamquam geminata alteri cedat, avertunt.*

13. Plutarch, *Quaestiones convivales* 5.7.4; see also *Anthologia Palatina* 7.170 and 11.76.

14. Perhaps a fragment of Euphorion; see Scheidweiler 185 (= Powell 175).

15. See F. T. Elworthy, *The Evil Eye* (1895), pp. 13 ff.; S. Seligmann, *Der böse Blick und Verwandtes* (1910), vol. 1, pp. 66 ff.; A. Delatte, *La catoptromancie grecque et ses dérivés* (1932), p. 152; A. Dundes, ed., *The Evil Eye: A Casebook* (1992). It is worth recalling here Theocritus's Dametas (*Carmina* 6.39) who, having seen himself reflected in the water of the sea, spat three times to ward off the evil eye.

16. Ovid, *Metamorphoses* 3.440.

17. J. G. Frazer, in his essay "Some Popular Superstitions of the Ancients" (1931), pp. 134 f., singled out a possible connection between the myth of Narcissus and the Pythagorean precept against looking at one's image in the waters of a river (number 24 in Mullach, vol. 1, p. 510; see p. 243n. 43). Frazer linked this precept to a series of primitive beliefs (see also *The Golden Bough* [1922], vol. 1, pp. 144 ff.) to which one could also add Artemidorus, *Oneirocritica* 2.7, who states that to dream of seeing one's reflection in water means one's own death or the death of one's relatives (see also the Pythagorean *symbolon* that forbids "looking at one's reflection in the light of a lamp" in Boehm pp. 51 f.). See also J. von Negelein, "Bild, Spiegel und Schatten im Volksglauben" (1902), p. 25 and the entry for "Narcissus" (Eitrem) in Pauly-Wissowa (vol. 16, col. 1727). There is an extensive comparative study in A. Wesselski, "Narkissos oder der Spiegelbild" (1935), pp. 37 ff. and 328 ff. See also the brief but not especially clear observations of H. Jeanmaire, *Dionysos: Histoire du culte de Bacchus* (1951 = 1978), citing Paul of Aegina. Regarding the mortal dangers of being reflected, one can consider also the famous Orphic story of the trick played on Dionysos by the Titans, who were able to slay him by causing him look at his reflection, as mentioned by Clement of Alexandria, *Protrepticus ad Hellenos* 2.18.1, and also Nonnus, *Dionysiaca* 6.172 f. (= frag. 209 in Kern); see also A. B. Cook, *Zeus: A Study in Ancient Religion* (1914), vol. 2, p. 251; M. Detienne, *Dionysos mis à mort* (1977), pp. 166 f.; M. Meslin, "Significations rituelles et symboliques du miroir" (1980). For the distorting mirror, see V. J. Propp, *Problemy komizma i smekha* (1976 = *Comicità e riso* [1988], p. 53). To speak to oneself in a mirror was also understood as an act of stupidity (and was attributed to the comic folk figure Akko): see E. Pellizer, *Favole di identità e favole di paura* (1982), p. 153. E. Pellizer's two readings of the Narcissus myth—"L'eco, lo specchio e la reciprocità amorosa" (1985) and "Narciso e le figure della dualità" (1991)—are the most interesting items written in recent years on the subject of Narcissus, along with the elegant article of F. Frontisi-Ducroux, "Du simple au double" (1980).

18. Ovid, *Metamorphoses* 3.466.

19. Pausanias, *Graeciae descriptio* 9.31.8. Unfortunately, in his commentary on Pausanias (*Pausanias' Description of Greece* [1898 = 1965], vol. 5, p. 159), Frazer does not devote even a single word to this version of the myth, but there are some observations in F. Frontisi-Ducroux, "Du simple au double" (1980). Pausanias's version served as the subject for one of Pascoli's *Poemi conviviali*, "I gemelli" (see G. Pascoli, *Opere* [1980], vol. 1, pp. 982 ff.), but Pausanias is not mentioned in the commentary.

20. See pp. 102–7.

21. As P. Zanker has shown, at a certain point in the history of its iconography (i.e., the early Empire) the figure of Narcissus became in some sense con-

fused with that of Hermaphroditus (*"Iste ego sum"* [1966]). This can be clearly seen in a painting found in the Museo Nazionale in Naples (G. E. Rizzo, *Pittura ellenistico-romana* [1929], fig. 128b; reproduced in Zanker *"Iste ego sum"* [1966], p. 167, appearing here as Fig. 3) in which Narcissus is shown standing and staring intently at his own reflection, and depicted with undeniably female breasts. I would not exclude the possibility that the version of the story reported in Pausanias, in which Narcissus had a female as his perfect copy, might also be in some way responsible for this development. Regarding the connections between Narcissus, his twinness, and the world of *erōs*, see F. Frontisi-Ducroux, "Du simple au double" (1980).

22. "Wälsungenblut," in T. Mann, *Sämtliche Erzählungen* (1987), vol. 1, p. 421: "sein kostbar geschmucktes, dunkel liebliches Ebenbild."

23. Malalas, *Chronographia* 7.172 (Migne vol. 97). See E. Jeffreys, M. Jeffreys, and R. Scott, *The Chronicle of John Malalas* (1986) for an English translation and notes.

24. Apollodorus, *Bibliotheca* 3.12.3.

25. It is well known, in fact, that milk was supposedly able to transmit physiognomic features, which was used as an argument against the use of wet nurses (see Favorinus in Gellius, *Noctes Atticae* 12.1.15; see also pp. 200–1).

26. As discussed by J. Rendel Harris, *The Twelve Apostles* (1927), p. 52, cited by A. H. Krappe, "Notes sur la légende de la fondation de Rome" (1933).

27. Ibid.

28. Ibid. See also J. von Negelein, "Bild, Spiegel und Schatten im Volksglauben" (1902), p. 10.

29. Regarding the representations of twins in the ancient world, see F. Mencacci, *I fratelli amici: La rappresentazione dei gemelli nella cultura romana* (1996, following her 1989 Ph.D. dissertation, "Omnes congeminavimus: Rappresentazioni dei gemelli nella cultura e nella letteratura Romana"). I owe much of the material and the references to twins used in this chapter to Mencacci's work and to her valuable suggestions.

30. R. Zazzo, *Les jumeaux: Le couple et la personne* (1960), p. 450.

31. This perhaps adds further interest to F. Frontisi-Ducroux's suggestion in "Du simple au double" (1980) that the pair of Ajaxes described in Homer, *Iliad* 12.269 ff., is an expression of "a single voice and as if a single man."

32. R. Zazzo, *Les jumeaux: Le couple et la personne* (1960), p. 450.

33. Ibid., p. 467.

34. Ibid., p. 473.

35. Plutarch, *De Iside et Osiride* 12. Another case of incestuous (twin?) siblings can be found in pseudo-Plutarch, *De fluviis* 11.3. See also E. Pellizer, "Narciso e le figure della dualità" (1991), especially pp. 20 ff.

36. Ovid, *Metamorphoses* 9.453; Antoninus Liberalis, *Metamorphoses* 30.14; etc. In the various sources for the myth (collected and discussed in F. Bömer, *P. Ovidius Naso: Metamorphosen, Buch VIII–IX* [1977], pp. 411 ff.), the erotic initiative is sometimes attributed to the sister for her brother, and sometimes to the brother for his sister. As for Canace and Macareus, a famous case of brother-sister incest, Ovid (*Heroides* 11) does not say if they are twins or not, but they do become twins in the *Canace* of Sperone Speroni. Needless to say, it is

love between a brother and a sister that is at the center of the *Volsungasaga,* the work that inspired R. Wagner's *Die Walküre.*

37. Ovid, *Metamorphoses* 9.548ff.

38. Plautus, *Cistellaria* 451.

39. Propertius, *Elegiae* 2.18.33f.

40. Lygdamus, *Corpus Tibullianum* 3.1.23ff. I am reading the *quondam* of 3.1.23 in the only way that seems to me possible: that is, as a reference to the future. This is an interpretation that goes back at least to Justus Lipsius ("Variae Lectiones" [1613], pp. 437ff.); but see also J. A. Vulpius, *Albius Tibullus* (1749, p. 217, with a full discussion); C. G. Heyne, *Albi Tibulli carmina libri tres* (1817, p. 272); L. Dissenius, *Albii Tibulli carmina* (1865, p. 323). The exegetical question is inescapably bound up with the biographical question, and the possibility of reconstructing (but how?) the details of Lygdamus and Neaera's love affair: see A. Cartault, *Tibulle* (1909), pp. 71f.; L. Pepe, *Tibullo minore* (1948), pp. 13f.; G. Baligan, *Il terzo libro del corpus Tibullianum* (1948), pp. 3ff. Judging by the bibliography, in recent decades the biographical question seems fortunately to have lost much of its appeal.

41. It is worth noting here a singular analogy with Goethe, in his poem "An Charlotte von Stein" (see J. W. Goethe, *Selected Poems* [1983], containing the German text with an English verse translation): "Ach, du warst in abgelegten Zeiten / meine Schwester oder meine Frau" ("Ah, in an earlier age you must have been / my sister, or my wife"). Evidently the young Goethe was profoundly sensitive to the inability of traditional nomenclature to express the relations and feelings that romantic love engendered between a man and a woman. As he wrote in a letter to Augusta Stolberg (dated January 26, 1775, in *Goethe-Briefe* [1902], vol. 1, pp. 249f.): "Meine Teure—ich will Ihnen keinen Nahmen geben, denn was sind die Nahmen Freundin, Schwester, Geliebte, Braut, Gattin, oder ein Wort das einen Complex von all diesen Nahmen begriffe, gegen das unmittelbare Gefühl, zu dem—ich kann nicht weiter schreiben . . ." ("My dear—I do not want to call you by any name, because what are those names, 'friend,' 'sister,' 'beloved,' 'fiancee,' or 'wife,' or even a word that could contain them all, with respect to this immediate feeling, to which—but I cannot write any more . . .").

42. It was already clear to Lipsius, Vulpius, and Heyne (see p. 268n. 40) that *frater* and *soror* here would mean *amasius* and *amasia* (whether in a more or less chaste sense, it is impossible to say), and that *vir* would mean *maritus.* J. A. Vulpius (*Albius Tibullus* [1749], p. 217) reports that Jacobus Mazzonius already suggested (in his *Defensionis comoediae Dantis libri tres* III.23) that Lygdamus and Neaera were *frater* and *soror patrueles,* a quite original idea (also in M. Antonius Muretus, *Albi Tibulli carmina* [1558], ad loc.). Without making any specific citations, H. Wagenwoort argues against this reading in "De Lygdamo poeta eiusque sodalicio" (1917). G. Baligan (*Il terzo libro del corpus Tibullianum* [1948], p. 6) took up the suggestion, again without citing a specific source, and made Lygdamus and Neaera into cousins who at one time (the famous *quondam*) had been man and wife, but who were no longer married.

43. Seneca, *Phaedra* 608ff.

44. Petronius, *Satyricon* 127.1ff.

45. On the *ius osculi*, see M. Bettini, *Antropologia e cultura Romana* (1986, pp. 33 ff. = *Anthropology and Roman Culture* [1991], pp. 21 ff.) and "il divieto fino al sesto grado incluso nel matrimonio romano" (1988, with bibliography). The importance of the kiss between brother and sister is clearly demonstrated in the legend of Horatia, who according to some sources was killed by her brother precisely for having refused to offer him the ritual kiss (Festus 380 in Lindsay); for an analysis of the legend, see M. Bettini, "Il racconto di Orazia" (1988).

46. See Petronius, *Satyricon* 9.2, 9.9; 11.2; 91.2; etc.

47. Ibid., 24.6.

48. Martial 10.65.14 f.

49. Ibid., 2.4.

50. Plutarch, *De fraterno amore* 2.

51. Plato, *Symposium* 189b ff.

52. Ibid., 191b. See F. Frontisi-Ducroux, "Du simple au double" (1980).

Chapter 10.   The Insult

1. Propertius, *Elegiae* 4.7. See R. Dimundo, *Properzio 4.7* (1990).

2. Propertius, *Elegiae* 4.7.23 ff. Some useful exegetical observations can be found in M. Rothstein, *Die Elegien des Sextus Propertius* (1898), vol. 2, pp. 262 ff. An almost entirely literary study of this section is provided by M. Komp, *Absage an Cynthia* (1988), pp. 59 ff. See also R. Dimundo's analysis in *Properzio 4.7* (1990), pp. 128 ff.

3. So perhaps we might understand the *fissa harundine* in Propertius, *Elegiae* 4.7.25, if for no other reason than out of respect for the old folkloric exegesis by V. Padula (*Pauca quae in Sexto Propertio Vincentius Padula ab Acrio animadvertebat* [1871]; see also B. Croce, *Poesia antica e moderna* [1941], pp. 71 ff.), which provides a precious comparison to "the reed instrument with a cogged wheel that emits a hollow noise as it whirls around," as used in various parts of Italy during the Easter holidays. On Padula's Latin studies, see A. La Penna in *L'integrazione difficile* (1977), pp. 300 ff. Of course, there is no doubt that this *fissa harundine* is difficult to understand; see the note by R. Dimundo in *Properzio 4.7* (1990), pp. 132 ff.

4. Again, we should keep in mind here the observations of V. Padula, *Pauca quae in Sexto Propertio Vincentius Padula ab Acrio animadvertebat* (1871), who mentions the brick placed under the heads of monks as a sign of their humble burial.

5. Propertius, *Elegiae* 4.7.47 ff.

6. There is even more to admire in this elegant phrase if we think that here Cynthia is basically paraphrasing a stinging insult: *petere cibum e flamma*, "snatching food from the pyre" (Donatus, *Commentum Terenti in Eunuchum* 490; Catullus, *Carmina* 59.2, etc.), that is, to pillage the tombs of the dead, which was considered a serious business at Rome. See also the use of *bustirape!* ("you grave-robber!") as an insult in Plautus (*Pseudolus* 361).

7. Juvenal, *Saturae* 11.17 f.: *ergo haud difficile est perituram arcessere sum-*

mam / lancibus oppositis vel matris imagine fracta, "It is not any trouble to raise the sum (soon to be squandered) hocking the family plates or putting the shattered image of his mother up for sale."

8. See the *scholia vetera* to Juvenal, *Saturae* 11.17 ad loc.: *vendet . . . matris suae imaginem, si in argento picta est aut in auro.*

9. Pliny, *Naturalis historia* 35.4: *ipsi honorem non nisi in pretio ducentes, ut frangat heres furisque detrahat laqueo,* "they think that the honor consists only in the price, so that the heir breaks up [the statue] and the thief drags it away with a noose."

10. See pp. 32–33.

11. On the subject of the profanation of images, nothing can match the twisted treachery of the ritual insults to which Mlle. Vinteuil and her friend subjected the portrait of her father, M. Vinteuil (M. Proust, *Du coté de chez Swann* [1954], pp. 159ff.). There is a fine analysis of this famous episode in M. Lavagetto, *Stanza 43* (1991), pp. 72ff.

12. In "Cynthia's Ghost: Propertius 4.7 Again" (1977), J. C. Yardley suggests that the poet put the words of this reproach in Cynthia's mouth only in order to make a learned allusion ("and he expected the readers to recognize the allusion") to the myth of Protesilaus and Laodamia. But this is an impoverished sort of solution: why after all should literature only be about itself? The same interpretation is found again in M. Komp, *Absage an Cynthia* (1988), pp. 77f.

13. Ovid, *Remedia amoris* 723f. See P. Pinotti, *P. Ovidio Nasone: Remedia amoris* (1988), pp. 306ff.

14. See Vergil, *Aeneid* 4.508 and 4.640.

15. Artemidorus, *Oneirocritica* 5.53.

16. Propertius, *Elegiae* 4.7.75ff. *Latris,* in Greek, means "a hired servant," and Propertius is playing here with a speaking name: *Latris, cui nomen ab usu est,* "Latris, who has her name from her work." See R. Dimundo, *Properzio 4.7* (1990), p. 185, with a discussion of the mirror on pp. 73ff.

17. See the scene in Petronius's *Satyricon* in which Circe, confronted with her lover's frigidity, seeks a confirmation of her beauty in the mirror (Petronius, *Satyricon* 128.4): "She snatched a mirror from the hands of her stupefied maid, and tried on all those faces that usually make lovers smile" (*rapuit deinde tacenti speculum, et postquam omnes vultus temptavit, quos solet inter amantes risus fingere*). On making faces in the mirror to express a desire for difference and to chase away an unsatisfactory double, see E. Pellizer, "Narciso e le figure della dualità" (1990), p. 16.

18. The cup dates from the second half of the fifth century B.C.E.; see A. Pontrandolfo, "Amore e morte allo specchio" (1987), p. 56.

19. See A. Pontrandolfo, "Amore e morte allo specchio" (1987). On the erotic value of the mirror, see M. Meslin, "Significations rituelles et symboliques du miroir" (1980), pp. 334f. Consider also the observation by F. Frontisi-Ducroux, "Senza maschera nè specchio: L'uomo greco e il suo doppio" (1991), p. 136: "the mirror forms a part of the female body." It is worth noting, in this sense, that according to Artemidorus (*Oneirocritica* 4, *proem.*), the mirror symbolizes a woman, while *Anthologia Palatina* 6.1.8 provides evidence for the practice of offering a mirror to Aphrodite when one's beauty has faded: once again, the mirror is connected with love (Aphrodite).

20. See C. Gallini, "Immagini da cerimonia: Album e videocassette da matrimonio" (1991).

21. See J. von Negelein, "Bild, Spiegel und Schatten im Volksglauben" (1902); O. Rank, *Der Doppelgänger* (1914 = *The Double* [1971]); A. Delatte, *La catoptromancie grecque et ses dérivés* (1932), pp. 149 ff.; W. Deonna, *Le symbolisme de l'oeil* (1965), pp. 290 ff.; F. Frontisi-Ducroux, "Du simple au double" (1980); J. P. Vernant, "Au miroir de Méduse" (1989); M. Meslin, "Significations rituelles et symboliques du miroir" (1980); A. Baltrusaitis, *Le miroir: révélations, science-fiction et fallacies* (1979); A. M. Di Nola, "La magia dello specchio" (1987); B. Goldberg, *Mirror and Man* (1985); U. Eco, *Sugli specchi e altri saggi* (1985); etc.

22. See W. Deonna, *Le symbolisme de l'oeil* (1965), p. 294 (citing E. Reclus, *Croyances populaires*).

23. Aristotle, *De insomniis* 2.459b.26.

24. Pliny, *Naturalis historia* 7.64.

25. Proclus, *In Platonis Rempublicam commentarii XII*, in Kroll p. 290; see p. 43.

26. G. B. Della Porta, *Magia naturale* (1677), p. 26.

27. *Anthologia Palatina* 5.266. See also p. 43.

28. Statius, *Silvae* 3.4.93 ff.

29. The mirror used here appears to be the sort that could be closed inside a case (*lopheion*): for information on this type of object, see the entry for "Speculum" (Ridder) in Daremberg-Saglio (vol. 4, p. 1425). In Aristophanes' *The Clouds* (749 ff.) there is a plan to magically capture the moon and enclose it in an analogous *lopheion*. Needless to say, the mirror was also supposedly able to gather up the souls of the dead, and thus contain the final trace of their presence: for this reason, the mirrors in a house recently plunged into grief would be veiled or kept rigorously empty of any images. One might mention in this regard the suggestive iconography of an Attic red-figure vase discussed by A. B. Cook, *Zeus: A Study in Ancient Religion* (1914), vol. 2, p. 206 n. 2: it shows Orestes pursued by the Furies, while the face of Clytemnestra appears to be reflected in a mirror.

30. U. Eco, *Sugli specchi e altri saggi* (1985), pp. 19 f. On the power of the mirror to exalt the presence of the divine and to make the presence of mortal things opaque, see J. P. Vernant, "Au miroir de Méduse" (1989). The essay includes a discussion of Pausanias, *Graeciae descriptio* 8.37.1 ff., regarding the mirror in the temple of Despoena at Lycosura, in which the statues of the gods shine resplendently with a brilliant light while the person who looks at them appears to be veiled in a fog.

31. Apuleius, *Apologia* 14 ff.

32. This is precisely the famous invention that underlies Oscar Wilde's *Picture of Dorian Gray*, in which the portrait is transformed into a mirror, able to produce a painted figure that shares the same age as its referent, coordinated with its referent in time, something that by its nature a painting should not be able to do. In his youth, standing in front of an extraordinarily successful portrait of himself, Dorian expresses a dreadful desire: to remain always in possession of his beauty, and to transfer to the portrait all the grim furrows of old age. The fixed image in the mirror thus becomes able to move, equal to the passing

of years, while the moving image outside the mirror will continue to remain identical to itself. The result of this magical game of metamorphosis, in which the changing image takes on the features of the image that stays the same and vice versa, the subject will miraculously succeed in escaping from time: Dorian will cease to share the same age as himself. There is a vast bibliography on Wilde's novel: see, for example, T. Ziolkowski, *Disenchanted Images* (1977), pp. 128 ff. A recent Lacanian interpretation can be found in E. Ragland-Sullivan, "The Phenomenon of Aging in Oscar Wilde's *Picture of Dorian Gray*" (1986).

33. The clear analogical relationship between Propertius's *Elegiae* 4.7 and 4.11 has often been noted by the critics. See, for example, D. K. Lange, "Cynthia and Cornelia: Two Voices from the Grave" (1979) and M. Komp, *Absage an Cynthia* (1988), pp. 188 ff. (with bibliography). For the connections to Euripides' *Alcestis*, see P. Fedeli, *Properzio: Elegie libro IV* (1965), pp. 244 ff. and p. 258; along with G. Paduano, "Le reminiscenze dell'Alcesti nell'elegia 4.11 di Properzio" (1968).

34. Seneca the Elder, *Controversiae* 2.7.3, characterizes the proper behavior of a Roman woman in the presence of strangers as follows: "in confronting someone who greets her indiscreetly it is better for her to appear more impolite than shameless, and when it is necessary to return the greeting [because of a kinship relation], she does well to blush visibly" (*adversus officiosum salutatorem inhumana potius quam inverecunda sit: etiam in necessaria resalutandi vice multo rubore confusa <sit>*).

35. Propertius, *Elegiae* 4.11.31: *ipsa loquor pro me,* "I myself speak on my own behalf." A woman, in fact, was not able to defend herself in court; see Valerius Maximus, *Facta et dicta memorabilia* 8.3, for a description of Afrania who pleaded her own case because she was utterly shameless (*quod impudentia abundabat*); Plutarch (*Comparatio Lycurgi et Numae* 3.10 f.) also reports that "when in Rome a woman pleaded her own cause in the forum," the Senate immediately sent someone to consult the oracle, trying to find out what such a prodigy foretold for the city. See pp. 123–24.

36. Propertius, *Elegiae* 4.11.77 ff.

37. See pp. 9–14.

38. For colloquies with the portrait of the deceased, see Ovid, *Heroides* 13.157 (for Ovid's Laodamia, see pp. 10–11); Statius, *Silvae* 3.3.203 f.

39. Propertius, *Elegiae* 4.11.84. I am reading *singula verba iace,* and not *tace.* The *consensus codicum* reads *tace,* while *iace* appears only as a correction in some manuscripts; but this is clearly a case in which correction is required by the sense. See the critical apparatus in P. Fedeli, *Propertius* (1984), p. 282.

40. See pp. 4–6.

41. Seneca, *Epistulae ad Lucilium* 40.1; see p. 240 n. 20.

42. This allowed C. Lévi-Strauss to locate forgetting (i.e., the loss of memory) under the heading of "lack of communication with oneself," as discussed in "La geste d'Asdiwal" (1973).

43. Cicero, *Rhetorica ad Herennium* 4.52.65: *Sermocinatio est, cum alicui attribuitur personae sermo et is exponitur cum ratione dignitatis.* See P. M. Forni, "Zima sermocinante (*Decameron,* III.5)" (1986).

44. *Laudatio Thuriae* 2.48 (*Corpus inscriptionum Latinarum* VI 1527). See

M. Durry, *Eloge funèbre d'une matrone romaine* (1950), p. 23 and D. Flach, *Die sogenannte Laudatio Turiae* (1991).

45. Propertius, *Elegiae* 4.11.69. See M. Rothstein's *Die Elegien des Sextus Propertius* (1898), ad loc.

Chapter 11.   Seduction and Vendetta

1. Tirso de Molina, *El burlador de Sevilla y convidado de piedra* (1989, L. Vázquez, ed.), 153 ff. "Ah, pobre honor! si eres alma / del honor, por qué te dejan / en la mujer inconstante, / si es la misma ligereza?" Vázquez keeps the reading "del honor" following the editio princeps; "hombre" was a conjecture by Surià. For the reasons supporting the reading of "honor" and the various meanings attributed to that word in these two lines ("honestidad" in 153 and "honra" in 154), see Vázquez's note, p. 113. The subject of Don Juan is extraordinarily vast, also from the bibliographical point of view: "If literally thousands of books, articles, and reviews exist on the Don Juan theme, it may be asked whether any just, valid, or even useful reason exists to single out so few for listing on these pages," as A. E. Singer observed in "The Present State of Don Juan Studies" (1988), p. 1. In any case, there is a rich bibliography collected in A. E. Singer's *A Bibliography of the Don Juan Theme: Versions and Criticism* (1954, with supplements). Among the works that are concerned more strictly with the relationship between the Don Juan theme and the ancient vendettas carried out by statues, we should note, in addition to D. Paulme's "La statue du Commandeur" (1958), the study by H. Heckel, *Das Don Juan–Problem in den neueren Dichtung,* (1915), pp. 6 ff. On the Italian side, there is now a fine book by R. Raffaelli, *Variazioni sul Don Giovanni* (1990).

2. See pp. 189–98.

3. Euripides, *Hippolytus* 616 ff.; see also Lucian (or pseudo-Lucian), *Amores* 38.

4. Lucian, *De vera historia* 21 ff.

5. In Roman culture the problem of female chastity involved the question of *turbatio sanguinis:* that is, the confusion in the blood of a lineage that occurred when the woman engaged in irregular sexual relations with someone other than her husband. The term is used by Ulpian, *Digesta* 1.2.11, to describe what happens when a widow remarries before the prescribed limit of 10 months (and thus runs the risk of superimposing new sexual relations on a possible conception from her prior husband). But female adultery in general, not only in cases of premature remarriage, constituted a debasement and a cause for uncertainty in the blood of the lineage, as can be seen quite clearly in passages like the following from Seneca: *Thyestes* 241, "the blood is uncertain," *sanguis dubius est* (Atreus discovering that Thyestes seduced his wife) and in his *De matrimonio* (cited by Jerome, *Adversus Iovinianum* 2.319): [*mulier*] *bene meretur de maioribus, quorum sanguinem furtiva subole non vitiat,* "a woman is worthy of her ancestors, whose blood she does not defile with surrogate offspring," etc. See M. Bettini, "Lettura divinatoria di un incesto" (1984); G. Guastella, "La rete del sangue" (1985); F. Mencacci, "Sanguis/cruor: Desi-

gnazioni linguistiche e classificazione antropologica del sangue nella cultura romana" (1986).

6. Seneca the Elder, *Controversiae* 2.7.9. On female silence, and the rules of proper female behavior in Roman culture generally, see L. Beltrami, *L' 'impudicizia' di Tarpeia: Trasgressioni e regole del comportamento femminile a Roma* (1989), especially pp. 46 ff. (with a full bibliography and an extremely rich selection of materials).

7. I Corinthians 11.7 f.

8. Plutarch, *Coniugalia praecepta* 31 and 32; see also L. Beltrami, *L' 'impudicizia' di Tarpeia: Trasgressioni e regole del comportamento femminile a Roma* (1989), pp. 61 ff. A few verses after the passage cited in the text, in I Corinthians 14.35 ff., St. Paul orders that "if there is anything women desire to know, let them ask their husbands at home; it is shameful for a woman to speak in church."

9. Plutarch, *Comparatio Lycurgi et Numae* 3.10.

10. A. S. Pushkin, *Kamennyi gost'* (1936), scene 3.

11. See R. Jakobson, "The Statue in Pushkin's Poetic Mythology" (1975); H. Kucera, "Pushkin and Don Juan" (1956); L. Weinstein, *The Metamorphoses of Don Juan* (1959), pp. 91 f.; W. N. Vickery, *Alexander Pushkin* (1970), pp. 94 ff. (with some quite interesting observations); R. Gregg, "The Eudaemonic Theme in Pushkin's 'Little Tragedies' " (1976).

12. See W. N. Vickery, *Alexander Pushkin* (1970), pp. 94 ff.

13. Such a choice could be closely connected to Pushkin's past as a Don Juan on the one hand (love affairs and duels, as discussed in E. J. Simmons, *Pushkin* [1937], pp. 76 ff.), and to his decision to marry on the other. In 1830, the year of the composition of this "little tragedy," Pushkin was in fact engaged to Natalia Nikolaevna. But as W. N. Vickery emphasizes in *Alexander Pushkin* (1970), p. 96 (following Anna Akhmatova's observations in her *"Kamennyi gost'* Pushkina"), Pushkin was already obsessed by the thought of death, and by the thought of being one day replaced by another man at Natalia's side (a fear he expresses in a letter to his future mother-in-law, dated April 5, 1830; in particular, he was obsessed by the thought of leaving behind "a lovely widow, free to choose a new husband the day afterwards"). It is worth noting, moreover, that in the "little tragedy" Donna Anna had not married the Commendatore of her own free will, but at her mother's behest, which was precisely Pushkin's situation with Natalia. In the opposition between Don Juan–the-seducer and the Commendatore-husband, Pushkin thus seems to have found a way to project the ambivalence of his own psychological situation on the verge of getting married.

14. See pp. 55–58.

15. It makes little difference to the plot if he then does so as a father, a "giver" (who ought to be concerned with the purity of his daughter so as to bestow her on the honor of another man), or as a husband, a "taker" (who should thus be directly concerned with his own honor).

16. Ovid, *Heroides* 7.99 ff.

17. A. S. Pushkin, *Kamennyi gost'* (1936), scene 3.

18. Propertius's jealous preoccupation (*Elegiae* 2.6.9 ff.) is somewhat different: *me iuvenum pictae facies, me nomina laedunt,* "the portraits of the young

men wound me, as do their names." See E. Rohde, *Der griechische Roman* (1914), p. 174. We can perhaps find an analogous preoccupation on the part of the young lover in Plautus's *Asinaria* (763f.), who includes among the laws of love that he decrees for his girlfriend the following: *si qua inutilis pictura sit, eam vendat,* "if she has some useless picture in the house, let her sell it." There is, in fact, reason to suspect that the jealous young man might consider a very specific category of pictures to be especially useless.

19. Petronius, *Satyricon* 110.6ff.

20. Ovid, *Tristia* 2.296. For the text, which presents some slight difficulties, see the long note by S. G. Owen, *P. Ovidii Nasonis Tristium liber secundus* (1924), pp. 175f.

21. Ovid, *Metamorphoses* 5.227ff.

22. Pausanias, *Graeciae descriptio* 6.11.6; Dio Chrysostom, *Orationes* 31.95ff.; Eusebius, *Praeparationis evangelicae libri* 5.34. See also J. G. Frazer, *Pausanias' Description of Greece* (1898 = 1965), vol. 4, pp. 38ff.; E. Rohde, *Psyche* (1890–94 = *Psyche* [English translation, 1972]).

23. See Pausanias, *Graeciae descriptio* 5.27.10 (another case of a statue's responsibility for a homicide). See E. Rohde, *Psyche* (1890–94 = *Psyche* [English translation, 1972] with notes), along with J. G. Frazer's commentary on *Pausanias' Description of Greece* (1898 = 1965), ad 1.28.11; G. Glotz, *La solidarité de la famille dans le droit criminel en Grèce* (1904 = 1973), pp. 184ff.; D. M. McDowell, *Athenian Homicide Law* (1963), pp. 85–89. For information regarding other laws, see W. Brückner, "Bildnisstrafe" (1972). The subject of punishment inflicted on an image would cross over into that adjacent topic (but one rather outside our interests here) of punishing *in effigie* guilty parties who are absent or dead (so, for example, the Scriptores Historiae Augustae, *Tyranni triginta* 29 describing the crucifixion of Celsus *in effigie*). See also pp. 163–64. On this topic, it is worth consulting at a minimum W. Brückner, *Bildnis und Brauch* (1966), pp. 191ff. Brückner's works, focused on medieval and Renaissance culture, are extremely useful in defining the anthropological values associated with the image in European society.

24. Eusebius, *Praeparationis evangelicae libri* 5.34. The story was apparently also treated in Callimachus's *Aetia* (frag. 84 in Pfeiffer).

25. See *Diēgēseis* to Callimachus, *Aetia* 1.37.

26. Lucian, *Deorum concilium* 12: the same powers were attributed to the statue of another athlete, Polydamas, at Olympia.

27. Lucian, *Philopseudes* 46.

28. This statue was also reported to have thaumaturgical powers.

29. For the functional equivalence of the phantom and the image, see pp. 9–17.

30. Philostratus, *Heroicus* 3.21f. and 19.3ff. in Kayser, p. 152.

31. See p. 126.

32. See p. 274n. 17.

33. See pp. 44–48 and especially p. 45.

34. *Anthologia Palatina* 9.67.

35. See p. 45.

36. D. Paulme, "La statue du Commandeur" (1958), pp. 299ff.

37. William of Malmsbury, *De gestis regum Anglorum* 2.205 (1889 = 1964),

vol. 2, pp. 256 ff.; see also L. Radermacher, "Aus Lucians Lügenfreund" (1902). A full study of this story (and of its later recurrences) can be found in P. F. Baum, "The Young Man Betrothed to a Statue" (1919), which provides the richest and most detailed collection of materials. There are useful comments in A. Graf, *Roma nella memoria e nelle immaginazioni del medio evo* (1923), pp. 665 ff. and in F. von Bezold, *Das Fortleben der antiken Götter im mittelalterliche Humanismus* (1922 = 1962), pp. 64 ff. See also D. Paulme, "La statue du Commandeur" (1958); M. Camille, *The Gothic Idol* (1989), pp. 57 ff.; D. Freedberg, *The Power of Images* (1989), pp. 334 f. This medieval story enjoyed a notable success in modern literature (retold by Eichendorff, Brentano, Heine, Mérimée, Flaubert, D'Annunzio, etc.), as discussed in the works just cited by F. von Bezold (p. 71) and L. Radermacher. The poorest reworking of this legend would appear to be J. von Eichendorff's *Das Marmorbild* (1955); despite von Eichendorff's notable predilection for stories about statues, this reworking of the ancient story is rather modest. The list of modern reworkings can be further augmented with examples discussed in T. Ziolkowski, *Disenchanted Images* (1977), pp. 18 ff. For more general observations on the symbolism of the statue in literature, see E. Celiberti, "Le antinomie della statua" (1990).

38. See pp. 50–54.

39. See D. Paulme, "La statue du Commandeur" (1958), pp. 299 ff.

40. Vincent of Beauvais, *Speculum historiale* 8.87, and others. See also L. Radermacher, "Aus Lucians Lügenfreund" (1902); P. F. Baum, "The Young Man Betrothed to a Statue" (1919); A. Graf, *Roma nella memoria e nelle immaginazioni del medio evo* (1923), pp. 674 f.; D. Paulme, "La statue du Commandeur" (1958); M. Camille, *The Gothic Idol* (1989), pp. 222 ff., with interesting observations on the relationship between Venus and the Virgin. See also D. Freedberg, *The Power of Images* (1989), pp. 317 ff. This variation of the story was included by G. Keller in his *Sieben Legenden* (1872).

41. *Capitulare de imaginibus* 4.17 (Migne vol. 98, col. 1219).

42. Epiphanius is a frequent laughingstock in these stories.

43. See p. 276 n. 40.

Chapter 12.   The Justice of Death Standing Up

1. Aristotle, *De arte poetica* 9.1452a; pseudo-Aristotle, *De mirabilibus auscultationibus* 156.22; Plutarch, *De sera numinis vindicta* 8.

2. Pseudo-Theocritus, *Carmina* 23 in Gow.

3. See M. Bettini, *Antropologia e cultura Romana* (1986), p. 240 and n. 8.

4. Plutarch, *Vita Caesaris* 66.12 f.

5. Because of the success of *Don Giovanni*, the subject of the justice of the statue, or of justice finally being carried out at the foot of a statue, came to enjoy a certain popularity in the European theatrical tradition. For example, it would also become a feature in the story of Semiramis, whose death at the hands of her son often took place at the feet of a statue of Ninus. See C. Questa, *Semiramide redenta* (1989), pp. 162 ff.

6. See pp. 128–31.

7. E. Benveniste, "L'expression du sarment dans la Grèce ancienne" (1948),

reprinted in *Le vocabulaire des institutions indo-européennes* (1969 = *Indo-European Language and Society* [1973]). See pp. 50–54.

8. On the Erinyes as a personal agent guaranteeing the fulfillment of a *moira*, see E. R. Dodds, *The Greeks and the Irrational* (1951).

9. E. T. A. Hoffmann, *Die Serapionsbrüder* (1957). On the importance of the wax figures in the works of Jean Paul, and his analogous aversion to these figures, see O. Rank, *Der Doppelgänger* (1914 = *The Double* [1971]).

10. E. Jentsch, "Zur Psychologie des Unheimlichen" (1906). On the equivalence of death and stone in Greek culture, see again J. P. Vernant, "La figuration de l'invisible et catégorie psychologique du double: Le colossos" (1966), especially pp. 259 ff.

11. R. Jakobson, "The Statue in Pushkin's Poetic Mythology" (1975), 34 f.

12. See pp. 13–14.

Chapter 13.   The Gaze

1. Ovid, *Metamorphoses* 10.293 f.

2. Homer, *Iliad* 18.417 ff. and also 18.376 ff. (the semimobile tripods also belonging to Hephaestus); Homer, *Odyssey* 7.91 (the golden guard dogs at the palace of Alcinous); along with Talos, the man of bronze watching over Crete found in Apollodorus, *Bibliotheca* 1.140. On the subject of automata that look like humans, see J. D. Bruce, "Human Automata in Tradition and Romance" (1912–13). There are two studies by A. Chapuis—A. Chapuis, *Les automates dans les oeuvres d'imagination* (1947), and A. Chapuis and E. Droz, *Les automates, figures artificielles d'hommes et d'animaux* (1949)—that are both useful works but with a tendency to popularize. On an interesting legend from the Swiss Alps, see E. Campi, *La poupée du vacher: Étude ethnopsychanalytique* (1979). See pp. 222–24.

3. Pindar, *Olympica* 7.52 f.

4. The evidence is collected in J. Overbeck, *Die antiken Schriftquellen zur Geschichte der bildenden Künste* (1868), n. 67–73. It might also be observed that according to Heliodorus, *Ethiopica* 3.13, the gods, when they descend among mortals, do not move by alternating their steps but by coursing along with their feet together, which is meant to explain why the Egyptians depict the gods with their feet joined together.

5. J. Overbeck, *Die antiken Schriftquellen zur Geschichte der bildenden Künste* (1868) n. 119–42. See F. Frontisi-Ducroux, *Dédale: Mythologie de l'artisan en grèce ancienne* (1975), especially pp. 95 ff. and R. L. Gordon, "The Real and the Imaginary: Production and Religion in the Graeco-Roman World" (1979). See also the remarks of D. Freedberg, *The Power of Images* (1989), pp. 283 ff. (live images in the Christian and modern tradition, with interesting suggestions for the ancient world). We can also note a Turkish superstition (cited by J. von Negelein, "Bild, Spiegel und Schatten im Volksglauben" [1902], p. 11): the artist pursued and punished by the image that he has created. Among the Greeks there must have been a long-standing and lingering suspicion that images could run away: on several occasions Pausanias tells stories about statues that, in various places of Greece, were tied down with chains, such as the statue

erected to the cruel ghost of Actaeon, which was then chained to a rock, or the simulacrum of Enyalius that the Spartans chained down so that "he would never run away from them," much like the wingless Victory of Athens (Pausanias, *Graeciae descriptio* 9.38.11 and 3.15.7; see also 8.41.6). Stories about statues that were bound to keep them from running away were also told concerning the island of Rhodes: see the scholia to Pindar, *Olympica* 7.54. On this subject, see also W. Crooke, "The Binding of a God" (1897), p. 336.

6. Ovid, *Metamorphoses* 10.250: *virginis est verae facies, quam vivere credas, / et, si non obstet reverentia, velle moveri*, "the face is that of a true maiden, and you would think she was alive and that she wanted to move, if reverence did not prevent it."

7. Euripides, *Eurystheus* frag. 372 in Nauck. In place of the *blepei* <n> which is found in the codices, Nauck corrected his text to follow the *legein* of F. G. Schmidt, but it seems inappropriate; see the scholia to Plato, *Meno* 367.73; Diodorus Siculus, *Bibliotheca historica* 4.76 (with a discussion in J. Overbeck, *Die antiken Schriftquellen zur Geschichte der bildenden Künste* [1868], pp. 119ff).

8. For the meaning of *blepō* and the difference between this verb and the verb *horaō*, "to look," see Chantraine (vol. 1, p. 179). On the gaze of the statue there are some observations in F. Frontisi-Ducroux, *Dédale: Mythologie de l'artisan en grèce ancienne* (1975), pp. 108ff.

9. E. Kris and O. Kurz, *Die Legende vom Künstler: Ein historischer Versuch* (1934 = *Legend, Myth, and Magic* [1979]). On the connection between the life of the image on the one hand and the eyes of the image on the other, there is apparently also an allusion in an episode from Plutarch (*De Pythiae oraculis* 8): shortly before the death of Hiero the Spartan, the eyes fell out of his statue at Leuctra.

10. W. Brückner, "Bild, Bildzauber" (1979).

11. For the importance of the eyes and the capacity to see as part of the simulation of life, one naturally thinks of the story by E. T. A. Hoffmann, "Der Sandmann" (1957). The contribution that the sinister optician Coppola-Coppelius makes to the creation of the doll/automaton Olympia is a determining factor. See pp. 222–24.

12. Pliny, *Naturalis historia* 35.120: *huius erat Minerva spectantem spectans quacumque aspiceretur*. See the entry for "Famulus" (Rossbach) in Pauly-Wissowa (vol. 6, col. 1985).

13. O. Söring, "Werke bildender Kunst in altfranzösischen Epen" (1900), p. 111.

14. M. Bettini, *Antropologia e cultura Romana* (1986), pp. 134ff.

15. Festus 152 in Lindsay: *malivoli autem quod in nullius tabernam spectabat*.

16. Pliny, *Naturalis historia* 11.150: *ut neque ab homine supremum eos spectari fas sit et caelo non ostendi nefas*.

17. Vergil, *Georgica* 4.485ff. See M. Bettini, *Antropologia e cultura Romana* (1986), p. 135, n. 12.

18. Frag. 43 in Boehm. See also Homer, *Odyssey* 23.198 (and also the scholia ad loc.), Apollodorus 244 F 129 in Jacoby; Hesychius, *Lexicon* s.v. *Epithalamitēs* (to sleep with the bed turned toward the image of Hermes): perhaps turned toward the one who directs dreams, and thus to assure oneself of positive visions? See C. Brillante, "Scene oniriche nei poemi omerici" (1990), especially p. 44.

19. B. Malinowski, "The Problem of Meaning in Primitive Language" (1953) and R. Jakobson, "Closing Statements: Linguistics and Poetics" (1960).

20. C. Mugler, "La lumière et la vision dans la poésie grecque" (1960), especially pp. 59ff. and S. Darup, "L'espressione tragica del desiderio amoroso" (1984). On theories and conceptions of optics in antiquity, see G. Simon, *Le regard de l'autre et l'apparence* (1988); for the gaze of love in the Greek novel, M. Fusillo, *Il romanzo greco* (1988), pp. 198ff.; for its role in modern literature, J. Rousset, *Leurs yeux se rencontrèrent: La scène de première vue dans le roman* (1984), which actually begins with the "rencontre exemplaire" between Theagenes and Chariclea in Heliodorus's *Ethiopica*, 3.4ff. There appears to be a fine example in Plutarch, *Quaestiones convivales* 5.7.2: in matters of love "the wounds received through touch or through hearing are not as deep as those received through looking and being looked at."

21. Ovid, *Metamorphoses* 14.695ff.

22. Antoninus Liberalis, *Metamorphoses* 39 = Hermesianax frag. 4 in Powell. Antoninus tells the same version of the story that we find in Ovid, but with different names, following Hermesianax's *Leontium*. For a discussion, see E. Rohde, *Der griechische Roman* (1914), pp. 84f. Another source of the myth can be found in Plutarch, *Amatorius* 20. On the Ovidian retelling of the story (which has seemed to some to be inaccurate, incoherent, etc.), see F. Bömer, *P. Ovidius Naso: Metamorphosen, Buch XIV–XV* (1986), pp. 214ff., with an ample discussion of earlier bibliography.

23. Ovid, *Metamorphoses* 14.718ff.

24. Ovid, *Metamorphoses* 14.744ff.: *postquam miserarum verba parentum / edidit et matrum miserarum facta peregit,* "after she spoke the words spoken by wretched mothers, and did the things that wretched mothers do."

25. Ovid, *Metamorphoses* 14.751ff.

26. F. Bömer, *P. Ovidius Naso: Metamorphosen, Buch XIV–XV* (1986), tries to maintain that at 14.753 *prospiciens* does not mean "to look from a distance," based on the argument that "from a distance the corpse would not have been able to be identified." In this portion of his excellent commentary, Bömer is strangely hostile to the text under discussion (see p. 280n. 37). For a clear illustration of the meaning of *prospicere,* see Seneca, *Epistulae ad Lucilium* 5.49.6.

27. See pp. 15–57.

28. Plutarch, *Amatorius* 20.

29. Antoninus Liberalis, *Metamorphoses* 39.

30. Ibid., 39.6: *pros hybrin.*

31. Ovid, *Metamorphoses* 14.751ff.

32. The connection between the Eastern iconographic representation and the cult of Cyprus was attested in classical sources as R. Herbig has clearly shown in "Aphrodite Parakyptousa" (1927); the subject was taken up again by H. Zimmermann, *Die babilonische Göttin im Fenster* (1928), pp. 2f., who makes a connection as well to the *kilili* at the window in the Assyrian tradition. But this Assyrian connection appears rather doubtful; see the entry for *kilili* in *The Assyrian Dictionary* (vol. 8, p. 371) with new iconographic material and further observations by R. D. Barnett in "The Nimrud Ivories and the Art of the Phoenicians" (1935, especially pp. 182f. and pp. 203f.), and also his "Ancient

Ivories in the Middle East" (1982), p. 48. Reproductions of the goddess at the window can be found in J. G. Pritchard, *The Ancient Near East in Picture* (1954), plate 131, p. 39; M. E. L. Mallowan, *Nimrud and Its Remains* (1966), plate V, p. 434; S. Moscati, ed., *The Phoenicians* (1988), plate 81.

33. See the valuable work by W. Fauth, *Aphrodite Parakyptousa* (1966), pp. 329 ff. See also E. Rohde, *Der griechische Roman* (1914), pp. 86 f.

34. See R. Herbig, "Aphrodite Parakyptousa" (1927) and also W. Fauth, *Aphrodite Parakyptousa* (1966).

35. But we will shortly return to this question; see pp. 156–57.

36. See Aristophanes, *Pax* 980 ff.; *Ecclesiazusae* 924 f. For *diakyptein* see the Septuagint, *Libri regum* 2.30. In this passage, the situation is quite interesting: the queen Jezebel appears in fact to be awaiting Jehu at the window of the palace, in the position of Astarte *prospiciens:* "she adorned her head / and looked out [*diekypsen*] from the window." W. Fauth, in *Aphrodite Parakyptousa* (1966), pp. 31 ff., is inclined to see here a further reflection of the Phoenician goddess, but the recent commentary by M. Cogan and H. Tadmor (*II Kings: The Anchor Bible* [1988], pp. 111 ff.) seems resolutely to exclude this possibility.

37. See W. Fauth, *Aphrodite Parakyptousa* (1966), pp. 362 ff. See also R. Herbig, "Aphrodite Parakyptousa" (1927). There seems little point to the supposed "Zwischenquelle" in F. Bömer, *P. Ovidius Naso: Metamorphosen, Buch XIV–XV* (1986), p. 215, to which Bömer would apparently attribute the connection ("Verbindung") between the Venus of Salamis and the story told by the poets. Bömer's "Zwischenquelle" is nothing other than an imaginary (but reassuring) hypostasis of the very question that we are asking. Even less useful is Ovid's supposed slovenliness (what Bömer calls "Sorglosigkeit") in having treated his sources too freely (the evidence that Bömer supplies in support of this supposed slovenliness is particularly incongruous: p. 215).

38. See Ovid, *Metamorphoses* 14.756 f.

39. What W. Fauth (*Aphrodite Parakyptousa* [1966], p. 366) describes as "merely a literal translation of the local cult-designation *Aphrodite parakyptousa.*"

40. The phrase "to look sideways," *transversa tueri,* is found, for example, in Vergil, *Eclogae* 3.8; Valerius Flaccus, *Argonautica* 2.154; etc. In Ovid, *Amores* 3.1.33, the figure of Elegy is said to "have smiled, casting sidelong glances" at the poet (*limis subrisit ocellis*) who is being castigated by the stern figure of Tragedy. One cannot help but recall Naevius's Tarentilla (see p. 262n. 17) and her skill in the art of *adnictare,* of winking.

41. See pp. 59–65.

42. As opposed to the mythical tales recounted above; for a discussion, see p. 148.

43. Xenophon, *Respublica Lacedaemoniorum* 3.

Chapter 14.   Respect

1. Dio Chrysostom, *Orationes* 31.152 ff. See pp. 54–58.
2. On the speech and its contents, see pp. 54–58.

3. Lysias, *Orationes* 6.15.

4. Compare the analogous logic in Dio Chrysostom, *Orationes* 31.82: if someone damages a statue, or steals some part of it, you punish him immediately in the same manner as someone who robs the temples; but if someone steals the statue from its owner, dedicating it to another person or erasing the inscription, then you do nothing? In any case the problem continually revolves around the respect that one owes to the images (and the respect that they are unjustly denied).

5. G. Glotz, *La solidarité de la famille dans le droit criminel en Grèce* (1904), p. 186. See Plutarch, *De sera numinis vindicta* 16. See also p. 275n. 23.

6. Suetonius, *Vita Tiberii* 58: *nummo vel anulo effigiem impressam latrinae vel lupanare intulisse.* See G. Lahusen, *Schriftquellen zum römischen Bildnis* (1984), vol. I, pp. 11ff.

7. Seneca, *De beneficiis* 3.26.2: *rem ineptissimam fecero, si nunc verba quaesiero quemadmodum dicam illum matellam sumpsisse,* "I would be acting in a very silly fashion if I tried to find a polite way of saying that he picked up a chamber pot."

8. Ibid., 3.26.2.

9. See perhaps also Pliny, *Naturalis historia* 33.41.

10. Suetonius, *Vita Tiberii* 58.

11. Pliny, *Naturalis historia* 35.70.

12. Suetonius, *Vita Tiberii* 44. See also Pliny, *Naturalis historia* 34.62 (and see p. 65). On obscene pictures in houses, see the condemnation of Propertius, *Elegiae* 2.6.27ff. (see also *Priapea* 4; Pliny, *Naturalis historia* 35.72; *Anthologia Latina* 4.39.9f.).

13. Suetonius, *Vita Tiberii* 43f.

14. Frag. 9 in Boehm.

15. Iamblichus, *Vita Pythagorae* 256.

16. Ibid., 84 (in Boehm pp. 13f.). See also Macrobius, *Saturnalia* 7.13.11.

17. Dio Chrysostom, *Orationes* 31.42; see pp. 54–58.

18. Scribonius Largus, *Compositiones* 9: *raro enim aliquis, priusquam se suosque tradat medico, diligenter de eo iudicat, cum interim nemo ne imaginem quidem suam committat pingendam nisi probato prius artifici per quaedam experimenta atque ita electo.*

19. This naturally suggests the so-called edict of Alexander, according to which the handsome general decreed that no one but Apelles could paint his portrait, no one but Pyrgoteles could make an engraving of his effigy, and no one but Lysippus could cast his statue in bronze (see Cicero, *Epistulae ad familiares* 5.12.7; Horace, *Epistulae* 2.1.237ff.; Valerius Maximus, *Facta et dicta memorabilia* 8.11 ext. 2; Pliny, *Naturalis historia* 7.125). The same problem presents itself when contemporary men of power, even if less handsome than the legendary Alexander, nevertheless entrust their image only to a responsible agent who is exclusively dedicated to its care.

20. See pp. 77–81.

21. See pp. 109–20.

22. Plutarch, *De Pythiae oraculis* 8.

23. Ibid.

24. Cassius Dio, *Historia Romana* 44.18.2.

25. Suetonius, *Vita Vitellii* 9: *ipso movente statuae equestres, cum plurifariam ei ponerentur, fractis repente cruribus pariter corruerunt.*

26. Suetonius, *Vita Domitiani* 15.2.

27. See pp. 45–48.

28. Pausanias, *Graeciae descriptio* 6.11.6 (see pp. 128–29).

29. Plutarch, *Vita Timoleontis* 23. On punishments carried out *in effigie,* see p. 275n. 23.

30. G. Glotz, *La solidarité de la famille dans le droit criminel en Grèce* (1904), p. 185 (citing Michel 364.4ff.).

31. Suetonius, *Vita Galbae* 10: *conscendisset tribunal, propositis ante se damnatorum occisorumque a Nerone quam pluribus imaginibus.*

32. Suetonius, *Vita Othonis* 7 (see also 3): *certe et imagines statuasque eius reponi passus est.* Compare Cassius Dio, *Historia Romana* 64.6.1 and Tacitus, *Historiae* 1.78. For a discussion of the image as faithfulness, see pp. 50–58.

33. See pp. 23–24.

34. Suetonius, *Vita Caligulae* 22: *In templo simulacrum stabat aureum iconicum amiciebaturque cotidie veste, quali ipse uteretur.* See also Cassius Dio, *Historia Romana* 59.28.3; Josephus, *Antiquitates Iudaicae* 19.1. For the iconographic tradition of this subject in the Middle Ages see M. Camille, *The Gothic Idol* (1989), p. 55. Regarding Caligula, see the commentary by G. Guastella, *Suetonio: Vita di Caligola* (1992).

35. Suetonius, *Vita Caligulae* 22: *interdiu vero cum Capitolino Iove secreto fabulabatur, modo insusurrans ac praebens in vicem aurem, modo clarius nec sine iurgiis. Nam vox comminantis audita est:* ἤ μ᾿ ἀνάειρ᾿ ἤ ἐγώ σέ? (the reference is to Homer, *Iliad* 23.724).

36. Suetonius, *Vita Caligulae* 34: *statuas virorum inlustrium ab Augusto . . . in campum Martium conlatas . . . subvertit atque disiecit . . . vetuitque posthac viventium cuiquam usquam statuam aut imaginem nisi consulto et auctore se poni.*

37. Ibid.

38. Quintilian, *Institutio oratoria* 7.7.5: <similes> *contra quas nihil opponi potest nisi lex altera. 'Tirannicidae imago in gymnasio ponatur. Mulieris imago in gymnasio ne ponatur. Mulier tyrannum occidit.' Nam neque mulieris imago ullo alio casu poni potest, nec tyrannicidae ullo alio casu summoveri.*

39. See J. Cousin, *Quintilien: Institution oratoire* (1977), vol. 4, p. 172 n. 2.

40. Plutarch, *Amatorius* 11.

41. See Pliny, *Naturalis historia* 34.18 (the *Achilleae,* thus named because Achilles constituted the ideal of masculine beauty, and was a hero especially dear to the ephebes).

42. Ibid., 35.5.

43. See Juvenal, *Saturae* 6.340 and the scholia ad loc.; Seneca, *Epistulae ad Lucilium* 97.2; Festus 348 in Lindsay; Ovid, *Ars amatoria* 3.243ff.; etc. On the Bona Dea and her characteristic features, see G. Piccaluga, "Bona dea: Due contributi all'interpretazione del suo culto" (1964); H. H. J. Brower, *Bona Dea* (1989); L. Beltrami, *L' 'impudicizia' di Tarpeia: Trasgressioni e regole del comportamento femminile a Roma* (1989), pp. 79ff.

44. Cicero, *De domo sua* 105; *De legibus* 2.14.36; etc. See H. H. J. Brower, *Bona Dea* (1989), pp. 158 ff.

45. Lactantius, *Divinae institutiones* 1.122. 10 f.

46. Juvenal, *Saturae* 6.340 f.: *ubi velari pictura iubetur / quaecumque alterius sexus imitata figuras.* See also the scholia ad loc.

47. Seneca, *Epistulae ad Lucilium* 97.2: *sic summotis extra consaeptum omnibus viris ut picturae quoque masculorum animalium contegantur.* It seems likely that *animalium* should mean "animal" here, give the context, referring to any male "life form," man or animal (but H. H. J. Brower disagrees [*Bona dea* (1989), p. 192]).

48. See pp. 122–25.

49. Juvenal, *Saturae* 6.309 ff. On the vice that characterizes these two ladies, see J. Gérard, *Juvenal et la réalité contemporaine* (1976), p. 273.

50. This scornful gesture was quite common: see Juvenal again, *Saturae* 1.131; Horace, *Sermones* 1.8.38; Suetonius, *Vita Neronis* 56; etc. (see also E. Courtney, *A Commentary on the Satires of Juvenal* [1980], p. 298).

51. Valerius Maximus, *Facta et dicta memorabilia* 2.1.7: *inter ista tam sancta vincula* [of kinship] *non magis quam in aliquo sacrato loco nudare se fas esse credebatur,* "it was believed to be no more permissible to undress in a sacred place than it was in the presence of those bound to us by the sacred bonds of kinship" (the context is the practice of Roman fathers not bathing with their adult sons, or the father-in-law with his son-in-law).

Chapter 15. Premonition

1. Terence, *Eunuchus* 583 ff. On the phrase *quo pacto Danaen misisse,* etc., see E. Fraenkel, "The Giants in the Poem by Naevius" (1964). This passage from Terence was obviously much cited as a result of having been sharply criticized by Augustine in his *Confessiones* (1.16 and 26.11), and in his *De civitate dei* (11.7), as an example of lascivious painting capable of corrupting morals. See P. Courcelle, *Recherches sur le Confessions de Saint Augustin* (1950), p. 55. Regarding Augustine and the subject of images, see M. Bettini, "Fra Plinio a S. Agostino: Francesco Petrarca sulle arti figurative" (1984), especially pp. 240 ff.

2. Donatus, *Commentum Terenti in Eunuchum* ad loc. (Ennius, *Scenica* 380 in Vahlen).

3. On the anthropological tracks along which the plots of Roman comedy run, see M. Bettini, "Verso un'antropologia dell'intreccio" (1990).

4. Plautus, *Mostellaria* 832 ff.

5. The *cornix* may perhaps have been considered especially astute and malicious. See the proverb *cornicum oculos configere,* "to dig out crows' eyes," or sometimes simply *cornici oculum,* "the crow's eyes," meaning to prove oneself more shrewd than someone already known for shrewdness (Cicero, *Pro Murena* 11.25; *Pro Flacco* 20.41; Quintilian, *Institutio oratoria* 8.3.2: A. Otto, *Die Sprichwörter und die sprichwörtlichen Redensarten der Römer* (1890), p. 33). The slave's invention corresponds to what in the Second Sophistic would come to be called allegorical painting, or enigmatic painting, which as such demands an

exegesis. See p. 286n. 46. In "Notes on Plautus" (1941), E. Riess seems to have thought that Plautus was alluding to some fable, but without proposing a specific reference.

6. Pliny, *Naturalis historia* 35.89f. See Lucian's description of the painting "Slander" (*Calumniae non temere credendum* 2ff.), in which Apelles was supposed to have depicted his own misadventures at the court of Ptolemy.

7. Pliny, *Naturalis historia* 35.140.

8. Fishermen and the like seem to have held a particular attraction for women of royal rank, as also in the case of Faustina, the wife of Marcus Aurelius (as reported in the Scriptores Historiae Augustae [Julius Capitolinus], *Vita Marci Antonini philosophi* 19.7). Aurelius Victor, *De Caesaribus* 16.2f., provides an interesting explanation: *quia plerumque nudi agunt, flagitiis aptiores* ("because for the most part they do their work in the nude, which makes them suited to vice").

9. Pliny, *Naturalis historia* 35.88 (about Apelles); *imagines adeo similitudinis indiscretae pinxit,* "he painted portraits that were perfect likenesses," and 35.140 (about Ctesicles): *utriusque similitudine mire expressa,* "the likeness of each portrait was extraordinary."

10. Plautus, *Epidicus* 624: *estne consimilis quasi cum signum pictum pulcre aspexeris?*

11. Plautus, *Mercator* 313: *si umquam vidistis pictum amatorem, em illic est.*

12. Plautus, *Poenulus* 1271ff. For the meaning of *exemplum* (which surely here means something like "model," "subject"), see H. Kornhardt, *Exemplum* (1936), p. 56. On the difficulty of depicting (or describing) everything that stands outside the sphere of familiar experience, see the observations of L. Marin, *Le portrait du roi* (1981).

13. This pair of painters had a sort of mythological significance; see E. Fraenkel, *Elementi Plautini in Plauto* (1960), pp. 16ff.

14. For the use of the word *graphicus* in Plautus see *Epidicus* 410; *Pseudolus* 519, 700; *Stichus* 570; *Trinummus* 936, 1024. For *pergraphicus* see *Trinummus* 1139. For *graphice: Persa* 306, 464, 836; *Trinummus* 767.

15. Plautus, *Persa* 843.

16. Plautus, *Stichus* 570.

17. Plautus, *Epidicus* 410.

18. Plautus, *Trinummus* 1024.

19. See pp. 171–72.

20. Plautus, *Persa* 843.

21. Plautus's use of *graphicus* is altogether unknown in Greek, even though the Latin word itself has a Greek derivation. In Greek *graphikos* can mean simply the painter, someone who knows the art of painting; as an adjective, it can refer at most to some subject that is particularly well suited to being painted (Plato, *Theaetetus* 144e; Aelian, *Varia historia* 14.37; Diodorus Siculus, *Bibliotheca historica* 2.53.7; Plutarch, *Vita Antonii* 24, etc.). But there is nothing in Greek like Plautus's use of the word (and perhaps also its popular usage?): that is, nothing that expresses perfection or some other sort of unqualified success.

22. Plautus's attitude toward painting, as well as metaphors and idioms about painting in the comedies, perhaps deserve to be better studied than they have been: see C. Knapp, "References to Painting in Plautus and Terence"

(1917). For the meaning of *graphicus* there are some observations in E. Fraenkel, *Elementi plautini in Plauto* (1960), p. 185 n. 1. For the use of analogous metaphors from painting in Dante (not "la pittura" but "lo scritto" in *Purgatorio* 2.44), see A. Menichetti, "Tre note di filologia italiana" (1969). The history of literary English perhaps presents something comparable to the evolution of Greek *graphikos* into Plautus's use of *graphicus*. In eighteenth-century writers the Italian term "pittoresco" (which meant only "pertaining to painting") began to appear widely in the English form "picturesque," referring to things that were not beautiful in a straightforward way, but somehow suggestive, unusual, like the old Gypsy in the shade of an oak tree, the parson's crosseyed daughter, and so on. See M. Praz, *La morte, la carne e il diavolo nella letteratura romantica* (1969), pp. 16 ff.

23. Suetonius, *Vita Galbae* 10: *repertus anulus opere antiquo, scalptura gemmae Victoriam cum tropaeo exprimente.*

24. Suetonius, *Vita Vespasiani* 7: *effossa sunt sacrato loco vasa operis antiqui atque in iis assimilis Vespasiano imago.*

25. Pliny, *Naturalis historia* 36.14: *glaeba lapidis unius cunei dividentium soluta, imaginem Sileni intus extitisse.* See Cicero, *De divinatione* 1.23 and 2.48, and Quintilian, *Institutio oratoria* 2.19.3. An inscription from Magnesia describes the interrogation of the god by the inhabitants of the city after a plane tree fell down and a tiny image of Dionysus was discovered inside it (as cited by A. S. Pease, *M. Tulli Ciceronis De divinatione libri duo* [1920/23 = 1977], p. 124, following Michel 856).

26. Pliny, *Naturalis historia* 37.15 ff.: *E margaritis, Magne, tam prodiga re et feminis reperta, quas gerere te fas non sit, fieri tuos vultus? . . . Grave profecto, foedum probrum erat, ni verius saevum irae deorum ostentum id credi oporteret clareque intellegi posset iam tum illud caput orientis opibus sine reliquo corpore ostentatum.* See S. Citroni Marchetti, *Plinio il vecchio e la tradizione del moralismo romano* (1991), p. 284.

27. Jerome, *Vulgata, Epistula ad Colossenses* 2.17 and Augustine, *Enarrationes in psalmos* 67.

28. Augustine, *De civitate dei* 17.8: Solomon foretold Christ, adumbrating the future.

29. On these powers of the mirror, see especially A. Delatte, *La catoptromancie grecque et ses dérivés* (1932); M. Meslin, "Significations rituelles et symboliques du miroir" (1990), and A. Baltrusaitis, *Le miroir: Révélations, science-fiction et fallacies* (1979); see also pp. 111–16. See also E. R. Dodds, *The Ancient Concept of Progress* (1973), chapter 10. An important passage can be found in Lucian, *De vera historia* 1.26.

30. Vergil, *Aeneid* 1.450 ff.

31. The bibliography on the exegesis of this passage is endless; see W. Suerbaum, "Hundert Jahre Vergils Forschung" (1980). Even so, A. M. Negri has made one attempt at further probing into the matter in "Sunt lacrimae rerum et mentem mortalia tangunt" (1988), with bibliography that supplements the materials collected in Suerbaum.

32. Vergil, *Aeneid* 1.464: *animum pictura pascit inani.*

33. Ibid., 1.488: *se quoque principibus permixtum agnovit Achivis.*

34. Ibid., 1.562 ff.

35. Ibid., 1.575 f.: *Atque utinam rex ipse Noto compulsus eodem / adforet Aeneas!*

36. Homer, *Odyssey* 8.72 ff. and 8.492 ff.

37. Ibid., 8.492 ff.

38. On the function of *phēmē*, see M. Detienne, *L'écriture d'Orphée* (1989).

39. See Vergil, *Aeneid* 1.463: *feret haec aliquam tibi fama salutem* ("this renown will bring you a sort of salvation").

40. Petronius, *Satyricon* 83: *In pinacothecam perveni vario genere tabularum mirabilem. Nam et Zeuxidos manus vidi nondum vetustatis iniuria victas, et Protogenis rudimenta cum ipsius naturae veritate certantia non sine quodam horrore tractavi. Iam vero Apellis quam Graeci 'monocnemon' appellant, etiam adoravi. Tanta enim subtilitate extremitates imaginum erant ad similitudinem praecisae, ut crederes etiam animorum esse picturam. Hinc aquilam ferebat in caelum sublimis Idaeum, illinc candidus Hylas repellebat improbam Naida. Damnabat Apollo noxias manus lyramque resolutam modo nato flore honorabat. Inter quos etiam pictorum amantium vultus tamquam in solitudine exclamavi: "ergo amor etiam deos tangit?"* . . . *Ecce autem, dum ego cum ventis litigo, intravit pinacothecam senex canus.* There are some observations regarding this episode in N. W. Slater, *Reading Petronius* (1990), pp. 91 ff. and pp. 201 ff.

41. Propertius, *Elegiae* 1.17.1 f.: *et merito, quoniam potui fugisse puellam / nunc ego desertas alloquor alcyonas* ("deservedly: because I was able to abandon my girlfriend, now I address the solitary halcyons").

42. Achilles Tatius, *Leucippe and Clitophon* 1.1.2. The text follows that established by E. Vilborg, *Achilles Tatius: Leucippe and Clitophon* (1955).

43. Achilles Tatius, *Leucippe and Clitophon* 1.2.1.

44. Ibid., 1.3 ff.

45. In contrast to the modern usage of *ekphrasis,* rhetorical treatises of the second century C.E. do not seem to apply this term only to descriptions of works of art, but also to the description of any subject in general (a landscape, an animal, an inanimate object, etc.): see H. C. Harlan, *The Description of Paintings as a Literary Device and Its Application in Achilles Tatius* (1965); H. Maguire, *Art and Eloquence in Byzantium* (1982), pp. 22 f.; S. Bartsch, *Decoding the Ancient Novel* (1989), p. 10 and pp. 31 f.

46. On this subject, see especially the useful work by S. Bartsch, *Decoding the Ancient Novel* (1989), which not only analyzes the strict relationship between description and plot that is especially characteristic of *Leucippe and Clitophon* and Heliodorus's *Ethiopica,* but also provides an analysis of the way in which the reader, confronted with descriptions of works of art that have a function inside the text, is often provoked to discover a "deeper meaning [than that] uncovered by the interpretative activity of either the author himself or an exegete supplied in the text" (p. 171). Another interesting aspect of this work is the constant parallel (including parallel terminology) between the description / interpretation carried out in the novel, the literary practices of the Second Sophistic, and the techniques of dream interpretation. On the function of description in the Greek novel, see also M. Fusillo, *Il romanzo greco* (1989), pp. 83 ff.

47. Longus, *Daphnis and Chloe,* proem. 1.

48. See pp. 73, 259n. 63 regarding Barthes's observation that "at first we love a picture."

49. Achilles Tatius, *Leucippe and Clitophon* 1.4.3. The manuscript tradition is divided, and Vilborg accepts, instead of *Eurōpēn*, the variant *Selēnēn*. Despite the fact that this second reading appears to have greater support in the manuscripts (see E. Vilborg, *Achilles Tatius: Leucippe and Clitophon, A Commentary* [1962], p. 20), it nevertheless seems to me that the first reading yields a better text from the point of view of literary consistency. In any case, as Vilborg himself notes, "the author certainly intended to allude to the picture of Europa."

50. Achilles Tatius, *Leucippe and Clitophon* 2.15.4

51. Ibid., 3.6.3f. Regarding this description, see S. Bartsch, *Decoding the Ancient Novel* (1989), p. 55.

52. Achilles Tatius, *Leucippe and Clitophon* 5.3.4: *hētis hypēinitteto prosomoion*. On the enigmatic image that is in need of *exēgēsis*, or interpretation (instead of a mere *diēgēsis*, or description), see S. Bartsch, *Decoding the Ancient Novel* (1989), pp. 27ff.

53. Achilles Tatius, *Leucippe and Clitophon* 5.3.5ff. For the sign of the swallow (which is a bad omen), see M. Bettini, "Turno e la rondine nera" (1988).

54. Achilles Tatius, *Leucippe and Clitophon* 5.4.1f.

55. The phrase that Menelaus uses to describe the interpreters of these signs is *exēgētai tōn symbolōn* (Achilles Tatius, *Leucippe and Clitophon* 5.4.1).

56. See Artemidorus, *Oneirocritica* 2.25.

57. Ibid., 1.2 (*ainissomenēs . . . psychēs*) and 4.1 (*di' ainigmatōn*).

58. See, for example, Philostratus, *Vita Apollonii* 2.37.

59. See pp. 177–79.

60. See A. Bouché-Leclerq, *Histoire de la divination dans l'antiquité* (1882), vol. 4, pp. 77ff.; W. R. Halliday, *Greek Divination* (1913 = 1967), pp. 229f.; R. Bloch, *Les prodiges dans l'antiquité classique* (1963), pp. 79ff.; E. Benveniste, *Hittite et indo-européen* (1962), pp. 10ff. and *Le vocabulaire des institutions indo-européennes* (1969 = *Indo-European Language and Society* [1973]).

61. Cicero, *De divinatione* 2.84. For other famous *omina* of this type, see also 1.103 and 1.104; Valerius Maximus, *Facta et dicta memorabilia* 1.5.4; etc.

62. In addition to *katoptromanteia*, Pliny refers to another practice of divination using an image: the *metōposkopoi*, that is, those people who practice divination by means of observing faces. One such person, observing the people painted by Apelles, was able to say how many years each of them had left to live, or how long they had already lived; see Pliny, *Naturalis historia* 35.88, with additional observations in A. E. Wardman, "Description of Personal Appearance in Plutarch and Suetonius: The Use of Statues as Evidence" (1967). See also pp. 210–12.

Chapter 16.   Resemblance

1. Augustine, *Soliloquia*, 2.10f. Ratio: *Dicimus item falsam arborem quam pictam videmus, et falsam faciem quae de speculo redditur, et falsum turrium motum navigantibus falsamque infractionem remi nihil ob aliud, nisi quod verisimilia sunt.* Augustinus: *Fateor.* Ratio: *Ita et in geminis fallimur, et in ovis, et in sigillis uno anulo impressis et <in> ceteris talibus.* Aug.: *Sequor omnino, atque*

concedo. Ratio: *Similitudo igitur rerum, quod ad oculos pertinet, mater est falsistatis.* Aug.: *Negare non possum.* Ratio: *Sed haec omnis silva, nisi me fallit, in duo genera dividi potest. Nam partim aequalibus in rebus, partim vero in deterioribus est. Aequalia sunt, quando tam hoc illi quam illud huic simile dicimus, ut de geminis dictum est, vel de impressionibus anuli. In deterioribus autem, quando illud quod deterius est, simile esse dicimus meliori. Quis enim in speculum attendat, et recte dicat se esse illi imagini similem, ac non potius illam sibi? . . . Natura gignendo vel resultando similitudines deteriores facit. Gignendo, cum parentibus similes nascuntur; resultando, ut de speculis cuiuscemodi . . . Iam vero animantium opera sunt in picturis, et huiscemodi quibusque figmentis: in quo genere includi etiam illa possunt, si tamen fiunt, quae demones faciunt.* The text is taken from the recent edition by W. Hörmann, *Soliloquiorum libri duo: De immortalite animae; De quantitate animae* (1986), pp. 58 f. (but not all the editorial choices are to be commended; see the observations of J. P. Bouhot and G. Madec [1987], pp. 332 f.). For the problem of resemblance in Augustine's thought (central to his notion of the *prima similitudo* and the impulse to imitate from which the entire universe derives), see *De vera religione* 66; *De trinitate* 6.10; *De immortalitate animae* pp. 19 ff.: E. Gilson, *Introduction à l'étude de Saint Augustin* (1943), pp. 275 ff.

2. Augustine, *De trinitate* 6.10: *Imago enim si perfecte implet illud cuius imago est, ipsa coaequatur ei, non illud imagini suae.* For a similar idea, see Quintilian, *Institutio oratoria* 10.2.10.

3. But a falsehood in the sense of a falsehood due to the simple incapacity to "fill," *implere*, the object that one wants to reproduce, not because of an intention to deceive. See, for example, Augustine again in *De vera religione* 66.

4. Catullus, *Carmina* 61.216 ff. A valuable commentary on this passage can be found in P. Fedeli, *Catullus: Carmen 61* (1983), pp. 138 ff.

5. Vergil, *Eclogae* 4.60.

6. Servius (auctus) *ad Eclogas* 4.60: *sicut enim maiores se sermone cognoscunt, ita infantes parentes risu se indicant agnoscere.*

7. In more general terms, the topic of paternal resemblance also constitutes one of the many applications of the principle according to which the masculine prevails over the feminine. See F. Héritier, *L'exercice de la parenté* (1981). This principle is operative in Roman kinship terms; see M. Bettini, "Il divieto di matrimonio fino al sesto grado incluso nel matrimonio romano" (1988). On the influence of this principle on ancient medical theories, see G. E. R. Lloyd, *Science, Folklore and Ideology* (1983), pp. 58 ff. But there is no better illustration of the presence and function of this rule than Augustine's observation, *De civitate dei* 16.8, that androgynous beings combine the two genders perfectly, but nevertheless they are assigned accordingly to the "more noble gender" (*meliore*), that is, to the masculine gender. As a result, no one says *una androgynus* or *una hermaphroditus;* the androgyne and the hermaphrodite are always he, never she.

8. Ovid, *Heroides* 6.123 ff.

9. Ovid, *Tristia* 4.5.31 ff. The same is found at 2.8.31 f.

10. The physical and moral are found together in Pliny the Younger, *Epistulae* 5.16.9: *filiam quae non minus mores eius quam os vultumque referebat, totumque patrem mira similitudine exscripserat,* "a daughter who reproduced not only the face and features but also the moral character, a perfect transcription

of her father in every way" (and thus we see also the topic of resemblance as a copy or transcription). Suetonius's Caligula (*Vita Caligulae* 25.4) also had a daughter who was similar to him: in brutality, of course, which prompted her even as a child to poke her fingers in the eyes of the other children who played with her.

11. See pp. 121–25.

12. This goes along with the belief that in procreation the dominant role is played by the paternal seed, and that the mother is called upon only to supply a receptacle. This belief is attested in ancient Greek and Roman culture, e.g., Aeschylus, *Eumenides* 658 ff. See E. Lesky, *Die Zeugungs- und Vererbungslehren der Antike und ihr Nachwirken* (1950), p. 54; G. E. R. Lloyd, *Science, Folklore and Ideology* (1983), pp. 86 ff. See also J. P. Vernant, *Mythe et pensée chez le grecs* (1966 = *Myth and Thought Among the Greeks* [1983]). On the identificatory value of blood in Roman culture, see G. Guastella, "La rete del sangue" (1985), especially the excellent observations on pp. 76 ff. regarding resemblances at Rome in terms of blood and lineage.

13. Apuleius, *Apologia* 14.

14. In the cases in which maternal resemblance is victorious (Theocritus, *Carmina* 18.21; Statius, *Silvae* 1.2.271 ff. and 3.3.11 ff.) the beauty of the newborn is explicitly emphasized; see P. Fedeli, *Catullus: Carmen 61* (1983), p. 139. The same holds true, for example, in Shakespeare, *Sonnets* 3, in which a handsome friend reflects the prettiness of his mother: "Thou art thy mother's glass, and she in thee / calls back the lovely April of her prime." It is also interesting to consider Seneca, *Phaedra* 658 ff. in this regard: Hippolytus contains "his father entire," *genitor totus* (Theseus; see also 646 ff.), but nevertheless "a part of his grim mother mingles her beauty [*decus*] to an equal degree." Once again, the presence of maternal features is realized in terms of beauty.

15. Ovid, *Metamorphoses* 4.290 f.

16. Horace, *Carmina* 4.5.21 ff.

17. L. Mueller observed this ellipsis with a certain amazement: "But that plain *similis* is striking, since ordinarily the term 'father' is added" (*Q. Horatius Flaccus: Oden und Epoden* [1900], vol. 2, p. 368).

18. Catullus, *Carmina* 61.226 ff. (see pp. 189–90). See also Macrobius, *Saturnalia* 2.5.3.

19. Martial, 6.27.3 f.: *est tibi, quae patria signatur imagine vultus, / testis maternae nata pudicitiae.*

20. In the choice of *argumenta*, Quintilian observes (*Institutio oratoria* 5.10.24), it is first of all necessary to consider the *genus*, "for people are generally believed to be like their parents and ancestors," *nam similes parentibus et maioribus, suis plerumque creduntur.* The *genus* immediately supplies a frame of reference for the argument's demonstration of individual characteristics.

21. Seneca, *Troades* 461 ff.

22. See Euripides, *Troades* 1178; Vergil, *Aeneid* 3.490. This inventory of features presents various analogies with that scene in the *Odyssey* (3.149 f.) when Helen recognizes Telemachus as a son of Odysseus; for additional such situations in Homer see the references in H. Hayman, *The Odyssey of Homer* (1866), vol. 1, p. 113.

23. Pliny, *Naturalis historia* 7.54.

24. Quintus Cicero, *Commentariolum petitionis* 11.44: *animi ianua*. See A. Otto, *Die Sprichwörter und die sprichwörtlichen Redensarten der Römer* (1890), p. 130 and p. 147; R. Lamacchia, "Aspetti di civiltà diverse in alcune espressioni idiomatiche" (1978).

25. Aeschylus, *Choephori* 205 ff. See pp. 16–17. Hands, feet, and the head constituted specific marks of personal identity and recognizability for each individual. In the appalling stories of children devoured by their father, these are generally the elements by which the parent / inadvertent cannibal realizes the crime he has committed (Herodotus 1. 119; Aeschylus, *Agamemnon* 1591 ff.; Seneca, *Thyestes* 1038 ff.). Likewise, the feet constitute one of the arguments in favor of the stranger who pretends to be Odysseus (*Odyssey* 19.379 f.); see also M. M. Sassi, *La scienza dell'uomo nella Grecia antica* (1988), pp. 70 ff. Finally, it is worth mentioning the famous topic of the footprints used as proof that a hero passed through a certain place, such as the footprint of Perseus at Chemnis (Herodotus 2.91), or the footprint of Heracles by the river Tyras (Herodotus 4.82), and the ironical observations of Lucian in *De vera historia* 7. As a result, these same features by which an individual was able to be recognized could also be used, vertically, as the identifiable features for a group or a lineage, something that the individual possessed as part of the entire semiotic device of family resemblances.

26. *Mahabharata, Śantiparvan* 12.1.13 ff.; see D. Silvestri, "Riflessi onomastici indomediterranei" (1986).

27. Theocritus, *Carmina* 17.43 ff. The adjective *rhaidioi* seems rather unusual here: why should a woman "without love" have easy or abundant births? A. S. F. Gow, *Theocritus* (1950), vol. 2, p. 334, suggested the possibility that it is more a question of births that are careless rather than easy, given that it is "not asserted elsewhere that unchaste wives are necessarily prolific." Actually, I suspect that Theocritus is here alluding to the prolific production of twins that is typical of unfaithful women (see pp. 201–2). As for the missing resemblance connected to thinking about another man, see pp. 199–200.

28. Pliny, *Naturalis historia* 7.49: *in ea quae gemino partu alterum maritu similem alterumque adultero genuit*. On the serious suspicions attached to twin births, see pp. 202–3.

29. Martial 6.39.6 ff.

30. Aristotle, *De generatione animalium* 4.3.767b.

31. Ibid., 4.3.767b.

32. Plutarch, *Vita Bruti* 1.1 and 1.7 (citing Posidonius).

33. M. Bettini, *Antropologia e cultura romana* (1986), pp. 182 ff. and also "Sosia e il suo sosia: Pensare il doppio a Roma" (1991), especially pp. 39 ff.

34. Lucretius, *De rerum natura* 4.1218 ff. See Aristotle, *De generatione animalium* 4.3.769a (markedly different from Lucretius). See also J. Blayney, "Theories of Conception in the Ancient Roman World" (1986), pp. 233 ff.

35. W. E. Leonard and S. B. Smith, *T. Lucreti Cari De rerum natura* (1942), p. 632. They do not directly consider here the ancient scientific theories involving genetics; for this, see E. Lesky, *Die Zeugungs- und Vererbungslehren der Antike und ihr Nachwirken* (1950), pp. 136 ff., and two works by G. E. R. Lloyd: *Science, Folklore and Ideology* (1983), pp. 86 ff., and *Magic, Reason and Experi-*

ence (1979). Analogous theories can be found in Hippocrates, *De genitura* 7 ff.; Censorinus, *De die natali* 6; etc. See H. A. J. Munro, *T. Lucreti Cari De rerum natura* (1928), p. 564; H. Diels and W. Kranz, *Die Fragmente der Vorsokratiker* (1934), vol. 1, p. 300; C. Bailey, *Lucreti De rerum natura libri sex* (1947), vol. 3, pp. 1313 ff. Above all, see the extensive commentary by R. D. Brown, *Lucretius on Love and Sex* (1987), pp. 320 ff.

36. Lucretius, *De rerum natura* 4.1211 ff.

37. See pp. 192–93.

38. See pp. 191–92.

39. As a pure conduit for male resemblances, the woman is also a conduit for male words. Cicero (*De oratore* 3.46) noted that women more easily preserved the ancient ways of speaking, because they were excluded from many spheres of speech and thus generally maintained what they had learned to start with. Therefore, when listening to his mother-in-law, Laelia, Cicero had the feeling that he was listening to the Latin of Plautus or Naevius: *ex quo sic locutum esse eius patrem iudico, sic maiores,* "consequently I thought this was the way her father spoke, and likewise her ancestors." It is the language of the father that the woman transmits, making her once again the mediator of something that does not belong to her gender. For female language in general, see M. E. Gilleland, "Female Speech in Greek and Latin" (1980); and M. Bettini and L. Ricottilli, "Elogio dell'indiscrezione" (1987).

40. Cassius Dio, *Historia Romana* 56.3.4.

41. Cicero, *De officiis* 1.121, records the case of Africanus's son, who "on account of his poor health could not be as similar to his father as his father had been to his," *propter infirmitatem valetudinis, non tam potuit patris similis esse quam ille fuerat sui.* The defining role played by the paternal presence is made quite clear in one of the *elogia Scipionum,* in which it is said of Gn. Cornelius Scipio that he "produced an heir, and aspired to the deeds of his father," *progeniem genui, facta patris petiei (Corpus inscriptionum Latinarum* I 15). Together with the generation of offspring (in order to continue the lineage), there is also the tension produced by the need to repeat the paternal *facta.*

42. Pliny, *Naturalis historia* 7.52 ff.: *similitudinum quidem immensa reputatio est et in qua credantur multa fortuita pollere, visus, auditus, memoria haustaeque imagines sub ipso conceptu. Cogitatio etiam utriuslibet animum subito transvolans effingere similitudinem aut miscere existimatur, ideoque plures in homine quam in ceteris omnibus animalibus differentiae, quoniam velocitas cogitationum animique celeritas et ingenii varietas multiformes notas imprimit, cum ceteris animantibus immobiles sint animi et similes omnibus singulis in suo cuique genere.* See the discussion of *similitudines* in the entry for "Pliny the Elder" (Kroll) in Pauly-Wissowa (vol. 21, col. 308), which suggests that Pliny's chapters on the subject of *similitudines* (7.50–56) are often based on materials gathered by Pliny himself (but see, for example, the general discussion in Aristotle, *De historia animalium* 7.6.585b ff. and *De generatione animalium* 1.16.721b ff. and 4.3.769a ff.). The occasional presence of parallels with Valerius Maximus might suggest a common source in Varro (but it is also entirely possible that Pliny himself made use of Valerius Maximus).

43. Aetius, *De placitis philosophorum* 5.12 (= *Doxographi Graeci* 423). On the

authorship of the work, attributed in our sources to Plutarch, see the entry for "Plutarch" (Ziegler) in Pauly-Wissowa (vol. 21, cols. 879 f.). On a lack of resemblance to one's parents, see also pp. 194–95.

44. Empedocles, A 81 in Diels-Kranz.

45. This Stoic attestation appears as II 752 in Von Arnim.

46. Heliodorus, *Ethiopica* 10.14.

47. Ibid., 10.14.7. The story of gazing at the painting of Andromeda at the moment of conception is also told at 4.8.5. This is also the source, of course, for Tasso's story of the conception of Clorinda, in his *Gerusalemme liberata*, 12.24.

48. The kings of Ethiopia considered Perseus and Andromeda to be the founders of their lineage. For a discussion of Greek and Roman views of Ethiopians and their mythological status, see F. M. Snowden, *Blacks in Antiquity* (1970), pp. 144 ff. and L. A. Thompson, *Romans and Blacks* (1989), pp. 88 ff.

49. Montaigne, "Of the Power of Imagination," in his *Essais* (1933 = *Essays* [1958]).

50. Jerome, *Quaestiones Hebraicae* 3.1: [*feminae*] *quales perspexerint sive mente conceperint in extremo voluptatis aestu, quae concipiunt, talem subolem procreant, cum hoc ipsum etiam in equarum gregibus apud Hispanos dicatur fieri, et Quintilianus in ea controversia in qua accusabatur matrona quod Aethiopem peperit, pro defensione illius argumentatur hac conceptum esse natura quam supra diximus.*

51. Quintilian, *Declamationes* frag. 8 in Lehnert.

52. Once again, horses appear to resemble humans; see p. 96. Aristotle reports a pastoral belief shared by horse breeders (*De generatione animalium* 4.2.767a) that "there is supposed to be a difference regarding the gender of the offspring based on whether they are looking to the south or the north when they copulate." The influences transmitted by means of the gaze affect here not only the resemblance to the parents but also serve to determine the type of offspring. It is also worth noting as well the famous trick used by Jacob (Genesis 30.37 ff.), who obtained lambs of variegated color by planting multicolored rods where the sheep came to drink, with the result that the mothers "looked at the rods in the heat of coupling and gave birth to spotted offspring, variegated and of different colors."

53. The same situation occurs again in Plutarch, *De sera numinis vindicta* 21, but with a more scientific explanation: it turns out that the woman had had Ethiopian ancestors four generations removed (see Aristotle, *De historia animalium* 7.6; Antigonus of Carystus, *Historiarum mirabilium collectanea* 122; Pliny, *Naturalis historia* 7.51). This topic (*matrona Aethiopem peperit*) constituted a subject much beloved by the rhetoricians; for another example, see Calpurnius Flaccus, *Declamationes, excerpta* 2 in Lehnert.

54. Favorinus in Gellius, *Noctes Atticae* 12.1.14 ff.: *sicuti valeat ad fingendas corporis atque animi similitudines vis et natura seminis, non secus ad eandem rem lactis quoque ingenia et proprietates valere. Neque in hominibus id solum, sed in pecudibus quoque animadversum. Nam si ovium lacte haedi aut caprarum agni alantur, constat ferme in his lanam duriorem, in illis capillum gigni teneriorem. . . . Id hercle ipsum est, quod saepe numero miramur, quosdam pudicarum mulierum liberos parentum suorum neque corporibus neque animis similes exsistere.* An extensive commentary on this chapter in Gellius (also in relation to

the topos of rejecting the use of wet nurses) can be found in W. Schick, *Favorin Peri paidon trophes und die antike Erziehungslehre* (1911); see also K. R. Bradley, "Wet-Nursing at Rome: A Study in Social Relations" (1986). In an essay entitled "On the Affection of Fathers for Their Children," Montaigne provides an even darker picture of this disparaged practice: "It is an everyday thing within the environs of my estate to see the peasant women call the she-goats to aid them when they cannot nurse their infants with their own breasts. At this moment I actually have two men in my service who did not drink women's milk for longer than a week. These goats straightaway become used to nursing these infants, and come running when they cry, recognizing their voices; they refuse to nurse any other children but their own, and the infant likewise refuses to nurse with any other goat. I saw one of them the other day from whom they had taken away his usual goat. . . . In the end, he could not manage to accustom himself to the other that had been brought to him, and died, surely from hunger" (*Essais* [1933] = *Essays* [1958]).

55. Favorinus in Gellius, *Noctes Atticae* 12.1.20: *natura lactis . . . quae iam a principio imbuta paterni seminis concretione ex matris etiam corpore et animo recentem indolem configurat.* W. Schick, *Favorin Peri paidon trophes und die antike Erziehungslehre* (1911), p. 23, notes that there do not appear to be parallels for this notion in the other scientific authors of antiquity (but see p. 293n. 56, regarding Nigidius in Pliny), in which case Favorinus (or Gellius) would be speaking with "rhetorische Undeutlichkeit," a rhetorical lack of clarity. It should be noted that Macrobius, who repeats this paragraph almost to the letter, does introduce a significant variation (*Saturnalia* 5.11.15): *natura lactis . . . quae infusa tenero et mixta parentum semini adhuc recenti ex hac gemina concretione unam indolem configurat,* "the nature of the milk given to the infant and combining the seeds of both parents shapes the single personality of the newborn from this double concretion." The dominance of the male seed has disappeared, and is replaced instead by a balanced *gemina* concretion that derives from both parents, sounding altogether more reasonable.

56. Pliny, *Naturalis historia* 7.67 (= Swoboda, frag. 3): *idem* [Nigidius] *lac feminae non corrumpi alenti partum, si ex eodem viro rursus conceperit, arbitratur.*

57. See p. 273n. 5.

58. Scriptores Historiae Augustae (Julius Capitolinus), *Vita Marci Antonini philosophi* 19.3.

59. For another example of a Roman noble's resemblance to a gladiator, see Juvenal, *Saturae* 6.81: *nobilis Euryalum mirmillonem exprimat infans,* "so that the aristocratic infant recalls Euryalus the gladiator" (but the story in this case does not involve blood or Chaldeans). For the attraction that gladiators held for Roman aristocratic matrons in the imperial period, see J. P. V. D. Balsdon, *Life and Leisure in Ancient Rome* (1969), p. 297.

60. Scriptores Historiae Augustae (Aelius Lampridius), *Vita Commodi Antonini* 1.2; Fronto, *Epistulae ad M. Antoninum imperatorem* 1.3 (94 Van den Hout = 234 Portalupi). For a discussion, see L. Robert, *Hellenica* (1946), p. 42 and F. Mencacci, "Il sangue del gladiatore: Commodo e la doppia identità" (1989).

61. Fronto, *Epistulae ad M. Antoninum imperatorem* 1.3 (94 Van den Hout = 234 Portalupi): *vidi pullulos tuos, quod quidem libentissime in vita mea*

viderim, tam simili facie tibi, ut nihil sit hoc simili similius. . . . vidi te non exadversum modo, sed locupletius, sive me ad dexteram sive ad sinistram convertissem. . . . panem alter tenebat bene candidum, ut puer regius, alter autem cibarium, plane ut a patre philosopho prognatus. Deos quaeso sit salvus sator, salva sint sata, salva seges sit, quae tam similes procreat. Nam etiam voculas quoque eorum audivi tam dulcis, tam venustas, ut orationis tuae lepidum illum et liquidum sonum nescio quo pacto in utriusque pipulo adgnoscerem.

62. On the antinomies of twin births, see the comprehensive study by F. Mencacci, *I fratelli amici: La rappresentazione dei gemelli nella cultura romana* (1996).

63. Pliny, *Naturalis historia* 7.53 f.

64. Valerius Maximus, *Facta et dicta memorabilia* 9.14.2.

65. Ibid., 9.14 ext. 3.

66. Pliny, *Naturalis historia* 7.55. In Macrobius, *Saturnalia* 2.4.20, the anecdote is told instead about Augustus.

67. The joke is absolutely identical to one studied by S. Freud in *Der Witz und seine Beziehung zum Unbewussten* (1905 = *Wit and Its Relation to the Unconscious* [1916]). As an example of a tendentious joke used against persons whom it is not possible to attack directly: His Highness sees among the crowd a man of imposing aspect who resembles him to an extraordinary degree. He beckons the man and asks: "Your mother was a servant in the palace, was she not?" "No, Your Highness," the man answers, "but my father was." In other cases, the adulterous resemblance (or the resemblance that is believed to be the product of adultery) not only fails to produce embarrassment but even results in a sort of advantage: by unexpectedly displacing the progression of the lineage it can sometimes favor rather than undermine the line of descent. Suetonius, for example, reports (*Vita Othonis* 1) that the father of the future emperor Otho, "was extremely wellborn on his mother's side, with many important family connections, and was so beloved by Tiberius and so similar to him in his features, that many supposed him to be Tiberius's son" (*pater L. Otho, materno genere praeclaro multarumque et magnarum propinquitatum, tam carus tamque non absimilis facie Tiberio principi fuit, ut plerique procreatum ex eo crederent*). In some sense this illicit but imperial resemblance foresaw Otho's rise to power.

68. On the Saturnalia king and his capricious powers, see Seneca, *Apocolocyntosis* 8.21; Tacitus, *Annales* 13.15; Lucian, *Saturnalia* 4. See also M. Bettini, "Iacta alea est: Saturno e i Saturnali" (1990). For other indecorous resemblances among the Roman nobility, see Plutarch, *Vita Ciceronis* 25 and *Vita Galbae* 9.

69. Apuleius, *Apologia* 14.2: *an tu ignoras nihil esse aspectabilius homini nato quam formam suam?*

70. That is, if any importance is granted to the addition found in the margin to the manuscript of Pliny designated as *Leidensis Lipsi* n. 7 (7.55 *in fine*), in which it is said that Senator Agrippinus could not be distinguished from Paris the mime. See the note by R. Schilling, *Pline l'ancien: Histoire naturelle, livre VII* (1977), p. 151.

71. I have pursued this subject, and the representations of the double in Roman culture, at much greater length in "Sosia e il suo sosia: Pensare il doppio a Roma" (1991).

72. Diodorus Siculus, *Bibliotheca historica* (fragmenta libri XXXI) 31.25.2.

73. Suetonius, *Vita Vespasiani* 19: *in funere . . . archimimus personam eius ferens imitansque, ut est mos, facta ac dicta vivi.* This passage in Diodorus is not given much credit in A. N. Zadoks and J. Jitta, *Ancestral Portraiture in Rome* (1932), p. 25. The authors assume (without saying why) that this mimic practice cannot be dated to the historical era supposed by Diodorus. In a different cultural context, this practice of creating a *persona ficta* of the dead king can be usefully compared with the ceremonies described by E. H. Kantorowicz in *The King's Two Bodies: A Study in Mediaeval Political Theology* (1957), in the medieval courts both of France and of England.

74. Chariton, *Chaereas and Callirhoe* 1.14.9 f.

75. Ibid., 4.1.10.

76. Callirhoe's faithfulness is of course a principal feature of the story; see J. Helms, *Character Portrayal in the Romance of Chariton* (1966), pp. 46 ff.

77. Chariton, *Chaereas and Callirhoe* 2.11.1 ff.

78. See pp. 13–14.

79. Chariton, *Chaereas and Callirhoe* 3.8.7.

80. Vergil, *Aeneid* 4.82 ff.

81. Seneca, *Phaedra* 646 f.: *sic est, Thesei vultus amo, / illos priores quos tulit quondam puer.*

82. J. P. Vernant, "Au miroir de Méduse" (1989).

83. Suetonius, *Vita Neronis* 28: *meretricem quam fama erat Agrippinae simillimam, inter concubinas recepit.* The same is found in Cassius Dio, *Historia Romana* 61.11.2 (Xiphilinus).

84. Scriptores Historiae Augustae (Aelius Lampridius), *Vita Commodi Antonini* 5.8.

85. Vergil, *Aeneid* 4.327 ff. (of which Ovid's *Heroides* 7.135 ff. is only a poor comparison). See also Tacitus, *Annales* 12.68 (*Agrippina, velut dolore victa et solacia conquirens, tenere amplexu Britannicum veram paterni oris effigiem appellare,* "Agrippina, as if stricken by grief and seeking to console herself, held Britannicus in a tender embrace, saying that he was the true image of his father's features") and Ausonius, *Parentalia* 22.1 ff.

86. Augustine, *Soliloquia* 2.10 ff. (see pp. 187–88).

87. Artemidorus, *Oneirocritica* 3.31.

88. Ibid., 2.7; see also 2.12. On the powers of the mirror, see pp. 111–16.

89. The scholia to Callimachus, *Hymnus in Jovem* 13 (in Pfeiffer, p. 42). See pp. 44, 252n. 25.

90. Shakespeare, *Sonnets* 3.

91. Artemidorus, *Oneirocritica* 2.7.

92. Ibid., 5.67.

93. See pp. 113–14.

Chapter 17.   The Doll

1. R. Lanciani, "Delle scoperte avvenute nei disterri del nuovo Palazzo di Giustizia" (1889). For the excavation and findings, see especially *Crepereia Tryphaena: Le scoperte archeologiche nell'area del Palazzo di Giustizia* (1983).

2. *Crepereia Tryphaena,* in G. Pascoli, *Carmina* (1951). The notes by L. Vischi in G. Pascoli, *Carmi Latini* (1920), pp. 237 ff. are still useful, and see also the remarks of A. Ghiselli, *Crepereia Tryphaena* (1955) and M. Perugi in G. *Pascoli: Opere* (1982), vol. 2.

3. Ovid, *Fasti* 5.419 ff. The holiday of the Lemuria fell on May 9, 11, and 13; see F. Bömer, *P. Ovidius Naso: Die Fasten* (1958), p. 215. Pascoli follows Ovid extremely closely. We can compare, for example, *Crepereia Tryphaena* 26 f.: *nocte, cum pictae volucres tacebunt / et canes,* with the corresponding words in Ovid's *Fasti* 5.429 f.: *nox ubi iam media est somnoque silentia praebet / et canis et variae conticuistis aves.* As regards the ritual words themselves, they are taken entirely from Ovid; the words in the *Crepereia Tryphaena* 31 f.: *his fabis manes, redimo, Tryphaenae, / meque meosque* have been only slightly adapted (according to the context required) from the words in Ovid's *Fasti* 5.438 f.: *haec ego mitto, / his . . . redimo meque meosque fabis.*

4. This identification follows a theory proposed by A. Castellani, "Descrizione degli oggetti trovati nel sarcofago di Crepereia Tryphaena" (1889); Pascoli's poem is much indebted to Castellani and also to the observations in R. Lanciani, "Delle scoperte avvenute nei disterri del nuovo Palazzo di Giustizia" (1889), as discussed already by L. Vischi, in G. Pascoli, *Carmi Latini* (1920), pp. 237 ff.

5. Pliny, *Naturalis historia* 21.100, in which Pliny notes *quidam callitrichon vocant, alii polutrichon,* "others call it lovely-hair or thick-hair."

6. On this topic, see pp. 225–27.

7. A. Mura Sommella, "Crepereia Tryphaena" (1983), p. 29, and especially the same author's discussion of the doll, "Bambola in avorio" (1983).

8. See especially K. M. Elderkin, "Jointed Dolls in Antiquity" (1930). The bibliography on this topic does not appear to be very extensive: in addition to the standard entries in Daremberg-Saglio ("Figlinum opus," "Ludi," "Pupa") and the entry for "Giocattoli" in the *Enciclopedia dell'arte antica,* one can also consult W. Deonna, "L'enfance antique et ses jeux" (1932); J. Dörig, "Von griechischen Puppen" (1958, but Dörig's use of classical texts leaves much to be desired; unfortunately it has become part of the archaeological bibliography, creating some confusion); A. Andrén, "Classical Antiquities in the Zorn Collection" (1948), p. 61; M. R. Rinaldi, "Ricerche sui giocattoli nell'antichità, I: Le bambole" (1956, which is especially useful for its careful assembly of the evidence and textual references); A. Balil, "Munecas antiguas en España" (1962); U. Scamuzzi, "Studio sulla mummia di bambina (la cosiddetta 'Mummia di Grottarossa')" (1964, especially the *Appendix* on the doll discovered in the tomb, although Scamuzzi is not always reliable); M. Manson, "Histoire d'un mythe: Les poupées de Maria femme d'Honorius" (1978, but the comprehensive work on this topic that the author promises in the notes has apparently not been published); A. Mura Sommella, "Bambola in avorio" (1983, with extensive references to other publications and archaeological catalogs); R. Danese, "Intorno al latino 'pupa': Linee per una ricerca" (1986, with a very valuable analysis of literary evidence). On archaeological finds involving dolls (or figures similar to dolls, given that it is a distinction difficult to establish in some cases), in addition to the bibliography cited above, see especially the work by H. B. Walters, *Catalogue of the Terracottas in the Department of Greek and Roman Antiq-*

uities (1903), p. 233, n. C 460–C 462; D. Burr, *Terra-cottas from Myrina* (1934), pp. 30f.; D. Thompson, *Troy: The Terracotta Figurines of the Hellenistic Period* (1963), pp. 89f.; E. Töpperwein, *Terrakotten von Pergamon* (1976), especially pp. 56ff.; and D. Thompson's review of Töpperwein in the *American Journal of Archaeology* (1979). In the Archaeological Museum of Syracuse one can see a mold used to produce dolls. On the doll in general, there is a brief but profound study by J. M. Lotman, "Le bambole nel sistema della cultura" (1984). On the doll in folklore, there are some useful observations in V. J. Propp, *Istoričeskie korni volšebnoj skazki* (1946 = *Le radici storiche dei racconti di fate* [1972], pp. 317ff.).

9. K. M. Elderkin ("Jointed Dolls in Antiquity" [1930], p. 468ff.) cites only one case of a baby doll. It is quite unusual that U. Scamuzzi, "Studio sulla mummia di bambina (la cosiddetta 'Mummia di Grottarossa')" (1964), denies that the figurine found in the tomb of Grottarossa is a doll, based on the bizarre argument that because the figurine is precisely a girl (rather than a baby) it cannot be a doll.

10. M. R. Rinaldi, "Ricerche sui giocattoli nell'antichità, I: Le bambole" (1956), p. 109.

11. See pp. 226–27.

12. See especially Plato, *Alcibiades* 1.132–1.33a (the Platonic authorship of this dialogue has been discussed at length: see P. Friedländer, *Platon*, II, *Die platonischen Schriften, Erste Periode* (1957, pp. 213ff. = *Plato*, vol. 2 [1964], pp. 237ff.). Socrates wants to demonstrate to Alcibiades that the soul (*psychē*), in order to truly know itself, must be reflected in another soul. To illustrate his argument, Socrates uses the *korē* and the way it is produced as a metaphor for this process: "Have you observed that the face of the person who looks in the eye of another person is seen in the aspect [*opsis*] of the person he is facing, as in a mirror? This is what we call *korē*, and that is the image [*eidōlon*] of the person who is looking at the eye. . . . Therefore an eye that looks into another eye, and turns its gaze toward the most important part of it, that through which one looks, is thus able to see itself. . . . But if it turns its gaze to another part of the human body, or toward some other thing different from what makes it similar to another eye, then it will not be able to see itself." The *korē*, the girl in the eye, is thus the image of someone who looks at another: its existence demands a reciprocity, an encounter between two organs of perception that—as privileged mirrors—combine to form the face of the looker in the form of an *eidōlon*/girl in the eye of the looked upon. The action, of course, is imagined as reciprocal: at the same time that a *korē* is created in one person's eye, there is necessarily another *korē* produced in the eye of the other. But it can happen—and here we discover some of the more marvelous beliefs about the girl in the eye—that this is not always the kind *korē*, but rather a horrible figure of the Gorgon that appears at the center of the eye, as discussed in J. P. Vernant and P. Vidal-Naquet, *Mythe et tragédie deux* (1986), p. 28, and F. Frontisi-Ducroux, "Senza maschera nè specchio: L'uomo greco e i suoi doppi" (1991); or the fabulous peoples mentioned by Pliny who have more than one pupil in each eye, or whose pupils display the likenesses of animals (*Naturalis historia* 7.16ff.; see K. F. Smith, "Pupula duplex" [1902], for a discussion). For the contrary possibility of an eye that possesses no pupil at all as a sign of imminent death see the Scriptores His-

toriae Augustae (Julius Capitolinus), *Vita Pertinacis* 14. On the related topic of an actual pupil-soul, see E. Monseur, "L'âme pupilline" (1905); W. Deonna, "L'âme pupilline et quelques monuments figurés" (1957) and *Le symbolisme de l'oeil* (1965), pp. 28ff., and also G. Guidorizzi, "Lo specchio e la mente: Un sistema di intersezioni" (1991).

13. Homer, *Iliad* 14.494 and *Odyssey* 9.390. See also Sophocles, *Oedipus rex* 1277; Artemidorus, *Oneirocritica* 2.39; Rufus of Ephesus, *Peri onomasias* 24; Pollux 2.70.

14. Homer, *Iliad* 8.164. See also the comments of W. Leaf, *The Iliad* (1900), vol. 1, p. 343.

15. See Hesychius, *Lexicon*, *s.v. glēnē;* scholia to Homer, *Iliad* 24.192 in Erbse, p. 552; Rufus of Ephesus, *Peri onomasias* 24; Pollux 2.70.

16. Homer, *Iliad* 24.192; Apollonius of Rhodes, *Argonautica* 4.424.

17. See Chantraine, *Dictionnaire Etymologique de la langue grecque* (vol. 1, p. 227).

18. See, for example, *Anthologia Palatina* 14.52 and (perhaps) Xenophon, *Respublica Lacedaemoniorum* 3.4f. For a discussion, see L. Spina, "L'incomparabile pudore dei giovani Spartani" (1985).

19. K. M. Elderkin, "Jointed Dolls in Antiquity" (1930), p. 456 and M. R. Rinaldi, "Ricerche sui giocattoli nell'antichità: Le bambole" (1956).

20. L. Pirzio Biroli Stefanelli, "Anellino d'oro con chiave" (1983), p. 65.

21. K. M. Elderkin, "Jointed Dolls in Antiquity" (1930), p. 456 and A. Andrén, "Classical Antiquities in the Zorn Collection" (1948), p. 64. For a different opinion, see D. Burr, *Terra-cottas from Myrina* (1934), p. 30, who argues that normal votive statues could also have articulated limbs, but the explanation provided is only that taken from an old theory of Heuzey, who held that mobile limbs could increase "the religious or magical potency of the figures." But the reference is to *paignia kampesigyia,* "toys with bendable limbs," which an Orphic text includes among the toys with which the Titans attracted the attention of the baby Dionysos (frag. 34 in Kern).

22. K. M. Elderkin, "Jointed Dolls in Antiquity" (1930).

23. Ibid.

24. A. Mura Sommella, "Bambola in avorio" (1983), p. 50.

25. K. M. Elderkin, "Jointed Dolls in Antiquity" (1930).

26. *Anthologia Palatina* 6.280 (see p. 225). It does not appear that Sappho (in Athenaeus, *Deipnosophistae* 9.410e) is speaking of an analogous offering of doll clothes to Aphrodite, although M. Manson does make this argument in "Histoire d'un mythe: Les poupées de Maria femme d'Honorius" (1978). The text (Sappho, frag. 101 in Lobel-Page) is badly corrupted, and the one likely interpretation—found in Athenaeus's remarks on the passage—is that she is speaking of veils for the head (*cheiromaktra;* see also A. Mura Sommella, "Bambola in avorio" [1983], p. 50).

27. K. M. Elderkin, "Jointed Dolls in Antiquity" (1930), p. 460.

28. Ibid., p. 459.

29. But there is evidence for statues being dressed. On the difficult interpretation of the statue of Fortuna in the Forum Boarium, which was covered by two togas, see J. Champeaux, *Le culte de la Fortune à Rome et dans le monde romain* (1982), pp. 274ff. For other dressed statues, see Pausanias, *Graeciae de-*

scriptio 1.8.15 and 7.23.5. For statues that are undressed and washed (or the bathing of statues of the gods), see J. G. Frazer's commentary on Ovid's *Fasti* (1929 = 1973) ad 4.136 and also P. Boyancé, "Théurgie et télestique néoplatoniciennes" (1955). As regards the general problem of the simulacrum of the god, there has been a long debate about whether a consecrated statue implied the presence of the god. The problem is too large to address here, and goes far beyond the bounds of this discussion. There are, however, interesting observations in R. L. Gordon, "The Real and the Imaginary: Production and Religion in the Greco-Roman World" (1979), and the more recent contribution of C. Brillante, "Metamorfosi di un'immagine: Le statue animate e il sogno" (1988, with bibliography and a discussion of the evidence). For a recent discussion of the problem of iconoclasm in the Christian tradition, see J. Goody, *Representations and Contradictions* (1997). Among the ancient Christian writers, Minucius Felix provides a discussion in his *Octavius* 24.8, and there is also an important fragment reported in Suidas s.v. *Heraiskos* in Adler 579 f.

30. The hair brings us back to the discovery of Crepereia's sarcophagus, and the way that the filaments of the plant in the water resembled waving hair, which was perhaps the most striking detail in the mythology of this archaeological find. The motion of the hair is a sign of life.

31. On this aspect of the doll's function, see especially J. M. Lotman, "Le bambole nel sistema della cultura" (1984).

32. Persius, *Saturae* 2.69 f. (see pp. 225–26). The text cited by Lactantius (*Divinae institutiones* 2.4.12) is partially paraphrased in prose: *hoc esse aurum in templis, quod sint Veneri donatae a virgine pupae.* I would also note that by substituting the phrase *in sacro* with *in templis,* Lactantius seems to recall the ancient exegetical tradition; see the scholia ad loc., in which the more difficult metaphorical expression used by the poet, *in sancto,* is glossed precisely as *in templis.*

33. Lactantius, *Divinae institutiones* 2.4.12 ff.: *quas ille ob minutiem fortasse contempserit. Non videbat enim simulacra ipsa et effigies deorum Polycleti et Euphranoris et Phidiae manu ex auro atque ebore perfectas nihil aliud esse quam grandes pupas non a virginibus, quarum lusibus venia dari potest, sed a barbatis hominibus consecratas.... Ergo his ludicris et ornatis et grandibus pupis unguenta et tura et odores inferunt, his opimas et pingues hostias immolant, quibus est quidem os, sed carens officio dentium, his peplos et indumenta pretiosa, quibus usus velaminis nullus est, his aurum et argentum consecrant, quae tam non habent qui accipiunt quam qui illa donarunt.* J. Dörig, "Von griechischen Puppen" (1958), p. 41, misunderstands the text completely, thinking that Lactantius says there were dolls in the temples honored by bearded men (which he took as proof of the fact that the dolls had a religious function in addition to being playthings).

34. Lactantius, *Divinae institutiones* 2.4.12: *Nam cum Iovi Olympio aureum amiculum detraxisset, laneum iussit imponi dicens aestate grave esse aurum, hieme frigidum, laneum vero utrique tempori aptum.* See Cicero, *De natura deorum* 3.34.83; Valerius Maximus, *Facta et dicta memorabilia* 1.1 ext. 3; Arnobius, *Adversus nationes* 6.21.

35. Lucilius frag. 15, in Marx 486 ff. The fragment is cited by Lactantius, *Divinae institutiones* 1.22.13 (see also Nonius 56.7), but the text is not without difficulties, and the version known to Lactantius was probably already corrupt.

On this point, the notes of F. Charpin, *Lucilius: Satires, Livres IX–XXVIII* (1979), pp. 246 f., are not especially helpful, and it is necessary to consult instead F. Marx, *C. Lucilii Carminum Reliquiae* (1904), vol. 2, pp. 180 ff. See also J. J. O'Hara, "Somnia ficta in Lucretius and Lucilius" (1987) and G. Mazzoli, "Reale, verum, pictum, falsum in Lucilio" (1989).

36. E. T. A. Hoffmann, "Der Sandmann" (1957). Regarding "Androiden" in Hoffmann, see H. Grob, *Puppen, Engel, Enthusiasten* (1984), pp. 70 ff.

37. E. Jentsch, "Zur Psychologie des Unheimlichen" (1906).

38. Heron, *De automatis,* in W. Schmidt, *Herons von Alexandria: Druckwerke und Automatentheater* (1899), pp. 338 ff. On the Western tradition of *automata* see E. Battisti, *L'antirinascimento* (1989), vol. 1, pp. 249 ff. (with the relevant notes) and M. G. Losano, *Storie di automi: Dalla Grecia classica alla Belle Époque* (1990). See also pp. 148–49.

39. Vitruvius, *De architectura* 9.8.5 and 10.7.4. The figures involved seem to be those of animals. For a discussion, see L. Callebat, *Vitruve: De l'architecture livre X* (1986), pp. 159 f. On the *automata* of Vitruvius and Heron, see H. Diels, *Antike Technik* (1914), pp. 54 ff.

40. Heron, *De automatis* 22.

41. Pseudo-Aristotle, *De mundo* 6. The passage is translated verbatim by Apuleius in *De mundo* 27; see also Tertullian, *De anima* 6.3 and the *sigillarius motus* that he discusses in a completely analogous context (a passage that was completely misunderstood by U. Scamuzzi, "Studio sulla mummia di bambina (la cosiddetta 'Mummia di Grottarossa')" [1964], who took this to be an allusion to the *sigilla* that were given to children for the festival of the Sigillaria).

42. Likewise H. von Kleist, in his *Aufsatz über das Marionettentheater* (1978), explains that one should not "imagine that each limb [of the marionette] is individually stopped and started by the puppeteer in the various moments of the dance. Rather, each movement has a center of gravity: only this center must be regulated inside the figure and its limbs, which are nothing more than pendulums that follow along in an entirely mechanical fashion." Thus also for von Kleist the movement of the marionette is marked by its extreme economy of mechanical effort. But in this unusual study the puppet is then taken as a symbol of the complete innocence and spontaneity that is possessed by everything that is unaware: a lost paradise, whose main gate was shut in antiquity, and which we can now only try to enter by some sort of back door. The topic of the marionette fascinated the literature and scholarship of the nineteenth century; see T. Gauthier, "Les marionnettes" (1903).

43. Eustathius, *Commentarii ad Homeri Iliadem* in Dindorf p. 457.38 (= Van der Valk p. 723): "the art of the puppet maker is undignified."

44. Plato, *De legibus* 1.644e. On the metaphorical use of *neurospasma,* particularly in philosophical debates, see H. O. Schröder, "Marionetten: Ein Beitrag zur Polemik des Karneades" (1983). There are frequent (and often dismissive) references to marionettes in Marcus Aurelius (see, for example, 7.3).

45. Horace, *Sermones* 2.7.80 ff.: *nempe / tu mihi qui imperitas alii servis miser atque / duceris ut nervis alienis mobile lignum.*

46. Aulus Gellius, *Noctes Atticae* 14.1.23: *ludicra et ridenda quaedam neurospasta.* See also Persius, *Saturae* 5.129 ff.; Marcus Aurelius 7.3 and 10.38; etc. There are other comparisons in the entry for "Neurospasta" in Pauly-Wissowa

(vol. 17, col. 162f.). As regards the general topic of animated statues (which goes beyond the limits of our study here) see also P. Boyancé, "Théurgie et télestique néoplatoniciennes" (1955) and pp. 135–37. Herodotus 1.48 describes the *neurospasta* that had for their one moving part a mobile phallus, which Egyptian women carried in the processions of Dionysus. In Euripides, *Phoenissae* 1123ff., the shield of Polynices has as its *episēma* the horses of Glaucus, which were rendered mobile by means of pivots that were controlled from inside the shield, making it possible for the horses to look as if they were running wildly.

47. For H. Bergson, the poorly concealed mechanical quality of life was the basis of everything that produces a comic effect, as discussed in *Laughter: An Essay on the Meaning of the Comic* (1913).

48. Petronius, *Satyricon* 34.8: *larvam argenteam attulit servus sic aptatam, ut articuli eius vertebraeque laxatae in omnem partem flecterentur. Hanc cum super mensam semel iterumque abiecisset, et catenatio mobilis aliquot figuras exprimeret, Trimalchio adiecit: 'eheu nos miseros, quam totus homuncio nihil est!'*

49. See M. Manson, "Histoire d'un mythe: Les poupées de Maria femme d'Honorius" (1978).

50. Persius, *Saturae* 2.69f., and the scholia ad loc. in Jahn pp. 291f.; the scholia to Horace, *Sermones* 1.5.65; *Anthologia Palatina* 6.280. It is perhaps useful to compare Plato, *Phaedrus* 230b; *Anthologia Palatina* 9.326. On the literary evidence, see especially R. Danese, "Intorno al latino 'pupa': Linee per una ricerca" (1986).

51. See K. M. Elderkin, "Jointed Dolls in Antiquity" (1930), p. 455, for dolls in the temples of Aphrodite, Artemis, Athena, and Demeter. For the dolls discovered in the temple of Artemis in Ephesus, see H. B. Walters, *Catalogue of the Terracottas in the Department of Greek and Roman Antiquities* (1903); and for recent discoveries in Lavinium of hands holding a ball, see *Enea nel Lazio: Archeologia e mito* (1981), p. 218. See also A. Mura Sommella, "Bambola in avorio" (1983), p. 51.

52. A. Van Gennep, *Les rites de passage* (1909 = *The Rites of Passage* [1966]).

53. See pp. 220–1.

54. Scholia to Persius, *Saturae* 2.69f. in Jahn pp. 291 f.: *quibus diis tam sunt opes supervacuae quam Veneri puppae, quas virgines nubentes donant. Solebant enim virgines antequam nuberent quaedam virginitatis suae dona Veneri consecrare. Hoc et Varro scribit.*

55. See also the scholia to Horace, *Sermones* 1.5.69: the boys "having completed their childhood and having already put on the toga of a man consecrated their *bullae* to the Penates, just as the girls did their dolls" (*egressi annos pueritiae iam sumpta toga dis Penatibus* ["*apud Lares*" Porph.] *bullas suas consecrabant, ut puellae pupas*). See E. Tabeling, *Mater Larum* (1932 = 1975), pp. 16ff. B. L. Gildersleeve made a very amusing academic comment regarding this ancient practice of dedicating to the gods these dolls that were no longer used as playthings: "the practice of publishing a list of commentators in editions of the classics is a survival of this usage" (*The Satires of A. Persius Flaccus* [1875], p. 117).

56. *Anthologia Palatina* 6.280, with a discussion in M. Manson, "Histoire d'un mythe: Les poupées de Maria femme d'Honorius" (1978). J. Dörig ("Von griechischen Puppen" [1958], p. 44) once again misunderstands the text. For a study of this specific text and a general discussion of the adolescent character of

the cult of Artemis Limnatis, see especially C. Calame, *Les choeurs de jeunes filles en Grèce archaïque* (1977), vol. 1, pp. 257 ff. See also Varro, *Sesculixes* frag. 463 Buecheler.

57. M. Manson, "Histoire d'un mythe: Les poupées de Maria femme d'Honorius" (1978).

58. See pp. 215–16.

59. In addition to the passage cited above from Persius, and the relevant scholia (see p. 301n. 54), one can compare the scholia to Clement of Alexandria, *Protrepticus ad Hellenos* 45.22, along with material from the *Anecdota Graeca* in Bekker p. 102; the scholia to Theocritus, *Carmina* 2.110 in Wendel, p. 288; etc.

60. For the use of *pupa* to mean "girl," see R. Danese, "Intorno al latino 'pupa': Linee per una ricerca" (1986), which draws on materials from the *Thesaurus linguae Latinae,* as yet unpublished. Less useful in this regard is the discussion in J. A. Davison, "Meanings of the Word 'kore' in Plato, *Republic* 3.404c–e and Plutarch, *Moralia* 528e" (1966).

61. See, for example, Menander, *Dyscolus* 430, *Heros* 24, *Samia* 630.

62. Scholia to Theocritus, *Carmina* 2.110 in Wendel, p. 288.

63. Liddell-Scott-Jones, Supplement, s.v. *korokosmion.*

64. The term *kosmia* is actually used by Leonidas of Tarentum (*Anthologia Palatina* 9.326) to indicate a group of objects located inside a fountain where there were also statues of the nymphs (see Plato, *Phaedrus* 230b). There is a strong wordplay between the vocative *kourai* that immediately follows, "O nymphs!"; the poet is apparently referring to *korokosmia,* "dolls" or "figurines" offered "in great numbers" (*myria*) to the nymphs, who are themselves called *kourai* (the interpretation goes back to Meineke: see A. S. F. Gow and D. L. Page, *The Greek Anthology* [1965], vol. 2, p. 314). It is well known that the nymphs were the object of a particular cult practiced by young girls (recall, for example, Menander's *Dyscolus*); one can thus suppose that the name *korokosmia* used to indicate dolls derives precisely from their function as objects destined to be dedicated to the nymphs, also called *korai,* and thus adorning the places dedicated to their cult.

65. We cannot help but note that Persius, in his scorn for this practice, was perhaps exaggerating (as often) in order to make life seem more coarse and crude.

66. R. Danese, "Intorno al latino 'pupa': Linee per una ricerca" (1986). There is an impressive comparison reported in A. Van Gennep, *Les rites de passage* (1909 = *The Rites of Passage* [1966]), regarding puberty rites in China: "A wooden statue is made that represents the child in whose honor the ceremony is taking place; this statue is kept until the child is sixteen years old. . . . If the child dies before turning sixteen, the statue is buried with him; if he becomes gravely ill, the statue is made to pass through the door [the central element of the ceremony]." Also, in this case the wooden statue functions as a double of its owner. And just as with the ancient *pupa,* its temporal *excursus* oscillates between either abandonment at puberty or burial with the child if puberty is not reached, precisely what happened to Crepereia.

67. See pp. 12–13.

Chapter 18.   Image, Mirror, and *Homo Suus*

1. Seneca, *Naturales quaestiones* 1.16.1 ff.: *Hostius fuit Quadra, obscenitatis in scaenam usque productae.... Non erat ille ab uno tantummodo sexu impurus, sed tam virorum quam feminarum avidus fuit, fecitque specula ... imagines longe maiores reddentia, in quibus digitus brachii mensuram et crassitudinem excederet. Haec autem ita disponebat, ut cum virum ipse pateretur, aversus omnes admissarii sui motus in speculo videret ac deinde falsa magnitudine ipsius membri tamquam vera gaudebat.* "There was a man named Hostius Quadra whose obscenities even were staged as the subject of a theatrical piece. He engaged in debauched behavior not just with one gender, but lusted after both men and women. He had magnifying mirrors made in which a finger would look bigger in size and thickness than an arm. He even arranged these mirrors so that when he was acting as woman to some man, he could see in the mirror all the movements of the stallion behind him and so enjoy the false size of his lover's member as if it really were that large." See F. P. Weiblingen, *Senecas Naturales Quaestiones: Griechische Wissenschaft und römische Form* (1977), pp. 69 ff. See also the valuable commentary by D. Vottero, *L. Anneo Seneca, Questioni naturali* (1989), pp. 274 ff.

2. L. Fromond, in the edition of *Naturales quaestiones* edited by Justus Lipsius (with notes by Fromond), ad Anversa 1632, ad loc.: *Honestius tacuisses, Seneca. Pudet enim haec commentari aut legere; raptim saltem facio, et oculo conniventi.*

3. Antonio Rocco, "Amore è un puro interesse" (1635 = 1990), p. 171.

4. Seneca, *Naturales quaestiones* 1.16.4: *specula sibi per quae flagitia sua divideret disponeretque circumdedit.*

5. See F. Petrella, "Il sosia perturbante: Note sul 'doppio' di O. Rank" (1986), p. 66. For the importance of this theme in the works of Jean Paul, see O. Rank, *Der Doppelgänger* (1914 = *The Double* [1971]). On exhibitionism and scopophilia in the ancient world in general, one can also consult W. Krenkel, "Exhibitionismus in der Antike" (1977) and also his "Skopophilie in der Antike" (1977).

6. Suetonius, *De poetis* 47, in Reifferscheid, pp. 12–15. G. E. Lessing refused to accept Suetonius, and attempted to defend Horace by correcting the text of the biography, proposing a possible confusion between *Horatius* and *Hostius* ("Rettungen des Horaz" [1967], vol. 2, p. 559). Meanwhile, F. Algarotti limited himself to the observation that Horace was not unacquainted with "those refinements that are believed to be the discoveries only of more modern times, multiplying by means of mirrors the image of one's pleasures, and in this way as it were augmenting their reality" (*Saggio sopra Orazio* [1791 = 1990], p. 52).

7. Seneca, *Naturales quaestiones* 1.16.7: *Oculi quoque in partem libidinis veniant et testes eius exactoresque sint; etiam ea, quae a conspectu corporis nostri positio submovit, arte visantur, ne quis me putet nescire, quid faciam.*

8. Ibid., 1.16.9: *ad speculum suum immolandus fuit.*

9. Ibid., 1.16.5: *quem num putas in ipso habitu pingi noluisse?*

10. Apuleius, *Apologia* 13.1 ff.

11. Ibid., 14.5 ff.: *deest enim et luto vigor et saxo color et picturae rigor et mo-*

tus omnibus . . . cum in eo visitur imago mire relata, ut similis, ita mobilis, et ad omnem nutum hominis sui morigera; eadem semper contemplantibus aequaeva est ab ineunte pueritia ad obeuntem senectam, tot aetatis vices induit, tam varias habitudines corporis participat, tot vultus eiusdem laetantis vel dolentis imitatur. Enimvero quod luto fictum vel aere infusum vel lapide incussum vel cera inustum vel pigmento illitum vel alio quopiam humano artificio adsimulatum est, non multa intercapedine temporis dissimile redditur et ritu cadaveris unum vultum et immobilem possidet.

12. It is well known that in Plato's *Republic* the reproductions of the mirror and those of painting are not yet opposed to one another but are assimilated into the same category, and are equally condemned (10.596b ff.). For Leonardo da Vinci, on the other hand, the mirror becomes the master of painters (*Trattato della pittura* [1804], p. 165 f.).

13. Ovid, *Metamorphoses* 3.432 f.: *nihil habet ista sui: tecum venitque manetque / tecum discedet.*

14. Augustine, *Soliloquia* 2.17: *Annon tibi videtur imago tua de speculo quasi tu ipse velle esse?* See pp. 187–88.

15. Apuleius, *Apologia* 14.5: [*imago*] *ad omnem nutum hominis sui morigera.*

16. See U. Eco, *Sugli specchi e altri saggi* (1985), pp. 20 ff. This discussion is obviously much indebted to Eco's observations.

17. Ovid, *Metamorphoses* 3.466 (see p. 98).

18. Plautus, *Amphitruo* 441 ff.

19. Plautus, *Amphitruo* 600 f.

20. Pliny, *Naturalis historia* 35.4: *adeo materiam conspici malunt omnes quam se nosci.*

21. See M. Bettini, "Sosia e il suo sosia: Pensare il doppio a Roma" (1991).

22. Apollodorus, *Bibliotheca* 2.6.3; Hesychius, *Lexicon s.v. plēxanta kai plēgeenta;* see also Pausanias, *Graeciae descriptio* 9.11.4 and the discussion in C. Brillante, "Metamorfosi di un immagine: Le statue animate e il sogno" (1988), p. 23.

23. Eustathius, *Commentarii ad Homeri Iliadem* 11.749 in Dindorf, p. 882.38.

24. See pp. 7–9, 41–42.

25. See M. Bettini, "Sosia e il suo sosia: Pensare il doppio a Roma" (1991).

26. Plato, *Phaedrus* 275d ff.

27. Concerning this, see p. 240n. 20.

28. See N. Demand, "Plato and the Painters" (1975), according to whom the negative painting to which Plato refers here would be once again the illusionistic *skiagraphia*. This work actually attempts to identify two distinct phases of Platonic thought about painting: the first phase being favorable (*Io, Gorgias, Cratylus, Respublica* 2–6), in which Plato conceived of the painter as a respectable member of the community, as opposed to the second phase (*Phaedo, Respublica* 7–10, *Theaetetus, Parmenides, Phaedrus*), in which he shows himself to be on the contrary very critical of the painter as a type of illusionist (along with some positions between these two extremes). The comparison between the letters of the alphabet and painting appears again in the *Cratylus,* 424d–425a, with a discussion by Demand in her "Plato and the Painters" (1975). On the relationship between Plato and painting, and concerning expressions such as *skia-*

graphia, skēnographia, zōgraphia, there is a quite vast bibliography: see most recently E. C. Keuls, "Plato on Painting" (1974); followed by E. C. Keuls, "Skiagraphia Once Again" (1975) with a response by E. G. Pemberton, "A Note on Skiagraphia" (1976); L. Golden, "Plato's Concept of Mimesis" (1975); C. Karelis, "Plato on Art and Reality" (1975–76, especially concerning *Respublica* 10.595a–602b); W. Trimpi, "The Early Metaphorical Use of Skiagraphia and Skenographia" (1978); and again E. C. Keuls, *Plato and Greek Painting* (1978). Finally, concerning Platonic *mimēsis* and its relationship to the world of images see J. P. Vernant, *Religions, histoire, raisons* (1979). This attitude is rooted in a general "cognitive ambivalence" about images that is shared by many cultures; for a discussion, see J. Goody, *Representations and Contradictions* (1997), pp. 1–74.

29. See also Plato, *Phaedrus* 276a ff.

30. Favorinus, *Corinthiaca* 95.43 in Barigazzi.

31. The anecdote is reported several times by Plutarch: *Vita Agesilai* 2; *Regum et imperatorum apophthegmata* 191d; *Apophthegmata Laconica* 79.

32. See pp. 54–58.

33. See pp. 59–69.

34. See pp. 159–61.

35. See pp. 125–31.

36. The reference is naturally to the famous passage from Plato's *Respublica* 10.596a ff.

Works Cited

Abel, E., ed. *Orphica*. Leipzig 1885. Reprint: Hildesheim 1971.
Adler, A., ed. *Suidae Lexicon*. Stuttgart 1928. Reprint: Leipzig 1967.
Algarotti, F. *Saggio sopra Orazio*. Venice 1791. Reprint: Venosa 1990.
Andreae, B. *Studien zum römischen Grabkunst*. Heidelberg 1963.
Andrén, A. "Classical Antiquities in the Zorn Collection." *Opuscula Archaeologica* 5 (1948): 61ff.
Arnim, H. F. A., von ed. *Stoicorum veterum fragmenta*. Stuttgart 1964.
Assyrian Dictionary. Chicago 1956–92.
Babelon, E. *Catalogue des camées de la Bibliothèque Nationale*. Paris 1897.
Babelon, J. "Protésilas à Scioné." *Revue Numismatique* 13 (1951): 6ff.
Bailey, C. *Lucreti De rerum natura libri sex*. Oxford 1947.
Baldwin, B. *The Philogelos or Laughter Lover*. Amsterdam 1983.
Baligan, G. *Il terzo libro del corpus Tibullianum*. Bologna 1948.
Balil, A. "Munecas antiguas en España." *Archivio Español de Arqueologia* 35 (1962); 70ff.
Balsdon, J. P. V. D. *Life and Leisure in Ancient Rome*. London 1969.
Baltrusaitis, A. *Le miroir: Révélations, science-fiction et fallacies*. Paris 1979.
Balzac, H. de. "Le chef-d'oeuvre inconnu." In *Oeuvres,* vol. 9: 389ff. Paris 1965.
Barchiesi, M. *La Tarentilla rivisitata*. Pisa 1978.
Barigazzi, A., ed. *Opere di Favorino di Arelate*. Florence 1966.
Barnett, R. D. "Ancient Ivories in the Middle East." *Iraq* 14 (1982): 48.
———. "The Nimrud Ivories and the Art of the Phoenicians." *Iraq* 2 (1935): 179ff.
Barone, C. "Le spese e le illusioni degli amanti (Lucrezio IV.1123–1130, IV.1160–1169)." *Studi Urbinati di Storia, Filosofia e Letteratura* 52 (1978): 75ff.
Barthe, N. T. *L'amateur: Comédie en vers*. Paris 1870.
Barthes, R. *Fragments d'un discours amoureux*. Paris 1977.
Bartsch, S. *Decoding the Ancient Novel*. Princeton 1989.
Battisti, E. *L'antirinascimento*. Milan 1989.

Baum, P. F. "The Young Man Betrothed to a Statue." *Publications of the Modern Language Association* 34 (1919): 523 ff.

Beecher, D., and M. Ciavolella. *J. Ferrand: A Treatise on Lovesickness.* Syracuse 1990.

Beekes, R. S. P. "You Can Get New Children." *Mnemosyne* 39 (1986): 225 ff.

Bekker, I., ed. *Anecdota Graeca.* Berlin 1814. Reprint: Graz 1965.

Beltrami, A. "Clemente alessandrino nell'Ottavio di Minucio Felice." *Rivista di Filologia e di Istruzione Classica* 48 (1920): 239 ff.

Beltrami, L. "L' 'impudicizia' di Tarpeia: Trasgressioni e regole del comportamento femminile a Roma." Ph.D. dissertation. Pisa 1989.

Benveniste, E. "L'expression du sarment dans la Grèce ancienne." *Revue de l'Histoire des Religions* 134 (1948): 81 ff. Reprinted in *Le vocabulaire des institutions indo-européennes* (Paris 1969). (English translation: *Indo-European Language and Society,* trans. E. Palmer. London 1973.)

———. *Hittite et indo-européen.* Paris 1962.

———. "Le sens du mot 'kolossos' et les mots grecs de la statue." *Revue de Philologie* 6 (1932): 118 ff.

———. *Le vocabulaire des institutions indo-européennes.* Paris 1969. (English translation: *Indo-European Language and Society,* trans. E. Palmer. London 1973.)

Bergk, T. *Poetae lyrici Graeci.* 4th ed. Leipzig 1878–82.

Bergson, H. *Laughter: An Essay on the Meaning of the Comic.* Trans. C. Brereton and F. Rothwell. New York 1913.

Bertolucci Pizzorusso, V. "La clergie di Thomas: L'intertesto agiografico-religioso." In L. Rossi, ed., *Ensi firent li ancessor: Mélanges de philologie médiévale offerts à Marc-René Jung:* 335–48. Turin 1996.

Bettini, M. *Antropologia e cultura Romana.* Rome 1986. (English translation: *Anthropology and Roman Culture,* trans. J. van Sickle. Baltimore 1991.)

———. "Il divieto fino al sesto grado incluso nel matrimonio romano." *Athenaeum* 66 (1988): 69 ff.

———. "Fra Plinio e S. Agostino: Francesco Petrarca sulle arti figurative." In S. Settis, ed., *Memoria dell'antico nell'arte italiana:* 221 ff. Turin 1984.

———. "Iacta alea est: Saturno e i Saturnali." In *Verso un'antropologia dell'intreccio:* 99 ff. Urbino 1990.

———. "Lettura divinatoria di un incesto." *Materiali e Discussioni per l'Analisi dei Testi Classici* 12 (1984): 145 ff.

———. "Il racconto di Orazia." In *Primordia urbium:* 9 ff. Pavia 1988.

———. "Il sistema della parentela e la struttura della famiglia." In S. Settis, ed., *Storia e civiltà dei romani,* vol. 1. Milan 1992.

———. "Sosia e il suo sosia: Pensare il doppio a Roma." In R. Oniga, ed., *Plauto: Anfitrione:* 9 ff. Padua 1991.

———. "Turno e la rondine nera." *Quaderni Urbinati di Cultura Classica* 3 (1988): 7 ff.

———. "Verso un'antropologia dell'intreccio." In *Verso un'antropologia dell'intreccio:* 11 ff. Urbino 1990.

Bettini, M., and L. Ricottilli. "Elogio dell'indiscrezione." *Studi Urbinati di Storia, Filosofia e Letteratura* 60 (1987): 11 ff.

Bezold, F. von. *Das Fortleben der antiken Götter im mittelalterliche Humanismus.* Bonn 1992. Reprint: Aalen 1962.

Birt, T. *Laienurteil über bildende Kunst bei den Alten.* Marburg 1902.

Blaydes, F. H. M. *Aristophanis Nubes.* Halle 1890.

Blayney, J. "Theories of Conception in the Ancient Roman World." In B. Rawson, ed., *The Family in Ancient Rome: New Perspectives:* 230 ff. Ithaca 1986.

Bloch, R. "De Pseudo-Luciani Amoribus." Ph.D. dissertation. Strassbourg 1907.

———. *Les prodiges dans l'antiquité classique.* Paris 1963.

Blome, P. *Zur Umgestaltung griechischen Mythe in der römischen Sepulkralkunst: Alkestis-, Protesilaus- und Proserpinasarkophage.* Heidelberg 1978.

Boehm, F. "De symbolis Pythagoreis." Ph.D. dissertation. Berlin 1905.

Bollack, J., and P. Judet de la Combe. *L'Agamemnon d'Eschyle: Le texte et ses interpretations.* Lille 1981.

Bollack, M. *La raison de Lucrèce.* Paris 1978.

Bömer, F. *P. Ovidius Naso: Die Fasten.* Heidelberg 1958.

———. *P. Ovidius Naso: Metamorphosen, Buch VIII–IX.* Heidelberg 1977.

———. *P. Ovidius Naso: Metamorphosen, Buch XIV–XV.* Heidelberg 1986.

Borthwick, E. K. "Meleager's Lament: A Note on Anth. Pal. 5.166." *Classical Philology* 64 (1969): 173 ff.

Bouché-Leclercq, A. *Histoire de la divination dans l'antiquité.* Paris 1882.

Bouhot, J. P., and G. Madec. Review of *Soliloquiorum libri duo,* by W. Hörmann. *Revue des Études Augustiniennes* 33 (1987): 332 f.

Bowra, C. M. *Greek Lyric Poetry.* 2d ed. Oxford 1961.

Boyancé, P. "L'Apollon solaire." In *Mélanges d'archéologie, d'épigraphie et d'histoire offerts à Jérôme Carcopino:* 166 f. Paris 1966.

———. "Théurgie et télestique néoplatoniciennes." *Revue de l'Histoire des Religions* 147 (1955): 189 ff.

Bradley, K. R. "Wet-Nursing at Rome: A Study in Social Relations." In B. Rawson, ed., *The Family in Ancient Rome:* 201 ff. Ithaca 1986.

Brillante, C. "Metamorfosi di un'immagine: Le statue animate e il sogno." In G. Guidorizzi, ed., *Il sogno in Grecia:* 17 ff. Rome 1988.

———. "Scene oniriche nei poemi omerici." *Materiali e Discussioni per l'Analisi dei Testi Classici* 24 (1990): 31 ff.

Brilliant, R. *Portraiture.* London 1991.

Brower, H. H. J. *Bona Dea.* Leiden 1989.

Brown, R. D. *Lucretius on Love and Sex.* Leiden 1987.

Bruce, J. D. "Human Automata in Tradition and Romance." *Modern Philology* 110 (1912–13): 511 ff.

Brückner, W. "Bild, Bildzauber." In *Enzyklopaedie des Märchens,* vol. 2: 319 ff. Berlin 1979.

———. *Bildnis und Brauch.* Berlin 1966.

———. "Bildnisstrafe." In E. von Adalbert and E. Kaufmann, eds., *Handwörterbuch zur deutschen Rechtsgeschichte,* vol. 1-B: 424 ff. Berlin 1972.

———. "Cera—Cera Virgo—Cera Virginea." *Zeitschrift für Volkskunde* 59 (1963): 233 ff.

Brunn, G. *Geschichte der griechischen Künstler.* 2d ed. Stuttgart 1889.

Buecheler, F., ed. *Petronii Saturae; Adiectae sunt Varronis et Senecae saturae similesque reliquiae*. Zurich 1963.

Bühler, K. *Sprachtheorie: Die Darstellungsfunktion der Sprache*. Jena 1934. (English translation: *Theory of Language: The Representational Function of Language*, trans. D. F. Goodwin. Amsterdam 1990.)

Bunte, B., ed. *Hygini fabulae*. Leipzig 1856.

Buonamici, C. *La leggenda di Protesilao e Laodamia*. Pisa 1902.

Burkert, W. *Homo necans: Interpretationen altgriechischer Opferriten und Mythen*. Berlin 1972. (English translation: *Homo Necans: The Anthropology of Ancient Greek Sacrificial Ritual and Myth*, trans. P. Bing. Berkeley and Los Angeles 1983.)

———. *Weisheit und Wissenschaft*. Nuremberg 1962. (English translation: *Lore and Science in Ancient Pythagoreanism*, trans. E. L. Minar. Cambridge, Mass., 1972.)

Burr, D. *Terra-cottas from Myrina*. Vienna 1934.

Caillois, R. *Les démons de midi*. Saint Clément la Rivière 1991.

Calame, C. *Les choeurs de jeunes filles en Grèce archaïque*. Rome 1977. (English translation: *Choruses of Young Women in Ancient Greece*, trans. D. Collins and J. Orion. Lanham 1977.)

Callebat, L. *Vitruve: De l'architecture, livre X*. Paris 1986.

Camille, M. *The Gothic Idol*. Cambridge 1989.

Campi, E. "La poupée du vacher: Étude ethnopsychanalytique." Ph.D. dissertation. Paris 1979.

Canali, L. *Orazio: Anni fuggiaschi e stabilità di regime*. Venosa 1988.

Carmina Latina epigraphica. Göteborg 1912.

Cartault, A. *Tibulle*. Paris 1909.

Castellani, A. "Descrizione degli oggetti trovati nel sarcofago di Crepereia Tryphaena." *Bulletino della Commissione Archeologica Comunale in Roma* 17 (1889): 17ff.

Celiberti, E. "Le antinomie della statua." *Studi di Letteratura e di Linguistica* 4 (1990): 221ff.

Champeaux, J. *Le culte de la Fortune à Rome et dans le monde romain*. Rome 1982.

Chantraine, P. *Dictionnaire étymologique de la langue grecque*. Paris 1968–80.

———. "Grec 'kolossos.'" *Bulletin de l'Institut Français d'Archéologie Orientale* 30 (1931): 449ff.

Chapuis, A. *Les automates dans les oeuvres d'imagination*. Neuchâtel 1947.

Chapuis, A., and E. Droz. *Les automates, figures artificielles d'hommes et d'animaux*. Neuchâtel 1949. (English translation: *Automata*, trans. A. Reid. Neuchâtel 1958.)

Charpin, F. *Lucilius: Satires, livres IX–XXVIII*. Paris 1979.

Chiovenda, L. "Die Zeichnungen Petrarcas." *Archivum Romanicum* 17 (1933): 1ff.

Clarke, G. W. *The Octavius of Minucius Felix*. New York 1974.

Cogan, M., and H. Tadmor. *II Kings: The Anchor Bible*. New York 1988.

Conacher, D. J. *Euripidean Drama: Myth, Theme and Structure*. Toronto 1967.

———. *Euripides: Alcestis*. Warminster 1988.

Cook, A. B. *Zeus: A Study in Ancient Religion*. Cambridge 1914.

Cooke, J. D. "Euhemerism: A Medieval Interpretation of Classical Paganism." *Speculum* 2 (1927): 396 ff.

Corpus inscriptionum Latinarum. Berlin 1956.

Courcelle, P. *Recherches sur le Confessions de Saint Augustin.* Paris 1950.

Courtney, E. *A Commentary on the Satires of Juvenal.* London 1980.

Cousin, J. *Quintilien: Institution oratoire.* Paris 1977.

Crepereia Tryphaena: Le scoperte archeologiche nell'area del Palazzo di Giustizia. Exhibition catalog, Rome 1983. Venice 1983.

Croce, B. *Ariosto, Shakespeare e Corneille.* Bari 1929.

———. *La poesia.* Bari 1930.

———. *Poesia antica e moderna.* Bari 1941.

Croisille, J. M. *Pline l'ancien: Histoire naturelle, livre XXXV.* Paris 1985.

Crooke, W. "The Binding of a God." *Folklore* 8 (1897): 336.

Dalzell, A. "A Bibliography of Work on Lucretius, 1945–1972." *Classical Weekly* 66 (1972–73): 402 ff.

Dam, H. J. van. *P. Papinius Statius: Silvae, Book II.* Leiden 1984.

ad-Damiri. *Hayat al-hayawan: A Zoological Lexicon.* Trans. A. S. G. Jayakar. London 1908.

Danese, R. "Intorno al latino 'pupa': Linee per una ricerca." *Studi Urbinati di Storia, Filosofia e Letteratura* 59 (1986): 47 ff.

Da Ponte, L. "Don Giovanni." In P. Lecaldano, ed., *Tre libretti per Mozart.* Milan 1956.

Daremberg, C., and E. Saglio, eds. *Dictionnaire des antiquités grecques et romaines.* Paris 1877. Reprint: Graz 1963.

Darup, S. "L'espressione tragica del desiderio amoroso." In C. Calame, ed., *L'amore in Grecia:* 144 ff. Rome 1984.

Daut, R. *Imago: Untersuchungen zum Bildbegriff der Römer.* Heidelberg 1975.

Davison, J. A. "Meanings of the Word 'kore' in Plato, *Republic* 3.404c–e and Plutarch, *Moralia* 528e." *Classical Review* 16 (1966): 138 ff.

Degani, E. "Introduzione." In E. Cavallini, ed., *Luciano: Questioni d'amore:* 9 ff. Padua 1991.

Delatte, A. *La catoptromancie grecque et ses dérivés.* Paris 1932.

Della Porta, G. B. *Magia naturale.* Naples 1677. (English translation: *Natural magick.* New York 1957.)

Demand, N. "Plato and the Painters." *Phoenix* 29 (1975): 1 ff.

Deonna, W. "L'âme pupilline et quelques monuments figurés." *L'Antiquité Classique* 26 (1957): 59 ff.

———. "L'enfance antique et ses jeux." *Genava* 10 (1932): 113 ff.

———. *Le symbolisme de l'oeil.* Paris 1965.

Detienne, M. *Dionysos mis à mort.* Paris 1977. (English translation: *Dionysos Slain,* trans. M. Muellner and L. Muellner. Baltimore 1979.)

———. *L'écriture d'Orphée.* Paris 1989.

———. *Homère, Hésiode et Pythagore.* Brussels 1962.

Devereux, G. *Dreams in Greek Tragedy: An Ethno-Psychoanalytical Study.* Oxford 1976.

Diels, H. *Antike Technik.* Leipzig 1914.

Diels, H., and W. Kranz, eds. *Die Fragmente der Vorsokratiker.* Berlin 1934.

Dieterich, A. "Ueber eine Scene der aristophanischen Wolken." *Rheinisches Museum* 49 (1893): 275 ff.

Dimundo, R. *Properzio 4.7.* Bari 1990.

Dindorf, G., ed. *Aristides.* Leipzig 1829. Reprint: Hildesheim 1964.

―――. *Scholia Graeca in Homeri Iliadem.* Oxford 1875.

―――. *Scholia Graeca in Homeri Odysseam.* Oxford 1885. Reprint: Amsterdam 1962.

Di Nola, A. M. "La magia dello specchio." In *Lo specchio e il doppio: Dallo stagno di Narciso allo schermo televisivo,* exhibition catalog, Turin 1987: 71 ff. Milan 1987.

Dissenius, L. *Albii Tibulli carmina.* Göttingen 1835.

Dodds, E. R. *The Ancient Concept of Progress.* Oxford 1973.

―――. *The Greeks and the Irrational.* Berkeley and Los Angeles 1951.

Dörig, J. "Von griechischen Puppen." *Antike Kunst* 1 (1958): 41 ff.

Dörrie, H. *Pygmalion: Ein Impuls Ovids und seine Wirkungen bis in die Gegenwart.* Opladen 1974.

Dundes, Alan, ed. *The Evil Eye: A Casebook.* Madison 1992.

Durrieu, P., and J. J. Marquet de Vasselot. "Les manuscrits à miniatures des Héroides d'Ovide traduites par Saint-Gelais, et un grand miniaturiste français du XVIe siècle [Robinet Testard]." *L'Ariste* 64 (1894): 331 ff.

Durry, E. *Éloge funèbre d'une matrone romaine.* Paris 1950.

Eco, U. *Sugli specchi e altri saggi.* Milan 1985.

Eichendorff, J. von. *Das Marmorbild.* Munich 1955.

Elderkin, K. M. "Jointed Dolls in Antiquity." *American Journal of Archaeology* 34 (1930): 455 ff.

Ellmann, R. *Oscar Wilde.* London 1988.

Elworthy, F. T. *The Evil Eye.* London 1895.

Enciclopedia dell'arte antica. Rome 1958–66.

Enea nel Lazio: Archeologia e mito. Exhibition catalog. Rome 1981.

Enger, R. *Aeschyli Agamemnon.* 2d ed. Leipzig 1863.

Erbse, H., ed. *Scholia Graeca in Homeri Iliadem: Scholia vetera.* Berlin 1969–88.

Ernout, A. *Pline l'ancien: Histoire naturelle, livre XXVII.* Paris 1962.

Fauth, W. *Aphrodite Parakyptousa: Untersuchungen zum Erscheinungsbild der vorderasiatischen Dea prospiciens.* Mainz 1966.

Fedeli, P. *Catullus: Carmen 61.* Amsterdam 1983.

―――. *Propertius.* Stuttgart 1984.

―――. *Properzio: Elegie, libro IV.* Bari 1965.

Fehr, B. *Studien zur Oscar Wildes Gedichten.* Berlin 1918.

Ferrand, J. *Traité de l'essence et guérison de l'amour ou mélancolie érotique.* Toulouse 1610.

Ferri, S. "Alcune iscrizioni di Cirene." *Abhandlungen der Preussischen Akademie der Wissenschaften* (1925): 39; *Sitzungsberichte der Deutschen Akademie der Wissenschaften zu Berlin* (1927): 169.

―――. *Plinio il vecchio e la storia delle arti antiche.* Rome 1946.

Festugière, A. J., ed. *Proclus: Commentaire sur la République.* Paris 1970.

Flach, D. *Die sogenannte Laudatio Turiae.* Darmstadt 1991.

Forni, P. M. "Zima sermocinante (*Decameron*, III.5)." *Giornale Storico della Letteratura Italiana* 163 (1986): 63 ff.

Forster, R., ed. *Libanii opera*. Leipzig 1903. Reprint: Hildesheim 1963.

Foucault, M. *L'usage des plaisirs*. Paris 1984. (English translation: *The History of Sexuality*, vol. 2, *The Use of Pleasure*, trans. R. Hurley. New York 1988.)

Foucher, L. "Le culte de Bacchus sous l'empire romain." *Aufstieg und Niedergang der Römischen Welt* 17.2 (1981): 684 ff.

Fraenkel, E. *Aeschylus: Agamemnon*. Oxford 1962.

———. *Elementi Plautini in Plauto*. Florence 1960.

———. "The Giants in the Poem by Naevius." In *Kleine Beiträge zur klassischen Philologie*, vol. 2, *Zur römischen Literatur*: 22 ff. Rome 1964.

Franciosi, G. *Clan gentilizio e strutture monogamiche a Roma*. 2d ed. Naples 1978.

Franco, C. "Una statua per Admeto (Euripides, *Alcestis* 348–354)." *Materiali e Discussioni per l'Analisi dei Testi Classici* 13 (1984): 131 ff.

Frazer, J. G. *Apollodorus: The Library*. Cambridge, Mass., 1922.

———. *The Fasti of Ovid*. London 1929. Reprint: Hildesheim 1973.

———. *The Golden Bough: A Study in Magic and Religion*. London 1922.

———. *Pausanias' Description of Greece*. London 1898. Reprint: New York 1965.

———. "Some Popular Superstitions of the Ancients." In *Garnered Sheaves*: 128 ff. London 1931.

Freedberg, D. *The Power of Images*. Chicago 1989.

Freud, S. *Der Wahn und die Träume in Wilhelm Jensens "Gradiva."* In *Gesammelte Werke*, vol. 7. Frankfurt 1960. (English translation: *Delusion and Dream: An Interpretation in the Light of Psychoanalysis of "Gradiva," a Novel by Wilhelm Jensen*, trans. H. M. Downey. New York 1927.)

———. *Der Witz und seine Beziehung zum Unbewussten*. Vienna 1905. (English translation: *Wit and Its Relation to the Unconscious*, trans. A. A. Brill. New York 1916.)

Friedländer, P. *Platon*. Vol. 2, *Die platonischen Schriften: Erste Periode*. Berlin 1957. (English translation: *Plato, vol. 2, The Dialogues: First Period*, trans. H. Meyerhoff. Princeton 1969.)

Fromond, L. "Commentarius." In Justus Lipsius, ed., *Naturales quaestiones*. Antwerp 1632.

Frontisi-Ducroux, F. *Dédale: Mythologie de l'artisan en Grèce ancienne*. Paris 1975.

———. "Du simple au double." *Revue d'Esthétique* 1 (1980): 111 ff.

———. "Senza maschera nè specchio: L'uomo greco e i suoi doppi." In M. Bettini, ed., *La maschera, il doppio e il ritratto*: 131 ff. Bari 1991.

Fusillo, M. *Il romanzo greco*. Venice 1988.

Galletier, E. *Étude sur la poésie funéraire latine*. Paris 1922.

Gallini, C. "Immagini da cerimonia: Album e videocassette da matrimonio." In M. Bettini, ed., *La maschera, il doppio e il ritratto*: 85 ff. Bari 1991.

Gauthier, T. "Les marionnettes." In *Souvenirs de théâtre, d'art et de critique*: 215 ff. Paris 1903.

Gentili, B. *Poesia e pubblico nella Grecia antica*. 2d ed. Bari 1989. (English translation: *Poetry and Its Public in Ancient Greece*, trans. A. T. Cole. Baltimore 1988.)

Gérard, J. *Juvénal et la réalité contemporaine*. Paris 1976.

Gernet, L. "Droit and prédroit en Grèce ancienne." In *Anthropologie de la Grèce ancienne:* 213 ff. Paris 1976. (English translation: *The Anthropology of Ancient Greece,* trans. J. Hamilton and B. Nagy. Baltimore 1981.)

———. "Mariages de tyrans." In *Anthropologie de la Grèce ancienne:* 344 ff. Paris 1976. (English translation: *The Anthropology of Ancient Greece,* trans. J. Hamilton and B. Nagy. Baltimore 1981.)

Ghiselli, A. *Crepereia Tryphaena.* Bologna 1955.

Gide, A. *Le traité de Narcisse.* Lausanne 1946.

Gildersleeve, B. L. *The Satires of A. Persius Flaccus.* New York 1875.

Gilleland, M. E. "Female Speech in Greek and Latin." *American Journal of Philology* 101 (1980): 180 ff.

Gilson, E. *Introduction à l'étude de Saint Augustin.* Paris 1943.

Glotz, G. *La solidarité de la famille dans le droit criminel en Grèce.* Paris 1904. Reprint: New York 1973.

Goethe, J. W. "An Charlotte von Stein." In C. Middleton, ed., *Selected Poems:* pp. 60–63. Boston 1983.

———. *Goethe-Briefe.* Ed. P. Stein. Berlin 1902.

———. *Leiden des jungen Werthers.* In *Sämtliche Werke,* vol. 2.2: 361 ff. Munich 1987.

Goldberg, B. *Mirror and Man.* Charlottesville 1985.

Golden, L. "Plato's Concept of Mimesis." *Journal of British Aesthetics* 15 (1975): 118 ff.

Goody, J. *Representations and Contradictions.* London 1997.

Gordon, R. L. "The Real and the Imaginary: Production and Religion in the Graeco-Roman World." *Art History* 2 (1979): 5 ff.

Gow, A. S. F., ed. *Bucolici Graeci.* Oxford 1952.

———. *Theocritus.* Cambridge 1950.

Gow, A. S. F., and D. L. Page, eds. *The Greek Anthology.* Cambridge 1965.

Graf, A. *Roma nella memoria e nelle immaginazioni del medio evo.* Turin 1923.

Gregg, R. "The Eudaemonic Theme in Pushkin's 'Little Tragedies.'" In A. Kodjak and K. Taranovsky, eds., *Alexander Pushkin: A Symposium on the 175th Anniversary of His Birth:* 184 ff. New York 1976.

Greimas, A. J. *Sémantique structurale.* Paris 1966. (English translation: *Structural Semantics,* trans. D. McDowell, R. Schleifer, and A. Velie. Lincoln 1983.)

Grob, H. *Puppen, Engel, Enthusiasten.* Bern 1984.

Guastella, G. *La contaminazione e il parassita.* Pisa 1989.

———. "La rete del sangue." *Materiali e Discussioni per l'Analisi dei Testi Classici* 15 (1985): 49 ff.

———. *Suetonio: Vita di Caligola.* Rome 1992.

Guidorizzi, G. "Lo specchio e la mente: Un sistema di intersezioni." In M. Bettini, ed., *La maschera, il doppio e il ritratto:* 31 ff. Bari 1991.

Halliday, W. R. *Greek Divination.* London 1913. Reprint: Chicago 1967.

———. *The Greek Questions of Plutarch.* Oxford 1928.

Hanson, A. E. "The Medical Writers' Woman." In D. Halperin, J. Winkler, and F. Zeitlin, eds., *Before Sexuality:* 309 ff. Princeton 1990.

Harlan, H. C. "The Description of Paintings as a Literary Device and Its Application in Achilles Tatius." Ph.D. dissertation, Columbia University. New York 1965.

Harris, J. Rendel. *The Twelve Apostles.* Cambridge 1927.

Harrison, J. *Themis.* Cambridge 1927.

Haupt, M., ed. *Aeschyli tragoediae.* Leipzig 1852.

Hayman, H. *The Odyssey of Homer.* London 1866.

Heckel, H. *Das Don Juan–Problem in den neueren Dichtung.* Stuttgart 1915.

Helm, R., ed. *Fabii Planciadis Fulgentii opera.* Leipzig 1898. [Reprint: Stuttgart 1970.]

Helms, J. *Character Portrayal in the Romance of Chariton.* The Hague 1966.

Herbig, R. "Aphrodite Parakyptousa." *Orientalistische Literaturzeitung* 11 (1927): 918 ff.

Héritier, F. *L'exercice de la parenté.* Paris 1981.

Heyne, C. G. *Albi Tibulli carmina libri tres.* 4th ed. Leipzig 1817.

Hijmans, B. L., Jr. "Charite Worships Tlepolemus-Liber." *Mnemosyne* 39 (1986): 350 ff.

Hijmans, B. L., Jr., R. T. van der Paardt, V. Schmidt, C. B. J. Settels, B. Wesseling, and R. E. H. Westendorp Boerma. *Apuleius Madaurensis: Metamorphoses, Book VIII.* Groningen 1985.

Hoffmann, E. T. A. "Der Sandmann." In *Poetische Werke,* vol. 3: 3 ff. Berlin 1957.

———. *Die Serapionsbrüder.* In *Poetische Werke,* vol. 8. Berlin 1957.

Hörmann, W. *Soliloquiorum libri duo: De immortalite animae; De quantitate animae.* Vienna 1986.

Horsfall, N. "CIL VI 3795 = CLE 1988 (Epitaph of Allia Potestas): A Commentary." *Zeitschrift für Papyrologie und Epigraphik* 61 (1985): 251 ff.

Hout, M. P. J., van den, ed. *M. Cornelii Frontonis Epistulae.* Leipzig 1988.

Jacoby, F., ed. *Die Fragmente der griechischen Historiker.* Leiden 1927.

Jahn, O., ed. *Persius: Satirarum liber, cum scholiis antiquis.* Leipzig 1843. Reprint: Hildesheim 1967.

Jakobson, R. "Closing Statements: Linguistics and Poetics." In T. Sebeok, ed., *Style in Language.* London 1960.

———. "The Statue in Pushkin's Poetic Mythology." In *Pushkin and His Sculptural Myth,* trans. J. Burbank: 9 ff. The Hague 1975.

Jeanmaire, H. *Dionysos: Histoire du culte de Bacchus.* Paris 1951. Reprint: Paris 1978.

Jeffreys, E., M. Jeffreys, and R. Scott, eds. and trans. *The Chronicle of John Malalas.* Melbourne 1986.

Jentsch, E. "Zur Psychologie des Unheimlichen." *Psychiatrisch-neurologische Wochenschrift* 8 (1906): 195.

Jouan, F. *Euripide et les légendes des chants cypriens.* Paris 1966.

Kantorowicz, E. H. *The King's Two Bodies: A Study in Mediaeval Political Theology.* Princeton 1957.

Karelis, C. "Plato on Art and Reality." *Journal of Aesthetics and Art Criticism* 34 (1975–76): 315 ff.

Kayser, C. L., ed. *Flavii Philostrati opera auctiora.* Leipzig 1870. Reprint: Hildesheim 1964.

Keller, G. *Sieben Legenden.* Stuttgart 1872.

Kerényi, K. *Griechische Grundbegriffe.* Zurich 1964.

Kern, O., ed. *Orphicorum fragmenta.* Berlin 1922.

Keuls, E. C. *Plato and Greek Painting.* Leiden 1978.

————. "Plato on Painting." *American Journal of Philology* 95 (1974): 100 ff.

————. "Skiagraphia Once Again." *American Journal of Archaeology* 79 (1975): 1 ff.

von Kleist, H. *Aufsatz über das Marionettentheater*. In *Werke und Briefe*, vol. 3. Berlin 1978.

Klossowski, P. *La ressemblance*. Marseilles 1984.

Knapp, C. "References to Painting in Plautus and Terence." *Classical Philology* 12 (1917): 156 ff.

Kock, T., ed. *Comicorum Atticorum fragmenta*. Leipzig 1880. Reprint: Hildesheim 1976.

Komp, M. *Absage an Cynthia*. Frankfurt 1988.

Kornhardt, H. "Exemplum." Ph.D. dissertation. Göttingen 1936.

Krappe, A. H. "Notes sur la légende de la fondation de Rome." *Revue des Études Anciennes* 35 (1933): 146 ff.

Krenkel, W. "Exhibitionismus in der Antike." *Wissenschaftliche Zeitschrift der Wilhelm-Pieck-Universität, Rostock,* 26 (1977): 613 ff.

————. "Skopophilie in der Antike." *Wissenschaftliche Zeitschrift der Wilhelm-Pieck-Universität, Rostock,* 26 (1977): 619 ff.

Kris, E. *Psychoanalytic Explorations in Art*. New York 1952.

Kris, E., and O. Kurz. *Die Legende vom Künstler: Ein historischer Versuch*. Vienna 1934. (English translation: *Legend, Myth, and Magic in the Image of the Artist: A Historical Experiment*. New Haven 1979.)

Kroll, W. "Die Grabschrift der Allia Potestas." *Philologus* 73 (1914): 274 ff.

Kroll, W., ed. *Proclus: In Platonis Rempublicam commentarii*. Leipzig 1899. Reprint: Amsterdam 1965.

Kucera, H. "Pushkin and Don Juan." In M. Halle, ed., *For Roman Jakobson:* 273 ff. The Hague 1956.

Laclos, P. A. F. Choderlos de. *Les liaisons dangereuses*. In *Oeuvres complètes,* ed. L. Versini. Paris 1979.

Lahusen, G. *Schriftquellen zum römischen Bildnis*. Bremen 1984.

Lamacchia, R. "Aspetti di civiltà diverse in alcune espressioni idiomatiche." *Rivista di Cultura Classica e Medioevale* 20 (1978): 957 ff.

Lanciani, R. "Delle scoperte avvenute nei disterri del nuovo Palazzo di Giustizia." *Bulletino della Commissione Archeologica Comunale in Roma* 17 (1889): 175 ff.

Lange, D. K. "Cynthia and Cornelia: Two Voices from the Grave." *Studies in Latin Literature and Roman History* 1 (1979): 335 ff.

La Penna, A. *L'integrazione difficile*. Turin 1977.

Lavagetto, M. *Stanza 43*. Turin 1991.

Lazzeroni, R. "Per l'etimologia di 'hórkos': Una testimonianza ittita." *Studi e Saggi Linguistici* 29 (1989): 87 ff.

Leaf, W. *The Iliad*. London 1900.

Le Boulluec, A. *Clémente d'Alexandrie: Les Stromates*. Paris 1981.

Lehnert, G., ed. *Calpurnii Flacci declamationes*. Leipzig 1903.

————. *Quintiliani quae feruntur declamationes XIX maiores*. Leipzig 1905.

Leonard, W. E., and S. B. Smith. *T. Lucreti Cari De rerum natura*. Madison 1942.

Leonardo da Vinci. *Trattato della pittura*. Milan 1804. (English translation: *Treatise on Painting*, trans. A. P. McMahon. Princeton 1956.)

Lesky, A. *Alkestis: Der Mythus und das Drama*. Vienna 1925.

Lesky, E. *Die Zeugungs- und Vererbungslehren der Antike und ihr Nachwirken*. Wiesbaden 1950.

Lessing, G. E. "Rettungen des Horaz." In *Schriften*, vol. 2: 559. Frankfurt 1967.

Le Suffleur, A. David. "Les camées de la Collection de Luynes." *Arethusa* 10 (1926): 119 ff.

Lévi-Strauss, C. "Four Winnebago Myths." In S. Diamond, ed., *Culture and History:* 181 ff. New York 1960.

———. "La geste d'Asdiwal." In *Anthropologie structurale deux*. Paris 1973. (English translation: *Structural Anthropology* 2, trans. C. Jacobson and B. G. Schoepf. New York 1976. See also "The Story of Asdiwal," trans. N. Mann, in E. Leach, ed., *The Structural Study of Myth and Totemism*. London 1967: 1 ff.)

———. *La potière jalouse*. Paris 1985. (English translation: *The Jealous Potter*, trans. B. Chorier. Chicago 1988.)

———. *Les structures élémentaires de la parenté*. 2d ed. Paris 1968. (English translation: *The Elementary Structures of Kinship*, trans. J. H. Bell, J. R. von Sturmer, and R. Needham. Boston 1969.)

Liddell, H. G., R. Scott, and H. S. Jones, eds. *A Greek-English Lexicon, with Supplement*. 9th ed. Oxford 1968.

Lier, B. *Ad topica carminum amatoriorum symbolae*. Stettin 1914. Reprint: New York 1973.

Lindsay, W. M., ed. *Sexti Pompei Festi De verborum significatu quae supersunt, cum Pauli epitome*. Leipzig 1913. Reprint: Hildesheim 1978.

Linforth, I. M. *The Arts of Orpheus*. Berkeley and Los Angeles 1941.

Lipsius, Justus. "Variae lectiones." In *Iusti Lipsi opera*, vol. 2: 437 ff. Leiden 1613.

Lloyd, G. E. R. *Magic, Reason and Experience*. Cambridge 1979.

———. *Science, Folklore and Ideology*. Cambridge 1983.

Lobeck, A. *Aglaophamus*. Königsberg 1829.

Lobel, E., and D. Page, eds. *Poetarum Lesbiorum fragmenta*. Oxford 1955.

Loisy, A. *Les mystères païens et le mystère chrétien*. Paris 1914.

Losano, M. G. *Storie di automi: Dalla Grecia classica alla Belle Époque*. Turin 1990.

Lotman, J. M. "Le bambole nel sistema della cultura." In *Testo e contesto:* 175 ff. Bari 1984.

MacFarlane, K. N. "Isidore of Seville on the Pagan Gods." *Transactions of the American Philological Association* 70 (1980): 3 ff.

Maguire, H. *Art and Eloquence in Byzantium*. Princeton 1982.

Malinowski, B. "The Problem of Meaning in Primitive Language." In C. K. Ogden and I. A. Richards, eds., *The Meaning of Meaning:* 296 ff. London 1953.

Mallowan, M. E. L. *Nimrud and Its Remains*. New York 1966.

Mancini, G. "Anno 1912." *Notizie degli Scavi di Antichità* 5 (1912): 155 ff.

Mann, T. "Wälsungenblut." In *Sämtliche Erzählungen*, vol. 1: 421 ff. Darmstadt 1987.

Manson, M. "Histoire d'un mythe: Les poupées de Maria femme d'Honorius."

Mélanges d'Archéologie et d'Histoire de l'École Français de Rome, Antiquité, 90 (1978): 863 ff.

Marchetti, S. Citroni. *Plinio il vecchio e la tradizione del moralismo romano.* Pisa 1991.

Marcovich, M. *Alcestis Barcinonensis: Text and Commentary.* Leiden 1989.

———. *Athenagoras: Legatio pro Christianis.* Berlin 1990.

Marin, L. *Le portrait du roi.* Paris 1981. (English translation: *Portrait of the King*, trans. M. Houle. Minneapolis 1988.)

de Martino, E. *Morte e pianto rituale nel mondo antico.* Turin 1958. Reprint: Turin 1975.

Marx, F., ed. *C. Lucilii Carminum reliquiae.* Leipzig 1904. Reprint: Amsterdam 1963.

Mayer, M. "Der Protesilaos des Euripides." *Hermes* 20 (1885): 101 ff.

Mazzoli, G. "Reale, verum, pictum, falsum in Lucilio." In D. Lanza and O. Longo, eds., *Il meraviglioso e il verisimile:* 113 ff. Florence 1989.

McDowell, D. M. *Athenian Homicide Law.* Manchester 1963.

Méautis, G. *Recherches sur le pythagorisme.* Neuchâtel 1922.

Meineke, A., ed. *Fragmenta poetarum comoediae mediae.* Berlin 1840.

Mencacci, F. *I fratelli amici: La rappresentazione dei gemelli nella cultura romana.* Venice 1996.

———. "Omnes congeminavimus: Rappresentazioni dei gemelli nella cultura e nella letteratura romana." Ph.D. dissertation. Pisa 1989.

———. "Il sangue del gladiatore: Commodo e la doppia identità." In *Sangue e antropologia nella teologia medioevale:* 657 ff. Rome 1991.

———. "Sanguis/cruor: Designazioni linguistiche e classificazione antropologica del sangue nella cultura romana." *Materiali e Discussioni per l'Analisi dei Testi Classici* 17 (1986): 25 ff.

Menichetti, A. "Tre note di filologia italiana." *Cultura Neolatina* 29 (1969): 163 ff.

Meslin, M. "Significations rituelles et symboliques du miroir." In *Perennitas: Studi in onore di A. Brelich:* 327 ff. Rome 1980.

Mette, H. J. "Protesilaus (Euripides)." *Lustrum* 23/24 (1982): 228 ff.

Michel, C., ed. *Recueil d'inscriptions grecques.* Brussels 1990. Reprint: Hildesheim 1976.

Momigliano, A. "How Roman Emperors Became Gods." *American Scholar* 55 (1986): 181 ff.

Monseur, E. "L'âme pupilline." *Revue de l'Histoire des Religions* 51 (1905): 1 ff.

de Montaigne, Michel. *Essais.* Ed. A. Thibaudet. Paris 1933. (English translation: *Essays.* Stanford 1958.)

Moscati, S., ed. *The Phoenicians.* New York 1988.

Mueller, L. *Q. Horatius Flaccus: Oden und Epoden.* St. Petersburg 1900.

Mugler, C. "La lumière et la vision dans la poésie grecque." *Revue des Études Grecques* 73 (1960): 40 ff.

Mullach, F. G., ed. *Fragmenta philosophorum Graecorum.* Paris 1875. Reprint: Chicago 1968.

Müller, C., ed. *Fragmenta historicorum Graecorum.* Paris 1841. Reprint: Frankfurt 1975.

Munro, H. A. J. *T. Lucreti Cari de rerum natura libri sex.* 4th ed. London 1928.

Münzer, F. "Zur Kunstgeschichte des Plinius." *Hermes* 30 (1895): 499 ff.

Muretus, M. Antonius. *Albi Tibulli carmina.* Venice 1558.

Nauck, A., ed. *Tragicorum Graecorum fragmenta.* Hildesheim 1962.

Negelein, J. von. "Bild, Spiegel und Schatten im Volksglauben." *Archiv für Religionswissenschaft* 5 (1902): 2 ff.

Negri, A. M. "Sunt lacrimae rerum et mentem mortalia tangunt." *Studi Italiani di Filologia Classica* 81 (1988): 240 ff.

Nietzsche, F. *Also sprach Zarathustra.* In *Werke,* vol. 6. Berlin 1968.

de Nolhac, P. "Les mémoriaux intimes de Pétrarque." In *Pétrarque et l'humanisme,* vol. 2: 287 ff. Paris 1907.

Novakova, J. *Umbra: Ein Beitrag zur dichterischen Semantik.* Berlin 1964.

O'Hara, J. J. "Somnia ficta in Lucretius and Lucilius." *Classical Quarterly* 37 (1987): 517 ff.

Oniga, R. *I composti nominali latini: Una morfologia generativa.* Bologna 1988.

———. *Il confine conteso.* Bari 1990.

Otto, W. *Die Sprichwörter und die sprichwörtlichen Redensarten der Römer.* Leipzig 1890.

Overbeck, J. *Die antiken Schriftquellen zur Geschichte der bildenden Künste bei den Griechen.* Leipzig 1868. Reprint: Hildesheim 1971.

Owen, S. G. *P. Ovidii Nasonis Tristium liber secundus.* Oxford 1924.

Paduano, G. "Le reminiscenze dell'Alcesti nell'elegia 4.11 di Properzio." *Maia* 20 (1968): 21 ff.

Padula, V. *Pauca quae in Sexto Propertio Vincentius Padula ab Acrio animadvertebat.* Naples 1871.

Page, D. *Poetae melici Graeci.* Oxford 1962.

Pais, E. *Ancient Legends of Roman History.* London 1906.

Pascoli, G. *Carmi Latini.* Ed. L. Vischi. Bologna 1920.

———. *Carmina.* Ed. M. Valgimigli. Milan 1951.

———. *Poemi conviviali.* In *Opere.* Ed. M. Perugi. Naples 1980–82.

Pastorino, A. *Iuli Firmici Materni: De errore profanarum religionum.* Florence 1956.

Paulme, D. "La statue du Commandeur." *Revue de l'Histoire des Religions* 153 (1958): 34 ff. [Reprinted in *La statue du commandeur: Essais d'ethnologie* (Paris 1984).]

von Pauly, A. F., G. Wissowa, et al., eds., *Pauly's Realencyclopädie der classischen Altertumswissenschaft.* Stuttgart 1893–.

Pease, A. S. *M. Tulli Ciceronis De divinatione libri duo.* Champaign 1923. Reprint: Darmstadt 1977.

Peirce, C. S. "Speculative Grammar." In *Collected Papers,* vol. 2: 156 f. Cambridge, Mass., 1931–35.

Pellegrino, M. *M. Minucii Felicis Octavius.* Turin 1947.

Pellizer, E. "L'eco, lo specchio e la reciprocità amorosa." *Quaderni Urbinati di Cultura Classica* 46 (1985): 21 ff.

———. *Favole di identità e favole di paura.* Rome 1982.

———. "Narciso e le figure della dualità." In M. Bettini, ed., *La maschera, il doppio e il ritratto:* 13 ff. Bari 1991.

Pemberton, E. G. "A Note on Skiagraphia." *American Journal of Archaeology* 80 (1976): 82 ff.

Pepe, L. *Tibullo minore.* Naples 1948.

Perelli, L. *Lucrezio poeta dell'angoscia.* Florence 1969.

Petrella, F. "Il sosia perturbante: Note sul 'doppio' di O. Rank." In E. Funari, ed., *Il doppio fra patologia e necessità:* 66 ff. Milan 1986.

Pfeiffer, R., ed. *Callimachus.* Oxford 1985.

Picard, C. "Le cénotaphe de Midéa et les 'colosses' de Ménélas." *Revue de Philologie* 7 (1933): 341 ff.

Piccaluga, G. "Bona dea: Due contributi all'interpretazione del suo culto." *Studi e Materiali di Storia delle Religioni* 35 (1964): 195 ff.

Pichon, R. *Lactance.* Paris 1901.

Pigeaud, J. "Il sogno erotico nell'antichità greca e romana." In G. Guidorizzi, ed., *Il sogno in Grecia:* 143 ff. Rome 1988.

Pinotti, P. *P. Ovidio Nasone: Remedia amoris.* Bologna 1988.

Poe, E. A. "Marginalia." In *The Complete Works of E. A. Poe,* ed. J. H. Harrison, vol. 16. New York 1902.

———. "The Oval Portrait." In *The Complete Works of E. A. Poe,* ed. J. H. Harrison, vol. 4: 245 ff. New York 1902.

Ponnau, G. "Pygmalion." In *L'idolatrie:* 97 ff. Paris 1990.

Pontrandolfo, A. "Amore e morte allo specchio." In *Lo specchio e il doppio: Dallo stagno di Narciso allo schermo televisivo,* exhibition catalog, Turin 1987: 55 ff. Milan 1987.

Portalupi, F., ed. *Opere di Marco Cornelio Frontone.* Turin 1974.

Powell, J. U., ed. *Collectanea Alexandrina.* Oxford 1925.

Praz, M. "L'amore delle statue." In *Fiori freschi:* 423 ff. Milan 1982.

———. *La morte, la carne e il diavolo nella letteratura romantica.* Florence 1969.

Price, S. R. *Rituals and Power: The Roman Imperial Cult in Asia Minor.* Cambridge 1984.

Pritchard, J. G. *The Ancient Near East in Pictures.* Princeton 1954.

Propp, V. J. *Istoričeskie korni volšebnoj skazki.* Leningrad 1946. (Italian translation: *Le radici storiche dei racconti di fate.* Torino 1972.)

———. *Morfologija skazki.* Leningrad 1928. (English translation: *Morphology of the Folktale,* trans. L. Scott. Austin 1968.)

———. *Problemy komizma i smekha.* Moscow 1976. (Italian translation: *Comicità e riso.* Torino 1988.)

Prost, W. A. "The EIDOLON of Helen: Diachronic Edition of a Myth." Ph.D. dissertation, Catholic University of America. Washington, D.C., 1977.

Proust, M. *Du côté de chez Swann.* Paris 1954.

Proust, M. *La fugitive.* Paris 1954.

Pucci, G. "La statua, la maschera, il segno." In M. Bettini, ed., *La maschera, il doppio e il ritratto:* 107 ff. Bari 1991.

Pushkin, A. S. *Kamennyi gost'.* Moscow 1936.

Questa, C. *Semiramide redenta.* Urbino 1989.

Radermacher, L. "Aus Lucians Lügenfreund." In *Festschrift für Theodor Gomperz:* 197 ff. Vienna 1902.

———. *Hippolytos und Tekla.* Vienna 1916.

Radin, P. *The Culture of the Winnebago: As Described by Themselves.* Bloomington 1949.

Raffaelli, R. *Variazioni sul Don Giovanni.* Urbino 1990.

Ragland-Sullivan, E. "The Phenomenon of Aging in Oscar Wilde's Picture of Dorian Gray." In K. Woodward and M. M. Schwartz, eds., *Memory and Desire:* 184 ff. Bloomington 1986.

Rank, O. *Der Doppelgänger.* Leipzig 1914. (English translation: *The Double,* trans. Harry Tucker, Jr. Chapel Hill, N.C., 1971.)

Reifferscheid, A., ed. *C. Suetoni Tranquilli praeter Caesarum libros reliquiae.* Leipzig 1860. Reprint: Hildesheim 1971.

Reinach, S. *Cultes, mythes et religions.* Paris 1912.

Ribbeck, O., ed. *Tragicorum Romanorum fragmenta.* 3d ed. Leipzig 1897.

Riess, E. "Notes on Plautus." *Classical Quarterly* 35 (1941): 150 ff.

Rinaldi, M. R. "Ricerche sui giocattoli nell'antichità, I: Le bambole." *Epigraphica* 18 (1956): 104 ff.

Rizzo, G. E. *La pittura ellenistico-romana.* Milan 1929.

Robert, C. *Die antiken Sarkophagreliefs.* Rome 1969.

Robert, L. *Hellenica.* Vol. 2. Paris 1946.

Roca-Puig, R. *Alcestis: Hexámetres llatins.* Barcelona 1982.

Rocco, Antonio. "Amore è un puro interesse." In F. W. Lupi, ed., *Discorsi academici de' Signori Incogniti:* 171. Venice 1635. Reprint: Pisa 1990.

Rohde, E. *Der griechische Roman.* Leipzig 1914.

——. *Psyche.* Freiburg 1890–94. (English translation: *Psyche,* trans. W. B. Hillis. Freeport 1972.)

Rosati, G. *Narciso e Pigmalione.* Florence 1983.

Roscher, W. H. *Ausführliches Lexikon der griechischen und römischen Mythologie.* Leipzig 1884. Reprint: Hildesheim 1965.

——. "Die Schattenlosigkeit des Zeus-Abatons auf dem Lykayon." *Jahrbücher für Classiche Philologie* 38 (1892): 701 ff.

Rose, H. J. "Euripides, *Alcestis* 340 ff." *Classical Review* 41 (1927): 58.

——. *Hygini fabulae.* 3d ed. Leiden 1963.

Rothstein, M. *Die Elegien des Sextus Propertius.* Berlin 1898.

Rousset, J. *Leurs yeux se rencontrèrent: La scène de première vue dans le roman.* Paris 1984.

Roux, G. "Qu'est-ce qu'un kolossos?" *Revue des Études Anciennes* 62 (1960): 5 ff.

Saïd, S. "EIDOLON: Du simulacre à l'idole." In *L'idolatrie:* 9 ff. Paris 1990.

Salomies, O. *Die römische Vornamen.* Helsinki 1987.

Salvadore, M. *Due donne romane.* Palermo 1990.

——. *Il nome e la persona.* Rome 1987.

Sassi, M. M. *La scienza dell'uomo nella Grecia antica.* Turin 1988.

Scamuzzi, U. "Studio sulla mummia di bambina (la cosiddetta 'Mummia di Grottarossa')." *Rivista di Studi Classici* 12 (1964): 264 ff.

Scheidweiler, F., ed. *Euphorionis fragmenta.* Bonn 1908.

Schick, W. "Favorin Peri paidon trophes und die antike Erziehungslehre." Ph.D. dissertation. Leipzig 1911.

Schilling, R. *Pline l'ancien: Histoire naturelle, livre VII.* Paris 1977.

Schmid, W., and O. Stählin. *Geschichte der griechischen Literatur.* Munich 1940.

Schmidt, W. *Herons von Alexandria Druckwerke und Automatentheater.* Leipzig 1899.

Schmidt-Berger, U. "Philia: Typologie der Freundschaft und Verwandtschaft bei Euripides." Ph.D. dissertation. Berlin 1973.

Schröder, H. O. "Marionetten: Ein Beitrag zur Polemik des Karneades." *Rheinisches Museum* 126 (1983): 1ff.

Seeck, G. A. *Unaristotelische Untersuchungen zu Euripides.* Heidelberg 1985.

Segal, C. *Lucretius on Death and Anxiety.* Princeton 1990.

Seligmann, S. *Der böse Blick und Verwandtes.* Berlin 1910.

Sellers, E., ed. *The Elder Pliny's Chapters on the History of Art.* London 1896. Reprint: Chicago 1967.

Servais, J. "Les suppliants dans la loi de Cyrène." *Bulletin de Correspondance Hellénique* 84 (1960): 112ff.

Settis, S. "Presentazione." In J. Seznec, *La sopravvivenza degli antichi dei.* Turin 1981.

Seznec, J. *La survivance des dieux antiques.* Paris 1980. (English translation: *The Survival of the Pagan Gods,* trans. B. F. Sessions. New York 1953.)

Shulman, J. "Te quoque falle tamen: Ovid's anti-Lucretian Didactics." *Classical Journal* 76 (1981): 242ff.

Silvestri, D. "Riflessi onomastici indomediterranei." *Atti del Sodalizio Glottologico Milanese* 27 (1986): 138ff.

Simmons, E. J. *Pushkin.* Cambridge, Mass. 1937.

Simon, G. *Le regard de l'autre et l'apparence.* Paris 1988.

Singer, A. E. *A Bibliography of the Don Juan Theme: Versions and Criticism.* Morgantown 1954–80.

———. "The Present State of Don Juan Studies." In J. M. Sola-Solé and G. E. Gingras, eds., *Tirso's Don Juan:* 1ff. Washington, D.C., 1988.

Sinisi, S. *Le figure dell'ombra.* Rome 1982.

Slater, N. W. *Reading Petronius.* Baltimore 1990.

Smith, C. "Pictura." In W. Smith, W. W. Wayte, and G. E. Marindin, eds., *A Dictionary of Greek and Roman Antiquities,* vol. 2: 401ff. London 1890.

Smith, K. F. "Pupula duplex." In *Studies in Honor of B. L. Gildersleeve:* 287ff. Baltimore 1902.

Snowden, F. M. *Blacks in Antiquity.* Cambridge, Mass., 1970.

Sommella, A. Mura. "Bambola in avorio." In *Crepereia Tryphaena: Le scoperte archeologiche nell'area del Palazzo di Giustizia,* exhibition catalog, Rome 1983: 49ff. Venice 1983.

———. "Crepereia Tryphaena." In *Crepereia Tryphaena: Le scoperte archeologiche nell'area del Palazzo di Giustizia,* exhibition catalog, Rome 1983: 29. Venice 1983.

Söring, O. "Werke bildender Kunst in altfranzösischen Epen." *Vollmöllers Jahresberichte* 1 2 (1900): 111.

Spina, L. "L'incomparabile pudore dei giovani Spartani." *Quaderni Urbinati di Cultura Classica* 19 (1985): 167ff.

Stefanelli, L. Pirzio Biroli. "Anellino d'oro con chiave." In *Crepereia Tryphaena: Le scoperte archeologiche nell'area del Palazzo di Giustizia,* exhibition catalog, Rome 1983: 65. Venice 1983.

Suerbaum, W. "Hundert Jahre Vergils Forschung." *Aufstieg und Niedergang der Römischen Welt* 2 (1980): 208 ff.

Swift, Jonathan. "The Lady's Dressing Room." In H. Williams, ed., *The Poems of Jonathan Swift,* vol. 2: 524 ff. Oxford 1937.

Swoboda, A., ed. *Operum reliquiae P. Nigidii Figuli.* Paris 1889. Reprint: Amsterdam 1964.

Tabeling, E. *Mater larum.* Frankfurt 1932. Reprint: New York 1975.

Tennyson, A. "Lucretius." In *The Poetic and Dramatic Works of Alfred Lord Tennyson,* vol. 3: 253 ff. Boston 1929.

Thesaurus linguae Latinae. Leipzig 1900 –.

Thomas, Y. "À Rome, pères citoyens et cité des pères." In A. Burguière, ed., *Histoire de la famille,* vol. 1: 195 ff. Paris 1986. (English translation: *A History of the Family,* trans. S. Hanbury-Tenison, R. Morris, and A. Wilson. vol. 1 Cambridge, Mass., 1996.)

Thompson, D. Review of *Terrakotten von Pergamon,* by E. Töpperwein. *American Journal of Archaeology* 83 (1979): 117 ff.

———. *Troy: The Terracotta Figurines of the Hellenistic Period.* Princeton 1963.

Thompson, L. A. *Romans and Blacks.* London 1989.

Tirso de Molina. *El burlador de Sevilla y convidado de piedra.* With introduction and notes by L. Vázquez. Madrid 1989.

Tolman, J. A. *A Study of the Sepulchral Inscriptions in Buecheler's Carmina Latina Epigraphica.* Chicago 1910.

Töpperwein, E. *Terrakotten von Pergamon.* Berlin 1976.

Touchmann, J. "Le fascinés, 4." *Melusine* 9 (1898–99): 79.

Traina, A. "Sul linguaggio lucreziano dell'eros." In *Poeti latini e neolatini,* vol. 2: 22 ff. Bologna 1981.

Trenkner, S. *The Greek Novella in the Classical Period.* Cambridge 1958. Reprint: London 1987.

Trimpi, W. "The Early Metaphorical Use of Skiagraphia and Skenographia." *Traditio* 34 (1978): 403 ff.

Turcan, R. *Firmicus Maternus: L'erreure des religions païennes.* Paris 1982.

Turner, F. M. "Lucretius among the Victorians." *Victorian Studies* 16 (1973): 329 ff.

Vahlen, J., ed. *Ennianae Poesis reliquiae.* Leipzig 1903. Reprint: Amsterdam 1963.

Van der Valk, M., ed. *Eustathius: Commentarii ad Homeri Iliadem pertinentes.* Leiden 1971.

Van Gennep, A. *Les rites de passage.* Paris 1909. (English translation: *The Rites of Passage,* trans. M. B. Wizedom and G. L. Caffe. Chicago 1966.)

Verducci, F. *Ovid's Toyshop of the Heart.* Princeton 1985.

Vernant, J. P. "Au miroir de Méduse." In *L'individu, la mort, l'amour:* 117 ff. Paris 1989. (English translation: "In the Mirror of Medusa," in F. Zeitlin, ed., *Mortals and Immortals:* 141 ff. Princeton 1991.)

———. "Figuration de l'invisible et catégorie psychologique du double: Le colossos." In *Mythe et pensée chez les grecs:* 251 ff. Paris 1966. (English translation: "The Representation of the Invisible and the Psychological Category of the Double: The Colossos," in *Myth and Thought among the Greeks:* 305 ff. London 1983.)

———. "Figures féminines de la mort en Grèce." In *L'individu, la mort, l'amour:* 131 ff. Paris 1989. (English translation: "Feminine Figures of Death in Greece," in F. Zeitlin, ed., *Mortals and Immortals:* 95 ff. Princeton 1991.)

———. *Figures, idoles, masques.* Paris 1990.

———. *Mythe et pensée chez les grecs.* Paris 1966. (English translation: *Myth and Thought among the Greeks.* London 1983.)

———. "Psyche: Simulacro del corpo o immagine del divino?" In M. Bettini, ed., *La maschera, il doppio e il ritratto:* 3 ff. Bari 1991. (English translation: "Psyche: Simulacrum of the Body or Image of the Divine?" in F. Zeitlin, ed., *Mortals and Immortals:* 186 ff. Princeton 1991.)

———. *Religions, histoire, raisons.* Paris 1979.

Vernant, J. P., and P. Vidal-Naquet. *Mythe et tragédie deux.* Paris 1986. (English translation: *Myth and Tragedy in Ancient Greece,* vol. 2, trans. J. Lloyd. New York 1990.)

Verrall, A. W. V. *The Agamemnon of Aeschylus.* London 1889.

Vickery, W. N. *Alexander Pushkin.* New York 1970.

Vilborg, E. *Achilles Tatius: Leucippe and Clitophon.* Stockholm 1955.

———. *Achilles Tatius, Leucippe and Clitophon: A Commentary.* Stockholm 1962.

Vinge, L. *The Narcissus Theme in Western European Literature.* Lund 1967.

Vollmer, F. *P. Papini Stati Silvarum liber.* Leipzig 1898.

Vottero, D. *L. Anneo Seneca: Questioni naturali.* Turin 1989.

Vulpius, J. A. *Albius Tibullus.* Padua 1749.

Vürtheim, J. *Stesichoros' Fragmente und Biographie.* Leiden 1919.

Wagenwoort, H. "De Lygdamo poeta eiusque sodalicio." *Mnemosyne* 45 (1917): 102 ff.

Walters, H. B. *Catalogue of the Terracottas in the Department of Greek and Roman Antiquities.* London 1903.

Wardman, A. E. "Description of Personal Appearance in Plutarch and Suetonius: The Use of Statues as Evidence." *Classical Quarterly* 17 (1967): 414 ff.

Weiblingen, F. P. *Senecas Naturales Quaestiones: Griechische Wissenschaft und römische Form.* Munich 1977.

Weinstein, L. *The Metamorphoses of Don Juan.* Stanford 1959.

Wendel, C., ed. *Scholia in Theocritum vetera.* Leipzig 1914. Reprint: Stuttgart 1967.

Wesselski, A. "Narkissos oder der Spiegelbild." *Archiv Orientàlní* 7 (1935): 37 ff.

Wilamowitz, U. "Sepulchri Portuensis imagines." In *Kleine Schriften,* vol. 5.1: 523 ff. Berlin 1937.

Wilde, Oscar. *Charmides and Other Poems.* London 1913.

———. *Picture of Dorian Gray.* Oxford 1994.

William of Malmesbury. *De gestis regum Anglorum.* Ed. W. Stubbs. London 1889. Reprint: London 1964.

Wohlers, C. Roeder. "A Commentary on Apuleius' Metamorphoses, Book VIII." Ph.D. dissertation, Rutgers University. New Brunswick 1986.

Wrede, H. *Consecratio in formam deorum.* Mainz 1981.

Yardley, J. C. "Cynthia's Ghost: Propertius 4.7 Again." *Bulletin of the Institute of Classical Studies, London,* 24 (1977): 83 ff.

Zadoks, A. N., and J. Jitta. *Ancestral Portraiture in Rome.* Amsterdam 1932.

Zanker, P. "*Iste ego sum:* Der naive und der bewusste Narcissus." *Bonner Jahr-bücher* 166/67 (1966): 152ff.

Zazzo, R. *Les jumeaux: Le couple et la personne.* Paris 1960.

Zimmermann, H. "Die babilonische Göttin im Fenster." *Orientalistische Lite-raturzeitung* 31 (1928): 2ff.

Ziolkowski, T. *Disenchanted Images.* Princeton 1977.

Index

absence, 5–6, 16–17, 20–25, 40–43, 47–51, 88–89, 91–92, 108, 113–14

Achilles, 47, 130

Achilles Tatius, 181–84, 259n64, 264n36, 286n46, 287n52–53

actors, 55–56, 203–6

Adaeus of Mitylene, 256n18

Admetus, 18–28, 40–41, 45, 48–51, 53, 81, 91, 103, 116, 134, 239n17, 242n34, 252n33, 252n40

adultery, 9–10, 14–15, 31, 50–51, 57, 112, 122, 127–28, 133–34, 170–71, 180–81, 191, 194–95, 201–4, 211–12, 262n14, 273n5, 290n27

aegis, 100

Aelian, 43, 61–62, 255n11, 256n14, 259n7, 265n10–11, 284n21

Aelius Aristides, 22–23, 239n14

Aeneas, 88, 112, 126, 149, 177–179, 207–9, 243n42, 263n24

Aeschylus, 14–16, 21–22, 193–94, 242n40, 242n33, 243n52, 244n53, 289n12, 290n25

Aetius, 199

Afrania, 272n35

afterlife, 9–10, 12, 25, 31, 44, 46, 111, 116, 271n29

Agathe Tyche, 62, 73

Agesilaus, 235

agnatio, 191, 196–97

Agrippa, 65

Agrippina, 208, 295n85

aithale, 36–37

Ajax, 267n31

Akko, 266n17

Alcestis, 18–28, 40–41, 45, 48–51, 53, 81, 91, 103, 116, 134, 239n17, 242n34, 252n33, 252n40

Alcestis Barcinonensis, 48, 252n40

Alexander the Great, 76, 281n19

Alexis, 256n19

Algarotti, F., 303n6

allegory, 283n5

Allia Potestas, 26

Allius, 26–28, 111

Amazon "of the lovely legs," 65

Ammianus, 106

anadyomene, 76

Anaxarete, 150–57

Andreae, B., 241n28

Andrén, A., 296n8, 298n21

Andromache, 193–94

Andromeda, 127, 183, 199

Anecdota Graeca, 249n28, 302n59

Anna Akhmatova, 274n13

Anthologia Latina, 4.39 281n12

Anthologia Palatina, 51, 96, 114, 131, 218, 225, 240n23, 253n47, 259n3, 265n10, 265n13, 270n19, 298n18, 301n50, 302n64

Antigonus of Carystus, 292n53

Antipater, 265n10

Antoninus Geminus, 202

Antoninus Liberalis, 73–74, 150, 153, 242n34, 267n36

Nigidius, 201
Ninus, 276n5
de Nolhac, P., 253n48
Nonius, 299n35
Nonnus, 249n31–32, 266n17
Novakova, J., 252n21
novel (Greek), 91, 181–86, 199–200, 206

Octavia, 53
Odysseus, 178–79, 289n22
Odyssey, 178–79, 242n33, 246n23, 277n2,
   278n18, 289n22, 290n25, 298n13
Oedipus, 71, 255n11
O'Hara, J. J., 299n35
Olympicus, 96
omen, 185–86
Oniga, R., 253n55, 261n13
Onomacritus, 249n21
Onomarchus, 64, 69, 156
Orestes, 17, 194, 271n29
Orpheus, 149
Orphic fragments, 36, 240n36, 248n18,
   249n31–32, 266n17, 298n21
Orphic Hymn to Helios, 240n40
Orphism, 33–37, 298n21
Osiris, 102–3
Ostyak, 241n32
Otho, 163–64
Otto, A., 283n5, 290n24
Overbeck, J., 255n3, 277n4–5, 278n7
Ovid, 280n40, 282n43, 288n9, 296n3,
   298n29
Ovid: *Heroides*, 11–14, 27, 126, 190–91,
   240n22, 243n42, 246n28, 267n36,
   272n38, 295n85; *Metamorphoses*, 59, 68,
   94, 98, 103, 127, 147–48, 151–53, 155–56,
   192, 230–31, 237n1, 265n1, 266n16,
   267n36, 279n24; *Remedia amoris*, 84–
   85, 87, 261n8, 261n9, 84, 112, 240n23
Owen, S. G., 275n20

Paduano, G., 272n33
Padula, V., 269n3–4
Page, D. L., 302n64
Pais, E., 255n11
Palladium, 99–100
Palladius, 96
Pallas, 99–101, 103
parakyptousa, 153–56
Paris, 20, 22–23, 113
Parrhasius, 65, 79, 160
parthenos, 217

Pascoli, G., 214–16, 266n19, 296n4
Pasiteles, 8
Pastorino, A., 249n23
Pater, W., 254n2
patrilineal, 121, 190–93, 196–97, 202
Patroclus, 47, 130
Paul (Biblical), 123
Paul of Aegina, 266n17
Paulme, D., 52, 131, 273n1, 275n37, 276n39,
   276n40
Paulus Silentiarius, 114
Pausanias, 44, 98, 242n34, 249n21,
   249n27, 253n55, 259n7, 271n30, 275n22,
   275n23, 277n5, 282n28, 298n29, 304n22
Pausias, 76–77
Pease, A. S., 285n25
Peirce, C. S., 49–50
Pellegrino, M., 251n10
Pellicus of Corinth, 129
Pellizer, E., 240n23, 266n17, 267n35
Pemberton, E. G., 304n28
Penelope, 189
Pepe, L., 268n40
Perelli, L., 262n16
Perseus, 127–28, 199, 208, 290n25, 292n48
Persius, 220, 225, 300n46, 302n65
Perugi, M., 296n2
Petrarch, 1, 3–5, 23–24, 59, 75, 99, 102,
   118, 186, 237n2, 253n48, 263n28
Petrella, F., 303n5
Petroma, 253n55
Petronius, 105, 126–27, 180–81, 185–86,
   224, 243n42, 269n46, 269n47, 270n17
Phaedra, 104–5, 208
phantom, 11–13, 14, 20–23, 27, 32–33, 46–
   47, 67–68, 118, 129, 149, 215–16
pharmakos, 71
phatic function, 149
Phidias, 46, 220
Philemon, 256n19
Philogelos, 95
Philomela, 183–84
Philostephanus, 255n3
Philostratus, 64, 66–67, 95, 130, 248n11,
   255n4, 287n58
Phineus, 127
photography, 49–50
Phryne, 259n3
Picard, C., 242n38
Piccaluga, G., 282n43
Pichon, R., 251n9
Pigeaud, J., 260n2, 264n37

Reinach, S., 257n28
Remus, 99, 101, 103
resemblances, 187–212
respect, 52–53, 112, 114, 119, 123–24, 158–68, 203–4, 235, 281n4
respicere, 149–50, 156–57, 262n17
revenge, 30–32, 41, 54, 128–31, 136, 173, 235, 276n5
Ricottilli, L., 291n39
Riess, E., 283n5
Rinaldi, M. R., 296n8, 297n10, 298n19
Rizzo, G. E., 266n21
Robert, C., 241n28
Robert, L., 293n60
Roca-Puig, R., 252n38
Rocco, A., 228
Rohde, E., 258n39, 274n18, 275n22–23, 279n22, 280n33
Roman comedy, 170–71, 173–74
Roman de Tristan, 10, 246n26
Roman elegy, 104, 109, 116, 121, 123, 150–51, 181, 280n40
Romulus, 99, 101, 103
Rosati, G., 254n2, 265n4
Roscher, W. H., 252n23
Rose, H. J., 239n16, 244n5
Rothstein, M., 269n2, 273n45
Rousset, J., 279n20
Roux, G., 241n32
Rufus of Ephesus, 298n13, 298n15

sacralizing object, 51–54, 133, 136, 253n55
Saïd, S., 245n15
saliva, 266n15
Salvadore, M., 246n28, 254n77
Sappho, 261n10, 298n26
sarcophagus (Vatican), 12, 27, 33
Sassi, M. M., 243n52, 290n25
Saturnalia, 204–5
Scamuzzi, U., 296n8, 297n9, 300n41
scapegoat, 71
Scheffer, J., 239n16
Schick, W., 292n54, 293n55
Schilling, R., 294n70
Schmid, W., 240n22
Schmidt, W., 300n38
Schmidt-Berger, U., 244n3
Schröder, H. O., 300n44
scopophilia, 303n5
Scott, R., 267n23
Scribonius Largus, 161–62
Scriptores Historiae Augustae, 19, 70–71,

201–2, 246n24, 275n23, 284n8, 293n60, 295n84, 297n12
Second Sophistic, 283n5, 286n46
Seeck, G. A., 244n3, 246n30
Segal, C., 261n10, 264n33–34
Seligmann, S., 265n11, 266n15
Sellers, E., 238n2
semen, 200–1, 262n14
Semiramis, 276n5
Seneca, 41, 105, 159, 167, 193, 208, 228–29, 240n4, 240n20, 261n13, 272n41, 273n5, 282n43, 289n14, 290n25, 294n68
Seneca the Elder, 123, 244n11, 272n34
Serapis, 21
sermocinatio, 119
Servais, J., 253n53
Servius, 190, 209, 239n14, 246n23, 253n55
Settis, S., 257n37
Seznec, J., 240n7, 257n37
shade (of the dead), 9–13, 19, 21–22, 27, 30, 46–48, 111, 116–17, 119, 215
shadow, 7–8, 12–13, 16, 21–22, 42–47, 49–50, 89, 114, 178, 210
Shakespeare, W., 211, 264n39, 289n14
Shulman, J., 262n20
siblings, 98, 103–8, 267n36
Silenus, 175
Silvestri, D., 290n26
similitudo, 40, 206, 209–10, 230–31, 284n9, 286n40, 287n1, 288n10, 291n42
Simmons, E. J., 274n13
Simon, G., 279n20
Singer, A. E., 273n1
Sinisi, S., 252n30
skēnographia, 304n28
skia, 12–13, 21–22, 43–44, 95
skiagraphia, 304n28
Slater, N. W., 286n40
Smith, C., 238n2
Smith, K. F., 297n12
Smith, S. B., 290n35
Snowden, F. M., 292n48
solitary lover, 5–6, 10, 21–24, 38–39, 50–51, 53, 61, 88–89, 91, 97–99, 118–19, 181, 207–8, 234
Sophocles, 255n11, 298n13
Söring, O., 278n13
Sosia, 231–33
Sparta, 258n47
Speroni, S., 267n36
Spina, L., 298n18
spit, 266n15

Compositor:	G & S Typesetters, Inc.
Text:	10/13 Galliard
Display:	Galliard
Printer:	Malloy Lithographing, Inc.
Binder:	Malloy Lithographing, Inc.